Paralegal Ethics

Angela Schneeman

Paralegal Ethics

Angela Schneeman

Africa • Australia • Canada • Denmark • Japan • Mexico • New Zealand • Philippines
Puerto Rico • Singapore • Spain • United Kingdom • United States

NOTICE TO THE READER

West Legal Studies Staff:
Business Unit Director: Susan L. Simpfenderfer
Executive Editor: Marlene McHugh Pratt
Acquisitions Editor: Joan M. Gill
Editorial Assistant: Lisa Flatley
Executive Marketing Manager: Donna J. Lewis
Channel Manager: Nigar Hale
Executive Production Manager: Wendy A. Troeger
Production Editor: Betty L. Dickson
Cover Design: Connie McKinley

Library of Congress Cataloging-in-Publication Data

Schneeman, Angela.
      Paralegal ethics / Angela Schneeman.
         p.   cm.
      Includes bibliographical references and index.
      ISBN 0-7668-0949-8
      1. Legal assistants—United States.   2. Legal ethics—United States.   I.   Title.

KF320.L4 S358 1999
174'.3'0973—dc21   99-055790

To the memory of my mother-in-law, Margery Schneeman

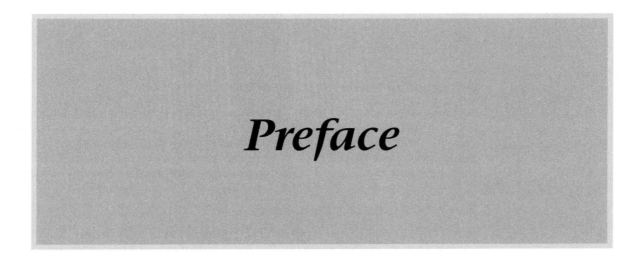

Preface

Paralegal Ethics is a readable, concise study of legal ethics from the perspective of the paralegal. This text prepares paralegal students for the ethical dilemmas they will face on the job with a practical approach relying heavily on situations actually faced by paralegals. Several resources included throughout the text make *Paralegal Ethics* an excellent resource to take from the classroom to the office.

The paralegal profession is still growing and evolving. Because of the increasing level of responsibility being assumed by many paralegals, legal ethics is of paramount importance. *Paralegal Ethics* emphasizes the importance of ethical behavior and the basic rules applicable to attorneys and paralegals.

TEXT CONTENTS

Because paralegals must abide by the rules of ethics established for attorneys, the text focuses on the codes of ethics applicable to attorneys as well as the rules of ethics adopted by the national paralegal associations.

- The basic rules of ethics discussed in this text include:
- Unauthorized Practice of Law
- Confidentiality
- Conflicts of Interest
- Competence, Diligence, and Zealousness
- Financial Dealings with Clients (including legal fees and trust accounting)
- Maintaining Integrity and Public Respect for the Legal Profession
- Advertising and Solicitation

In addition, *Paralegal Ethics* includes an overview of business ethics and a chapter focusing on legal ethics issues that will be of special concern in the future.

CHAPTER CONTENTS

Most chapters focus on a certain rule, or set of rules, of ethics and include the following:

Hypothetical Situations

Most chapters include two main hypothetical situations and several examples concerning the topic rule or rules of ethics. An Ethical Dilemma at the beginning of each chapter is a hypothetical situation that brings the student's focus to the topic rule, and A Question of Ethics is a second hypothetical situation in each chapter that focuses on the same rule of ethics from the paralegal's perspective.

Discussion of Pertinent Rules of Ethics

Special emphasis is given to the Model Rules of Professional Conduct, which have been adopted by the vast majority of jurisdictions in the United States, with discussion of the variances that may exist from the Model Rules. Examples and hypothetical situations are included throughout each chapter to illustrate how the rules being discussed actually affect paralegals and the attorneys they work for.

From the Paralegal's Perspective

Most chapters include a special section, From the Paralegal's Perspective, that includes the pertinent rules of ethics adopted by the national paralegal associations and practical advice on how paralegals can adhere to the rules. Resources for further information and assistance to paralegals who are struggling with questions of ethics are included throughout the text.

Cases and Discussion

Each chapter that discusses a rule or set of rules of ethics includes at least one case and a brief discussion. Wherever possible, a second case involving a paralegal and the topic of legal ethics is included. These cases have been edited liberally to draw attention to the rule of ethics being discussed within the chapter.

Chapter Summaries and Summary Questions

Chapter Summaries summarize the important points made in each chapter as a study aid for students. The Summary Questions at the end of each chapter include several hypothetical questions that require the student to give practical application to the material covered throughout the chapter.

Chapter Features

Preceding each chapter is a one- or two-page Feature designed to pique the interest of the students in the topic of legal ethics. These features are magazine-style stories based on legal ethics topics from the headlines. These features can be optional reading for the students, or they can be used to spark a class discussion before beginning a new chapter. For example, the feature preceding Chapter 7 (Maintaining Integrity and Public Respect for the Legal Profession) focuses on Matthew Hale. How do your students feel about a self-admitted bigot and white supremacist who has applied for admission to the bar in Illinois? Does he have a *right* to be admitted to bar (against the recommendation of the Illinois Bar Association Committee on Character and Fitness)?

Chapter 8 on Advertising and Solicitation is preceded by a feature on a New York attorney who uses suggestive advertising to promote her law practice. What do your students think? Do they find it offensive? Should the bar try to regulate this type of advertising?

Discussion concerning these and others features focusing on interesting topics from national headlines are one way to get students interested in the topic being studied and to show students that legal ethics has very real and important applications.

ANCILLARY MATERIALS

Instructor's Guide

A convenient Instructor's Guide with suggested test questions, supplementary activities, and suggestions for discussion is available with this text.

West Publishing's Web Site

Another excellent feature available with *Paralegal Ethics* is West Publishing's Web site at **www.westlegalstudies.com.** This unique resource, which will be updated quarterly, includes new information and developments in several topics addressed in this text that are of great importance to the paralegal instructors, paralegal students, and paralegals. Links to several useful Web sites can also be found at the site.

ACKNOWLEDGMENTS

I would like to thank the National Federation of Paralegal Associations and the National Association of Legal Assistants for allowing me to include their model rules and codes of ethics in this text. Also, my special thanks go to everyone at West and Delmar who helped with each step of this project, especially Joan Gill and Lisa Flatley.

I would also like to thank the following reviewers:

Wendy Edson
Hilbert College

Holly Enterline
Memphis State Tech

Melynda Hill-Teter
Arizona Association of
   Professional Paralegals

Gayle Mozee
Graham & James

Kathryn Myers
Saint Mary of the Woods College

Anthony Piazza
David N. Myers College

Nicholas Riggs
Sullivan College

Constantinos Scaros
Interboro Institute

Paul Sedlacek
National American University

Barbara Smythe
College of Legal Arts

Linda Wimberly
Eastern Kentucky University

Angela Schneeman

Please note the Internet resources are of a time-sensitive nature
and URL addressess may often change or be deleted.

Contents

Preface   *viii*

Feature: The Importance of Legal Ethics   1
CHAPTER 1 AN INTRODUCTION TO LEGAL ETHICS   2
Introduction   3
Sources of Legal Ethics Regulation   3
Attorney Responsibility for Paralegal Ethics   6
An Ethical Dilemma   8
Paralegal Associations and Paralegal Ethics   9
Case and Discussion   10
Consequences of Unethical Attorney Behavior   14
Consequences of Unethical Paralegal Behavior   15
Paralegal Regulation   17
Resources for Legal Ethics Research   20
Chapter Summary   26
Summary Questions   27

Feature: Law Practice for Dummies: The Move Toward Self-Help
   Legal Services   30
CHAPTER 2 UNAUTHORIZED PRACTICE OF LAW   32
An Ethical Dilemma   33
Introduction   33
Basic Rules Concerning the Unauthorized Practice of Law   34
What Constitutes the Unauthorized Practice of Law?   35
Professions at Risk of Engaging in the Unauthorized
   Practice of Law   38
Self-Representation   38
Enforcing the Unauthorized Practice of Law Rules   39
Case and Discussion   40
Guidelines for Utilizing Paralegals   41
FROM THE PARALEGAL'S PERSPECTIVE   42
Independent Paralegals   43
Guidance from the Paralegal Associations   44
Avoiding the Unauthorized Practice of Law   45
Consequences to the Paralegal for the Unauthorized
   Practice of Law   49
Case Law Involving Paralegals   49

A Question of Ethics   *51*
Case and Discussion   52
Chapter Summary   53
Summary Questions   54

Feature: Mr. Butts   *56*
CHAPTER 3 CONFIDENTIALITY   **59**
An Ethical Dilemma   *60*
Introduction   60
The Ethical Duty to Confidentiality   61
Attorney–Client Privilege   67
Case and Discussion   70
Confidentiality and the Corporate Client   71
FROM THE PARALEGAL'S PERSPECTIVE   72
A Question of Ethics   *76*
Chapter Summary   77
Summary Questions   78

Feature: The Litigation Explosion   *80*
CHAPTER 4 CONFLICT OF INTEREST   **82**
An Ethical Dilemma   *83*
Introduction   83
The General Rule   84
Conflict of Clients' Interests   85
Conflicting Interests of Current and Former Clients   87
Imputed Disqualification   88
Detecting Conflicts of Interest   90
The Organization as a Client   91
Special Rules Concerning Government Lawyers   91
Conflict of Client's Interests and Attorney's Personal Interests 92
The Attorney as a Witness   95
Attorney's Employees and Agents   95
Case and Discussion   96
FROM THE PARALEGAL'S PERSPECTIVE   97
A Question of Ethics   *99*
Case and Discussion   100
Chapter Summary   101
Summary Questions   101

Feature: The Right to Effective Counsel and the Ethical
*   Challenges of Public Defenders*   *104*
CHAPTER 5 COMPETENT, DILIGENT, AND ZEALOUS
REPRESENTATION OF THE CLIENT   **106**
An Ethical Dilemma   *107*
Introduction   107
Competent Representation Defined   108
Case and Discussion   110
Accepting or Declining Representation   112
Maintaining Competence   114
Basic Rules Concerning Diligent Representation of Client 114
Case and Discussion   115
Zealous Representation   116
FROM THE PARALEGAL'S PERSPECTIVE   118
Paralegal Competence and Diligence   118

A Question of Ethics — *119*
Standards for Paralegal Competence — **121**
Maintaining Competence — **124**
Chapter Summary — **124**
Summary Questions — **125**

Feature: Contingent Fee Controversy — *127*
CHAPTER 6 THE ETHICS OF LEGAL FEES AND FINANCIAL MATTERS — **129**
An Ethical Dilemma — *130*
Introduction — **130**
Client Trust Accounts — **131**
Legal Fees and Billing — **134**
Fee Agreements — **139**
Fee Disputes — **139**
Division of Fees with Others — **141**
Case and Discussion — **142**
A Question of Ethics — *143*
FROM THE PARALEGAL'S PERSPECTIVE — **144**
Trust Accounting — **144**
Paralegals and Billing — **145**
Paralegal Fee Recoverability — **145**
Fee Splitting with Attorneys — **148**
Case and Discussion — **149**
Chapter Summary — **150**
Summary Questions — **150**

Feature: The Racist Who Wants to be a Lawyer — *153*
CHAPTER 7 MAINTAINING INTEGRITY AND PUBLIC RESPECT FOR THE LEGAL PROFESSION — **156**
An Ethical Dilemma — *157*
Introduction — **157**
Bar Admission — **157**
Disciplinary Matters — **159**
Misconduct — **159**
Reporting Misconduct — **161**
Case and Discussion — **163**
Pro Bono Service — **165**
FROM THE PARALEGAL'S PERSPECTIVE — **166**
A Question of Ethics — *166*
Maintaining the Integrity of the Paralegal Profession — **166**
Paralegal Misconduct — **167**
The Paralegal's Duty to Report Misconduct — **167**
Pro Bono for Paralegals — **170**
Chapter Summary — **171**
Summary Questions — **171**

Feature: You've Come a Long Way Baby? — *173*
CHAPTER 8 ADVERTISING AND SOLICITATION — **175**
An Ethical Dilemma — *176*
Introduction — **176**
Advertising Acceptance — **176**
Supreme Court Decisions Allowing Advertising — **177**
Current Rules Regulating and Restricting Advertising — **178**

False and Misleading Advertising 180
Case and Discussion 181
Advertising Media 182
Advertising Records and Reporting 183
Specialization 183
Advertising Costs and Referral Fees 184
Law Firm Names and Letterhead 184
Solicitation 185
FROM THE PARALEGAL'S PERSPECTIVE 187
Paralegal Advertising 187
A Question of Ethics 188
Solicitation 190
Case and Discussion 191
Chapter Summary 192
Summary Questions 193

Feature: Somebody's Watching You . . . 195
CHAPTER 9 BUSINESS ETHICS FOR EVERYONE 197
Introduction 198
The Importance of Business Ethics 198
Ethics for All Members of the Organization 198
Ethics Programs 199
Specific Issues in Ethics 201
Resolving Ethical Dilemmas 205
Chapter Summary 207
Summary Questions 207

Feature: Attorneys and Public Image 209
CHAPTER 10 ETHICS FOR THE TWENTY-FIRST
CENTURY 210
Introduction 211
Ethics 2000 211
Client Confidentiality and New Technology 211
The Internet and the Practice of Law 213
FROM THE PARALEGAL'S PERSPECTIVE 215
The Future of the Paralegal Profession 215
Chapter Summary 217
Summary Questions 217

Appendix A Missouri's Rules of Professional Conduct 219
Appendix B New Hampshire's Guidelines for the Utilization
of Legal Assistant Services 242
Appendix C Code of Ethics and Professional Responsibility
of the National Association of Legal Assistants 245
Appendix D National Federation of Paralegal Associations,
Inc. Model Code of Ethics and Professional Responsibility
and Guidelines for Enforcement 247
Appendix E Directory of Paralegal Associations 257
Glossary 271
Index 277

THE IMPORTANCE OF LEGAL ETHICS

When can you divulge information shared with you by a client? What should you do if your personal interests conflict with the interests of a client? Is it okay to give legal advice to clients on routine matters? These are all questions of ethics, the type of ethical dilemmas you will frequently be faced with as a paralegal.

Every day of your life you make ethical decisions, and you will be making important ethical decisions every day of your career as a paralegal. Most of these decisions will be easy and will be made with little thought. Many of the decisions you make will be made by relying on your education, experience, good judgment, and common sense. However, there are some decisions that you will be forced to make based on other criteria. Your common sense alone will not always be enough to help you make the right, moral, legal, and ethical decision in the complex environment in which you will be working. Rules of ethics, especially those dealing with client rights, are not always intuitive. Your instinct and gut feeling may tell you one thing, when the rules of ethics may prescribe another. For example, your personal ethics may tell you that it is the right thing to do to turn in your client when he or she is evading justice, but the rules of ethics may prescribe another course of action.

As a paralegal, it will be important for you to be familiar with all rules of ethics that apply to you and to follow those rules at all times. The ethical decisions you make will have an impact on you, your employer, your clients, and the public. Unethical behavior can cost you your reputation and your job. It could also subject you to lawsuits and even criminal prosecution in some instances. Your unethical behavior can also cause your supervising attorneys to be subject to discipline, including disbarment.

Both the National Association of Legal Assistants (NALA) and the National Federation of Paralegal Associations (NFPA) have established rules of ethics for their members. In addition, the rules of ethics applicable to the attorneys you work for will generally apply to you. It is important that you have an understanding of all these rules of ethics. The study of legal ethics and professional responsibility, which is an integral part of any paralegal's education, will assist you in making appropriate decisions when dealing with clients, the courts, the public, and the business of law practice that you will be concerned with every day.

Chapter 1

An Introduction to Legal Ethics

"In civilized life, law floats in a sea of ethics."

Earl Warren, New York Times, November 12, 1962

Introduction
Sources of Legal Ethics Regulation
  State Judicial System, Bar Association, and
  Legislature
  American Bar Association
    Model Code of Professional Responsibility
    Model Rules of Professional Conduct
    Ethics Opinions
Attorney Responsibility for Paralegal Ethics
  Rule 5.3 Responsibilities Regarding Nonlawyer
  Assistants
An Ethical Dilemma
Paralegal Associations and Paralegal Ethics
Case and Discussion
  The National Association of Legal Assistants
  The National Federation of Paralegal
  Associations
**Consequences of Unethical Attorney
  Behavior**
  Discipline by the Court or Court-Appointed Dis-
    ciplinary Agency
  Civil Lawsuits
  Criminal Prosecution
**Consequences of Unethical Paralegal
  Behavior**
  Loss of Respect
  Loss of Clients

Disciplinary Action Against Responsible
  Attorney
Loss of Employment
Criminal Prosecution
Civil Lawsuits
Discipline by Paralegal Association
Paralegal Regulation
  Paralegal Licensing
  Paralegal Certification
  Paralegal Registration
  The American Bar Association's Position
  The National Association of Legal Assistants'
    Position
  The National Federation of Paralegal
    Associations' Position
Resources for Legal Ethics Research
  Supervising Attorney or Ethics Committee
  State Code of Ethics
  State Bar Associations
  Paralegal Associations
Chapter Summary
Summary Questions

INTRODUCTION

The moral and ethical behavior of judges, attorneys, and paralegals is important to the success of our legal system and the administration of justice. **Legal ethics** form the code of conduct among members of the legal profession, which governs their moral and ethical behavior and their professional duties toward one another, toward their clients, and toward the courts. The role of legal ethics is to identify and remove inappropriate conduct from the legal profession and to protect clients and the public. Rules and guidelines for legal ethics are established in the codes of ethics and professional responsibility established by the professional associations of both attorneys and paralegals.

As a paralegal, it will be important for you to be familiar with the rules and guidelines for legal ethics to avoid unethical behavior that may result in sanctions against you or your supervising attorneys and to protect the rights and interests of clients.

This chapter introduces you to legal ethics by exploring the several sources of rules for legal ethics and your supervising attorney's responsibility for your ethical conduct. Next, this chapter focuses on the role the paralegal associations play in legal ethics and the consequences of unethical behavior by both attorneys and paralegals. After an examination of paralegal regulation, this chapter concludes with a discussion of several resources to assist you with questions you may have throughout your career concerning legal ethics.

Legal ethics
The standards of minimally acceptable conduct within the legal profession, involving the duties that its members owe one another, their clients, and the courts. Also termed etiquette of the profession. (Black's Law Dictionary, Seventh Edition)

SOURCES OF LEGAL ETHICS REGULATION

Ethical rules and guidelines for attorneys come from several sources, mostly at the state level. The standards of legal ethics and **professional responsibility** are established by each state and set forth in a **Code of Ethics,** Code of Professional Responsibility, or Code of Professional Conduct, as that document may be called. The code of ethics adopted by each state or jurisdiction is binding on every attorney licensed to practice law in that state. It is very important that paralegals are familiar with the code of ethics that dictates the ethical behavior for attorneys in the state in which they work.

The state judiciary, state **bar associations,** and state legislature all play a role in adopting the code of ethics for attorneys and for overseeing the ethical behavior of attorneys licensed to practice law in each state. However, the specific roles played by the judiciary, bar association, and state legislature varies from state to state.

Professional responsibility
A general term referring to the duties and obligations of those in the legal field; legal ethics.

Code of ethics
Code or set of rules setting forth the standards and guidelines for ethical behavior and professional responsibility for a certain profession. May also be referred to as a code of professional responsibility, code of conduct, or a similar name.

State Judicial System, Bar Association, and Legislature

The highest court of each state has the ultimate authority over attorney conduct, although at least a portion of that authority is usually delegated to other entities within the state. The state judicial system and bar association work together to oversee the ethical behavior of each state's attorneys. In some states, the highest court has adopted the code of ethics governing the ethical behavior of attorneys—often based on recommendations by the state bar association. In other jurisdictions, the court has delegated the authority to adopt the code of ethics to the state bar association. In any event, attorney conduct is regulated by the courts, which may interpret, modify, and even override the provisions of the state's code of ethics.

State bar associations are responsible for regulating attorneys and overseeing the continuing education of attorneys. State bar associations are often empowered by the courts or by legislation to adopt and enforce codes of ethics. To ensure compliance with the codes of ethics, each state that delegates authority to

Bar association
An organization of members of the bar of a state or county, or of the bar of every state, whose primary function is promoting professionalism and enhancing the administration of justice.

Integrated bar

A bar association in which membership is a statutory requirement for the practice of law. Also termed unified bar. (Black's Law Dictionary, Seventh Edition)

Nonintegrated bar

A type of voluntary bar association that exists in some states, to which membership by attorneys practicing in that state is optional.

Statute

A law passed by a legislative body. (Abbr. s.; stat.) (Black's Law Dictionary, Seventh Edition)

American Bar Association (ABA)

A voluntary national organization of lawyers. Among other things, it participates in law reform, law-school accreditation, and continuing legal education in an effort to improve legal services and the administration of justice. (Black's Law Dictionary, Seventh Edition)

Model Code of Professional Responsibility

Model code adopted by the ABA that became effective in 1970. The Model Code of Professional Responsibility (Model Code) is divided into nine canons, all of which broadly prescribe ethical conduct for lawyers. Within the canons are disciplinary rules (DRs) and ethical considerations (ECs), which provide more detailed guidance on ethical issues. The Model Code of Professional Responsibility was adopted or followed closely by most jurisdictions but has since been replaced by the Model Rules of Professional Conduct by the ABA and most states.

Model Rules of Professional Conduct

Model rules adopted by the ABA in 1983 to replace the Model Code of Professional Responsibility. Now adopted in some form in most jurisdictions in the United States.

the bar association to adopt and enforce the code of ethics requires membership in the bar association as a condition to the right to practice law in that state. State bar associations with mandatory membership for all attorneys licensed in that state are **integrated bars.** In states in which the judiciary maintains the authority to adopt and enforce the code of ethics, state bar membership is voluntary. These states have **nonintegrated bars.** Several state bar associations offer memberships to qualified paralegals in their state.[1] Membership in the state bar association is not a requirement for paralegals in any state.

The state judiciary or state bar association is also responsible for overseeing the admission of new attorneys to practice law in that state and for disciplining the unethical behavior of attorneys.

Many state bar associations have appointed committees to answer questions on ethics and to render opinions when requested to do so. These committees provide advice and guidance in the form of ethics opinions that are usually published for the benefit of all attorneys within the jurisdiction. Some may be accessed through the Internet. Because these opinions are not court opinions, but rather the opinions of a bar association ethics committee, they are not considered binding authority. However, they are considered very helpful in interpreting the code of ethics in the jurisdiction to which they apply.

State **statutes** also govern the ethical behavior of attorneys. Again, the exact role played by the state legislature varies by state. However, in every jurisdiction, legislative bodies pass laws concerning the ethical practice of law. Laws may be passed regarding the requirements for licensing attorneys and admitting attorneys to the state bar. In addition, state legislatures may pass laws regarding the unauthorized practice of law, handling trust account funds, and other matters that directly affect attorneys. In some instances the unethical action of an attorney is also a violation of the law.

American Bar Association

The **American Bar Association** (ABA) is the country's largest voluntary professional association of attorneys. More than half of the attorneys in this country are members of the ABA and its specialty sections. Qualified paralegals may become associate members. The ABA's influence in lawmaking and the practice of law, particularly through the development of model rules and guidelines, is substantial.

The first model code of ethics adopted by the ABA was the Canons of Professional Ethics adopted in 1908. These canons were based in large part on the code of ethics adopted by the Alabama State Bar Association in 1887. The Alabama State Bar Association was the first bar association in the country to adopt such a code of ethics. Subsequently the ABA has adopted first the **Model Code of Professional Responsibility** and then the **Model Rules of Professional Conduct.**

Model Code of Professional Responsibility. The Canons of Professional Ethics was amended numerous times, and in 1969 the House of Delegates of the American Bar Association adopted the new Model Code of Professional Responsibility (Model Code), which became effective January 1, 1970. The Model Code of Professional Responsibility is divided into nine canons, all of which broadly prescribe ethical conduct for lawyers. Within the canons are disciplinary rules and ethical considerations, which provide more detailed guidance on ethical issues. The ethical considerations are aspirational and represent the objectives toward which every member of the profession should strive. They constitute a body of principles upon which the lawyer can rely for guidance in many specific situations.[2] The disciplinary rules are mandatory. They state the minimum level of conduct below which no lawyer can fall without being subject to disciplinary action.[3]

The Model Code was adopted, sometimes with minor amendments, in nearly every state in the country and the District of Columbia. It has now been replaced in most states by the Model Rules of Professional Conduct (Model Rules), discussed below. Following is a list of the nine canons that make up the Model Code.

Canon 1: A Lawyer Should Assist in Maintaining the Integrity and Competence of the Legal Profession.
Canon 2: A Lawyer Should Assist the Legal Profession in Fulfilling Its Duty to Make Legal Counsel Available.
Canon 3: A Lawyer Should Assist in Preventing the Unauthorized Practice of Law.
Canon 4: A Lawyer Should Preserve the Confidences and Secrets of a Client.
Canon 5: A Lawyer Should Exercise Independent Professional Judgment on Behalf of a Client.
Canon 6: A Lawyer Should Represent a Client Competently.
Canon 7: A Lawyer Should Represent a Client Zealously Within the Bounds of the Law.
Canon 8: A Lawyer Should Assist in Improving the Legal System.
Canon 9: A Lawyer Should Avoid Even the Appearance of Professional Impropriety.

Model Rules of Professional Conduct. In August 1983 the ABA House of Delegates approved the Model Rules to replace the Model Code. These rules have been amended several times since 1983, and revisions continue on an ongoing basis. The Model Rules, although they use different phraseology, address concerns similar to the Model Code. The Model Rules are intended to serve as a national framework for implementation of standards of professional conduct.[4] The Model Rules (Figure 1–1) are organized under the following broad categories that cover many of the roles played by attorneys in their practice of law:

1. Client–Lawyer Relationship
2. Counselor
3. Advocate
4. Transactions with Persons Other Than Clients
5. Law Firms and Associations
6. Public Service
7. Information about Legal Services
8. Maintaining the Integrity of the Profession

Missouri is one of several states that modeled its Rules of Professional Conduct closely after the ABA's. The full text is included as Appendix A.

Membership in the ABA is voluntary, and the ABA has no actual authority to enforce its model codes and rules. However, by adopting model rules and codes, the ABA gives guidance to its members as to appropriate ethical behavior and guidance to state judicial systems and state bar associations in adopting their own enforceable codes of ethics.

Ethics Opinions. The ABA also provides ethical guidance to attorneys in the form of ethics opinions issued by its **Standing Committee on Ethics and Professional Responsibility.** The ethics opinions issued by the ABA have no binding authority but rather they interpret the standards of ethics established by the Model Rules adopted by the ABA (Figure 1–2). The ethics opinions of the ABA are often relied on by attorneys to answer questions they have concerning ethics, and they are an often-cited authority.

In addition to all of the sources of legal ethics for attorneys, they must look inward as well. As set forth in the preamble to the Model Rules, ". . . a lawyer is also guided by personal conscience and the approbation of professional peers. A lawyer should strive to attain the highest level of skill, to improve the law and the legal profession, and to exemplify the legal profession's ideals of public service."[5]

Standing Committee on Ethics and Professional Responsibility
Standing committee established by the American Bar Association to issue both formal and informal advisory opinions on ethical questions as guidance to attorneys.

Model Rules adopted (with amendments)	Model Code adopted (amended to include some substance of model rules)	State follows neither Model Rules nor Model Code
Alabama	Iowa	California
Alaska	Maine	Florida
Arizona	Nebraska	
Arkansas	New York	
Colorado	Ohio	
Connecticut	Oregon	
Delaware	Tennessee	
District of Columbia	Vermont	
Georgia	Virginia	
Hawaii		
Idaho		
Illinois		
Indiana		
Kansas		
Kentucky		
Louisiana		
Maryland		
Massachusetts		
Michigan		
Minnesota		
Mississippi		
Missouri		
Montana		
Nevada		
New Hampshire		
New Jersey		
New Mexico		
North Carolina		
North Dakota		
Oklahoma		
Pennsylvania		
Rhode Island		
South Carolina		
South Dakota		
Texas		
Utah		
Washington		
West Virginia		
Wisconsin		
Wyoming		

FIGURE 1–1

State adoptions of Model Rules and Model Code

ATTORNEY RESPONSIBILITY FOR PARALEGAL ETHICS

Attorneys in every state may be held directly responsible for the unethical actions of the paralegals and other nonlawyer personnel they employ. For that reason, your knowledge of legal ethics is of great importance to the attorneys to whom you report. Rule 5.3 of the Model Rules of Professional Conduct specifically addresses the attorney's responsibility for his or her nonlawyer assistants as follows:

Rule 5.3 Responsibilities Regarding Nonlawyer Assistants

With respect to a nonlawyer employed or retained by or associated with a lawyer:
    (a) a partner in a law firm shall make reasonable efforts to ensure that the firm has in effect measures giving reasonable assurance that the person's conduct is compatible with the professional obligations of the lawyer;

State Judicial System	State Bar Associations	State Legislature	American Bar Association
• The highest court in the state has the ultimate authority for regulating the ethical behavior of attorneys licensed within the state. • May adopt the code of ethics governing attorneys under its jurisdiction. • The courts have the authority to interpret, modify, and override provisions of the code of ethics. • May be responsible for overseeing admission of new attorneys to practice law in that state. • May be responsible for disciplining unethical attorneys or may delegate disciplinary authority to bar association and be required to approve serious disciplinary actions, especially disbarment.	• May adopt the code of ethics governing attorney members. • Often responsible for enforcing the state's code of ethics. • May be responsible for overseeing admission of new attorneys to practice law in that state. • May be responsible for disciplining unethical attorneys. • May have appointed committee to answer questions on ethics and to issue ethics opinions.	• May pass laws establishing the ethical behavior of attorneys. • May pass laws regarding requirements for licensing attorneys and admitting attorneys to the state bar association.	• Adopted Model Rules of Professional Conduct as guidance to the states in establishing their own codes of ethics. • Issues Ethics Opinions to answer questions and interpret the standards of ethics established by the Model Rules.

FIGURE 1–2

Sources of legal ethics legislation

(b) a lawyer having direct supervisory authority over the nonlawyer shall make reasonable efforts to ensure that the person's conduct is compatible with the professional obligations of the lawyer; and

(c) a lawyer shall be responsible for conduct of such a person that would be a violation of the Rules of Professional Conduct if engaged in by a lawyer if:

(1) the lawyer orders or ratifies the conduct involved; or

(2) the lawyer is a partner in the law firm in which the person is employed, or has direct supervisory authority over the person, and knows of the conduct at a time when its consequences can be avoided or mitigated but fails to take reasonable remedial action.

Attorneys are responsible for paralegal and other nonlawyer employees under this rule in three ways. First, the partner of a law firm has a duty to ensure that the firm's employees are reasonably familiar with the rules of ethics that apply to attorneys, and that the conduct of the firm's employees is expected to be compatible with the rules of ethics applicable to the attorneys. For example, law firms

An Ethical Dilemma

Adams, Brown, and Calder is a law firm of fifty attorneys in a major metropolitan area. Adams, Brown, and Calder has a litigation department that consists of fifteen attorneys and fifteen paralegals. Brown is the managing litigation partner in charge of supervising the attorneys and paralegals in the department. Brown is responsible for overseeing *Drew v. Evans*, a personal injury case that has recently come into the office. This case involves a long-time client of the firm's, Drew, who is suing Mr. Evans for damages Drew sustained when he was rear-ended by Evans in an automobile accident.

On a Thursday afternoon, when Brown is leaving and not expecting to be back in the office until Tuesday, she realizes that an answer is due from Evans' attorney on Friday. She asks Frank, one of the newer paralegals who has been closely working on the case, to contact Evans' attorney to find out if they are going to file their answer on time or request an extension. Brown then leaves the office.

Frank calls Evans' attorney's office only to be told that Evans' attorney will be out of the office for the rest of the week. There doesn't seem to be anyone in Evans' attorney's office who is familiar with the case, so Frank (who is unaware of the rule of ethics prohibiting personal contact with an adverse party who is represented by counsel) decides to contact Evans directly.

Evans was surprised to learn that his attorney was out of town, and he was a bit angry that his attorney hadn't filed an answer. "I just want to settle this matter," he tells Frank. "Tell Drew I'll give him $20,000."

Frank knows this is much more than Drew was expecting—and without even going to court! Frank knows he is unauthorized to accept the offer, but he tells Evans that the offer sounds great and he just needs to reach Brown to get her approval on the deal.

What basic rules of ethics have been broken, and who has broken them in this matter? What would you do if you were Brown?

Answer and Discussion: First and most obviously, Frank broke several rules of ethics, including contacting the adverse client directly. He shouldn't have contacted Evans directly, and he certainly should not have discussed negotiation or settlement with the adverse party. Not so obvious, however, is the fact that Brown is also in violation of the rules of ethics. As a partner of Adams, Brown, and Calder, and especially as the attorney responsible for the supervision of Frank, she is responsible for his unethical actions. Brown has apparently given responsibility to Frank without making sure that he has been educated about the basic rules of ethics regarding contact with the adverse party in a case. In addition, as supervising attorney, Brown has the duty to make reasonable efforts to ensure that her paralegal's conduct is compatible with her professional obligations as a lawyer. Brown should have given Frank appropriate instruction before leaving the office, taking Frank's inexperience into account. Frank's actions were not compatible with the professional obligations of Brown, and Brown could be held responsible.

may hold seminars on ethics for all employees and have a written policy stating the basic rules of ethics that employees are expected to comply with.

Second, supervising attorneys are expected to make reasonable efforts to ensure that the personnel for whom they are responsible are performing their duties in an ethical manner. For example, a supervising attorney may not turn his or her back on the unethical behavior of a subordinate. The level of supervision required will depend on the paralegal's level of experience and knowledge.

Finally, attorneys are responsible for actions of paralegals or other nonlawyer personnel if the attorney instructed the paralegal to act in an unethical manner or if the attorney was aware of unethical conduct and did nothing to prevent it. Attorneys may not avoid ethical rules by requesting their nonlawyer personnel to perform an unethical task for them.

Even before the promulgation of the Model Rules, the Model Code recognized the attorneys' responsibility for the actions of their employees. The preliminary statement to the Model Code states that "Obviously the Canons, Ethical Considerations, and Disciplinary Rules cannot apply to non-lawyers; however, they do define the type of ethical conduct the public has a right to expect not only of lawyers but also of their non-professional employees and associates in all matters pertaining to professional employment. A lawyer should ultimately be responsible for the conduct of his employees and associates in the course of the professional representation of the client."[6]

The **Model Guidelines for the Utilization of Legal Assistant Services** were drafted by the American Bar Association Standing Committee on Legal Assistants and adopted by the American Bar Association's House of Delegates in 1991. The Model Guidelines give further guidance to attorneys for the proper and ethical utilization of paralegals. Guideline 1 of the Model Guidelines states that "A lawyer is responsible for all of the professional actions of a legal assistant performing legal assistant services at the lawyer's direction and should take reasonable measures to ensure that the legal assistant's conduct is consistent with the lawyer's obligations under the ABA Model Rules of Professional Conduct." The ABA Standing Committee on Legal Assistants developed the Model Guidelines for use by attorneys to conform to the ABA's Model Rules of Professional Conduct, decided authority, and contemporary practice. Some states have adopted a version of these Model Guidelines as their own. New Hampshire is one state that has adopted its own guidelines. These guidelines are included as Appendix B.

Attorneys are not responsible for the conduct of their paralegals in all instances. The attorney's exact responsibility is defined by the code of ethics that is binding on him or her. If an attorney is using due care in supervising and directing a paralegal to act ethically, the attorney will probably not be responsible for the paralegal's unethical conduct.

Model Guidelines for the Utilization of Legal Assistant Services
Guidelines drafted by the American Bar Association Standing Committee on Legal Assistants and adopted by the American Bar Association's House of Delegates in 1991.

PARALEGAL ASSOCIATIONS AND PARALEGAL ETHICS

As a paralegal, you must be familiar with and abide by the code of ethics that is binding on your supervising attorneys. This code of ethics will be binding on you as an employee and agent of the attorney. In addition, national, state, and local paralegal associations adopt codes of ethics specifically for their paralegal members.

There are two main national paralegal associations in the United States: the National Association of Legal Assistants (NALA) and the National Federation of Paralegal Associations (NFPA). In addition, each state has at least one state paralegal association and several local associations. Although membership in a paralegal association is not mandatory for paralegals, the associations have done much

CASE AND DISCUSSION

In the following case, the respondent attorney was suspended indefinitely from the practice of law due to the unethical behavior of his paralegal and his own failure to act ethically and properly supervise his legal assistant.

In the Matter of Eloy F. MARTINEZ, an Attorney Admitted to Practice before the Courts of the State of New Mexico.
No. 17631.
Supreme Court of New Mexico.
May 5, 1988.
Rehearing Denied June 3, 1988.

OPINION

. . . The facts in this case are undisputed. Martinez filed no answer to the charges filed and did not deny the allegations against him. The facts as alleged were deemed admitted pursuant to SCRA 1986, 17-309(C)(2) and 17-310(C).

Martinez employed the services of legal assistant named John Felix, who is not a licensed attorney. Felix maintained his own office separate from the offices of Martinez. In January 1987, Rosalba Oritz contacted Felix (whom she believed to be a licensed attorney) to assist her with a claim against Allstate Insurance arising out of an accident in which she was involved.

Felix apparently advised Oritz that he had seven (7) years of experience in the law, worked with Martinez, and would handle her case for a contingency fee of one-third of any recovery. He did not advise her of his status as a non-lawyer.

At the time of her first meeting with Felix, Oritz had been offered $800 by Allstate to settle the property damage aspect of her claim. Felix advised her to accept that offer and, acting upon his advice, she did so. Felix then notified Allstate that he was representing Oritz and that she would accept the $800. Allstate issued a check to "Rosalba Oritz and John Felix, Her Attorney."

Felix then took the check to Martinez and requested permission to cash it and simply give the money to Oritz, whom he claimed needed it desperately. Martinez, who realized the check was improperly drawn, allowed Felix to cash it nonetheless. It was not placed in Martinez's trust account nor were any records of disbursement made. Felix pocketed $350 claiming entitlement to a fee (although he had nothing to do with obtaining the offer) and gave the remainder to Oritz.

Martinez subsequently wrote to Allstate advising that he and Felix represented the Oritz family and stating that Felix would visit with the claims representative about a settlement for Oritz. Nowhere in the letter did Martinez state that Felix was not an attorney or that he (Martinez) had never been retained by Oritz. Several days later, Felix negotiated a settlement of $5,500 for Oritz without her knowledge or approval. The checks were issued to Oritz and Martinez. Oritz, never having met or consulted with Martinez, became alarmed and refused to negotiate the checks despite the persistent efforts of Felix to induce her to do so.

[1] In that Felix was not privy to these proceedings, we do not decide whether he was engaging in the unauthorized practice of law thus make no finding that Martinez may have assisted in such an endeavor in violation of SCRA 1986, 16-505(B). We do, however, find that Martinez employed Felix as a legal assistant and failed to make reasonable efforts to ensure that the conduct of Felix comported with his own professional obligations. He therefore violated SCRA 1986, 16-503. Furthermore, the actions of Felix in making misrepresentations to Oritz and to Allstate are imputed to Martinez by SCRA 1986, 16-503(C). Martinez has, therefore, engaged in conduct involving misrepresentation and deceit in violation of SCRA 1986, 16-804(C) not only through his own failure to clarify the status of Felix in his communications with Allstate, but also by virtue of his responsibility for the dishonest conduct of Felix.

[2] When an attorney receives money in settlement of a client's claim, that money must be deposited into a trust account and records made of any disbursements, including payments to the attorney for fees claimed by the attorney. This rule is mandatory and is designed to preclude precisely what occurred in this situation: the mishandling of money belonging to a client. To allow one's assistant to simply cash a check made payable to a client with no documentation of the transaction is inexcusable and can lead to the misappropriation of funds. The conduct of Martinez in this instance was violative of SCRA 1986, 16-115. Any violation of this particular rule will generally result in a severe sanction for an attorney even in the absence of other misconduct. . . .

The record is void of any suggestion that Martinez was even remotely interested in the pending disciplinary action. While formal charges were personally served upon him, Martinez filed no response and, although notified of a hearing, did not appear. . . . All in all, he has ignored nearly twenty-five (25) communications from disciplinary counsel, the hearing committee, and the disciplinary board during the past year. . . .

We do not find cause to remand this case to the disciplinary board and request the attorneys who volunteer their time to these matters to devote more attention to Martinez. . . .

IT IS THEREFORE ORDERED that Eloy F. Martinez be and hereby is suspended indefinitely from the practice of law. . . . His reinstatement will not be automatic, but shall occur only after a reinstatement proceeding conducted pursuant to SCRA 1986, 17-214 where Martinez will have the burden of demonstrating by clear and convincing evidence that he has the requisite moral qualifications and is once again fit to resume the practice of law. . . .

IT IS FURTHER ORDERED that the Clerk of the Supreme Court strike the name of Eloy F. Martinez from the roll of those persons permitted to practice law in New Mexico and that this Opinion be published in the State Bar of New Mexico *News and Views* and in the *New Mexico Reports*. . . .

IT IS SO ORDERED.

to shape public opinion of paralegals, both with attorneys and with the public in general. The paralegal associations promote professionalism, offer continuing legal education to paralegals, set ethical guidelines for paralegals to follow, and offer assistance in many forms to paralegals.

The National Association of Legal Assistants

The **National Association of Legal Assistants (NALA)** was formed in 1975 and currently has approximately 18,000 paralegal members, both through individual memberships and through its 90 state and local affiliated associations. Student membership is available to individuals who are pursuing a course of study to become legal assistants. The NALA monitors events affecting paralegals and represents paralegals on some of the important national issues, including education and certification. The NALA publishes *Facts & Findings,* a quarterly journal for paralegals.

> **National Association of Legal Assistants (NALA)**
> A national association of legal assistants (paralegals) formed in 1975, currently representing over 18,000 members through individual memberships and 90 state and local affiliated associations.

The NALA has adopted a Code of Ethics and Professional Responsibility as well as Standards and Guidelines for Utilization of Legal Assistants. Members of the NALA are bound by the Code of Ethics and Professional Responsibility, and any violation of the code is cause for removal of membership. The NALA–affiliated associations must adopt the NALA Code of Ethics and Professional Responsibility as their standard of conduct.

Code of Ethics and Professional Responsibility. The NALA's Code of Ethics and Professional Responsibility, which is found in Appendix C, closely resembles the ABA Code of Professional Responsibility. It was initially adopted in 1975 and has been revised several times since. Canon 9 of the NALA's code specifically states that legal assistants are governed by the bar association's codes of professional responsibility and rules of professional conduct.

Model Standards and Guidelines for Utilization of Legal Assistants. The NALA's ongoing study of professional responsibility and ethical considerations has led to the NALA Model Standards and Guidelines for Utilization of Legal Assistants. The guide "provides an outline of minimum qualifications and standards necessary for legal assistant professionals to assure the public and the legal profession that they are, indeed, qualified."[7] These guidelines offer guidance on several matters concerning legal ethics, including:

- Disclosure of the legal assistant's status as a legal assistant
- Preserving the confidences and secrets of all clients
- Understanding the rules of ethics applicable to attorneys to avoid actions that would involve the attorney in a violation of the rules or give the appearance of professional impropriety.

The guidelines also assist in determining what duties may and may not be performed by a legal assistant. These guidelines can be found on NALA's Web site at **www.NALA.org.** See Figure 1–3.

The National Federation of Paralegal Associations

The **National Federation of Paralegal Associations (NFPA)** was formed in 1974, and its members consist primarily of state associations. The NFPA is a federation of 60 member associations representing over 17,000 individual members nationwide. Student memberships are available. Membership in some state associations automatically constitutes membership in the NFPA.

> **National Federation of Paralegal Associations (NFPA)**
> A national association of paralegals formed in 1974; currently has more than 55 state and local association members, representing more than 17,000 paralegals.

The NFPA has five official goals:

1. To advance, foster, and promote the paralegal profession with absolute dedication

> **The National Association of Legal Assistants:**
> - Prefers the title *Legal Assistant* to Paralegal
> - Defines the term Legal Assistant as follows: "Legal assistants, also known as paralegals, are a distinguishable group of persons who assist attorneys in the delivery of legal services. Through formal education, training and experience, legal assistants have knowledge and expertise regarding the legal system and substantive and procedural law which qualify them to do work of a legal nature under the supervision of an attorney."
> - Has over 18,000 paralegal members through individual memberships and through its 90 state and local affiliated associations
> - Is headquartered at 1516 S. Boston, #200, Tulsa, OK 74119, phone (918)587-6828; fax (918)582-6772, e-mail: nala@nala.org, Web site: **http://www.nala.org**
> - Prefers self-regulation for the paralegal profession
> - Offers the Certified Legal Assistant (CLA) credential to those who meet certain education requirements and pass a comprehensive test
> - Publishes *Facts & Findings*, a quarterly journal featuring how-to educational articles for legal assistants
> - Has adopted a Code of Ethics and Professional Responsibility that is binding on its members
> - Has adopted Model Standards and Guidelines for Utilization of Legal Assistants

FIGURE 1–3

The National Association of Legal Assistants

2. To monitor and participate in developments in the paralegal profession
3. To maintain a nationwide communication network among paralegal associations and other members of the legal community
4. To advance the education standards of the paralegal profession
5. To participate in, carry on, and conduct research, seminars, experiments, investigations, studies, or other work concerning the paralegal profession[8]

The NFPA monitors and reports on developments in courts, bar associations, and legislation that may affect paralegals and represents many paralegals in a national forum on the issues of education and licensing of paralegals. The NFPA publishes the *National Reporter,* a quarterly journal for paralegals. The NFPA has also adopted a code of ethics for paralegals' guidance (Figure 1–4).

Model Code of Ethics and Professional Responsibility. The NFPA's Model Code of Ethics and Professional Responsibility was adopted in 1993 to "delineate the principles for ethics and conduct to which every paralegal should aspire."[9] As with other model codes, NFPA's Model Code of Ethics and Professional Responsibility has no binding authority on paralegals. However, many state paralegal associations have adopted the NFPA's Model Code as their own code of ethics. The NFPA's Model Code follows the format of the ABA's Model Code, with eight canons. The canons are supplemented by ethical considerations. The full text of the NFPA Model Code with Ethical Considerations is found in Appendix D. The eight canons follow:

1.1 Paralegal Shall Achieve and Maintain a High Level of Competence.
1.2 A Paralegal Shall Maintain a High Level of Personal and Professional Integrity.
1.3 A Paralegal Shall Maintain a High Standard of Professional Conduct.
1.4 A Paralegal Shall Serve the Public Interest by Contributing to the Delivery of Quality Legal Services and the Improvement of the Legal System.
1.5 A Paralegal Shall Preserve All Confidential Information Provided by the Client or Acquired From Other Sources Before, During, and After the Course of the Professional Relationship.
1.6 A Paralegal Shall Avoid Conflicts of Interest and Shall Disclose any Possible Conflict to the Employer or Client, as Well as to the Prospective Employers or Clients.

The National Federation of Paralegal Associations:
- Prefers the title paralegal
- Defines the term *paralegal* as follows: "A paralegal is a person qualified through education, training or work experience to perform substantive legal work that requires knowledge of legal concepts and is customarily but not exclusively, performed by a lawyer. This qualified person may be retained or employed in a traditional capacity by a lawyer, law office, governmental agency, or other entity or is authorized by administrative, statutory or court authority to perform this work; or This qualified person may be retained or employed in a non-traditional capacity, provided that such non-traditional capacity does not violate applicable unauthorized practice of law statutes, administrative laws, court rules or case law."
- Is a federation of 60 member associations representing over 17,000 individual members nationwide
- Is headquartered in Kansas City, Missouri, mailing address: P.O. Box 33108, Kansas City, MO 64114, telephone (816)941-4000, fax (816)941-2725, e-mail: info@paralegals.org, Web site: **http://www.paralegals.org/**
- Prefers a two-tiered licensing plan, which constitutes mandatory regulation, recognizing that another form of regulation (e.g., certification or registration) may be appropriate in a given state
- Offers the Paralegal Advanced Competency Exam (PACE) as a means for experienced paralegals to validate their knowledge to themselves and their employers
- Publishes *National Paralegal Reporter*, a quarterly journal for paralegals
- Has adopted a Model Code of Ethics and Professional Responsibility and Guidelines for Enforcement
- Has appointed The Ethics and Professional Responsibility Committee, which responds to questions and renders opinions regarding ethical conduct, obligations, utilization, and/or discipline of paralegals

FIGURE 1–4
National Federation of Paralegal Associatons

1.7 A Paralegal's Title Shall be Fully Disclosed.
1.8 A Paralegal Shall Not Engage in the Unauthorized Practice of Law.

In 1997, the NFPA supplemented its Model Code with Guidelines for the Enforcement of the Model Code of Ethics and Professional Responsibility. These guidelines are discussed in this chapter under Consequences of Unethical Paralegal Behavior.

The NFPA has appointed an Ethics and Professional Responsibility Committee, which was formed for the purposes of accepting and responding to inquiries concerning ethical conduct, obligations, utilization, and/or discipline of paralegals.[10] This committee responds to inquiries from any paralegal, attorney, corporate, or government agency employing a paralegal, court, legislature, or bar association. The committee issues opinions based, in large part, on the following:

- The NFPA Model Code of Ethics and Professional Responsibility
- Other policy statements and/or positions by NFPA
- The ABA Model Guidelines for Utilization of Legal Assistant Services
- The code of ethics adopted by the state from which the inquiry arose
- The ABA Model Rules of Professional Conduct
- The ABA Model Code of Professional Responsibility
- Any published decision concerning paralegal and/or attorney ethics or discipline

The opinions issued by the NFPA Ethics and Professional Responsibility Committee are not binding. However, they may be used for guidance and as a persuasive argument in favor of the findings of NFPA. Opinions of this committee may be found on the NFPA Web site at **www.paralegals.org** without the names of the concerned parties. (See Figure 1–4).

CONSEQUENCES OF UNETHICAL ATTORNEY BEHAVIOR

There are several possible consequences to unethical behavior by attorneys, including disciplinary action by the court or court-appointed disciplinary agency, civil lawsuits for malpractice, and even criminal prosecution.

Discipline by the Court or Court-Appointed Disciplinary Agency

An attorney who acts unethically and violates the applicable code of ethics may be subject to disciplinary action and possible sanctions. Typically, complaints are heard by a court-appointed disciplinary agency, whose purpose is to investigate complaints and recommend appropriate sanctions when warranted. The recommended sanctions usually require court-approval, especially serious sanctions such as disbarment. The authority to discipline an attorney ultimately rests with the court authorized to admit the attorney to practice law.

There are several different options for **sanctions** against the attorney, including **disbarment** by the court, **suspension** of license to practice by the court, **probation,** or **reprimand. Admonition** is an option if formal charges have not been brought. This is the only type of sanction that is typically not made a public record.

A reprimand is somewhat more severe because of the implications to an attorney when the reprimand is made public. Public censure, or a public reprimand, is generally appropriate when an attorney acts negligently without reasonable diligence in representing a client and causes injury or potential injury to the client.[11]

Probation is often the sanction imposed when the **disciplinary board** determines that the attorney should be allowed to continue practicing law, with supervision.

Suspension of an attorneys' license is not permanent, and the suspension typically provides for a certain date on which the attorney's license will be reinstated.

Serious misconduct may lead to disbarment—the revocation of an attorney's license to practice law. Disbarment may be warranted for a continuing pattern of gross incompetence, neglect of client matters, negligence concerning supervision of office staff or maintaining adequate records, and for conversion of funds.[12] Many jurisdictions allow an attorney who has been disbarred to re-apply for a license to practice law after a prescribed amount of time has lapsed.

Civil Lawsuits

Unethical behavior that results in harm to a client or a third party may result in a civil action being brought against the attorney for monetary damages in a **legal malpractice** suit. Legal malpractice suits are usually filed on the basis of professional negligence or breach of fiduciary obligations. Negligence may be established in a legal malpractice suit when the following four elements are present:

1. **Duty.** There was an actual attorney-client relationship.
2. **Breach.** The attorney's actions involved a breach of duty to the client.
3. **Injury.** The client sustained actual damages.
4. **Causation.** The attorney's acts or omissions were the proximate cause of the damage.

As with the medical profession, a legal malpractice suit against an attorney can have devastating affects. A legal malpractice suit can result in damages being awarded against the attorney's law firm and against the attorney personally. At-

---

Sanction
A penalty or coercive measure that results from failure to comply with a law, rule, or order [a sanction for discovery abuse]. (Black's Law Dictionary, Seventh Edition)

Disbarment
The revocation of an attorney's right to practice law.

Suspension
The temporary cutting off or debarring a person, as from the privileges of that person's profession.

Probation
A period during which a person who holds a job, position, or license, who has failed to perform according to acceptable standards, must either conform to such standards or suffer termination or loss of the license.

Reprimand
In professional responsibility, a form of disciplinary action—imposed after trial or formal charges—that declares the lawyer's conduct improper but does not limit his or her right to practice law. (Black's Law Dictionary, Seventh Edition)

Admonition
Any authoritative advice or caution from the court to the jury regarding their duty as jurors or the admissibility of evidence for consideration [the judge's admonition that the jurors not discuss the case until they are charged]. A reprimand or cautionary statement addressed to counsel by a judge [the judge's admonition that the lawyer stop speaking out of turn]. (Black's Law Dictionary, Seventh Edition)

Disciplinary board
Court-appointed board, typically consisting of a mixture of attorneys and nonattorneys, to receive complaints about attorney misconduct and oversee the disciplinary process.

Legal malpractice
An attorney's failure to exercise on behalf of his client the knowledge, skill, and ability ordinarily possessed and exercised by members of the legal profession. Legal malpractice is a tort if it results in injury.

torneys, therefore, carry legal malpractice insurance to protect them in the event of a legal malpractice suit being brought against them.

A violation of the rules of ethics, in itself, does not establish a malpractice claim in a civil lawsuit.[13] Most courts, however, allow the rules of ethics to be used as evidence in legal malpractice cases. A breach of the code of ethics may be considered evidence that the conduct of the attorney has fallen short of professional standards, which can be considered legal malpractice.

Criminal Prosecution

Some types of unethical behavior are specifically prohibited by law and are considered crimes. Unethical acts that are considered to be the commission of a serious crime, such as **fraud,** may result in **felony** charges. When an attorney commits a crime, he or she may be subject to criminal prosecution and disciplinary action. If an attorney is found guilty of a crime in a court of law, he or she will have to pay the penalty prescribed by the court.

CONSEQUENCES OF UNETHICAL PARALEGAL BEHAVIOR

When a paralegal acts unethically, he or she is not in any danger of being disbarred or sanctioned by the state's disciplinary board. However, this does not mean that unethical behavior by a paralegal cannot have serious consequences. A paralegal's unethical behavior can result in a loss of respect for the paralegal, the loss of the employer's client, and disciplinary action against the responsible attorney. In addition, the paralegal may lose his or her employment and may even be subject to criminal prosecution or a civil lawsuit. In some jurisdictions, the paralegal may be subject to disciplinary action by a committee appointed by the paralegal association to which the paralegal belongs.

Loss of Respect

At a minimum, unethical behavior by a paralegal can lead to the loss of respect by the paralegal's superiors, co-workers, and local legal community and to a poor reputation with his or her peers. The legal community is often the target of negative stereotyping, and unethical behavior by one of its members reflects poorly on the entire profession.

Loss of Clients

In addition to losing co-workers' respect, unethical behavior can lead to the loss of clients by the paralegal's employer. Unethical behavior that jeopardizes a client's case will not be well regarded. Clients will hold their attorneys responsible for the behavior of their employees. If a paralegal breaks a client's trust by unethical behavior, the attorney may very well lose the client.

Disciplinary Action Against Responsible Attorney

As discussed earlier, unethical behavior by a paralegal can lead to disciplinary action against the attorney who is responsible for the paralegal. Attorneys can be disciplined and even disbarred for violations of the code of ethics in the state in which the attorney practices.

Fraud
Deceit, deception, or trickery to induce another to part with anything of value, or to surrender some legal right, to his or her detriment.

Felony
A serious crime, such as aggravated assault, rape, robbery, or murder, usually punishable by death or imprisonment for a term exceeding one year.

Loss of Employment

Behavior by a paralegal that is clearly unethical and damaging to a client, supervising attorney, or the paralegal's employer often leads to loss of employment. Not only does the paralegal become unemployed, but he or she also will probably not receive favorable recommendation from the discharging employer.

Criminal Prosecution

Some rules of ethics are also rules of law. Depending on the exact nature of the unethical behavior, these same acts may be criminal. Paralegals may find themselves facing criminal charges when their unethical behavior is also illegal behavior.

Civil Lawsuits

When the unethical behavior of a paralegal causes a client or another party to be injured, the injured party may sue the firm that employs the paralegal. Paralegals are rarely the target of legal malpractice suits, although they are often covered under the law firm's malpractice insurance. It is more likely that the attorneys who supervise the paralegal will be the targets of a civil action. However, if the client is damaged directly as a result of a paralegal's actions, the paralegal may also be named as a defendant.

No paralegal wants to be responsible for causing his or her employer to be sued, and no paralegal wants the task of having to defend his or her actions in a lawsuit.

Discipline by Paralegal Association

The possibility of being disciplined by a paralegal association is a relatively new development in the paralegal profession. In 1997 the NFPA adopted Guidelines for the Enforcement of the Model Code of Ethics and Professional Responsibility. The NFPA adopted these guidelines in response to its determination that the "NFPA Model Code of Ethics and Professional Responsibility should be recognized as setting forth the enforceable obligations of all paralegals."[14] The NFPA guidelines establish the following:

- Basis for discipline of paralegals
- Guidelines for the formation and operation of a Disciplinary Committee to oversee matters of discipline
- Procedures for the reporting alleged violations of the NFPA's Model Code of Ethics and Professional Responsibility/Disciplinary Rules
- Procedures for investigating charges of misconduct and conducting hearings before a tribunal
- Suggested sanctions for misconduct
- Procedures for appealing a decision of the Committee

Some of the suggested sanctions in the Guidelines include a letter of reprimand to the responding party, counseling, attendance at an approved ethics course, probation, suspension, imposition of a fine and referral to the appropriate authority in the event of criminal activity. The full text of these guidelines is found as part of Appendix D.

It is still too early to judge the full impact of the model guidelines. These guidelines are just a model that may be adopted by any state or local paralegal association affiliated with the NFPA. Obviously, a paralegal cannot be disciplined by an association to which he or she does not belong, and at this time, membership in all paralegal associations is still voluntary. Currently, the guidelines cannot be imposed on any paralegal without his or her consent.

PARALEGAL REGULATION

Attorneys must be licensed and admitted to the bar in the state in which they practice—but who sets the national standards for and regulates paralegals? At this time, the answer is no one. There are currently no minimum national requirements for education for paralegals, nor are there mandatory national guidelines for certification or licensing. In most jurisdictions, paralegals are subject to the same laws concerning the unauthorized practice of law that all nonattorneys are subject to. However, there is a movement underway in many states to change this. Regulation by means of licensing, certification, and registration are currently being discussed in several venues. Possibly by the time you read this text, some of these issues will have been resolved. You must be aware of any regulation requirements being considered, and comply with any requirements in place, in any jurisdiction in which you plan to work as a paralegal.

Almost certainly, any regulation of paralegals will include a scheme for mandating the ethical behavior of paralegals. Any state regulation of paralegals will probably include formal adoption of a code of ethics for all regulated paralegals, as well as a means for enforcing the code of ethics by sanctioning the unethical behavior of the regulated paralegals.

There are several different means by which paralegals might be regulated. Regulated paralegals may be required to fulfill minimum education requirements, licensing requirements, or certification requirements.

Paralegal Licensing

A **license** is a privilege conferred on a person by the government to do something that he or she otherwise would not have the right to do. No form of licensing for paralegals is currently required in any state in this country. However, two types of licensing have been proposed, and either or both may be adopted in several states in the near future.

The first type of proposed licensing covers a broader base of paralegals and requires that all paralegals must meet certain requirements and be licensed in the state in which they work. The second type of licensing requires that **independent paralegals,** or **legal technicians,** meet certain requirements and be licensed by the state. Legal technicians are those individuals who offer their services to the public without the supervision of an attorney.

The term *limited licensure* refers to a process currently utilized in a few jurisdictions that authorizes nonlawyers, who are often paralegals, to perform certain, specific functions that are customarily performed by attorneys. One example of limited licensure is Rule 12 (Limited Practice Rule for Closing Officers) of the Washington Court Rules. This rule authorizes nonattorneys in the State of Washington who meet certain conditions to perform specified functions incident to the closing of real estate and personal property transactions. The authorized functions, including preparation and completion of legal documents incident to the closing, are tasks traditionally considered to be the practice of law.[15]

Paralegal Certification

Certain groups, including the NALA, endorse the **certification** of paralegals, as opposed to licensing. Contrary to licensing, which involves permission from the state to perform certain functions, certification deals with self-regulation. Certification is usually considered to be a voluntary program, such as the Certified Legal Assistant (CLA) or Certified Legal Assistant Specialist (CLAS) certifications currently being granted by NALA. Certification is granted to individuals who meet predetermined qualifications, usually in the areas of education and experience,

License
Permission by competent authority, usually the government, to do an act which, without such permission, would be illegal or otherwise not allowable. Permission to exercise a certain privilege, to carry on a particular business, or to pursue a certain occupation.

Independent paralegal
A self-employed paralegal who works directly for the public to provide legal services not considered to be the practice of law. Also known as a legal technician.

Legal technician
A self-employed paralegal who works directly for the public to provide legal services not considered the practice of law. Also known as an independent paralegal.

Certification
Form of self-regulation whereby an organization grants recognition to an individual who has met qualifications specified by that organization.

and who pass a test established by the certifying group. Other groups have proposed voluntary certification by the state bar associations.

Paralegal Registration

Registration
The process by which individuals or institutions meeting with certain requirements list their names on a roster kept by an agency of government or by a nongovernmental organization. Registration provides the public with a list of individuals who have met with certain requirements.

Some proposals for regulation provide for the **registration** of paralegals. If paralegal registration were required in a particular jurisdiction, paralegals who fall under certain categories (most likely those offering their services directly to the public) would be required to register with the county clerk, or some similar officer, in any county or state in which they work. In order to properly register, a paralegal would likely be required to meet with certain education, bonding, and character requirements.

California has recently passed legislation requiring the registration of **legal document assistants,** paralegals who provide certain self-help services to individuals who represent themselves in legal matters. The registration requirements do not apply to paralegals who work under the supervision of an attorney.

Legal document assistant
Individual recognized in California who is authorized to provide or assist in providing, for compensation, self-help legal services to the public.

Although there are no licensing or certification requirements for paralegals at this time, both the NALA and the NFPA support minimum education standards and voluntary testing for different types of credentials. The NALA and the NFPA do not share the same positions with regard to licensing and certification.

The American Bar Association's Position

The ABA's position is that paralegal regulation is a matter best handled at the state level. It has not proposed a formal plan or model for paralegal regulation.

In 1992, the ABA established the Commission on Nonlawyer Practice consisting of sixteen lawyers and nonlawyers having diverse geographical and professional backgrounds to conduct research, hearings, and deliberations to determine the implications of nonlawyer practice for society, the client, and the legal profession. The Commission heard testimony in Washington, D.C., New York, Minneapolis, and seven other cities and collected extensive data from the testimony of witnesses, written submissions, and independent documents to form the basis for its findings and recommendations.

The Commission examined the nonlawyer activity in law-related situations by **self-represented persons, document preparers,** paralegals, and legal technicians.

Self-represented person
A person who represents himself or herself for the purpose of resolving or completing a process in which the law is involved.

The report issued by the Commission included three major conclusions:[16]

1. Increasing access to affordable assistance in law-related situations is an urgent goal
2. Protecting the public from harm from persons providing assistance in law-related situations is also an urgent goal
3. When adequate protections for the public are in place, nonlawyers have important roles to perform in providing affordable access to justice

Document preparer
An individual who prepares or assists in the preparation of legal documents at the direction of an individual who is representing himself or herself in a legal matter.

The report supports the expanded roles of paralegals, under the supervision of attorneys, and leaves the matter of regulation to the states.

The National Association of Legal Assistants' Position

Certified Legal Assistant (CLA)
Title awarded to paralegals who pass the CLA exam and meet with other criteria established by the National Association of Legal Assistants.

The NALA does not support licensing of paralegals or mandatory regulation of any type. Rather, the NALA prefers voluntary certification of paralegals who meet with certain requirements.

A top priority of the NALA since its formation has been the establishment of certain standards for the profession. The NALA developed a voluntary certification program with a designation of **Certified Legal Assistant** (CLA) and **Certi-**

fied Legal Assistant Specialist (CLAS) for those who successfully meet certain education requirements and pass the CLA or CLAS exam. As of September 1999, there were 9,993 Certified Legal Assistants in the United States and over 7,832 Certified Legal Assistant Specialists. Approximately 21,000 legal assistants had participated in the CLA program.[17] More information on the requirements for the CLA designation is included in Chapter 5.

The National Federation of Paralegal Associations' Position

In 1992 the NFPA passed a resolution that endorses a two-tiered regulatory scheme consisting of licensing and specialty licensing at the state level as the preferred form of regulation. The NFPA resolution outlines standards for the profession, including a minimum level of education, continuing legal education courses, requirements for experience, and standards of ethics and character. The NFPA concurs with the position of the ABA Commission on Nonlawyer Practice by supporting regulation so long as it expands the role of paralegals.

The NFPA's position on regulation favors a two-tiered licensing plan that constitutes mandatory regulation, while recognizing that another form of regulation, such as certification or registration, may be appropriate in a given state. The NFPA's policy on regulation includes:

- Standards for ethics
- Standards for discipline
- Standards for education
- A method to assess advanced competency of paralegals
- Establishing a disciplinary process
- Defining those tasks that paralegals may perform by paralegals in numerous specialty areas of law

More information on the NFPA's position on regulation can be found on the NFPA Web site at **www.paralegals.org.**

The **Paralegal Advanced Competency Exam (PACE)** was developed for the NFPA in 1996 as a means for paralegals to validate their knowledge to themselves and their employers. Also, the members of the NFPA believe that with the increasing numbers of states considering regulation of paralegals, the PACE exam may be one means for establishing competency for future regulation and licensing requirements. Unlike the NALA, which promotes voluntary certification through its CLA exam, the PACE exam is not intended to be used in place of regulation, but rather as a part of a regulation scheme. According to the NFPA, "It is not the intention of NFPA members to use PACE as a voluntary certification process. PACE is to be used in conjunction with a regulatory plan that will permit experienced paralegals to perform at higher levels of responsibility than now permitted."[18] More information on the PACE is included in Chapter 5.

At this time, no jurisdiction requires paralegals to pass either the CLA or PACE exam, and few paralegal employers require passing of either of the exams as a prerequisite to employment.

There are numerous arguments both for and against each type of regulation. Proponents of paralegal regulation believe that it will allow paralegals to expand their role without engaging in the unauthorized practice of law and that it will promote the profession while protecting the public. Many believe that certain legal services can be well performed by nonattorneys, making needed legal services more affordable and more available to the public, thus providing a valuable service to society.

Opposition to regulation comes from a diverse group of members of the legal community. Those who oppose paralegal regulation include attorneys, judges, and some paralegals themselves. Opponents to paralegal regulation argue that regulation is unnecessary and that it would increase legal fees and negatively im-

Certified Legal Assistant Specialist (CLAS)
Title awarded to paralegals who pass the CLA exam, at least one of the CLA specialty exams, and who meet with other criteria established by the National Association of Legal Assistants.

Paralegal Advanced Competency Exam (PACE)
Exam promoted by the NFPA as a means for experienced paralegals to validate their knowledge to themselves and their employers.

pact the paralegal profession. They feel that the provision of legal services should be restricted to licensed attorneys and that the provision of any legal services by paralegals without attorney supervision should be considered the unauthorized practice of law.

New proposals for regulation of paralegals are continually being introduced and considered. For the latest developments in paralegal regulation across the country and in your state, check out the companion Web site to this text at **www.westlegalstudies.com.**

RESOURCES FOR LEGAL ETHICS RESEARCH

As indicated throughout this chapter, there are numerous places to turn with questions concerning legal ethics. Perhaps one of the best resources is your supervising attorney or an ethics committee within the law firm or legal department where you work. The primary source for further research and information is the code of ethics that is binding on the attorneys for whom you work. Ethical advice and guidelines specific to paralegal concerns can be obtained through your local, state, or national paralegal association.

Supervising Attorney or Ethics Committee

A simple question of ethics may be answered verbally by your supervising attorney in most instances. If there is a more complex question involving a particular client or matter, you may be well advised to put the question in memorandum form to your supervising attorney. If your employer has an ethics committee, as do several large law firms and legal departments, you may find that this is the appropriate place to address questions concerning ethics. Again, this request for an opinion should be put in writing, being sure to adhere to any office policies in place.

State Code of Ethics

All paralegals must comply with the state code of ethics (Figure 1–5) that applies to attorneys in their jurisdiction. As discussed previously in this chapter, failure to do so can have serious consequences. A current copy of the state's code of ethics can usually be found in each law library. Many states have made their codes of ethics available over the Internet.

State Bar Associations

Your state's bar association may also make available copies of your state's code of ethics (Figure 1–6). In addition, many state bar associations have Web sites where they publish ethics opinions of the state ethics committee and provide other useful information concerning legal ethics in your state. Ethics opinions may help you to interpret the codes of ethics, and may even address your particular concern.

Paralegal Associations

If you have questions concerning ethical conduct specific to paralegals that are not sufficiently answered by your supervising attorney or ethics committee, the code of ethics of your paralegal association should be consulted. If you are not a member of a paralegal association, you may look to a local association, state association, or the NALA or NFPA for assistance (Figure 1–7). The NFPA Ethics Board will also give advice on specific ethical situations.

Appendix E provides a directory of state and local paralegal associations, along with their national affiliations.

STATE	CODE
Alabama	*Code of Ala.*, Rules of Alabama Supreme Court, vol. 23A (1996), p. 855
Alaska	*Alaska Stat.*, Alaska Court Rules – State and Federal (1999), p. 431 **http://touchngo.com/lglcntr/ctrules/profcon/htframe.htm**
Arizona	*Ariz. Rev. Stat.*, Supreme Court Rules, vol. 17A (1997), p. 375 **http://www.azbar.org/FindingLawyer/rules.asp#Rule42**
Arkansas	*Ark. Code Ann.*, Court Rules (1998), p. 1015
California	*Ann. Cal. Codes*, Professional Rules, vol. 23, pt. 3 (1996), p. 319 (and 1998 supp. p. 76) **Http://www.calbar.org/pub250/1995rpc.htm**
Colorado	*Colo. Rev. Stat.*, vol. 12 (1998), p. 711 **http://www.cobar.org/comms/ethics/rulesprof/rulprofc.htm**
Connecticut	*Conn. Gen. Stat. Ann.*, Connecticut Rules of Court – State and Federal (1998), p. 363
Delaware	*Del. Rules Ann.*, Delaware Rules Annotated (1998), p. 1127
District of Columbia	*D.C. Code*, D.C. Court Rules Annotated (1998), vol. 1, p. 157 **http://www.law.cornell.edu/cgi-bin/foliocgi.exe/DC-code?**
Florida	*Fla. Stat. Ann.*, Bar and Judiciary Rules (1994), vol. 35, p. 227 (and 1998 supp. p. 43) **http://www.flabar.org/newflabar/lawpractice/Rules**
Georgia	*Ga. Code*, Georgia Rules of Court Annotated (1998), p. 1028.
Hawaii	*Hawaii Rev. Stat. Ann.*, Court Rules Annotated (1998), p. 807 **http://www.state.hi.us/jud/hrpc-rls.htm**
Idaho	Idaho Rules of Court, Idaho Rules of Professional Conduct **http://www2.law.cornell.edu/cgi-bin/foliocgi.exe/rpc-idaho?**
Illinois	*Ill. Comp. Stat. Ann.*, State Court Rules Annotated, vol. 2 (1997), p. 562 **http://www.illinoisbar.org/CourtRules/Article8/home.html**
Indiana	*Burns Ind. Stat. Ann.*, Court Rules Annotated (1998), p. 205 **http://www.state.in.us/judiciary/courtrules**
Iowa	*Iowa Code Ann.*, Iowa Rules of Court (1999), p. 367 **http://www.judicial.state.ia.us/rules/iowarules.asp**
Kansas	*Kan. Stat. Ann.*, Kansas Court Rules and Procedure (1999), p. 473 **http://www.kscourts.org/ctruls/atrul226.htm**
Kentucky	*Ky. Rev. Stat. Ann.*, Kentucky Rules Annotated (1998), p. 1099
Louisiana	*La. Rev. Stat.*, vol. 21A (1988), p. 161 (and 1998 supp. p. 62) **http://lsba.org/html/rules_of_professional_conduct.html**
Maine	*Me. Rev. Stat. Ann.*, Maine Rules of Court (1998), p. 387
Maryland	*Ann. Code Md.*, Maryland Rules, vol. 2 (1997), p. 408
Massachusetts	*Mass. Gen. Laws Ann.*, Massachusetts Rules of Court (State) (1998), p. 280 **http://www.massbar.org/rules/contents.html**
Michigan	*Mich. Comp. Laws*, Michigan Rules of Court (State) (1998), p. 655 **Http://www.michbar.org/directory/rulescon.html**

FIGURE 1–5

State code of ethics

STATE	CODE
Minnesota	*Minn. Stat. Ann.,* Minnesota Court Rules, vol. 52 (1993), p. 169 (and 1998 supp. p. 187) **Http://www.courts.state.mn.us/lprb/conduct.html**
Mississippi	*Miss. Code Ann.,* Mississippi Rules of Court (1998), p. 327 **Http://www.mslawyer.com/mssc/index019.html**
Missouri	*Mo. Ann. Stat.,* Rules 1–26, Bar and Judiciary (1995), p. 26 (and 1998 Supp. p. 20)
Montana	*Mont. Code Ann.,* Annotations vol. 12 (1998), p. 606 **Http://www.montanabar.org/attorneyinfo/rulesandregs/indexrp.htm**
Nebraska	*Neb. Rev. Stat. Ann.,* Nebraska Court Rules and Procedure (1997), p. 545
Nevada	*Nev. Rev. Stat., Ann.,* Court Rules Annotated (1998), p. 143 **http://www.leg.state.nv.us/other/cr/scr.html**
New Hampshire	*N.H. Rev.Stat. Ann.,* New Hampshire Court Rules Annotated, vol. 2 (1998)
New Jersey	New Jersey Rules of Court, Rule 1:14 (1999) **http://www.njlawnet.com/nj-rpc/**
New Mexico	N.M. Stat. Ann., New Mexico Rules Annotated, vol. 2 (1998), p. 453
New York	*N.Y. Cons. Laws Ann.* (McKinney), New York Rules of Court, (1998) p. 645 **Http://www.nysba.org/opinions/codes/anchor1.html**
North Carolina	*Gen. Stat. N.C. Ann.,* Annotated Rules of North Carolina (1998), p. 495 **http://www.aoc.state.nc.us/www/public/aoc/barrules.html**
North Dakota	*N.D. Century Code Ann.,* North Dakota Court Rules Annotated, (1998–99) p. 791 **http://www.court.state.nd.us/Court/Rules/FRAMESET.HTM**
Ohio	*Ohio Rev. Code Ann. (Anderson),* tit. 19 (1994), p. 261 (and 1996 supp. p. 127)
Oklahoma	*Okla. Stat. Ann.,* tit. 5–6 (1996), p. 159 (and 1999 supp. p. 46)
Oregon	Oregon Rules of Court, Code of Professional Responsibility **www.osbar.org** (then click on OSB Reference Desk and then on Ethics Advice for Lawyers).
Pennsylvania	*Pa. Cons. Stat. Ann.,* tit. 42 (R. Civ. P. sec 2326–end) (1998 supp. p. 133) **http://members.aol.com/RulesPA/conduct.html**
Rhode Island	*Gen. Laws of R.I.,* Rhode Island Court Rules Annotated (1998), p. 93
South Carolina	*Code of Laws of S.C. Ann.,* Court Rules: Appellate Court Rules, vol. 22A (1996), p. 116
South Dakota	*S.D. Codified Laws,* vol. 7A (1995), p. 184 (and 1998 supp. 37)
Tennessee	*Tenn. Code Ann.,* Tennessee Court Rules Annotated (1998-99), p. 30 (and 1997 supp. p. 1)
Texas	*Vernon's Texas Codes Ann.,* Government Code, vol. 3A (1997 supp. p. 173) **http://www2.law.cornell.edu/cgi-bin/foliocgi.exe/rpc-texas?**

FIGURE 1–5—*cont'd*
State code of ethics

STATE	CODE
Utah	Utah Code Ann, *Utah Court Rules Annotated (1998)*, p. 1177 **http://www.utahbar.org/rules/index.html**
Vermont	*Vt. Stat. Ann.*, Admin. Orders & Rules (1986), p. 452 (and 1997 supp. p. 354) **http://www.vtbar.org**
Virginia	*Code of Va. Ann.*, Rules of Virginia Supreme Court, vol. 11 (1998), p. 310 **http://www.vsb.org/profguides/codeprof.html**
Washington	*Wash. Rev. Code Ann.*, Washington Court Rules (State) (1999), p. 33 **http://198.187.0.226/courts/rules/state/rpc/home.htm**
West Virginia	*W. Va. Code Ann.*, West Virginia Court Rules (1997), p. 583
Wisconsin	*Wis. Stat. Ann.*, Supreme Court Rules – 1997 Special Pamphlet, p. 94 **http://www.wisbar.org/rules/conduct.html**
Wyoming	*Wyo. Stat. Ann.*, Wyoming Court Rules (1998), p. 697 **http://courts.state.wy.us/RULES/18PROCO.HTM**

FIGURE 1–5—*cont'd*
State code of ethics

Alabama
Alabama State Bar
415 Dexter Avenue
P.O. Box 671
Montgomery, AL 36104
Tel: 334-269-1515
Fax: 334-261-6310
http://www.alabar.org/

Alaska
Alaska Bar Association
510 L Street #602
P.O. Box 100279
Anchorage, AK 99510
Tel: 907-272-7469
Fax: 907-272-2932
http://www.alaskabar.org/

Arizona
State Bar of Arizona
111 W. Monroe Street, Suite 1800
Phoenix, AZ 85003-1742
602-340-7200
Fax: 602-271-4930
http://www.azbar.org/

Arkansas
Arkansas State Bar Association
400 W. Markham, Suite 401
Little Rock, AR 72201
Tel: 501-375-4605
Fax: 501-375-4901
http://www.arkbar.com/

California
California State Bar Association
555 Franklin Street
San Francisco, CA 94102
Tel: 415-561-8200
Fax: 415-561-8305
http://www.calbar.org/

Colorado
Colorado Bar Association
1900 Grant Street, #950
Denver, CO 80203
Tel: 303-860-1115
Fax: 303-894-0821
http://www.cobar.org

Connecticut
Connecticut State Bar Association
101 Corporate Place
Rocky Hill, CT 06067
Tel: 860-721-0025
Fax: 860-257-4125
http://www.ctbar.org/

Delaware
Delaware State Bar Association
201 Orange Street, Suite 1100
Wilmington, DE 19801
Tel: 302-658-5279
Fax: 302-658-5212
http://www.dsba.org

FIGURE 1–6
State bar associations

District of Columbia
District of Columbia Bar Association
1819 H Street NW, 12th Floor
Washington DC 20006-3690
Tel: 202-223-6600
Fax: 202-293-3388
http://www.badc.org/

Florida
650 Apalachee Parkway
Tallahassee, FL 32399-2300
Tel: 904-561-5600
Fax: 904-561-5827
http://www.flabar.org/

Georgia
State Bar of Georgia
800 The Hurt Building
50 Hurt Plaza
Atlanta, GA 30303
Tel: 800-334-6865
Fax: 404-527-8717
http://www.gabar.org/

Hawaii
Hawaii State Bar Association
Penthouse 1, 9th Floor
1136 Union Mall
Honolulu, HI 96813
Tel: 808-537-1868
Fax: 808-521-7936
http://www.hsba.org/

Idaho
Idaho State Bar
P.O. Box 895
525 W. Jefferson Street
Boise, ID 83701
Tel: 208-334-4500
Fax: 208-334-4515
http://www2.state.id.us/isb/

Illinois
Illinois State Bar Association
424 S. Second Street
Springfield, IL 62701
Tel: 217-525-1760
Fax: 217-525-0712
http://www.illinoisbar.org/

Indiana
Indiana State Bar Association
230 E. Ohio, 4th Floor
Indiana Bar Center
Indianapolis, IN 46204-2199
Tel: 317-639-5465
Fax: 317-266-2588
http://www.ai.org/isba/

Iowa
Iowa State Bar Association
521 Locust, Suite 300
Des Moines, IA 50309-1939
Tel: 515-243-3179
Fax: 515-243-2511
http://www.iowabar.org/

Kansas
Kansas State Bar Association
1200 Harrison Street
P.O. Box 1037
Topeka, KS 66612
Tel: 785-234-5696
Fax: 785-234-3813
http://www.ink.org/public/cybar/

Kentucky
Kentucky Bar Association
514 West Main Street
Frankfort, KY 40601-1883
Tel: 502-564-3795
Fax: 502-564-3225
http://www.kybar.org/

Louisiana
Louisiana State Bar Association
601 St. Charles Avenue
New Orleans, LA 70130
Tel: 504-566-1600
Fax: 504-566-0930
http://www.lsba.org/

Maine
Maine State Bar Association
124 State Street
P.O. Box 788
Augusta, ME 04330
Tel: 207-622-7523
Fax: 207-623-0083
http://www.mainebar.org/

Maryland
Maryland State Bar Association
520 W. Fayette Street
Baltimore, MD 21201
Tel: 410-685-7878
Fax: 410-837-0518
http://www.msba.org/

Massachusetts
Massachusetts Bar Association
20 West Street
Boston, MA 02111-1218
Tel: 617-542-3602
Fax: 617-426-4344
http://www.massbar.org/

Michigan
Michigan State Bar Association
306 Townsend Street
Lansing, MI 48933-2083
Tel: 517-372-9030
Fax: 517-372-2410
http://www.michbar.org/

Minnesota
Minnesota State Bar Association
514 Nicollet Mall, Suite 300
Minneapolis, MN 55402
Tel: 612-333-1183
Fax: 612-333-4927
http://www.mnbar.org/

FIGURE 1–6—cont'd
State bar associations

Mississippi
Mississippi State Bar Association
643 N. State Street, P.O. Box 2168
Jackson, MS 39225-2168
Tel: 601-948-4471
Fax: 601-355-8635
http://www.msbar.org/

Missouri
Missouri State Bar Association
326 Monroe
Jefferson City, MO 65102
Tel: 314-635-4128
Fax: 314-635-2811
http://www.mobar.org/

Montana
State Bar of Montana
46 N. Last Chance Gulch
Suite 2A
P.O. Box 577
Helena, MT 59624
Tel: 406-442-7660
Fax: 406-442-7763
http://www.montanabar.org/

Nebraska
Nebraska State Bar Association
635 S. 14th Street, 2nd Floor
P.O. Box 81809
Lincoln, NE 68501
Tel: 402-475-7091
Fax: 402-475-7098
http://www.nebar.org

Nevada
State Bar of Nevada
201 Las Vegas Boulevard South
Suite 200
Las Vegas, NV 89101
Tel: 702-382-2200
Fax: 702-385-2878
http://www.nvbar.org/

New Hampshire
New Hampshire State Bar Association
112 Pleasant Street
Concord, NH 03301
Tel: 603-224-2942
Fax: 603-224-2910
http://www.nh.com/legal/idxbar.html

New Jersey
New Jersey State Bar Association
New Jersey Law Center
One Constitution Square
New Brunswick, NJ 08901-1500
Tel: 908-249-5000
Fax: 908-249-2815

New Mexico
State Bar of New Mexico
5121 Masthead N.E.
P.O. Box 25883
Albuquerque, NM 87125
Tel: 505-797-6000
Fax: 505-828-3765
http://www.technet.nm.org/sbnm/

New York
New York State Bar Association
One Elk Street
Albany, NY 12207
Tel: 518-487-5557
Fax: 518-487-5564
http://www.nysba.org

North Carolina
North Carolina State Bar Association
800 Weston Pkwy
Cary, NC 27519
Tel: 919-677-0561
Fax: 919-677-0761
http://www.barlinc.org/

North Dakota
State Bar Association of North Dakota
P.O. Box 2136
Bismarck, ND 58502-2136
Tel: 701-255-1404
Fax: 701-224-1621

Ohio
Ohio State Bar Association
1700 Lake Shore Drive
P.O. Box 1562
Columbus, OH 43216-6562
Tel: 614-487-2050
Fax: 614-487-1008
http://www.ohiobar.org/

Oklahoma
Oklahoma Bar Association
1901 N. Lincoln
Oklahoma City, OK 73105
Tel: 405-524-2365
Fax: 405-524-1115
http://www.okbar.org

Oregon
Oregon State Bar
5200 SW Meadows Road
Lake Oswego, OR 97035
Tel: 503-620-0222
Fax: 503-684-1366
http://www.osbar.org/

Pennsylvania
Pennsylvania State Bar Association
100 South Street
P.O. Box 186
Harrisburg, PA 17108-0186
Tel: 717-238-6715
Fax: 717-238-1204
http://www.pa-bar.org/

FIGURE 1–6—*cont'd*
State bar associations

Rhode Island
Rhode Island State Bar Association
115 Cedar Street
Providence, RI 02903
Tel: 401-421-5740
401-421-2703
http://www.ribar.com/

South Carolina
South Carolina Bar
950 Taylor Street, P.O. Box 608
Columbia, SC 29202
Tel: 803-799-6653
Fax: 803-799-4118
http://www.scbar.org/

South Dakota
South Dakota State Bar Association
222 E. Capitol
Pierre, SD 57501
Tel: 605-224-7554
Fax: 605-224-0282
http://www.sdbar.org/

Tennessee
Tennessee Bar Association
3622 West End Avenue
Nashville, TN 37205-2403
Tel: 614-383-7421
Fax: 615-297-8058
http://www.tba.org/

Texas
State Bar of Texas
1414 Colorado
P.O. Box 12487
Austin, TX 78711-2487
Tel: 512-463-1463
Fax: 512-473-2295
http://texasbar.com/start.htm

Utah
Utah State Bar
645 S. 200 East
Salt Lake City, UT 84111
Tel: 801-531-9077
Fax: 801-531-0660
http://www.utahbar.org/

Vermont
Vermont State Bar Association
35-37 Court Street
P.O. Box 100
Montpelier, VT 05602
Tel: 802-223-2020
Fax: 802-223-1573
http://www.vtbar.org/

Virginia
Virginia Bar Association
7th & Franklin Building
701 E. Franklin Street, Suite 1120
Richmond, VA 23219
Tel: 804-644-0041
Fax: 804-644-0052
http://www.vsb.org/

Washington
Washington State Bar Association
500 Westin Bldg.
2001 6th Avenue
Seattle, WA 98121-2599
Tel: 206-727-8200
Fax: 206-727-8320
http://www.wsba.org/

West Virginia
West Virginia State Bar Association
2006 Kanawha Boulevard E.
Charleston, WV 25311
Tel: 304-558-2456
Fax: 304-342-1474
http://www.wvbar.org/

Wisconsin
Wisconsin State Bar Association
402 W. Wilson
Madison, WI 53703
Tel: 608-250-6101
Fax: 608-257-5502
http://www.wisbar.org

Wyoming
Wyoming State Bar
500 Randall Avenue, P.O. Box 109
Cheyenne, WY 82001
Tel: 307-632-9061
Fax: 307-632-3737
http://www.wyomingbar.org/

FIGURE 1–6—cont'd
State bar associations

CHAPTER SUMMARY

- Legal ethics is the code of conduct among members of the legal profession that governs their moral and professional duties toward one another, toward their clients, and toward the courts.
- The role of legal ethics is to identify and remove inappropriate conduct from the legal profession and to protect the public.
- Professional responsibility is a general term that refers to the duties and obligations of those in the legal field.
- Attorneys are subject to the code of ethics adopted by the state in which they are licensed to practice.

American Bar Association	**http://www.abanet.org/**
National Association of Legal Assistants	**http://www.nala.org/**
National Federation of Paralegal Associations	**http://www.paralegals.org/**
Hieros Gamos	**http://www.hg.org/**
Katsuey Kat's Legal Links	**http://www.katsuey.com/**
The 'Lectric Law Library's Paralegal's Reading Room	**http://www.lectlaw.com/ppara.htm**
Legal Information Institute (links to state codes of ethics opinions)	**http://www.law.cornell.edu/ethics/**
Legalethics.com: The Internet Ethics Site	**http://www.legalethics.com/**
The Virtual Chase	**http://www.virtualchase.com/resources.ethics.shtml**
Stetson University College of Law	**http://legal.law.stetson.edu/litethics/ethicslinks.htm**

FIGURE 1–7

Online resources for paralegal ethics research

- The code of ethics adopted by most states follows either the ABA's Model Rules of Professional Conduct or the older Model Code of Professional Responsibility.
- Attorneys can be held responsible for the unethical behavior of their non-lawyer employees, including paralegals.
- The National Association of Legal Assistants and the National Federation of Paralegal Associations are both national paralegal associations that have adopted rules and guidelines for ethical behavior by paralegals.
- There are currently no state or national requirements that paralegals must be licensed or hold a certificate.
- Unethical behavior by an attorney may result in disciplinary action by the state disciplinary board, a civil suit against the attorney for legal malpractice, or even criminal prosecution.
- Unethical behavior by a paralegal may result in the loss of respect of co-workers and others, the loss of the firm's client, disciplinary action against the attorney to whom the paralegal reports, loss of employment, being named in a civil lawsuit, or criminal prosecution.

SUMMARY QUESTIONS

1. What is the role of legal ethics?
2. Suppose you have a question concerning the ethical handling of client trust account funds? Where might you look for an answer?
3. Which branch of law has the ultimate authority over the ethical behavior of attorneys?
4. Do the state paralegal associations have the same authority over ethical paralegal conduct as the state bar association has over ethical attorney conduct in most states? Why or why not?
5. If the Model Rules of Professional Conduct adopted by the ABA are not binding authority on the attorneys who are members of the ABA, why does the ABA adopt such rules?
6. Suppose that Lewis is a new paralegal working for Sandra's firm on a high-profile domestic abuse case involving a local politician. Lewis has never been cautioned about client confidentiality, and he is aware that others in the firm

have leaked information to the press on previous occasions. When a friend of a friend indicates that the local gossip paper would pay good money for the inside scoop on a case, Lewis accepts the offer and talks to a reporter. Could Sandra be held responsible for Lewis's actions?

7. Suppose that you work for a small law firm that specializes in estate planning. One of the duties you have assumed in the six months you have been on the job is attending the initial client interview. Recently you have been asked to conduct the initial interview on your own. your sister, who is in law school, tells you that she thinks that is considered the unauthorized practice of law in your state. How can you determine if she is right?

8. What are the possible consequences of unethical behavior by paralegals?

9. How could regulation of paralegals affect the enforcement of rules of ethics for paralegals?

10. A complaint has been filed by a former client with the state disciplinary board against attorney Mark Brown. The complaint alleges that Mark Brown's negligence caused her personal injury lawsuit to be dismissed, when she feels that the suit was worth several hundred thousand dollars to her. What are the possible dispositions of this matter?

ENDNOTES

[1]The states of Alaska, California, Colorado, Connecticut, Florida, Illinois, Kansas, Michigan, Minnesota, Montana, Nevada, New Jersey, New Mexico, North Carolina, North Dakota, Ohio, Rhode Island, Texas, Utah, Virginia, and Wisconsin currently have paralegal members.

[2]Preliminary Statement to the Model Code of Professional Responsibility, as amended through 1980.

[3]Ibid.

[4]Chair's Introduction to Model Rules of Professional Conduct, by Robert W. Meserve, then Chairman of the American Bar Association Commission on Evaluation of Professional Standards (1983).

[5]Preamble to Model Rules of Professional Conduct, as amended through 1996.

[6]Model Code of Professional Responsibility and Code of Judicial Conduct Preliminary Statement (1969).

[7]Preamble to NALA Model Standards and Guidelines for Utilization of Legal Assistants from the NALA Web site (1997).

[8]NFPA, An Association's Partner in Progress, NFPA Web site, **www.paralegals.org.**

[9]National Federation of Paralegal Associations, Inc. Model Code of Ethics and Professional Responsibility and Guidelines for Enforcement Preamble (1997).

[10]National Federation of Paralegal Associations Guidelines for Rendering Ethics and Disciplinary Opinions (1995).

[11]People v. Fry, 875 P.2d 222 (Colo. 1994).

[12]Disciplinary Board v. Nassif, 547 N.W.2d. 541 (N.D. 1996).

[13]Nagy v. Beckley, 578 N.E. 2d 1134 (Ill. App. 1991).

[14]National Federation of Paralegal Associations, Inc. Model Code of Ethics and Professional Responsibility and Guidelines for Enforcement Preamble (1997).

[15]Washington Local Rules of Court and West's Washington Court Rules, Part I, Rule 12 (1997).

[16]ABA Commission on Nonlawyer Practice. Nonlawyer Activity in Law-Related Situations A Report with Recommendations, 1995 American Bar Association.

[17]Professional Certification, Background and Numbers, NALA Web site September 1998, **www.nala.org/cert.htm**

[18]NFPA Response to the ABA Commission on Nonlawyer Practice, from the NFPA's Web site at **www.paralegals.org/Development/abaresponse.html** (1997)

[19]Selected definitions from Black's Law Dictionary, Seventh Edition, Copyright (c) 1999 West Group, Eagan, Minnesota, USA, with permission.

LAW PRACTICE FOR DUMMIES: THE MOVE TOWARD SELF-HELP LEGAL SERVICES

How to File for Bankruptcy, Do Your Own Divorce, How to Prepare Your Own Will, Fight Your Traffic Ticket—and Win! These are just a few of the titles you may find on the shelf in your neighborhood bookstore or library. The list of titles for self-help legal books continues to grow. And, increasingly, so does the number of software solutions to your legal problems.

Whereas the unauthorized practice of law, especially representing others in court or disseminating legal advice by lay persons, is illegal, individuals almost always have a right to self-representation. Legal self-help books and software are making self-representation an increasingly attractive alternative to hiring an attorney for many routine legal tasks. Self-help books and software are available on numerous topics. For example, there are many state-specific self-help books on drafting your own simple will. Divorces, bankruptcies, and small claims are other areas in which self-help books and software are becoming increasingly popular.

Another factor contributing to the rise in self-representation in the United States is the availability of information. In this information age, laws, court rules and procedures, forms, and advice are available over the Internet. The lay person is finding legal information more accessible and easier to understand.

In several states the court systems are also making an attempt to assist individuals, especially the poor, to access their court system and services. Small claims courts in several jurisdictions do not allow attorney representation—thereby giving all individuals a fair and equal chance to present their cases to the court.

Several federal courts and federal agencies have taken measures to increase access. In 1998 President Clinton directed the heads of executive departments and agencies to have all the federal government's documents in plain language. In his June 1, 1998, memo,[i] the president directed the use of plain language "in all new documents, other than regulations, that explain how to obtain a benefit or service or how to comply with a requirement you administer or enforce." The use of plain language in such documents makes it easier for the average person to understand his or her rights and how to obtain any benefits he or she is due.

Self-representation is a right that can benefit lay people when properly exercised. However, even the staunchest supporters of self-representation agree that it has its limits. For example, an educated lay person with adequate information and support can usually represent himself or herself in an amicable divorce. But when the other spouse hires an attorney and several issues, such as child custody and property settlement, are contested, it is time for the lay person to seek the assistance of an attorney. Most lay people are not equipped to represent themselves in a court of law, especially when the opposing party has attorney representation. Several areas of law are so complex that the advice of an attorney specializing in that area of law is imperative. Many attorneys hire specialists to represent them in matters outside their areas of expertise.

---

[i] memorandum for the Heads of Executive Departments and Agencies, from President Bill Clinton (June 1, 1998).

In Texas, a special committee of the bar association recently challenged the legality of self-help books and software. In 1998, the Texas Unauthorized Practice of Law Committee initiated investigations of Parsons Technology and Nolo Press to determine if the distribution of their products constituted the unauthorized practice of law in Texas. Parsons Technology is an Iowa company that markets Quicken Family Lawyer, self-help legal software. Nolo Press is the largest publisher of legal self-help books in the United States.

The Committee's investigation of Parsons resulted in a lawsuit in which a federal judge in Dallas, Texas issued a summary judgment preventing Parsons from distributing future copies of Quicken Family Lawyer software in Texas. Judge Barefoot Sanders found that distribution of such self-help legal software constituted the unauthorized practice of law under §§Tex. Gov't Code 81.101-.106 (Vernon's 1998).

Parsons Technology quickly appealed the Court's decision, which was vacated by the U.S. Court of Appeals for the Fifth Circuit. The appeal was based on an amendment to Tex. Gov't Code 81.101-106, which was signed into law in June 1999, immediately before the court's decision. The new law states, in part, that "the 'practice of law' does not include the design, creation, publication, distribution, display, or sale ... [of] computer software, or similar products if the products clearly and conspicuously state that the products are not a substitute for the advice of an attorney."

The amendment to the Texas statute also benefited Nolo Press. In a September 21, 1999, letter to Nolo's attorney, the Committee announced its decision to drop its investigation of Nolo Press and other self-help law publishers. At least for the immediate future, self-help law book and software publishers will continue to assist those who wish to handle their own routine legal matters.

Chapter 2

Unauthorized Practice of Law

"The prohibition against unauthorized law practice is within the state's police power and is designed to ensure that those performing legal services do so competently."

J.W. v. Superior Court, 17 Cal.App.4th 958 (1993)

An Ethical Dilemma
Introduction
Basic Rules Concerning the Unauthorized Practice of Law
  Attorneys Must Not Engage in the Unauthorized Practice of Law
  Attorneys Must Not Assist Others in the Unauthorized Practice of Law
    Attorney Supervision of Employees
What Constitutes the Unauthorized Practice of Law?
  Activities Considered *Practicing Law*
    Setting and Accepting Fees for Legal Work
    Giving Legal Advice
    Preparing or Signing Legal Documents
    In-Court Representation
  State Statute Definitions
  State Court Definitions
Professions at Risk of Engaging in the Unauthorized Practice of Law
Self-Representation
Enforcing the Unauthorized Practice of Law Rules
Case and Discussion
Guidelines for Utilizing Paralegals
From the Paralegal's Perspective

  Traditional Paralegals
  Paralegals in the Corporation
  Paralegals Employed by the Government
  Freelance Paralegals
Independent Paralegals
Guidance from the Paralegal Associations
Avoiding the Unauthorized Practice of Law
  Disclose Your Status
  Have Your Work Reviewed and Approved by an Attorney
  Communicate with Your Supervising Attorney
  Don't Give Legal Advice
  Never Discuss the Merits of a Client's Case with Opposing Counsel
  Never Agree to Represent a Client or Negotiate or Set Fees on Behalf of an Attorney
  Never Represent a Client at a Deposition, in Court of Law, or Before an Administrative Board or Tribunal Without Authorization
Consequences to the Paralegal for the Unauthorized Practice of Law
Case Law Involving Paralegals
A Question of Ethics
Case and Discussion

Chapter Summary

Summary Questions

An Ethical Dilemma

Attorney Christine Pearson specializes in real estate law, but occasionally she will bring in a family law case. Ms. Pearson knows very little about family law, but her paralegal, Wendy Roberts, has had extensive experience in the area. When Ms. Pearson brings in a family law case, she has Wendy handle the entire matter, including meeting with and giving advice to the clients, completing all pleadings, and settling the matter through **mediation.** When Wendy asks Ms. Pearson a question, the answer is usually, "I don't know, Wendy. You know more about family law than I do." When the case is over, Ms. Pearson bills the clients and collects the fee. Is Ms. Pearson acting unethically by her delegation to Ms. Roberts?

Answer and Discussion: Yes. Ms. Pearson is clearly assisting Wendy with the unauthorized practice of law by not supervising her or taking responsibility for the files handled by her.

INTRODUCTION

The authority to practice law is granted to attorneys through the issuance of a license by each state or territory in the United States and by each federal court. Licensing qualifications vary among jurisdictions, but usually include meeting minimum education, citizenship, residence, age, and character requirements and passing a bar examination. Anyone who practices law without the proper license is considered to be guilty of the **unauthorized practice of law.**

The unauthorized practice of law is a difficult issue that concerns both attorneys and paralegals in significant ways. Attorneys have an ethical duty to refrain from practicing law in any jurisdiction in which they are unauthorized to do so. In addition, attorneys must be responsible for the actions of their employees and supervise their work to ensure that they are not breaching any rules prohibiting the unauthorized practice of law. Paralegals, on the other hand, must be aware of any rules concerning the unauthorized practice of law and must be sure that they are performing their jobs to the best of their abilities, without *practicing law.*

Unauthorized individuals are prohibited from practicing law because it is assumed that they do not have the necessary knowledge and skill to adequately represent others in matters of a legal nature. Unauthorized practice of law rules are designed to protect the public from "rendition of legal services by unqualified persons."[1] Courts have enforced unauthorized practice of law statutes, stating that it is clear that their purpose is to ensure that "laymen would not serve others in a representative capacity in areas requiring the skill and judgment of a licensed attorney."[2]

Another function of the rules regarding the unauthorized practice of law is to protect the integrity of the judicial system and the legal profession. Although attorneys are subject to the code of ethics established in each state, lay persons cannot be held to that code.

This chapter begins with a look at the basic rules of ethics and laws concerning the unauthorized practice law and then examines what is generally considered to be the unauthorized practice of law. Next, this chapter focuses on some of the professions at risk of engaging in the unauthorized practice of law, the individual's right to self-representation, and the consequences to attorneys who engage in, or aid others in, the commission of the unauthorized practice of law. The first part of this chapter concludes with a look at the guidelines available to assist attorneys

Mediation
An alternative dispute-resolution process in which a neutral third person, the mediator, helps disputing parties to reach an agreement. The mediator has no power to impose a decision on the parties unless participation is voluntary.

Unauthorized practice of law
Engaging in the practice of law without the license required by law.

with the proper utilization of paralegals. The second part of this chapter explores the issue of the unauthorized practice of law from the paralegal's perspective, including traditional, freelance, and independent paralegals. This chapter concludes with a look at the guidance available from the paralegal associations and how you, as a paralegal, can avoid the unauthorized practice of law.

BASIC RULES CONCERNING THE UNAUTHORIZED PRACTICE OF LAW

Rules prohibiting attorneys to practice law in any state in which they are unauthorized, or to assist others who are unauthorized with the practice of law, are established by the code of ethics adopted by each state for attorneys, by case law, by court rules, and by general statutes. The rules in most states closely resemble Model Rule 5.5 of the Model Rules of Professional Conduct.

> 5.5 **Unauthorized Practice of Law.** A lawyer shall not:
> (a) practice law in a jurisdiction where doing so violates the regulation of the legal profession in that jurisdiction; or
> (b) assist a person who is not a member of the bar in the performance of activity that constitutes the unauthorized practice of law.

Attorneys Must Not Engage in the Unauthorized Practice of Law

Admission to the bar is done on a state by state basis, and attorneys who are admitted in one state are not authorized to practice law in any other state without special permission. Attorneys may be admitted to the bar in more than one state, allowing them to practice law in neighboring states or in states where it may be beneficial to their practice for other reasons. Attorneys whose practice brings them before federal courts must be admitted to practice before those courts. Federal courts usually admit all attorneys who are licensed in the state where the court is located.

Attorneys who have an occasional need to practice law in a state where they are not licensed may receive special permission from the court for handling a specific matter. Most states extend **reciprocity** to attorneys from neighboring states who have practiced for a minimum number of years. Attorneys who practice law in any state where they are not licensed, or do not otherwise have permission, are engaging in the unauthorized practice of law.

Attorneys Must Not Assist Others in the Unauthorized Practice of Law

Attorneys must not assist unauthorized individuals in practicing law. If an attorney is associated with a disbarred or suspended attorney, the licensed attorney must not in any way aid his or her unauthorized associate in any action that would constitute the unauthorized practice of law.

Attorney Supervision of Employees. As set forth in Rule 5.3 of the Model Rules of Professional Conduct and similar rules in each state, attorneys are responsible for the conduct of their nonattorney employees, and they may be held accountable for the unethical actions of their employees. Licensed attorneys must responsibly supervise the actions of any employees or agents to ensure that they are not engaging in the unauthorized practice of law or they will be in violation of the pertinent rules or statutes concerning the unauthorized practice of law.

Reciprocity
Mutual or bi-lateral action (the Arthurs stopped receiving social invitations from friends because of their lack of reciprocity). The mutual concession of advantages or privileges for purposes of commercial or diplomatic relations (Texas and Louisiana grant reciprocity to each other's citizens in qualifying for in-state tuition rates). (*Black's Law Dictionary, Seventh Edition*)

Just how close must the attorney supervision be? This question has been addressed in several venues, and there is some variance in the answers given. Generally, the attorney must have direct contact with his or her employees. It would not be acceptable for paralegals to run one or more offices for an attorney who would not be located on site. The ABA Commission on Professional Ethics, Opinion 316 (1967), states that lawyers can employ any number of lay employees to perform a wide variety of tasks "except counsel clients about law matters, engage directly in the practice of law, appear in court or appear in formal proceedings as part of the judicial process, so long as it is he who takes the work and vouches for it to the client and becomes responsible to the client." Attorneys cannot delegate their role of appearing in court on behalf of a client or of giving legal advice to a client. An attorney "must not under any circumstances delegate to such person the exercise of the lawyer's professional judgment on behalf of the client or even allow it to be influenced by the nonlawyer's assistance."[3]

WHAT CONSTITUTES THE UNAUTHORIZED PRACTICE OF LAW?

The term *unauthorized practice of law* simply means the practice of law by someone who is unauthorized. Anyone who is not a properly licensed attorney is unauthorized. The difficulty with the term *unauthorized practice of law* lies with the definition of the term *practice of law*. The practice of law, in general terms, is defined as "doing and performing services in and in conformity with the adopted rules of procedure."[4] While it is clear that representing others before a court of law constitutes the practice of law, the practice of law extends beyond litigation, and includes giving legal advice and counsel, rendering a service that requires the use of legal knowledge or skill and preparing instruments and contracts by which legal rights are secured, whether or not the matter is pending in a court.[5] The courts have identified the following general parameters to determine whether the unauthorized practice of law has been engaged in:

1. Was the service rendered a service typically performed by attorneys or commonly understood to involve the practice of law?
2. Did the service rendered require legal skills and knowledge beyond that of the average lay person?[6]
3. Was there harm done to the consumer as a result of the services rendered?

Activities Considered *Practicing Law*

The practice of law generally includes the following activities:

1. Setting fees for legal work
2. Giving legal advice
3. Preparing or signing legal documents
4. Representing another before a court or other **tribunal**

Tribunal
A court or other adjudicatory body. The seat, bench, or place where a judge sits. *(Black's Law Dictionary, Seventh Edition)*

Setting and Accepting Fees for Legal Work. Entering into an arrangement to accept a fee for work of a legal nature by anyone other than a duly licensed attorney is clearly the unauthorized practice of law. However, it has been found that accepting a fee is not necessary to the unauthorized practice of law. In a recent case in Florida, defendants were enjoined from giving legal advice even if no fee was charged. According to the court, compensation is not a necessary element to proving that an individual has engaged in the unlicensed practice of law.[7]

Giving Legal Advice. It is generally agreed that giving legal advice is considered to be practicing law. Several tests have been applied to determine whether an individual is giving legal advice, and different rules and tests may be applied in different jurisdictions. Generally, someone is giving legal advice if:

1. The knowledge of the information imparted generally requires an advanced legal knowledge and skill
2. The advice given is intended to advise someone of his or her legal rights
3. The advice is not advice normally given by a nonlawyer as part of another business or transaction

Preparing or Signing Legal Documents. The preparation of legal documents is considered the practice of law in nearly every jurisdiction. Many courts have found that the preparation of legal documents, including (1) pleadings and other papers incident to litigation; (2) deeds, mortgages, notes, and other documents related to mortgages and real estate transfers; and (3) legal documents for others to present in family court all constitute the practice of law.

There are several reasons why preparing legal documents, a task that might otherwise be considered a clerical task, is usually considered to be the practice of law.

1. The preparation of most legal documents requires a superior knowledge of the law not possessed by most lay people
2. The preparation of legal documents can affect the legal rights of those for whom they are prepared
3. Preparation of legal documents is often accompanied by legal judgment and legal advice as to which legal document to prepare and how the document should be prepared

It is not considered the practice of law for paralegals or other supervised employees to prepare legal documents for the review and approval of a licensed attorney.

In-Court Representation. In general, it is considered practicing law to appear on behalf of someone else in a court of law or before an administrative board or tribunal. There are, however, several notable exceptions to this rule.

1. Nonlawyers may represent others at administrative hearings if permitted by the administrative agency
2. In some jurisdictions it is permissible for nonlawyers to appear in front of the court on behalf of an attorney employer to request a continuance on the attorney's behalf
3. Some jurisdictions allow law clerks who are supervised by attorneys and certified as to having completed minimum education requirements to appear before certain courts
4. In some jurisdictions, it is permissible for nonlawyers to appear before the court if the court specifically grants permission
5. In some jurisdictions corporations may represent themselves on certain matters
6. In most instances individuals are guaranteed the right to appear **pro se**

Pro se
For oneself; on one's own behalf; without a lawyer (the defendant proceeded *pro se*; a *pro se* defendant). Also termed *pro persona; in propria persona.* (*Black's Law Dictionary, Seventh Edition*)

State Statute Definitions

All states have statutes providing that only duly licensed attorneys may practice law in that state. Most of these statutes do not define the practice of law, but leave that up to the state's courts. Statutes that specify activities constituting the practice of law are "neither all-exclusive nor all-inclusive, and it does not encroach on the power of the judiciary to determine that other acts may also constitute the practice of law."[8] Following are sample excerpts from some of the state unauthorized practice of law statutes:

California

"No person shall practice law in this state unless he is an active member of the State Bar." California Business & Professional Code, Div. 3, Chapter 4 (Attorneys), Art. 7 § 6125.

Kentucky

The practice of law is any service rendered involving legal knowledge or legal advice, whether of representation, counsel or advocacy in or out of court, rendered in respect to the rights, duties, obligations, liabilities, or business relations of one requiring the services. But nothing herein shall prevent any natural person not holding himself out as a practicing attorney from drawing any instrument to which he is a party without consideration unto himself therefor. An appearance in the small claims division of the district court by a person who is an officer of or who is regularly employed in a managerial capacity by a corporation or partnership which is a party to the litigation in which the appearance is made shall not be considered as unauthorized practice of law. KY ST S CT Rule 3.020

Louisiana

"It is a crime for a non-lawyer to practice law, hold himself out as an attorney, or advertise that he alone or jointly has an office for the practice of law." LA.R.S. 37:213

"The practice of law is defined as appearing as an advocate, drawing papers, pleadings or documents, performing any act in connection with pending or prospective court proceedings or, if done for consideration, the advising on the "secular" law and doing any act on behalf of another tending to obtain or secure the prevention or redress of a wrong or the enforcement or establishment of a right." LA.R.S. 37:212.

Missouri

"The 'practice of law' is hereby defined to be and is the appearance of an advocate in a representative capacity or the drawing of papers, pleadings or documents or the performance of any act in such capacity in connection with proceedings pending or prospective before any court of record, commissioner, referee or any body, board, committee or commission constituted by law or having authority to settle controversies." V.A.M.S. 484.010

State Court Definitions

The right to practice law in state courts is determined by the law of each state as interpreted by the state's courts. The right to define the practice of law generally lies with the state's highest court.

Although there is little controversy surrounding the general definition of the term *practice of law* the specific definition and application of the term varies from state to state and even from court to court. Following is a sample of how the courts have defined the practice of law in some of the states:

In a case recently heard in the Supreme Court of Indiana, the court held that a "person who gives legal advice to clients and transacts business for them in matters connected with the law is engaged in the practice of law." [9]

In a recent case in the California Court of Appeals, the court held that " 'Practicing law' means more than just appearing in court; practice of the law includes legal advice and counsel and the preparation of legal instruments and contracts by which legal rights are secured although such matter may or may not be pending in a court."[10]

The Washington Court of Appeals recently found that close friends who assisted a woman during her last hospitalization ". . . engaged in unauthorized practice of law by securing will kit, discussing distribution of her assets, obtaining inventory of investments, typing will and arranging for signing and witnessing of will."[11]

PROFESSIONS AT RISK OF ENGAGING IN THE UNAUTHORIZED PRACTICE OF LAW

Certain occupations put individuals at risk for crossing the line and engaging in the unauthorized practice of law. Paralegals and law clerks are among this group due to the nature of their work. Because paralegals and law clerks are not licensed to practice law, under most circumstances they are viewed in the same light as any lay person with regard to unauthorized practice of law rules. Although paralegals and law clerks who work under the close supervision of attorneys are usually at little risk of committing unauthorized practice of law, those who offer their services to the public, or who work with little day-to-day supervision, are constantly at risk. It is very important for you to understand the ethical and legal implications of unauthorized practice of law and the rules that are applied in the state in which you work.

Realtors, accountants, bankers, and other professionals whose work puts them in constant contact with individuals who are in the process of entering into contracts or in need of other legal documentation are also at risk for engaging in the unauthorized practice of law. Some jurisdictions have adopted legislation and special rules that apply to individuals in such professions who routinely prepare documents for others as incident to another business.

For example, it is usually permissible for a realtor to prepare purchase agreements for his or her clients, and most realtors receive special training in how to provide that service. However, it is generally not permissible for the realtor to give legal advice concerning title to the property or for the realtor to represent his or her client if a dispute over the property should result in a legal action.

Some courts have found that nonattorneys may perform certain functions that may otherwise be considered the practice of law, when those functions are incidental to another transaction and "when difficult or doubtful legal questions are not involved."[12]

However, in a Minnesota case the court determined that the resolution by a tax expert of difficult legal questions incidental to the preparation of an income tax return for another constituted the practice of law. In that case, the court found that "When an accountant or other layman who is employed to prepare an income tax return is faced with difficult or doubtful questions of the interpretation or application of statutes, administrative regulations and rulings, court decisions, or general law, it is his duty to leave the determination of such questions to a lawyer."[13]

Corporations must also abide by rules prohibiting the unauthorized practice of law. With the exception of professional corporations of attorneys, corporations may not offer services considered to be the practice of law. In a 1990 Kentucky case, a corporation (not a professional corporation of attorneys) that advertised the preparation of legal documents for bankruptcy was ordered to cease and desist the unauthorized practice of law and fined $5,000.[14]

SELF-REPRESENTATION

In most jurisdictions, self-representation is a right granted to individuals. The right of self-representation in federal court is granted by 28 USC 1654. The

- Increased availability of legal self-help books
- Increased availability of legal self-help software
- Increased availability of legal information over the Internet
- Attempts by the courts to be more accessible
- Availability of services of mediators, legal documents preparers, and independent paralegals

FIGURE 2-1

Factors Contributing to the Increase in Self Representation

Supreme Court has held that self-representation in the state courts is a constitutional right in criminal cases. Self-representation in legal matters is on the rise in the Untied States, especially in family courts, traffic courts, estate planning, and probate matters and also in matters involving federal agencies. Self-help books and software, the availability of information over the Internet, and an attempt by the courts to be more accessible have all contributed to the increase in self-representation (Figure 2–1). The services of **mediators,** legal document preparers, and independent paralegals have also had a significant impact.

In some jurisdictions, corporations may elect self-representation if they are represented by officers who are tending to the business of the corporation. Other jurisdictions allow corporations to be represented only by licensed attorneys; owners or officers who provide legal services to the corporation may be found to be guilty of the unauthorized practice of law.

ENFORCING THE UNAUTHORIZED PRACTICE OF LAW RULES

Methods for enforcing unauthorized practice of law rules are not uniform among the states, and neither are the consequences to attorneys and lay persons who are found to be in violation of those rules. Control of the unauthorized practice of law is the responsibility of the judiciary in most states. The courts have the authority to determine who is eligible to practice before them.

In many states, the bar association appoints a committee to oversee the enforcement of the state's unauthorized practice of law rules. The bar association and committee both derive their power from the state's highest court. Most actions against individuals are brought by a committee of the state's bar association.

Tools for enforcing unauthorized practice of law rules include injunctions, **civil contempt** proceedings, criminal prosecution, **writs of quo warranto,** and disciplinary actions.

An **injunction** is a court order prohibiting someone from doing some specified act or commanding someone to undo some wrong or injury. Individuals engaged in the unauthorized practice of law may be issued an injunction by the court with jurisdiction. Injunctions are often considered an effective deterrent from the unauthorized practice of law because violation of an injunction can result in civil or criminal contempt. Actions to obtain an injunction to prohibit someone from engaging in the unauthorized practice of law are typically brought by committees or boards appointed by the state bar associations to assist with the enforcement of unauthorized practice of law rules.

Citations for **direct contempt** may be issued by the court to individuals involved with the court who are found to be engaging in the unauthorized practice of law. For example, if a judge determines that someone bringing a case in his or her courtroom is not licensed to practice law in that jurisdiction, the court may issue a citation for contempt. In addition, the court may issue a citation for indirect, or **constructive contempt** as a result of a complaint filed by the state attorney general, a local prosecutor, a bar association, or an individual attorney. The penalties for contempt may include imprisonment, a fine, or both.

Mediator

Neutral third person who helps people involved in the mediation process to reach agreement.

Civil contempt

The failure to obey a court order that was issued for another party's benefit. A civil-contempt proceeding is coercive or remedial in nature. The usual sanction is to confine the contemner until he or she complies with the court order. *(Black's Law Dictionary, Seventh Edition)*

Writ of quo warranto

A court's written order issued to test whether a person or corporation exercising power is legally entitled to do so; intended to prevent a continued exercise of authority unlawfully asserted.

Injunction

A court order commanding or preventing an action. To get an injunction, the complainant must show that there is no plain, adequate, and complete remedy at law and that an irreparable injury will result unless the relief is granted. *(Black's Law Dictionary, Seventh Edition)*

Direct contempt

Contempt that is committed in open court, as when a lawyer insults a judge on the bench. *(Black's Law Dictionary, Seventh Edition)*

Constructive contempt

Contempt that is committed outside of court, as when a party disobeys a court order. Also termed *consequential contempt; indirect contempt. (Black's Law Dictionary, Seventh Edition)*

Misdemeanor

A crime that is less serious than a felony and is usually punishable by fine, penalty, forfeiture, or confinement (usually for a brief term) in a place other than prison (such as a county jail). Also termed *minor crime, summary offense. (Black's Law Dictionary, Seventh Edition)*

Per curiam

[Latin] By the court as a whole. *(Black's Law Dictionary, Seventh Edition)*

Censure

An official reprimand or condemnation; harsh criticism (the judge's careless statements subjected her to the judicial council's censure). *(Black's Law Dictionary, Seventh Edition)*

Individuals engaging in the unauthorized practice of law may be subject to criminal prosecution. Most states have unauthorized practice of law statutes in place that establish **misdemeanor** penalties for the unauthorized practice of law, including fines of up to $1,000 and/or imprisonment of up to one year.

When corporations exceed the authority of their corporate charters and are engaged in activities considered to be the practice of law, the state attorney general or other authorized individual may move the proper court to issue a writ of quo warranto. A writ of quo warranto is an order directing that certain illegal activity be ceased.

Disciplinary action by the state bar association may be brought against attorneys who engage in the unauthorized practice of law or who assist in the unauthorized practice of law. The options for sanctions against the attorney include disbarment, suspension of the attorney's license to practice law, probation, or a reprimand. Because nonattorneys are not members of the bar associations, bar association disciplinary boards have no authority over them. Disciplinary action may only be brought against licensed attorneys who are members of the bar of the state in question.

CASE AND DISCUSSION

In the following case, a complaint was brought against an attorney for neglecting a legal matter and aiding in the unauthorized practice of law. The attorney in this matter failed to adequately supervise his paralegal, who was found to be engaged in the unauthorized practice of law.

The PEOPLE of the State of Colorado, Complainant,

v.

Jeffry L. FRY, Attorney-Respondent,

No. 94SA185

Supreme Court of Colorado

En Banc.

June 6, 1994.

PER CURIAM.

The respondent, Jeffry L. Fry, was charged by formal complaint with neglecting a legal matter and with aiding a nonlawyer in the unauthorized practice of law. The respondent and the assistant disciplinary counsel subsequently entered into a stipulation, agreement, and conditional admission of misconduct. . . . In the stipulation, the parties recommended the imposition of discipline in the range of a public **censure** to a forty-five day suspension from the practice of law. An inquiry panel of the Supreme Court Grievance Committee approved the stipulation, with the recommendation that the respondent receive a public censure. We accept the stipulation and the recommendation of the inquiry panel.

I.

The parties stipulated to the following facts and conclusions. On December 8, 1990, Marlon and Annabel Broxton met with the respondent's paralegal at the respondent's office. The paralegal advised the Broxtons that a Chapter 13 bankruptcy proceeding would resolve their current financial problems. The Broxtons were told that the attorney's fee was $1,000 and the filing fee was $120

for the Chapter 13. The Broxtons did not meet with the respondent on that day. . . . Ms. Broxton sent the respondent the filing fee.

After the Broxtons continued to receive calls from their creditors, the respondent's paralegal advised the Broxtons to prepare a note to send to their creditors giving the name of the law firm and telling the creditors to contact the paralegal. Ms. Broxton sent the respondent $400 toward the outstanding attorney's fee and asked the paralegal to notify the Broxton's home mortgage and Ford Motor Company of the impending bankruptcy proceedings. In February 1991, the paralegal contacted Mr. Broxton and asked him to sign the bankruptcy documents. Ms. Broxton asked the paralegal how to make their house payments outside of the Chapter 13 plan.

The voluntary bankruptcy petition was filed on February 21, 1991 in the United States Bankruptcy Court, and on March 11 the proposed plan and schedules were filed. The Chapter 13 statement reflected that Mr. Broxton was unemployed, but indicated, incorrectly, that he was receiving unemployment benefits.

After the bank holding the mortgage initiated foreclosure proceedings on the Broxton's home, the respondent's paralegal wrote to the bank in April 1991 advising them of the bankruptcy proceedings.

Neither the respondent nor the Broxtons attended a scheduled meeting of the creditors in early April 1991, and only Mr. Broxton went to the rescheduled meeting later that month. Mr. Broxton agreed to go forward without counsel and testified that he was unemployed and had no income. When the bankruptcy trustee determined that there was a discrepancy in the pleadings regarding Mr. Broxton's income, Broxton called the respondent's paralegal and was told that the paralegal did not know what the discrepancy was. Up to this point, the respondent still had not seen the Broxtons, and, in fact, there is no evidence that the Broxtons ever personally met the respondent during the course of the representation.

The bank holding the mortgage on the Broxtons' home objected to the proposed plan and filed a motion to dismiss. The respondent filed an untimely motion to confirm the plan on the same day that the bankruptcy trustee filed an objection to confirming the plan. The respondent did not respond to the trustee's objections. He appeared for a hearing set in June 1991, however, when the court denied confirmation and ordered that amended documents be filed within fifteen days or the proceeding would be dismissed.

The respondent failed to reply to the bank's motion for relief from the automatic stay. . . . The respondent later informed Broxton that the bankruptcy case had to be converted to a Chapter 7 and that the Broxtons would lose their home.

The motion to convert to a Chapter 7 bankruptcy was filed in July 1991. The bankruptcy court subsequently entered an order of conversion, but also granted the ban relief from the automatic stay. The respondent did not file the Chapter 7 amended schedules on time and the case was dismissed in September 1991. The respondent took no further action on behalf of the Broxtons. Moreover, the respondent did not return any of the $520 paid by the Broxtons when they requested a refund.

The respondent has stipulated that his failure to supervise his paralegal resulted in the paralegal engaging in the unauthorized practice of law. The respondent essentially allowed the paralegal to handle the bankruptcy proceeding from the beginning to its admittedly "regrettable end." He therefore violated DRR 33-101(AAA) (a lawyer shall not aid a nonlawyer in the unauthorized practice of law). In addition, the respondent's lack of involvement in the bankruptcy proceeding and his failures to attend scheduled meetings and timely file pleadings and responses constituted the neglect of a legal matter, . . .

II.

In approving the stipulation, the inquiry panel unanimously recommended that the respondent be publicly censured. . . .

The assistant disciplinary counsel indicates that the Broxton case was apparently an aberration, and that the respondent's "conduct was atypical when compared to other cases." The respondent states that as a result of this matter he has changed his procedures to ensure that the misconduct will not be repeated. We note that the respondent has not been previously disciplined in nearly twenty years of practice. Id. . . . The respondent has also cooperated in this proceedings, id. At 9.32(e), and has demonstrated remorse, id. At 9.32(1). Taking these factors into account, we accept the stipulation, agreement, and conditional admission of misconduct, and the inquiry panel's recommendation. However, we point out that two members of the court would have imposed a more severe sanction. . . .

GUIDELINES FOR UTILIZING PARALEGALS

While common sense and general ethical guidelines often dictate how much supervision paralegals require, sometimes the issue is not so clear. Experienced paralegals may have the knowledge to perform some functions that they can not legally perform, and it is often hard for attorneys to know which tasks can be legally delegated and how much supervision is required. Attorneys may find some assistance in guidelines for utilization of paralegals adopted by the bar associations in the states in which they practice.

Many states have adopted guidelines for the utilization of paralegals. These guidelines are drafted for the benefit of attorneys and are meant to offer assistance on how to best utilize the services of paralegals without engaging in the unauthorized practice of law. The guidelines may be adopted as state statute or as part of the state's court rules. Appendix B is an example of guidelines adopted by one state. The ABA's Model Guidelines for the Utilization of Legal Assistant Services, adopted by the ABA in 1991, make it clear that attorneys are responsible for the conduct of legal assistants working under their supervision and that, provided the attorney maintains responsibility for the paralegal's work product, the attorney may delegate any tasks normally performed by attorneys unless the provision of such service by someone other than an attorney is specifically prohibited by statute, court rule, administrative rule or regulation, controlling authority, or the ABA Model Rules of Professional Conduct or by the state's guidelines.

The guidelines specifically prohibit attorneys from delegating to paralegals the responsibility for establishing an attorney–client relationship, for establishing the amount of a fee to be charged for a legal service, or for a legal opinion rendered to a client.

The Model Guidelines do not offer many specifics or much detail on the utilization of paralegals, nor have the guidelines been adopted by all states.

However, until a consensus is reached on paralegal regulation, guidelines for utilizing paralegals may be the best guidance attorneys have to define the legal possibilities, and limits, of paralegals.

FROM THE PARALEGAL'S PERSPECTIVE

As a paralegal, you have several sources to turn to for information on avoiding the unauthorized practice of law. Although rules concerning the unauthorized practice of law are addressed in the codes of ethics of the national, state, and local paralegal associations, the paralegal associations have no legal authority over paralegals. As a paralegal, you must be aware of the rules concerning the unauthorized practice of law established by the statutes, case law, and attorney codes of ethics in any state in which you work.

Traditional Paralegals

Traditional paralegal
An individual who works as a paralegal under the direct supervision of an attorney.

While it seems that unauthorized practice of law rules restrict the activities that may be performed by many paralegals, there are very few restrictions on the activities and responsibilities that may be assumed by properly supervised **traditional paralegals.** As a paralegal, you can use your knowledge of the law and of legal procedure to assist attorneys in various ways. Drafting legal documents and performing other law-related services may at first glance appear to be practicing law. However, if you work under the supervision of an attorney who is ultimately responsible for your actions, you are merely assisting attorneys with their practice of law. Therefore there is no question of unauthorized practice of law.

According to the ABA's Special Committee on Legal Assistants, a lawyer may permit a legal assistant to assist in all aspects of the lawyer's representation of a client, provided that:

- The status of the legal assistant is disclosed.
- The lawyer establishes the attorney-client relationship.
- The lawyer reviews and supervises the legal assistant's work.
- The lawyer remains responsible.
- The services performed become part of the attorney's work product.
- The services performed by the legal assistant do not require the exercise of *unsupervised* legal judgment.
- The lawyer instructs the legal assistant concerning standards of client confidentiality.[15]

Paralegals in the Corporation

Paralegals who work for corporations must also be aware of their legal and ethical boundaries. A corporation may not designate a nonattorney to represent it in matters of a legal nature. Again, if you work under the direct supervision of attorneys in a legal department, you probably need not be too concerned. However, if you find you are working on legal matters with very little or no attorney supervision, you must consider the possibility that the work you are performing could be considered the unauthorized practice of law.

Paralegals Employed by the Government

Both federal and state government agencies utilize paralegals in very responsible roles. Many of these paralegals work in specialized areas and become experts in their specialty. In effort to keep costs low and operate as efficiently as possible, paralegals and other nonlawyers who work for federal and state agencies are sometimes allowed to perform tasks typically considered to be the practice of law. Often, these paralegals and nonlawyers receive their authority to perform certain functions from the rules and regulations of the administrative agencies in which they work. For example, the following is an excerpt from Chapter 338 of the Minnesota Statutes, Family Law, Administrative Process—Rules of Court—

> . . . (f) Nonattorney employees of the public authority responsible for child support may prepare, sign, serve, and file complaints, motions, notices, summary notices, proposed orders, default orders, consent orders, orders for blood or genetic tests, and other documents related to the administrative process for obtaining, modifying, or enforcing child and medical support orders, orders establishing paternity, and related documents, and orders to enforce maintenance if combined with a child support order. The nonattorney employee may issue administrative subpoenas, conduct prehearing conferences, and participate in proceedings before an administrative law judge. This activity shall not be considered to be the unauthorized practice of law. Nonattorney employees may not represent the interests of any party other than the public authority, and may not give legal advice. The nonattorney employees may act subject to the limitations of section 518.5512.

In effect, this statute gives paralegals who work for the public authority responsible for child support in Minnesota the authority to perform several functions that might otherwise be considered the unauthorized practice of law. Paralegals who receive authority under this statute may prepare, sign, serve, and file complaints and other legal documents. In addition, they may issue subpoenas, conduct prehearing conferences, and appear before an administrative law judge as specifically permitted by the statute.

Freelance Paralegals

Freelance paralegals are self-employed paralegals who work for a number of attorneys on a temporary or contract basis. Freelance paralegals must follow the same general guidelines as traditional paralegals. In addition, they have the added concern of making sure that the attorneys they are reporting to understand that they must adequately supervise the paralegal's work.

Freelance paralegal
A self-employed paralegal who works for several different attorneys, law firms, or corporations under the supervision of an attorney.

INDEPENDENT PARALEGALS

Most of the real controversy surrounding paralegals and the unauthorized practice of law concerns independent paralegals—paralegals who offer their services directly to the public without attorney supervision. Many of the services offered by independent paralegals are self-help services. These services include furnishing and completing forms and offering self-help information written by attorneys. Independent paralegals do not represent individuals in legal matters; rather they assist their customers with self-representation. Although it is clear that, in most instances, individuals have the right of self-representation, the role of a lay person to assist them is less clear.

Independent paralegals are in constant danger of crossing the unauthorized practice of law line. For example, in most jurisdictions it is legal for independent paralegals to sell legal forms, sample legal forms, and printed material drafted by attorneys explaining legal practice and procedure to the public. However, if the independent paralegal dispenses legal advice, in addition to the legal forms, he or she will probably be committing the unauthorized practice of law. In Michigan, the court has ruled that "the advertisement and distribution to the general public of forms and documents utilized to obtain a divorce together with any related textual instructions does not constitute the unauthorized practice of law."[16]

However, offering counsel and advice in addition to the forms and documents *is* considered to be the unauthorized practice of law in that state.

The issue of unauthorized practice of law by independent paralegals was brought to the attention of the legal community and the entire country in the mid-1970s when a woman named Rosemary Furman, a former court reporter with more than 20 years' experience, opened a legal-typing business in Jacksonville, Florida. Ms. Furman founded her business on her strong belief that it was not necessary to retain an attorney to perform simple, routine legal services. Ms. Furman and her service provided and typed divorce, name change, adoption, and bankruptcy forms. She claimed that she did not give legal advice, but rather left all decisions to her clients. The Florida State Bar Association did not agree, and in 1977 it charged Rosemary Furman with practicing law without a license. In 1979, the Florida State Supreme Court affirmed a decision finding Ms. Furman guilty and sentenced her to four months in jail. Ms. Furman's plight earned her much publicity and even a feature on the television news show *60 Minutes*. Ms. Furman had public sympathy on her side, and the governor commuted her sentence with the understanding that she would shut her business down permanently.

More recently, Robin Smith, owner of an Oregon business entitled People's Paralegal Services, was found by the Oregon Court of Appeals to be practicing law, which effectively shut her business down. Ms. Smith fought back by backing and helping to draft legislation to allow paralegals who meet certain requirements to register with authorities in Oregon. The bill would have allowed independent paralegals to provide limited legal assistance and advice so long as they were registered with the Department of Consumer and Business Services. Although this bill died in committee in 1997, it may be a harbinger of things to come.[17]

If you are considering employment as an independent paralegal, you must be very sure of the precedence for independent paralegals in your state. You must know how the unauthorized practice of law has been defined in your state and be exceedingly careful that your services never meet with that definition. In addition, you must be aware of any registration requirements in your state. For example, beginning in 2000, California individuals who render the services of a legal document technician, as defined by statute, must meet certain registration requirements with the appropriate county clerk. The California requirement is one of the first of its kind, but there may be new legislation in your state, so you must keep current with any developments regarding paralegal regulation. For the latest developments in your state, keep current with your local paralegal association. You can also check the companion Web site to this text at **www.westlegal-studies.com.**

GUIDANCE FROM THE PARALEGAL ASSOCIATIONS

Both the NALA's Code of Ethics and Professional Responsibility and the NFPA's Model Code of Ethics and Professional Responsibility have provisions specifically prohibiting the unauthorized practice of law by their members. Legal assistants, under the definition adopted by the NALA, work under the supervision of an attorney. In addition, nearly every canon of the NALA's Code of Ethics and Professional Responsibility refers to the necessity for legal assistants to avoid the unauthorized practice of law. Canon 3 specifically states:

Canon 3
A legal assistant must not: (a) engage in, encourage, or contribute to any act which could constitute the unauthorized practice of law; and (b) establish attorney-client relationships, set fees,

give legal opinions or advice or represent a client before a court or agency unless so authorized by that court or agency; and (c) engage in conduct or take any action which would assist or involve the attorney in a violation of professional ethics or give the appearance of professional impropriety.

Although the NALA Code of Ethics and Professional Responsibility and the NFPA's Model Code of Ethics and Professional Responsibility are not legally binding on the members of those organizations, these documents do give some guidance to paralegals. In addition, the NFPA will issue opinions on questions concerning legal ethics, including the unauthorized practice of law.

AVOIDING THE UNAUTHORIZED PRACTICE OF LAW

There are certain activities that all paralegals must be cautious to avoid and some general rules to follow to be sure that you are not engaging in the unauthorized practice of law. In general, you will want to:

- Always disclose your status as a paralegal, including on letterhead and business cards
- Make sure that legal documents and any correspondence you prepare that express a legal opinion are reviewed, approved, and signed by your supervising attorney
- Communicate important issues concerning each case or legal matter on which you are working with your supervising attorney and see that your work is reviewed and approved by an attorney
- Never give legal advice
- Never discuss the merits of a case with opposing counsel
- Never enter into fee agreements for legal services or agree to represent a client (on behalf of a supervising attorney or law firm)
- Never represent a client at a deposition, in a court of law, or before an administrative board or tribunal (unless paralegals or other lay persons are specifically authorized to appear by the court's rules or agency regulations)

Disclose Your Status

When meeting or speaking with clients or attorneys, you must always introduce yourself as a paralegal. When signing correspondence, be sure to indicate your title below your signature. By not doing so, it may be assumed that you are an attorney. Merely holding yourself out to be an attorney may be considered the unauthorized practice of law.

Law firms often include the names of their paralegal employees on their letterhead, and they often provide business cards for their paralegals. In both instances, it is important that the paralegal's title is included beneath his or her name. If the title is omitted, it may be assumed that the paralegal is in fact an attorney, and it could expose the paralegal to charges of the unauthorized practice of law.

Including a paralegal's name and title on a law firm's letterhead is not permissible in every jurisdiction. A minority of jurisdictions in the United States, including the State of Georgia, have found it unethical for law firms to include the names of paralegals on their law firm letterhead.[18]

Freelance paralegals and independent paralegals must make sure that, in addition to their letterhead and business cards, any marketing materials they use include their title and clearly indicate that they are not attorneys and not authorized to give legal advice or practice law.

Have Your Work Reviewed and Approved by an Attorney

As a paralegal, a significant amount of your time may be spent drafting legal documents and correspondence. With very few exceptions, any legal documents you prepare must be reviewed and signed by an attorney. In addition, if you are asked to draft correspondence that gives legal advice to a client, the correspondence should be reviewed and signed by the responsible attorney. After you have been working with the same attorneys for a long time and they attain a high comfort level with your work, the tendency may be to skip over the review process. Be sure to remind the attorneys you work for from time to time (if necessary) that they are ultimately responsible for your work and that they are responsible for reviewing and approving your work.

Communicate with Your Supervising Attorney

It is important that you communicate clearly with your supervising attorney regarding any matters on which you are working. Your communication can include face-to-face meetings, memos, e-mails and other methods to keep the attorney apprised of any developments as necessary to allow him or her to adequately direct and supervise your work.

Don't Give Legal Advice

To avoid the unauthorized practice of law, you must not give legal advice. This is a challenge for many paralegals, especially those who meet regularly with clients. Most paralegals engage in frequent conversation with clients, and these conversations involve the exchange of information. Paralegals must be sure that the information they provide does not include their independent legal judgment or advice. When you meet with clients or speak to clients over the telephone to relay information about their cases, you must be sure that you qualify any information you give them that may constitute legal advice by saying that it is the attorney's opinion. If they ask for your opinion or advice on matters that you have not discussed with the responsible attorney, you must defer the question and say that you are unable to give advice, but that you will check with their attorney. Never give your opinion as to the merits of a client's case—even when the client asks and you are confident you know the answer.

For example, assume that you are a paralegal for a personal injury law firm and you have just taken a call from a prospective client because all attorneys in the firm are out. The caller is distraught. She was involved in an automobile accident when another driver ran a red light and broadsided the car she was driving. As a result of the accident, she has lost the use of both her legs. The other driver admitted liability, and his insurance company paid the caller's medical bills, but she believes she's entitled to more. The caller asks: Do I have a case? How much is it worth? Will your firm represent me? What will it cost? If you are an experienced personal injury paralegal, the answers to these questions may seem obvious to you, but to answer them would be considered giving legal advice and you would be engaging in the unauthorized practice of law.

Never Discuss the Merits of a Client's Case with Opposing Counsel

Discussing a client's case with opposing counsel can be considered the unauthorized practice of law, even if you identify yourself as a paralegal. In addition, it can have serious negative consequences to your client's case.

Never Agree to Represent a Client or Negotiate or Set Fees on Behalf of an Attorney

Although paralegals commonly meet with potential clients to gather information prior to meeting with an attorney, it is important that a paralegal not discuss fee arrangements with potential clients, or agree (on behalf of the attorney) that the attorney will take on representation of the individuals as clients. Initial client interviews are often handled by both the attorney and paralegal, or the attorney will meet with potential clients either immediately before or after the paralegal meets with potential clients. The State Bar of Michigan has given an opinion that a lawyer should not entrust to a paralegal the full responsibility for conducting the initial interview and passing the information on to the lawyer. The opinion emphasizes the importance of the direct attorney–client relationship necessary to exercise the attorney's trained professional judgment.[19]

Never Represent A Client at a Deposition, in a Court of Law, or Before an Administrative Board or Tribunal Without Authorization

Traditionally, it has been considered the unauthorized practice of law for a paralegal to appear in court or in front of an administrative agency board or tribunal to represent another. In recent years, many exceptions to this rule have arisen.

Many administrative agencies, especially federal agencies, allow paralegals to appear before their tribunals to represent the rights of individuals (Figure 2–2). Each federal administrative agency has the power to permit representation by paralegals and other lay persons in their proceedings. Many agencies, including the Internal Revenue Service, the Immigration and Naturalization Service, and the Social Security Administration, permit paralegal representation before their

---

Federal Agencies Permitting Nonlawyer Representation

Representation is allowed only as permitted by applicable federal statute or regulation by the following agencies:

- Board of Immigration Appeals
- Civil Aeronautics Board
- Comptroller of the Currency
- Consumer Product Safety Commission
- Department of Agriculture
- Department of Health and Human Services
- Department of Justice
- Department of Labor
- Department of Transportation
- Department of Veterans Affairs
- Federal Deposit Insurance Corporation[1]
- Federal Energy Regulatory Commission
- Federal Maritime Administration[2]

- Federal Mine Safety and Health Review Commission
- General Accounting Office
- Internal Revenue Service[3]
- Interstate Commerce Commission[4]
- National Credit Union Administration
- National Mediation Board
- National Transportation Safety Board
- Occupational Safety and Health Review Commission
- Small Business Administration
- U.S. Customs Service
- U.S. Environmental Protection Agency

Information compiled by the NFPA's Roles and Responsibilities Committee
Kim Nichols, Coordinator[5]

1 Only qualified nonlawyers are permitted to represent
2 Only registered nonlawyers are permitted to appear.
3 Nonlawyers must become enrolled agents.
4 Only registered nonlawyers are permitted to practice.
5 As reported in the National Paralegal Reporter, Agencies That Allow Nonlawyer Practice, Summer 1999, page 35.

FIGURE 2-2

Agencies Permitting Nonlawyer Representation and Those Requiring Lawyer Representation

FIGURE 2-2—cont'd

Agencies Permitting Nonlawyer Representation and Those Requiring Lawyer Representation

- Disclose your status as a paralegal
- Get the approval and signature of your supervising attorney for any legal documents and any correspondence you prepare that express a legal opinion
- Communicate important issues concerning each case or legal matter on which you are working with your supervising attorney
- Never give legal advice
- Never discuss the merits of a case with opposing counsel
- Never enter into fee agreements for legal services (on behalf of supervising attorney or law firm)
- Never agree to represent a client on behalf of an attorney
- Never represent a client at a deposition, in a court of law, or before an administrative board (unless specifically authorized by the court's or agency's rules)
- Make sure that any letterhead or business cards with your name on them indicate that you are a paralegal

FIGURE 2–3

Avoiding the Unauthorized Practice of Law

agenices. Some agencies, such as the U.S. Patent Office, require special education and certification before representation is allowed. Individual states must permit paralegal representation before federal agencies in accordance with the rules of the federal agency. However, state administrative agencies are not required to permit paralegal representation—and many do not. If you are asked to make an appearance in front of an administrative agency, you must make certain that the extent of your involvement is permissible under the agency's rules (Figure 2–3).

Another exception to the rule prohibiting court appearances by paralegals provides that, under certain circumstances, paralegals may appear before certain courts on behalf of their attorney–employers when their appearance is more in the nature of a messenger.

Some court rules provide that the courts may grant permission to specific individuals to appear in court on behalf of another for specific reasons.

If you are ever asked to appear in court or in front of any administrative agency, board, or tribunal, you must be *certain* that the rules of the court or tribunal permit such an appearance.

CONSEQUENCES TO THE PARALEGAL FOR THE UNAUTHORIZED PRACTICE OF LAW

There are negative consequences both for the paralegal who is found to be practicing law and for any attorney who is responsible for the paralegal's supervision (Figure 2–4). Where no harm has been done to anyone, the most likely consequence would be disciplinary action against the responsible attorney for assisting in the unauthorized practice of law by not supervising his or her employees adequately. Under some circumstances, the supervising attorney can be sued for malpractice by a dissatisfied client. Independent paralegals may have an injunction filed against them to cease their business, or they may be cited for contempt.

Paralegals who work without attorney supervision may be in danger of criminal prosecution for the misdemeanor crime of practicing law without a license. Additionally, paralegals deemed to be practicing law without a license may be sued for legal malpractice in some jurisdictions. In one case in the State of Washington, the court found that nonlawyers who attempt to practice law are liable for their negligence and must meet the same standard of care as that of a lawyer.[20]

CASE LAW INVOLVING PARALEGALS

It is important to know how paralegals and the unauthorized practice of law have been treated by the courts in your state. Following is a sample of some of the outcomes of cases involving paralegals and the unauthorized practice of law in a few of the states:

In *Ferris v. Snively,* 19 P.2d 942 (Wash. 1933), a case in which an unlicensed law clerk handled uncontested probate matters, gave oral opinions on abstracts of title and prepared wills, leases, mortgages, bills of sale, and contracts upon his own initiative with no supervision from his employer, the court held that the work of law clerks require attorney supervision to avoid the unauthorized practice of law. The court further found that his work would not have been the unauthorized practice of law if he would have limited it to "work of a preparatory nature, such as research, investigation of details, assemblage of data, and like work that would enable the attorney–employer to carry a given matter to a conclusion through his own examination, approval or additional effort."

In *People v. Alexander,* 53 Ill.App.2d 299, 202 N.E. 2d 841 (1964), the defendant appealed from a judgment order finding him guilty of contempt of court for the unauthorized practice of law. The defendant in this case prepared an order with the collaboration of opposing counsel and appeared before the court for the purpose of apprising the court of the engagement and unavailability of counsel. The appellate court overruled the lower court's decision and found that the conduct of a law clerk who prepared an order with collaboration of opposing

Consequences to the Attorney	**Consequences to the Paralegal**
• Disciplinary proceedings	• Injunction
• Injunction	• Contempt of court
• Contempt of court	• Criminal prosecution
• Criminal prosecution	• Disciplinary proceedings brought against supervising attorney
• Civil action brought against attorney	• Loss of employment

FIGURE 2-4

Consequences to Engaging in the Unauthorized Practice of Law

counsel for the benefit of the court and as a mere recordation of what had transpired, did not constitute the unauthorized practice of law.

In a 1967 case brought by the New York County Lawyers' Association, the court found the defendant, Norman Dacey, was not practicing law by authoring and selling approximately 600,000 copies of *How to Avoid Probate,* a self-help book containing forms of various legal documents, including trusts and wills. The text also included advice on how to use these forms. The court held that since there was no personal and confidential relationship established between a client and an adviser, there was no practice of law.[21]

In a 1982 Florida case, *Florida ar v. Pascual,* 424 So.2d 757 (1982), a paralegal who represented a party at a closing, gave legal advice, and signed correspondence *for the firm* without indicating her title as a legal assistant was found to be engaging in the unauthorized practice of law.

In *Louisiana State Bar Asso. v. Edwins,* 540 So2d 294 (1989, La), the court determined that the attorney involved assisted a freelance paralegal in the unauthorized practice of law by permitting the paralegal (1) to advise a personal injury client of merits of case, (2) enter a contract for performance of legal service, (3) prepare motions and pleadings, and (4) to handle and distribute the client's money without close supervision.

In a 1990 case in Connecticut, an independent paralegal brought suit against the Connecticut Statewide Grievance Committee and Statewide Bar Counsel, alleging they violated her civil rights by threatening her with prosecution for criminal contempt if she advertised an offer to prepare court documents in uncontested divorce actions. The Connecticut District Court that heard *Monroe v. Horwitch* found that under Connecticut law, preparation of documents in divorce action is practice of law and the award of sanctions was not justified.[22]

In 1991, in *Cleveland Bar Association v. Scali,* the Board of Commissioners on the Unauthorized Practice of Law found that a paralegal who prepared legal documents, gave legal advice, performed legal services in estate planning, preparation of a will and probating an estate was engaged in the unauthorized practice of law.[23]

In a 1993 case heard in federal bankruptcy court in Florida, the court held that

> . . . to avoid liability for unauthorized practice of law, typing or secretarial services may sell printed materials and sample legal forms, provide secretarial services and type bankruptcy forms from written information furnished by clients, and advertise these services; however, these businesses may not advise how best to fill out bankruptcy forms or otherwise complete bankruptcy schedules, and may not use the word "paralegal" in advertisements or mislead reasonable lay person into believing that legal assistance regarding bankruptcy is provided. . . .[24] 151 B.R. 622

In Connecticut in 1998 the Supreme Court held that the Commissioner of the Department of Children and Families's nonlawyer representatives were expressly permitted by statute to prepare and file termination petitions, and therefore such activities did not constitute the unauthorized practice of law.[25]

In a 1998 Texas case the court held that although it was permissible for a paralegal to sign and present habeas corpus petitions on behalf of others, he could not draft documents and appear in court on behalf of others.[26]

In a 1998 case before the Supreme Court of Kentucky, the court held that a statute authorizing nonlawyers to represent parties in workers' compensation proceedings violated the constitutional principle of separation of powers. The court further held that while nonlawyer workers' compensation specialists did not engage in unauthorized practice of law when processing claims under attorney supervision, nonlawyers could not represent parties before any adjudicative tribunal.[27]

In another 1998 case, this one brought against an attorney in New York, an attorney was suspended from practice of law for three months for failure to adequately supervise a paralegal who prepared a contract of sale and appeared on client's behalf in order to postpone a foreclosure sale.[28]

A synopsis of the latest developments in case law concerning paralegals and the unauthorized practice of law can be found at the companion Web site to this text at **www.westlegalstudies.com.**

A Question of Ethics

Suppose you are packing a briefcase for attorney Katherine Laurence for the Jacobson hearing. There is a pretrial hearing scheduled on this criminal misdemeanor case today, and you have been very involved with the preparation of the case to date. You know all the facts of the case and have discussed them very closely with Katherine. You have made sure that all the necessary motions and documents are in her brief case and everything is ready to go. Katherine is just coming to collect her brief case when the phone rings. It is her daughter's teacher calling with an emergency. Katherine's 10-year-old daughter has fallen while playing soccer and has been seriously injured. She is on her way to the hospital via ambulance. Katherine leaves her briefcase, tells you to "handle it," and rushes out the door.

The only other attorney in your office is in Puerto Rico, and the hearing starts in 20 minutes. You attempt to call the Judge's clerk to tell him that Ms. Laurence will not be able to attend the hearing, but you are unable to get through to anyone in the judge's chambers or the clerk's office. What should you do? Should you appear in court on behalf of Ms. Laurence?

Answer and Discussion: The answer to this question will depend on the jurisdiction in which Ms. Laurence practices. In most jurisdictions, appearing in court on behalf of Ms. Laurence would be considered the unauthorized practice of law. There are, however, some exceptions to this rule for nonattorneys who appear on behalf of an employer simply to ask for a continuance of the matter. If you know the rules in your jurisdiction, and they permit such appearances, you may want to go for it and make the appearance on behalf of Ms. Laurence. Your first item of business would necessarily be to explain to the judge what has transpired and let him or her direct you on how to proceed. If you are unsure of the rules in your jurisdiction, and you are unable to reach the judge or judge's clerk by telephone, you may want to go to the courthouse and try to personally locate the judge's receptionist, secretary, or clerk, present him or her with the situation and the documents, and ask that the message be relayed to the judge. If the motion is a very simple, uncontested matter, the judge may ask you to appear on behalf of the attorney, or he or she may schedule a new date for Ms. Laurence to appear.

The one thing you absolutely cannot do in any jurisdiction is to simply appear in court and represent Ms. Laurence's client without identifying yourself as a paralegal appearing on behalf of Ms. Laurence.

Although most actions involving the practice of law involve disciplinary actions against attorneys for failure to supervise their employees properly and aiding in the unauthorized practice of law, the following case was brought seeking an injunction against a South Carolina legal technician prohibiting the unauthorized practice of law and solicitation of clients.

The STATE, Plaintiff
v.
Melvin J. ROBINSON, Defendant
No. 24389
Supreme Court of South Carolina
Heard Dec. 6, 1995
Filed March 18, 1996.

INJUNCTION ISSUED

MOORE, Justice.

This case is before us in our original jurisdiction. The State seeks an injunction prohibiting the unauthorized practice of law and solicitation of clients by defendant Robinson. We grant the injunction as follows.

FACTS

This case was referred to a special master to make findings of fact and conclusions of law. After two evidentiary hearings, the master made findings of fact including the following: 1) Robinson is not licensed or qualified to practice law; 2) he has a business license from Anderson County and advertises in the yellow pages as a "paralegal." 3) Robinson performs services without attorney supervision; 4) he has represented more than sixteen clients in court; 5) when appearing in family or circuit court, Robinson does not charge a fee to his clients but requires reimbursement for costs; 6) Robinson obtains leave of court to appear pursuant to S.C. Code Ann. § 40-5-80 (1986); and 7) Robinson gives legal advice.

The master concluded as a matter of law that Robinson's appearances in court did not constitute the unauthorized practice of law because he sought and obtained leave of court in each instance. He found, however, that Robinson's solicitation of clients, giving of legal advice, and preparation and filing of legal documents constituted the unauthorized practice of law and recommended Robinson be enjoined from engaging in these activities.

Neither the State nor Robinson takes exception to any of the master's findings of fact.

ISSUES

1. Does Robinson have a first amendment right to advertise himself as a paralegal?
2. Are giving legal advice and preparing legal documents authorized under § 40-5-80?

DISCUSSION

The advertisement in question here is a yellow pages listing under "Paralegals" that reads as follows:

ROBINSON, MELVIN J.
"IF YOUR CIVIL RIGHTS HAVE BEEN VIOLATED—CALL ME."
1612 E RIVER ST..224-7800

Robinson also has a business card he distributes with the same message on it. His business card and letterhead refer to him as "Paralegal Consultant."

[1]   It is undisputed the First Amendment does not protect commercial speech that is false, deceptive, or misleading. . . .

Robinson contends, however, that advertising himself as a paralegal is not false since there are no regulations requiring any qualifications to be a paralegal in this State.

[2] [3]   This Court has addressed the function of a paralegal In re: Easler, 275 S.C. 400, 272 W.E.2d 32 (1980):

Paralegals are routinely employed by licensed attorneys to assist in the preparation of legal document such as deeds and mortgages. The activities of a paralegal do not constitute the practice of law as long as they are limited to work of a preparatory nature, such as legal research, investigation, or the composition of legal documents, which enable the licensed attorney–employer to carry a given matter to its conclusion through his own examination, approval or additional effort.

. . . While there are no regulations dealing specifically with paralegals, requiring a paralegal to work under the supervision of a licensed attorney ensures control over his or her activities by making the supervising attorney responsible. . . . Accordingly, to legitimately provide services as a paralegal, one must work in conjunction with a licensed attorney. Robinson's advertisement as a paralegal is false since his work product is admittedly not subject to the supervision of a licensed attorney.

[4]   Further, the ad's statement, "If your civil rights have been violated—call me," is an unlawful solicitation. It is unlawful for one who is not a licensed attorney to solicit the cause of another person. S.C. Code Ann. § 40-5-310 (Supp. 1994). We find Robinson should be enjoined from advertising himself as a paralegal or soliciting the representation of others.

[5]   Next, Robinson contends he should not be enjoined from giving legal advice and preparing legal documents since he obtains the right to represent others by leave of court under § 40-5-80. That section is entitled, "Citizens not prevented from appearing in person or for others without reward" and provides:

This chapter shall not be construed so as to prevent a citizen from prosecuting or defending his own cause, if he so desires, or the cause of another, with leave of the court first had and obtained; provided, that he declare on oath, if required, that he neither has accepted nor will accept or take any fee, gratuity or reward on account of such prosecution or defense or for any other matter relating to the cause.[29]

Robinson argues "defending or prosecuting necessarily includes giving legal advice and preparing and filing legal papers and therefore the leave granted by the court includes leave to engage in these activities.

This Court has defined the practice of law to include the preparation and filing of legal documents involving the giving of advice, consultation, explanation or recommendations on matters of law. . . . Clearly, one defending or prosecuting a cause of action must engage in these activities. We note, however, the express language of § 40-5-80 requires that leave be obtained first. The record indicates Robinson does not always obtain leave before giving advice and preparing pleadings. Accordingly, we find Robinson should be enjoined from preparing and filing legal documents and giving legal advice unless he first obtains leave of court pursuant to § 40-5-80. Further, we emphasize that it is within the trial judge's sound discretion whether to allow such representation.

INJUNCTION ISSUED.

FINNEY, C.J., and TOAL, WALLER and BURNETT, JJ., concur.

CHAPTER SUMMARY

For all the reasons discussed in this chapter, it will be important for you to avoid the unauthorized practice of law throughout your career. To do so, you will need to be up to date on the unauthorized practice statutes, rules of ethics, and case law in your jurisdiction. Remember, all of these factors are subject to change with time. To keep current with the rules for avoiding the unauthorized practice of law in your state, consult the current rules of ethics applicable to the attorneys for whom you work, or request guidance from your local or national paralegal association. The companion Web site to this text at **www.westlegalstudies.com** will also include information on new cases and legislation concerning the unauthorized practice of law.

- The authority to practice law is reserved for licensed attorneys who meet the requirements established by each jurisdiction, including any education, citizenship, residence, age, character, and bar examination requirements.
- Anyone who practices law without a license or special permission is considered to be engaged in the unauthorized practice of law.
- The codes of ethics in every state provide that attorneys have an ethical duty to not engage in the unauthorized practice of law and to not assist any individual in the unauthorized practice of law.
- Attorneys are responsible for supervising their nonattorney employees to the extent that their employees will not be *practicing law*.
- The main goal of laws prohibiting the unauthorized practice of law is to protect the public from representation by unqualified and unscrupulous individuals.
- In addition to representing individuals in a court of law or administrative tribunal, setting fees for legal work, giving legal advice, and preparing or signing legal documents are all activities considered to be practicing law.
- The legislature and the courts in each state define exactly what constitutes the practice of law.
- Actions brought against an individual for the unauthorized practice of law are usually brought by a special committee appointed by the state's bar association under the authority of the highest court in the state.
- Injunctions, citations for contempt of court, and criminal prosecution are the tools most often used for enforcing the unauthorized practice of law rules.
- Paralegals may assist in all aspects of an attorney's representation of a client provided that the paralegal's status is disclosed, the attorney establishes the attorney–client relationship, the paralegal is supervised by the attorney, the attorney remains responsible, the paralegal's work becomes the attorney's work product, the paralegal does not exercise unsupervised legal judgment, and the paralegal is instructed in the standards of client confidentiality.
- Paralegals may represent individuals in administrative agency proceedings if the administrative rules and regulations of that particular agency permit such representation.
- To avoid the unauthorized practice of law, paralegals must never give legal advice.
- Paralegals found to be practicing law may have an injunction filed against them to cease their business practice, they may be found in contempt of court, or they may be charged with a criminal offense.
- Paralegals who engage in the unauthorized practice of law may be personally liable for any damages they cause by rendering their services.
- More guidance on what constitutes the unauthorized practice of law may be forthcoming with any future regulation of paralegals.

SUMMARY QUESTIONS

1. Who is authorized to practice law?
2. Can a Minnesota attorney whose client gets arrested for driving under the influence of alcohol in Wisconsin represent his client in the case? What are the attorney's options?
3. Suppose you are hired by an attorney to run a new branch of her office. She will work in a neighboring suburb, stop in weekly to supervise your work, and approve any major legal decisions that must be made. Is this permissible? Why or why not?
4. Suppose that you are a paralegal working in a corporate legal department. The attorney you report to asks you to draft articles of incorporation for a new subsidiary (on your own) and leave them on his desk. Is this permissible? Why or why not?
5. Suppose you are an independent paralegal in Michigan and have two potential clients walk in the door. The first client wants an uncontested divorce. He gives you a form he received from the court clerk and asks you to help him complete it and assist him with the filing procedures. The second client also wants assistance with a divorce. She is not sure what uncontested means, and she would like you to explain to her what her options are and what would be her best course of action, then complete the necessary forms and file them for her. Can you assist either or both of these clients without engaging in the unauthorized practice of law?
6. How is it decided whether a particular activity constitutes the unauthorized practice of law?
7. What does the term *pro se* mean?
8. What are some possible consequences to attorneys who are found to be engaged in, or assisting others in, the unauthorized practice of law?
9. Where can paralegals look for guidance on how to avoid the unauthorized practice of law?
10. If you are meeting with a new client to gather information prior to the client's meeting with your supervising attorney, what are some rules you must keep in mind to avoid the unauthorized practice of law?

ENDNOTES

[1] Model Rules of Professional Conduct, Comment to Rule 5.5.

[2] State, ex. Rel. Porter v. Alabama Funeral Services, Inc., 338 So.2d 812.

[3] Louisiana State Bar Association v. Edwins, 540 So.2d 294 (La. 1989).

[4] 7 AMJUR ATTYS § 118 (1997).

[5] Ibid.

[6] The Florida Bar v. Brumbaugh, 355 So.2d 1186 (Fla. 1978).

[7] The Florida Bar v. Smania, 701 So.2d 835 (Fla. 1997).

[8] 7 Am Jur 2d § 118 (1997).

[9] Matter of Thonert, 693 N.E.2d 559 (Ind. 1998).

[10] Estate of Condon, 76 Cal.Rptr.2d 922 (1998).

[11] In Re Estate of Marks, 957 P.2d 235 (Wash. App. Div.3 1998)

[12] State Bar of Mexico v. Guardian Abstract and Title Co., Inc. 575 P2d 943 (1978).

[13] Gardner v. Conway, 48 N.W.2d 788 (Minn. 1951).

[14]Kentucky Bar Association v. Legal Alternatives, Inc., 792 S.W.2d 368 (Ky. 1990).

[15]A.B.A. Special Committee on legal Assistants "Proposed Curriculum for Training Law Office Personnel." (preliminary draft 1971).

[16]State Bar of Michigan v. Cramer, 249 NW2d 1 (Mich. 1976).

[17]Oregon State Bar v. Smith 942 P.2d 793 (Or. App. 1997).

[18]Georgia State Attorney Disciplinary Board Advisory Opinion No. 21 (undated, but prior to 1989).

[19]Op. RI-128 (4/21/92).

[20]Bowers v. Transamerica Title Insurance Company, 675 P.2d 193 (1983).

[21]NY County Lawyers' Asso. V. Dacey, 21 NY2d 694 (1967).

[22]Monroe v. Horwitch, et al, 820 F. Supp. 682 (Conn. 1990).

[23]Cleveland Bar Association v. Scali, 608 N.E.2d 865 (1991).

[24]In re Calzadilla, 151 BR 622 (Fl Bkr 1993).

[25]In Re Darlene C., 717 A2d 1242 (1998).

[26]Drew v. Unauthorized Practice of Law Committee, 970 S.W.2d 152 (Austin, Tx. 1998).

[27]Turner, et al v. Kentucky Bar, 980 SW2d. 560 (Ky. 1998).

[28]In Re: Parker, 670 N.Y.S. 2d 414 (N.Y. 1998).

[29]This Court has also construed § 40-5-80 to allow a nonlawyer officer, agent, or employee to represent a business in civil magistrate's court for compensation. In re: Unauthorized Practice of Law Rules, 309 S.C. 304, 422 S.E.2d 123 (1992).

MR. BUTTS

In recent years, billions of dollars have been awarded in tobacco litigation cases—lawsuits filed against the big tobacco companies for damage inflicted on smokers. Several similar suits are still pending and anticipated.

These cases are being heard in numerous courts and involve hundreds of attorneys, jurors, judges, and corporate executives. But one of the key players in the tobacco litigation is a paralegal by the name of Merrell Williams.

In 1988 Merrell Williams took a paralegal position with Wyatt, Tarrant & Combs, Kentucky's largest law firm and attorneys for Brown & Williamson Tobacco Company. Brown & Williamson is a British-owned tobacco company and the third largest U.S. cigarette maker. Mr. Williams was one of a group of paralegals employed by Wyatt, Tarrant & Combs who worked on a massive document coding project at Brown & Williamson's research center. The paralegals were given the task of reviewing thousands of documents and coding them according to their subject and sensitivity. Those documents considered to be the most sensitive (and incriminating according to Williams) were sent on for attorney review.

Williams quickly became upset by the nature of the documents he was reviewing. The documents Williams read indicated that the tobacco companies had known for decades that cigarettes caused cancer and other health problems and that they were addictive, yet company officials continued to publicly deny it. Williams reviewed memos detailing how the tobacco company research documents proving the dangers of smoking were being sent to the company's attorneys for review as a means of protecting them from discovery and hiding them from the attorneys for litigants of several suits against the tobacco companies. The information Williams read in the documents caused him to quit smoking cold turkey—something he had been trying to do for years.

From the spring of 1988 until February 1992, Williams took action that would irrevocably change the future for himself, the tobacco companies, and, to an extent, the way of life for Americans—he started sneaking confidential client documents out of the office, photocopying them, and returning them to the files. All together, Williams covertly photocopied over 4,000 tobacco company documents, which he stored in bankers boxes at his home and at the homes of friends.

Apparently, Williams had no clear-cut plan for the documents. He held on to the documents during his entire assignment at Brown & Williamson. He held on to the documents until after he was laid off by Wyatt, Tarrant & Combs for budgetary reasons. In fact, he secretly held on to the documents until after March of 1993, when he found himself suffering from chest pains that resulted in quintuple heart bypass surgery. Williams blamed his heart problems on the stress he suffered while working on the Brown & Williamson project and on the fact that he had smoked two packs of cigarettes per day for thirty years.

Williams wasn't sure what to do about the documents, but he decided he had to do something . . . he couldn't "let the bastards get away with this."[i]

When Williams decided to meet with Mr. J. Fox DeMoissey, his former divorce lawyer, Williams was in a poor state. He told DeMoissey that he was tired of being sick, poor, and unemployed. He wanted money for his troubles, and believed Brown & Williamson owed it to him. DeMoissey had Williams bring him the incriminating documents. DeMoissey sealed the box of documents and delivered them to Brown & Williams with a letter. Without identifying his client, DeMoissey indicated that he represented someone who used to work for the law firm representing Brown & Williamson and that his client had developed severe health problems from smoking—problems that were compounded due to his work at the law firm and learning of the "fraud and hoax being perpetrated upon the American people" by the tobacco company and their law firm. In his letter, DeMoissey said he was returning the documents with the condition that Brown & Williamson settle his client's claim. DeMoissey indicated that if Brown & Williamson did not settle, his client would sue them and demand production of the documents he had returned. By some accounts DeMoissey asked for $2.5 million to return the documents and settle the matter.[ii]

Brown & Williamson did not concede to DeMoissey's demand. Instead they quickly learned of Williams identity and sued him for stealing documents and attempting extortion. A court order was issued prohibiting Williams from disclosing the contents of the documents or discussing them with anyone—even DeMoissey.

Unknown to Brown & Williams and DeMoissey, Williams had kept a copy of the documents he turned over to DeMoissey. Contrary to the court order issued against him, in March 1994 Williams turned over his copy of the tobacco company's documents to someone who was very interested in them—Richard Scruggs. Mr. Scruggs is a famous litigator who was, at that time, working with the Mississippi Attorney General to sue the tobacco industry to recoup money paid out by Medicaid for smoking-related illnesses. Scruggs could see that Williams was desperate and he agreed to help him out by finding a paralegal position for him and giving him a little cash to hold him over. Scruggs also loaned money to Williams for a $109,000 house in Mississippi and cosigned on loans for a sailboat and two cars Williams bought. Scruggs indicated later that it was not a lot of money to him, "I thought the guy had done a real brave thing. He was in a lot of trouble and needed some safe harbor."[iii]

On May 6, 1994, Scruggs flew to Washington, D.C., to give copies of the documents to Representative Henry Waxman, who was chairing the committee conducting the tobacco hearings. The hearings featured testimony from representatives of several major tobacco companies who still denied that their products were addictive or harmful to smokers' health. Indications in the documents produced by Williams proved that, in fact, the tobacco companies knew that their products were both addictive and very dangerous. In addition, the stack of documents included memos detailing how Brown & Williams routed incriminating documents through their attorneys to prevent their discovery in litigation.

An article about the documents appeared the day after Scruggs turned them over to Waxman—on the front page of *The New York Times* . . . but that was just the beginning. On May 12, 1994, a copy of the same documents was delivered to Stanton Glantz, a medical professor at the University of California–San Francisco. The documents were delivered anonymously with the name *Mr. Butts* (a Doonesbury cartoon cigarette character) on the return address. On July 1, 1995, Professor Glantz had the documents indexed and put out on the Internet, where they could be viewed by the world. Previously, plaintiff attorneys were concerned with the problem of getting the stolen secret documents admitted to court. Once the documents were put on the Internet, they were no longer protected, and that problem disappeared. Merrell Williams' documents are currently on **http://galen.library.ucsf.edu/tobacco/bw.html.**

Merrell Williams' actions have had an incredible impact on the tobacco litigation in this country and on the tobacco industry. Thanks in large part to Merrell Williams, there was finally evidence available to assist litigants in their lawsuits against the tobacco companies. Since Merrell Williams brought the tobacco company documents to light, several billions of dollars have been awarded in suits against the tobacco companies.

But what about the ethical implications of Merrell Williams actions? Williams betrayed the trust of his supervising attorneys and their clients. He breached a confidentiality agreement he entered into by making confidential information public. Under Rule 1.6 of the Kentucky Rules of the Supreme Court, attorneys must keep client information confidential unless it is necessary to reveal the information to prevent the client from committing a crime likely to result in imminent death or substantial bodily harm. Confidential information may also be divulged to defend the attorney in civil or criminal suits, and as required by court order. Neither of these exceptions apply. Although Merrell Williams is not an attorney, the rule applies to the attorneys Williams worked for and the rule applies to him as an employee of those attorneys.

Technically, Merrell Williams was in violation of several rules of ethics. But even the experts are unsure about the ethics involved when looking at the big picture—did the end justify the means? Some agree with Deborah Orlik, Ethics Columnist for *Legal Assistant Today* and author of *Ethics for the Legal Assistant,* who commented on the matter, saying that "Sometimes protecting the public necessitates stretching the limits of the rules of professional responsibility. Merrell Williams' acts may be the best example of one of those times."[iv] Others agree with the position of Laurie L. Levenson, Associate Dean of the Loyola School in Los Angeles and Professor of Criminal Law and Ethics who stated that "Sneaking out with a client's documents, or exchanging them for money or a job position, is just the type of conduct that raises a red flag. Breaches in duties to clients must be explained by more than a proclamation that the offender wanted the world to know the 'truth.'"[v]

In the eyes of many, Merrell Williams was a true hero whose actions worked against the evil tobacco companies and possibly helped to save thousands of lives. According to supporters of the tobacco companies, Merrell Williams was a thief and an embezzler. The truth is probably somewhere between those two positions. Only time will tell how history views the paralegal who left the tobacco industry in a cloud of smoke.

---

[i] Curriden, Mark. The Paralegal Who Smoked the Tobacco Industry, *Legal Assistant Today,* May/June 1997, p. 42.

[ii] Mollenkamp, Carrick, *The People vs. Big Tobacco* (Bloomberg L.P. 1998).

[iii] Ibid.

[iv] Orlik, Deborah, Tobacco vs. Truth, *Legal Assistant Today,* May/June 1997, p. 46.

[v] Levenson, Laurie L., It May be Moral, But Is It Ethical, *Legal Assistant Today,* May/June 1997, p. 48.

Chapter 3

Confidentiality

Three may keep a secret if two of them are dead.

Benjamin Franklin: Poor Richard's Almanac (1735)

An Ethical Dilemma
Introduction
The Ethical Duty to Confidentiality
    Model Rule
    What Is Protected
    Attorney's Employees and Agents
    Exceptions
        Client Permission
        Implied Permission
        Prevention of Certain Criminal Acts
        Self-Protection
        To Rectify or Prevent a Fraud on a Tribunal
        Court Order
    Internal Revenue Service–Required Reporting of
      Cash Receipts

Attorney–Client Privilege
    Waiver of the Attorney–Client Privilege
    Work Product Rule
Case and Discussion
Confidentiality and the Corporate Client
From the Paralegal's Perspective
    The NALA's Rules
    The NFPA's Rules
    Practical Considerations
        Keeping Communications Confidential
        Talking to the Press
        Protecting Confidential Files and Documents
        Dealing with Outside Services
A Question of Ethics

Chapter Summary

Summary Questions

An Ethical Dilemma

The client of criminal defense attorney Jim Jensen is missing. Jim Jensen's client is Bart Simon, a man with a past record of criminal activity and possible connections with organized crime. Bart has been arrested on charges of conspiracy to commit murder and racketeering. Three days before the trial is to begin, Bart has jumped bail and disappeared. Mr. Jensen is surprised by Bart's disappearance, although he has some ideas as to where he may have gone and with whom he may be. Mr. Jensen is worried about the safety of the witnesses for the prosecution. Although Bart has never overtly threatened their lives or said anything specific to Mr. Jensen, Mr. Jensen fears that Bart is capable of harming them or at least threatening them to prevent their testimony against him. In addition, Mr. Jensen is somewhat fearful of what may happen to him should he tell what he suspects concerning Bart's whereabouts. Mr. Jensen has decided to keep quiet, citing client confidentiality. Is Mr. Jensen acting unethically?

Answer and Discussion: Probably not. In most jurisdictions Mr. Jensen has no obligation to tell what he suspects concerning the whereabouts of his client. In fact, he probably has an obligation to keep quiet. Although there is some controversy surrounding the question of whether a client's whereabouts should be protected information under the given circumstances, pursuant to the ABA's Model Rules of Professional Conduct, Mr. Jensen may not disclose confidential information concerning his client. Mr. Jensen has the *discretion* to reveal what he knows to prevent the murder or serious bodily harm of someone if he is reasonably certain that his silence would result in the same.[1] However, Mr. Jensen has no proof; in fact his client never even specifically told him that he was going to jump bail and harm or murder anyone. Under the Model Rules, the only time an attorney is *required* to disclose client information is when necessary to rectify a client's fraud on a tribunal[2] or when ordered by a court. If Bart were to contact Mr. Jensen, Mr. Jensen would have an ethical duty to counsel him to turn himself in. In addition, Mr. Jensen must not aid his flight in any way.

Confidential relationship
A fiduciary relationship that exists between client and attorney and others in similar circumstances. The law requires the utmost degree of good faith in all transactions between the parties in a confidential relationship.

Attorney–client privilege
The client's right to refuse to disclose and to prevent any other person from disclosing confidential communications between the client and the attorney. Also termed *lawyer–client privilege; client's privilege. (Black's Law Dictionary, Seventh Edition)*

INTRODUCTION

Although your common sense may tell you that our hypothetical Mr. Jensen should tell what he knows to protect potential witnesses and the public at large, attorneys and their employees have a primary duty to protect the confidentiality of their clients. Effective representation of a client requires the client to divulge all relevant facts to the attorney. Obviously, a client may be reluctant to do so if not assured of the attorney's complete confidentiality. For this reason, attorneys have an ethical duty to keep client confidences and secrets. Rules and guidelines concerning client confidentiality come from two sources. In this chapter, we will examine the broad ethical rules concerning client confidentiality and the **confidential relationship,** and the more narrow rules concerning **attorney–client privilege** in the law of evidence. The second part of this chapter focuses on the issue of confidentiality from the paralegal's perspective.

THE ETHICAL DUTY TO CONFIDENTIALITY

The client–lawyer relationship is based on loyalty and requires that the lawyer maintain confidentiality of information relating to the representation. The confidential relationship between the client and attorney encourages the client to communicate fully and frankly with the attorney, even with regard to matters that may be damaging or embarrassing to the client.

With some exceptions, information imparted to attorneys and paralegals in the course of representing the client must be kept **confidential** and may not be discussed with others outside of the office. The rule of confidentiality applies not only to information given to the attorney by the client but also to information relating to a client's case from other sources as well. The exact rule of confidentiality and the exceptions to the rule vary from state to state. It is important that the pertinent state code of ethics be consulted whenever a question arises.

Confidential
Entrusted with the confidence of another or with his or her secret affairs or purposes; intended to be held in confidence or kept secret; done in confidence.

Model Rule

Rule 1.6 of the Model Rules of Professional Conduct establishes the attorney's duty with regard to client confidentiality. Pursuant to Rule 1.6, attorneys may not reveal information relating to representation of a client unless the client consents after consultation (Figure 3–1).

In addition to an exception for disclosures that are implicitly authorized in order to carry out the representation, Rule 1.6 provides that the attorney may reveal information to the extent he or she reasonably believes necessary to:

1. Prevent the client from committing a criminal act that the attorney believes is likely to result in imminent death or substantial bodily harm.
2. Establish a claim or defense on behalf of the attorney in a controversy between the attorney and the client, to establish a defense to a criminal charge or civil claim against the attorney based upon conduct in which the client was involved, or to respond to allegations in any proceeding concerning the attorney's representation of the client.

The Model Rules vs. the Model Code	
Model Rule 1.6 Confidentiality of Information	***Canon 5—A Lawyer Should Preserve the Confidences and Secrets of a Client***
Protects all information relating to a client	Protects all information gained in the relationship that (1) the client requests to be confidential or (2) is likely to be detrimental to the client
Attorney permitted to disclose information where implicitly authorized to do so	No such provision for *implied* authorization
May disclose information to prevent client from committing a criminal act that the lawyer believes is likely to result in imminent death or substantial bodily harm	May reveal the intention of client to commit a crime and the information necessary to prevent the crime regardless of seriousness of the proposed crime
May disclose information to establish a claim or defense on behalf of attorney in a controversy between attorney and client, to establish a defense to criminal charge or civil claim against attorney based upon conduct in which client was involved, or to respond to allegations in any proceeding concerning attorney's representation of client	May reveal confidences or secrets necessary to establish or collect fee or defend him or herself or employers or associates against an accusation of wrongful conduct

FIGURE 3–1

The Ethical Duty to Client Confidentiality

Most jurisdictions have followed Rule 1.6 when adopting their own rules concerning client confidentiality, although there are some variances between the states—especially with regard to exceptions to the rules.

What Is Protected

In every instance information learned by an attorney from or about a client during the course of representation is presumed to be confidential. The scope of the attorney's ethical duty to confidentiality under ABA Model Rule 1.6 is very broad and includes all information relating to the representation regardless of its source. Information received by an attorney from conversations with a client, documents produced by a client, and even an outside source, all fall under the attorney's duty to confidentiality.

Canon 4 of the Code of Professional Responsibility, which is still followed in some jurisdictions, provides that an attorney should preserve the *"confidences and secrets* of a client." The term *confidences* includes "information protected by the attorney–client privilege under applicable law," and the term *secrets* includes "other information gained in the professional relationship that the client has requested be held inviolate or the disclosure of which would be embarrassing or would likely to be detrimental to the client."[3] This portion of the Model Code is more limiting than the Model Rules with regard to the information that must be kept confidential, as it requires that the information is protected by the attorney–client privilege or that the information fall into the definition of confidences or secrets. Information protected by attorney–client privilege is usually limited to information learned through communications from the client for the purposes of securing legal advice or assistance. Information obtained from outside sources, information that the client has not requested to be kept confidential, and information that may not be embarrassing or detrimental to the client may not be included under this rule.

The code of ethics applicable in your state may follow either one of these rules, or it may be slightly different from both rules. If you have a question concerning the rules in your jurisdiction, it is very important that you consult the applicable code of ethics or other sources to determine exactly what information must be kept confidential.

The attorney's duty of confidentiality usually begins with the first meeting with the client. The ethical duty of confidentiality also applies to prospective clients who consult an attorney in "good faith for the purpose of obtaining legal representation or advice" even if the attorney declines representation and performs no legal services for the individual.[4]

The duty of confidentiality continues after the client–lawyer relationship has terminated.[5] An attorney or paralegal may never divulge confidential client information, even after the attorney's representation has terminated. This rule is of special concern for paralegals who leave one law firm to work for another. The attorney or paralegal may never divulge confidential information learned through previous employment—especially if it would be to the detriment of former clients. At times, attorneys or paralegals who go to work for a new law firm find they have confidential information about previous clients that could affect clients in the new law firm. Such a situation could cause a conflict of interest and may disqualify the attorney or paralegal from working on certain files in the new law firm. Conflicts of interest are discussed in Chapter 4.

The attorney–client privilege generally continues even after the client's death. This rule was upheld in a 1998 United States Supreme Court decision, when the court held that Deputy White House Counsel Vincent Foster's attorney, James Hamilton, could not be compelled to turn over notes from a meeting between them. The notes in question, which had been subpoenaed as directed by

Independent Prosecutor Ken Starr, were from a July, 1993 meeting during which confidential matters were discussed, including various investigations of staff firings in the White House travel office. Mr. Foster committed suicide just nine days after the meeting.

In its ruling, the Supreme Court held that:

> Knowing that communications will remain confidential even after death encourages the client to communicate fully and frankly with counsel. While the fear of disclosure, and the consequent withholding of information from counsel, may be reduced if disclosure is limited to posthumous disclosure in a criminal context, it seems unreasonable to assume that it vanishes altogether. Clients may be concerned about reputation, civil liability, or possible harm to friends or family. Posthumous disclosure of such communications may be as feared as disclosure during the client's lifetime.[6]

Attorney's Employees and Agents

The attorney's ethical duty to confidentiality extends to the attorney's employees and agents, especially paralegals. Model Rule 5.3(b) States that "With respect to a nonlawyer employed or retained by or associated with a lawyer, a lawyer having direct supervisory authority over the nonlawyer shall make reasonable efforts to ensure that the person's conduct is compatible with the professional obligations of the lawyer. . . ." The ABA's Comment to that Model Rule indicates that "A lawyer should give such assistants appropriate instruction and supervision concerning the ethical aspects of their employment, *particularly regarding the obligation not to disclose information relating to representation of the client* . . . [emphasis added]."

In an ethics opinion by the Florida Bar concerning a paralegal who was hired by an opposing law firm, it was determined that both the hiring firm and the former firm had ethical obligations to see that confidences of the client were not divulged. The opinion indicated that "the former firm has a duty to admonish the departing employee that the employee has an ethical or moral obligation not to reveal confidences or secrets of any client to the hiring firm." And that "the hiring firm has a corresponding duty not to seek or permit a disclosure of confidences or secrets by the employee and not to use such information." [7]

Paralegals must be fully aware of the provisions of the state code of ethics that deal with client confidentiality and must be certain to abide by them. Failure to do so may have severe consequences to the client, the supervising attorney, and the paralegal.

> "The purpose of the privilege (regarding attorney–client communications) is to encourage full and frank communication between attorneys and their clients and thereby to promote broader public interests in observance of law and the administration of justice. The privilege recognizes that sound legal advice or advocacy serves public ends and that such advice or advocacy depends upon the lawyer being fully informed by the client . . ."
>
> Upjohn v. United States, 449 U.S. 383 (1981)

Exceptions

As with most important rules of ethics, there are exceptions to the rule of confidentiality. These exceptions vary from state to state, but the most common exceptions to the rule of confidentiality are:

1. Confidential information may be divulged with the client's permission
2. Confidential information may be disclosed when implicitly authorized in order to carry out the representation of the client

3. Confidential information may be disclosed to prevent the client from committing a criminal act that may result in imminent death or substantial bodily harm
4. Confidential client information may be disclosed to establish a claim or defense in a controversy between the lawyer and the client
5. Confidential information must be divulged to rectify or prevent a fraud on a tribunal
6. Confidential information must be divulged if so ordered by a court of law

The first two exceptions are common-sense exceptions to allow the attorney to better represent the client. The last four exceptions may be adverse to the client's interests but are allowed to protect the public or the integrity of the court.

Client Permission. Clients often give their counsel express permission to disclose information concerning their representation to third parties to further their interests. For example, a client may authorize his or her attorney to discuss confidential financial records with an accountant. In jurisdictions that follow the Model Rules, the client must consent to the divulgence of such information after consultation with the attorney. It should be explained to the client why it is advisable to release such confidential information and what information will be divulged.

Implied Permission. An attorney is implicitly authorized to make disclosures about a client when appropriate in carrying out the representation, except to the extent that the client's instructions or special circumstances limit that authority.[8] If attorneys did not have implied authorization to discuss their clients' matters with others, it would be most difficult for them to practice law. For example, while litigating a case for a client "a lawyer may disclose information by admitting a fact that cannot properly be disputed, or in negotiation by making a disclosure that facilitates a satisfactory conclusion.[9]

In addition, it may be in the client's best interest for his or her attorney to consult with other attorneys within the law firm who may have past experience in similar situations or a certain expertise that will assist the attorney's representation. Attorneys and paralegals within a firm may discuss a client's case among themselves unless circumstances warrant otherwise. If an attorney or paralegal needs to consult with an attorney outside of the firm, the client's permission must be obtained. It is usually considered proper for an attorney to give limited information to outside agencies for bookkeeping, accounting, data processing, photocopying, and similar reasons, so long as the agency is selected with due care and is warned concerning the confidential nature of the information. If you are ever in doubt, be sure to ask your supervising attorney or seek the answer from another source.

Prevention of Certain Criminal Acts. Under Rule 1.6 of the Model Rules of Professional Conduct, an attorney **may** divulge confidential information to prevent the client from committing a criminal act that the lawyer believes is likely to result in imminent death or substantial bodily harm. If a client confesses a murder to his or her attorney, the attorney has no right or duty to disclose that information. If, on the other hand, the client tells the attorney that he or she is going to commit murder after their meeting, the attorney may disclose that information to prevent the crime. The attorney must divulge no more information than absolutely necessary to prevent the crime from being committed.

This rule is a deviation from the prior Model Code that allowed the attorney to divulge information concerning a criminal act, without specifying that it is likely to result in imminent death or substantial bodily harm. Under the Model Rules, the attorney must use his or her judgment when deciding whether to divulge the information, and must divulge no more information than absolutely necessary to prevent the crime from being committed. It is not an obligation. Comments to Rule 1.6 of the Model Rules of Professional Conduct give reason for the permissive nature of this exception as follows:

> In becoming privy to information about a client, a lawyer may foresee that the client intends serious harm to another person. However, to the extent a lawyer is required or permitted to disclose a client's purposes, the client will be inhibited from revealing facts which would enable the lawyer to counsel against a wrongful course of action. The public is better protected if full and open communication by the client is encouraged than if it is inhibited.

An attorney whose client consults him about intentions for future criminal behavior must attempt to counsel the client from committing such a crime. Rule 1.2(d) of the Model Rules sets forth the attorney's obligation as follows:

> (d) a lawyer shall not counsel a client to engage, or assist a client, in conduct that the lawyer knows is criminal or fraudulent, but a lawyer may discus the legal consequences of any proposed course of conduct with a client and may counsel or assist a client to make a good faith effort to determine the validity, scope, meaning or application of the law.

Many jurisdictions that have adopted the Model Rules have not adopted this rule verbatim. Some states allow an attorney to divulge confidential information to prevent **any** future crime, and some states **require** attorneys to divulge confidential information to prevent certain crimes.

Self-Protection. Where a legal claim or disciplinary charge alleges complicity of the attorney in a client's conduct or other misconduct of the attorney involving representation of the client, the attorney may respond to the extent he or she reasonably believes necessary to establish a defense.[10] If an attorney is involved in a civil action, which he or she must personally defend due to the representation of a client, the attorney may divulge such information as necessary to defend himself or herself. Attorneys may divulge only as much information as necessary for their defense.

An attorney entitled to a fee is also permitted to divulge the minimum information necessary to prove the services rendered to collect that fee.

To Rectify or Prevent a Fraud On a Tribunal. In addition to the attorney's duty to client confidentiality, as an officer of the court, the attorney has an ethical duty of candor toward the tribunal or court. At times, these two ethical duties can cause conflicts for attorneys who are trying to keep confidential information concerning the representation of their clients while preventing any fraud upon the court. Under Model Rule 3.3, attorneys must not knowingly:

1. Make a false statement of material fact or law to a tribunal
2. Fail to disclose a material fact to a tribunal when disclosure is necessary to avoid assisting a criminal or fraudulent act by the client
3. Fail to disclose to the tribunal legal authority in the controlling jurisdiction known to the lawyer to be directly adverse to the position of the client and not disclosed by opposing counsel
4. Offer evidence that the lawyer knows to be false. If a lawyer has offered material evidence and comes to know of its falsity, the lawyer shall take reasonable remedial measures

These duties "continue to the conclusion of the proceeding and apply even if compliance requires disclosure of information otherwise protected by Rule 1.6."[11]

Statements of Material Fact or Law to Tribunal by Attorney. An attorney must represent his or her client's interest without making any untrue statements of material fact or law to a tribunal. This would apply to statements made in court

Pleadings
A formal document in which a party to a legal proceeding (especially a civil lawsuit) sets forth or responds to allegations, claims, denials, or defenses. In federal civil procedure, the main pleadings are the plaintiff's complaint and the defendant's answer. *(Black's Law Dictionary, Seventh Edition)*

by the attorney and **pleadings** and other documents entered by the attorney. The attorney cannot be responsible for the truthfulness of every document he or she enters with the court, as much of this information is outside of the attorney's personal knowledge. However, any information within the attorney's scope of knowledge, such as affidavits signed by the attorney, or a statement in open court made by the attorney, must be truthful. Under most circumstances, an attorney may refuse to offer evidence that he or she reasonably believes is false.[12]

Disclosure to Prevent Assisting Client with Criminal Activity or Fraud. While an attorney has a duty to keep client information confidential, the attorney must not assist his or her client with a criminal or fraudulent act. For example, in *Minnesota v. Casby*, the attorney was found to be perpetrating a fraud on the court when he learned that the court was mistaken as to the true identity of his client and he did not disclose that information.[13]

Disclosure of Legal Authority Adverse to Client. Using false legal arguments in a case amounts to dishonesty toward the court. Under the Model Rules, an attorney has the duty to disclose directly adverse authority in the controlling jurisdiction that has not been disclosed by the opposing party.[14]

Evidence
The means by which any matter of fact may be established or disproved. Such means include testimony, documents, and physical objects. The law of evidence is composed of rules that determine what evidence is to be admitted or rejected in the trial of a civil action or a criminal prosecution and what weight is to be given to admitted evidence.

False Evidence and Perjury. Even the attorney's duty of confidentiality may be overridden by the attorney's duty to be honest to the court. An attorney must not knowingly offer false evidence. If an attorney has offered evidence and later comes to know of its falsity, the attorney must take reasonable remedial measures.[15] The issues of false **evidence** and **perjury** have always been surrounded by controversy and uncertainty. When false testimony or evidence is offered by a third party, it is clear that the attorney must reject that evidence, regardless of the client's wishes. However, the ethical course of action is not so clear when the client intends to commit perjury. The generally recognized rule is that, if necessary to rectify the situation, an attorney must disclose the existence of the client's deception to the court or to the other party. However, this rule does not always apply—especially in criminal defense matters.

Rule 3.3(a)(4) states that "If a lawyer has offered material evidence and comes to know of its falsity, the lawyer shall take reasonable remedial measures. The exact remedial measures to be taken can be problematic. The ABA Comments to the Model Rules address the matter as follows:

> If perjured testimony or false evidence has been offered, the advocate's proper course ordinarily is to remonstrate with the client confidentially. If that fails, the advocate should seek to withdraw if that will remedy the situation. If withdrawal will not remedy the situation or is impossible, the advocate should make disclosure to the court. It is for the court then to determine what should be done. . . ."

Perjury
Giving false testimony in a judicial proceeding or an administrative proceeding; lying under oath as to a material fact; swearing to the truth of anything one knows or believes to be false. Perjury is a crime. A person who makes a false affirmation is equally a perjurer.

Perjury by Client in Criminal Defense Matter. Criminal defense attorneys representing a client who may commit perjury have a special set of problems. The general rule is that the attorney must disclose the existence of perjury with respect to a material fact, even perjury of a client. This rule also applies to defense counsel in criminal cases. However, the attorney's ethical duty in such a situation may be qualified by constitutional provisions for due process and the right to counsel in criminal cases. "In some jurisdictions these provisions have been construed to require that counsel present an accused as a witness if the accused wishes to testify, even if counsel knows the testimony will be false."[16] The attorney clearly has an ethical duty to try to persuade the client not to commit perjury, including counseling the client as to the possible negative consequences that may occur, especially the penalty for perjury. If the client still insists on offering false testimony, the proper course of action is not so clear. The Supreme Court has determined that an attorney is acting ethically if he threatens to withdraw from representation and expose a client's perjured testimony should the client insist on making false testimony before the court.[17] Attorneys must follow the code of ethics that applies to them in their jurisdictions, as well as **precedent** set by the courts in such matters.

Court Order. An attorney must turn over information otherwise considered confidential if ordered to do so by a court of law. When the release of potentially confidential information in open court is in dispute, the court may hear the matter **in camera.** This means the attorney may have the chance to plead his or her argument to the judge in private, in the judge's chambers. If the court then finds that the information is not privileged and if the court orders the attorney to disclose it, the attorney must disclose or face civil contempt charges. If a court has properly found, after an in camera inspection, that information is not privileged, and has ordered a lawyer to disclose it, the rule of confidentiality does not protect the lawyer from a contempt finding.

Internal Revenue Service–Required Reporting of Cash Receipts

Under 26 U.S.C.A. § 6050I, attorneys must report to the Internal Revenue Service (IRS) cash receipt in excess of $10,000 in payment of fees on IRS Form 8300 (Figure 3–2). The attorney must report such cash receipt, along with the name of the paying client. Many attorneys have attempted to fight this rule, claiming that it breaches their duty to client confidentiality, but few have prevailed with this claim. It has been recommended in ethics opinions that attorneys inform new clients of their duty to report cash receipts in excess of $10,000 at the outset of representation, to give the client fair warning that if they do not wish to have such a disclosure made they should not pay in cash or they should seek other counsel. An ethical opinion of the Florida Bar advises as follows:

> An attorney who has claimed confidentiality and/or privilege in filing an incomplete IRS Form 8300 must, if served with a facially sufficient summons, make a good faith attempt to determine whether a legally recognized privilege applies. If the attorney determines that a privilege might apply, it should be asserted on the client's behalf. If the attorney determines that no privileges are applicable, the attorney acts ethically in complying with the summons. If the court rules that an asserted privilege is inapplicable and orders disclosure, the attorney must either comply with the court's order or appeal the order.[18]

ATTORNEY–CLIENT PRIVILEGE

In addition to the ethical rule of client confidentiality, the attorney–client relationship is subject to the attorney–client privilege (Figure 3–3), which includes the **work product rule.**

The attorney–client privilege is a privilege found in evidence law that governs the use of information in a court proceeding. The attorney–client privilege may be claimed by an attorney who is called on to testify or provide evidence concerning the attorney's representation of the client. The burden of proof concerning the attorney–client privilege is usually on the party claiming the privilege, but the court will make the final determination as to whether the testimony being sought is protected by the privilege. The attorney–client privilege provides that the attorney may not be called on to give testimony concerning confidential information disclosed to the attorney by the client during the course of representation.

The attorney–client privilege is more limited than the attorney's ethical duty to confidentiality and applies only in judicial and other proceedings in which an

Precedent
1. The making of law by a court in recognizing and applying new rules while administering justice. 2. A decided case that furnishes a basis for determining later cases involving similar facts or issues. *(Black's Law Dictionary, Seventh Edition)*

In camera
In chambers; in private. A term referring to a hearing or any other judicial business conducted in the judge's office or in a courtroom that has been cleared of spectators.

Work product rule
The rule providing for qualified immunity of an attorney's work product from discovery or other compelled disclosure. Fed. R. Civ. P. 26(b)(3). The exemption was primarily established to protect an attorney's litigation strategy. *Hickman v. Taylor,* 329 U.S. 495, 67 S.Ct. 385 (1947). Also termed *work product immunity; work-product privilege; work product exemption. (Black's Law Dictionary, Seventh Edition)*

Form 8300

(Rev. August 1997)

Department of the Treasury
Internal Revenue Service

Report of Cash Payments Over $10,000 Received in a Trade or Business

▶ See instructions for definition of cash.
▶ Use this form for transactions occurring after July 31, 1997.
Please type or print.

OMB No. 1545-0892

1 Check appropriate box(es) if: **a** ☐ Amends prior report. **b** ☐ Suspicious transaction.

Part I — Identity of Individual From Whom the Cash Was Received

2 If more than one individual is involved, check here and see instructions . . . . ▶ ☐

3 Last name	**4** First name	**5** M.I.	**6** Taxpayer identification number

7 Address (number, street, and apt. or suite no.) | **8** Date of birth . ▶ (see instructions) M M D D Y Y Y Y

| **9** City | **10** State | **11** ZIP code | **12** Country (if not U.S.) | **13** Occupation, profession, or business |

14 Document used to verify identity: **a** Describe identification ▶
b Issued by _____ **c** Number

Part II — Person on Whose Behalf This Transaction Was Conducted

15 If this transaction was conducted on behalf of more than one person, check here and see instructions . . . . . ▶ ☐

16 Individual's last name or Organization's name	**17** First name	**18** M.I.	**19** Taxpayer identification number

20 Doing business as (DBA) name (see instructions) | Employer identification number

21 Address (number, street, and apt. or suite no.) | **22** Occupation, profession, or business

| **23** City | **24** State | **25** ZIP code | **26** Country (if not U.S.) |

27 Alien identification: **a** Describe identification ▶
b Issued by _____ **c** Number

Part III — Description of Transaction and Method of Payment

| **28** Date cash received M M D D Y Y Y Y | **29** Total cash received $ .00 | **30** If cash was received in more than one payment, check here . . . ▶ ☐ | **31** Total price if different from item 29 $ .00 |

32 Amount of cash received (in U.S. dollar equivalent) (must equal item 29) (see instructions):

a U.S. currency $ _____ .00 (Amount in $100 bills or higher $ _____ .00)
b Foreign currency $ _____ .00 (Country ▶ _____)
c Cashier's check(s) $ _____ .00
d Money order(s) $ _____ .00   Issuer's name(s) and serial number(s) of the monetary instrument(s) ▶ _____
e Bank draft(s) $ _____ .00
f Traveler's check(s) $ _____ .00

33 Type of transaction
a ☐ Personal property purchased
b ☐ Real property purchased
c ☐ Personal services provided
d ☐ Business services provided
e ☐ Intangible property purchased
f ☐ Debt obligations paid
g ☐ Exchange of cash
h ☐ Escrow or trust funds
i ☐ Bail bond
j ☐ Other (specify) ▶

34 Specific description of property or service shown in 33. (Give serial or registration number, address, docket number, etc.) ▶ _____

Part IV — Business That Received Cash

35 Name of business that received cash | **36** Employer identification number

37 Address (number, street, and apt. or suite no.) | Social security number

| **38** City | **39** State | **40** ZIP code | **41** Nature of your business |

42 Under penalties of perjury, I declare that to the best of my knowledge the information I have furnished above is true, correct, and complete.

Signature of authorized official _____   Title of authorized official _____

43 Date of signature M M D D Y Y Y Y | **44** Type or print name of contact person | **45** Contact telephone number ( )

For Paperwork Reduction Act Notice, see page 4.   Cat. No. 62133S   Form **8300** (Rev. 8-97)

FIGURE 3-2

Attorneys must report cash receipts in excess of $10,000 on IRS form 8300.

Ethical Rule of Confidentiality	Attorney–Client Privilege
Found in the pertinent code of ethics	Found in evidence law
Concerns all actions of the attorney regarding confidential information concerning the client	Concerns judicial and other proceedings in which an attorney may be called as a witness or required to provide evidence concerning a client
Protects all information the attorney has relating to a client, regardless of its source	Concerns communications made by the client in a confidential setting for the purpose of securing legal advice or assistance
Applies to past wrongdoings and the contemplation of certain future wrongdoings	Applies to past wrongdoings—not to contemplation of future wrongdoings
With limited exceptions, prevents all disclosures of confidential information	Does not prevent disclosures outside the judicial process or information received from sources other than the client

FIGURE 3–3

Ethical Rule of Confidentiality vs. Attorney–Client Privilege

attorney may be called as a witness or required to provide evidence concerning a client. The scope of the information that is protected under this privilege is also more limited. The privilege applies only to communications made by the client in a confidential setting for the purpose of securing legal advice or assistance. It does not prevent disclosures outside the judicial process or information received from sources other than the client. As with the ethical duty to client confidentiality, the attorney–client privilege applies to past wrongdoings—not to the contemplation of future crimes.

> The attorney–client privilege protects the confidences of wrongdoers, but the reason for that protection—the centrality of open client and attorney communication to the proper functioning of our adversary system of justice ceases to operate at a certain point, namely, where the desired advice refers not to prior wrongdoing, but to future wrongdoing.[19]

Waiver of the Attorney–Client Privilege

The attorney–client privilege may be waived expressly or implicitly—but only by the client. The client owns the privilege; it may not be waived by the attorney. When the privilege is waived, it is given up by the client, and the attorney may disclose the confidential information in question.

The attorney–client privilege is waived expressly when the client, either verbally or in writing, gives the attorney permission to disclose confidential information otherwise covered by the privilege. Clients may do this for several reasons when they feel that it is to their advantage to disclose the information to the public or certain individuals. For example, clients involved in high-profile cases may give their attorneys permission to speak to the press regarding certain aspects of their cases to squelch rumors.

An implied waiver of the attorney–client privilege may be given by certain actions taken by the client. For example, if a client goes public with information otherwise covered by the privilege, the client has implicitly waived the privilege.

Work Product Rule

Before a case proceeds to trial, there is a period of **discovery.** Discovery is a "means for providing a party, in advance of trial, with access to facts that are within the knowledge of the other side, to enable the party to better try her case."[20] The discovery process may include **interrogatories, requests for pro-**

Discovery
A means for providing a party, in advance of trial, with access to facts that are within the knowledge of the other side, to enable the party to better try his or her case.

Interrogatories
Written questions put by one party to another or, in limited situations, to a witness in advance of trial. Interrogatories are a form of discovery and are governed by the rules of civil procedure.

Request for the production of documents
A request for the inspection or duplication of documents or other materials that are relevant to the subject matter of the litigation.

Deposition
The testimony of a witness given under oath outside of the courtroom, usually in advance of the trial or hearing, upon oral examination or in response to written interrogatories.

duction of documents, depositions, and other means prescribed by applicable law. In federal court the various instruments of discovery serve to "narrow and clarify the basic issues between the parties and as a device for ascertaining the facts, or information or as to the existence or whereabouts of facts, relative to those issues."[21]

Although the discovery process is far reaching, not all information in an attorney's possession is discoverable. The work product rule provides that an attorney's work product is privileged and not subject to discovery. Three criteria have been recognized as necessary to invoke the work product rule. The material in question must be:

1. Documents and tangible things otherwise discoverable
2. Prepared in anticipation of litigation
3. By or for another party or that party's representative[22]

The work product rule generally includes memoranda and other documents prepared by an attorney in preparation of litigation. The exact documentation that falls under the work product rule depends on the circumstances of each case and the importance of the documentation to the case. In one Supreme Court case, the court held that an attorney's notes concerning interviews with witnesses were not discoverable, partly because the petitioner's counsel (who requested the information) had access to the same witnesses. The court found that "forcing an attorney to repeat or write out all that witnesses have told him and to deliver an account to his adversary gives rise to grave dangers of inaccuracy and untrustworthiness" and that it was unwarranted under the circumstances. However, in a different Supreme Court case, where statements had been taken by government attorneys and approved by witnesses, the statements were not found to fall under the work product rule.[23]

Paralegals are often responsible for gathering documents for the discovery process under the supervision of an attorney. If you are assigned such a task, you must be sure that you know the pertinent work product rule. If in doubt, be sure to ask your supervising attorney.

CASE AND DISCUSSION

In the following case, an attorney indicated to the precinct police that he had brought his client in to surrender for the shooting of his wife. Testimony in this regard was deemed erroneously admitted into evidence in violation of the attorney–client privilege by the Court of Appeals, and a new trial was ordered.

84 N.Y.2d 718
The PEOPLE of the State of
New York, Respondent,
v.
James CASSAS, Appellant.
Court of Appeals of New York.
Jan. 17, 1995.

The primary issue here is whether an attorney's statement, incriminating his client in the murder of his wife and constituting the principal evidence against the defendant, was properly admitted into evidence. We conclude that it was not and we reverse.

Defendant was charged and convicted of firing four bullets into the back of the head and neck of his wife, Jan Cassas, at their Brooklyn home in the early morning hours of June 25,1987. Jan Cassas died as a result of her wounds.

Defendant and his then-attorney Samuel Hirsch on that same morning went to the police precinct nearest Hirsch's home and were directed to the precinct nearest defendant's home. At the second precinct, the attorney identified himself as a lawyer and inquired whether there had been any reported homicides or attempted homicides within the past 24 hours. Hirsch informed the desk sergeant that there was a problem at defendant's home and that a prompt police response was necessary. The attorney accompanied the police to defendant's home where the police found Jan Cassas dead in the master bedroom. The attorney then returned to the precinct where defendant was waiting.

There is evidence in the record that at the precinct, with defendant standing next to him, attorney Hirsch stated, "I brought my client in to surrender. I believe he shot his wife. You'll find the gun in the room. It will have my client's prints on it." The police arrested defendant. Later that day, the police returned to defendant's home and recovered a loaded gun from the master bedroom where Mrs.

Cassas' body was found. A second gun allegedly used in the killing was apparently never found.

Supreme Court denied defendant's motion to suppress the statements made by his attorney, finding that at the time the statements were made, Mr. Hirsch, as defendant's attorney, was his agent, authorized to speak about the subject matter within the scope of the parties' agency relationship. Therefore, the statement was binding on the defendant. The Appellate Division affirmed, 194 A.D.2d 685, 599 N.Y.S.2d 197. It concluded that the statement, admitted through the testimony of a detective, was direct evidence of guilt from a person acting as defendant's agent.

. . . In this case . . . we conclude that the oral assertions of defendant's attorney, introduced in the People's case-in-chief, were inadmissible. There was no evidence that the statement had been authorized by the defendant as a waiver of the attorney–client privilege. This is particularly important in criminal cases where a defendant retains the authority to make key choices about a defense against criminal charges.

. . . Significantly and key to the disposition of the instant case, the admissions would violate the attorney–client privilege because there is no evidentiary record support for a finding of waiver of the privilege by defendant. The attorney–client privilege "exists to ensure that one seeking legal advice will be able to confide fully and freely in his [or her] attorney, secure in the knowledge that his [or her] confidences will not later be exposed to public view to his [or her] embarrassment or legal detriment." (*Matter of Priest v. Hennessy*, 51 N.Y.2d 62, 67-68, 431 N.Y.S.2d 511, 409 N.E.2d 983.) . . .

The fact that the attorney is the agent of the client–principal does not alone equate to a waiver of this privilege. The specific authorization must come from defendant principal to attorney-agent to constitute a waiver of the attorney–client privilege. Mr. Hirsch was not called as a witness at trial, and no evidence was presented as to the full and detailed scope of the parties' relationship in the relevant context of the issue at hand. . . .

Accordingly, the order of the Appellate Division should be reversed, defendant's motion to suppress granted and a new trial ordered. . . .

Order reversed, etc.

CONFIDENTIALITY AND THE CORPORATE CLIENT

The ethical duty of confidentiality and the attorney–client privilege have several applications to attorneys and legal assistants working in the corporate law area. A Supreme Court decision in 1981 extended the attorney–client privilege to corporations, allowing corporations the right to keep confidential any information passed on to their attorneys. In effect, this ruling prevents attorneys from testifying against their corporate clients in a court of law or from disseminating unauthorized information about the corporation. The duty of confidentiality and the attorney–client privilege can extend to officers and directors of the corporation as well as to employees at various levels who are acting on behalf of the corporation. The Supreme Court has found that in addition to the officers, directors, and others controlling the actions in response to legal advice, middle-level and lower-level employees can involve the corporation in litigation and require the advice of attorneys.[24] Therefore the **confidential communication** between corporate counsel and employees at various levels who have relevant information needed by corporate counsel to adequately advise the client with respect to litigation may also be protected under the attorney–client privilege.

In recent years, corporate management has begun to hire outside counsel to perform internal investigations if it suspects wrongdoing within the company. Information uncovered by such outside counsel is usually considered privileged information and cannot be used against the corporation in any potential future lawsuits or criminal prosecutions. This allows the corporate management to attempt to put an end to any wrongdoing within the corporation or to attempt damage control before an official investigation begins.

Recent developments in several tobacco litigation cases have examined the issue of attorney–client privilege in a new light. Attorneys for the tobacco companies have been forced to turn over tens of thousands of documents that they had claimed inadmissible under the principle of attorney–client privilege. The attorney–client privilege was not granted with regard to these documents either

Confidential communication
A communication made within a certain protected relationship—such as husband-wife, attorney-client, or priest-penitent—and legally protected from forced disclosure. (*Black's Law Dictionary, Seventh Edition*)

because the court determined that the materials contained information relating to an ongoing crime or fraud, or because it was determined that the attorney involved was performing duties for the companies other than, or in addition to, providing legal advice.

FROM THE PARALEGAL'S PERSPECTIVE

The issue of client confidentiality is of special concern to paralegals because the privilege of confidentiality clearly extends to the lawyer's employees and law firm staff, especially paralegals. Paralegals are often in a position to receive confidential information and must at all times resist the temptation to disclose this information, either to the media, as a matter of convenience when working on a client's file, or as a source of interesting gossip with friends and family. Breaching a client's confidentiality can have serious consequences to paralegals and to the attorneys they work for.

Courts have found that paralegals are also subject to the principle of attorney–client privilege. In *AIG Life Insurance Company, et al. V. CUNA Mutual Insurance Company, 1996 WL 422297 (DKan.) 1996),* the court found the plaintiff could take the deposition of a paralegal working with attorneys for the defense, but that any question that inquired into matters protected by the attorney–client privilege may be objected to.

Special attention to client confidentiality must be given by the corporate paralegal working in the securities or merger and acquisition areas. Rumors regarding mergers and acquisitions can have a devastating effect on the outcome of the proposed transaction, as well as an effect on the price of the stock of either or both parties involved. Likewise, unauthorized leaks of information from a law firm that represents publicly held corporations, or corporations that are planning public offerings, can have significant financial implications for the client. All information regarding a publicly held corporation must be closely monitored and released only with forethought. Information passed on to third parties regarding a publicly held corporation may be considered "insider information" and could subject individuals purchasing stock based on that information to civil suits, criminal prosecution, or both.

Both of the national paralegal associations recognize the importance of maintaining client confidentiality in their codes of ethics.

The NALA's Rules

The paralegal's ethical duty to maintain client confidences is set forth in Canon 7 of the NALA Code of Ethics and Professional Responsibility, which must be adhered to by all members of the NALA.

Canon 7
A legal assistant must protect the confidences of a client and must not violate any rule or statute now in effect or hereafter enacted controlling

The NFPA'S Rules

Canon 1.5 of the NFPA's Model Code of Ethics and Professional Responsibility reads as follows:

1.5 A paralegal shall preserve all confidential information provided by the client or acquired from other sources before, during, and after the course of the professional relationship.

The NFPA provides the following ethical considerations as further guidance to paralegals:

EC-1.5(a)   A paralegal shall be aware of and abide by all legal authority governing confidential information in the jurisdiction in which the paralegal practices.

This ethical consideration is of the utmost importance to paralegals. It reaffirms that paralegals are subject to the code of ethics and case law in any jurisdiction in which they work. As discussed previously, although most states in the country have adopted the significant provisions of the ABA's Model Rules of Professional Conduct, there are many variations from the Model Rules among the states, especially in the area of attorney–client confidentiality. However, one rule that remains a constant among all jurisdictions is that the rules of attorney–client confidentiality apply to paralegals and other nonlawyer employees.

EC-1.5(b)   A paralegal shall not use confidential information to the disadvantage of the client.

As a paralegal, you will often be in a position to learn client confidences and secrets, many of which could be potentially harmful or damaging to a client. You must never use this information to the client's disadvantage. You must never disclose any confidential information that could be to the disadvantage of a client unless required by law.

EC-1.5(c)   A paralegal shall not use confidential information to the advantage of the paralegal or of a third person.

Paralegals are often in a position to learn confidential information that could be used to their advantages. This confidential client information must never be used to the advantage of the paralegal. For example, a paralegal could be in a position to learn inside information on a corporation that could affect the price of the corporation's stock. For a paralegal to act on that confidential information by buying or selling stock of that corporation, or recommending it to a friend, would not only be unethical, it would also be illegal.

EC-1.5(d)   A paralegal may reveal confidential information only after full disclosure and with the client's written consent; or, when required by law or court order; or, when necessary to prevent the client from committing an act that could result in death or serious bodily harm.

The same exceptions to the divulgence of confidential client information that apply to attorneys apply to paralegals. Generally, you may release client information:

1. With the client's written consent
2. When required by law or court order
3. When necessary to prevent the client from committing an act that could result in death or serious bodily harm

There will be times when the release of client information is required by law. This will almost always be a determination to be made by the supervising attorney.

A paralegal may release confidential information to prevent the client from committing an act that could result in death or serious bodily harm. Again, the supervising attorney should be consulted on this whenever possible.

> *EC-1.5(e)   A paralegal shall keep those individuals responsible for the legal representation of a client fully informed of any confidential information the paralegal may have pertaining to that client.*

To provide the client with the best possible representation, the attorney must be aware of all of the pertinent facts regarding the client. The rules of attorney–client confidentiality are designed to encourage the client to make full disclosures to the attorney, even if the information is embarrassing or damaging to the client. The paralegal need not be the gatekeeper of confidential information. In fact, the paralegal has a duty to keep the attorney apprised of any pertinent confidential information learned from or about the client.

> *EC-1.5(f)   A paralegal shall not engage in any indiscreet communications concerning clients.*

At times a paralegal may be in a position to learn confidential information that is almost overwhelmingly intriguing. Whether it is to your mother, your best friend, or a supermarket tabloid, you must always resist the temptation to talk about a client or client's case outside of the office.

Practical Considerations

A study of all the pertinent rules of ethics and laws still won't tell you everything you need to know concerning client confidentiality. In addition, you need common sense and an understanding of the practical issues you will face in keeping your client's confidential information confidential and avoiding any inadvertent disclosures.

Keeping Communications Confidential.   Modern law offices are usually designed with privacy and confidentiality in mind. Even so, you must be careful that confidential information is not accidentally leaked by conversations that may be overheard.

In the Office.   Even though it is permissible to discuss confidential client information with associates within the office, such conversations should be confined to those with a need to know. Idle gossip around the water cooler with coworkers who have nothing to do with a particular client can lead to leaks and to trouble.

All client conferences should be held in private offices or in a private conference room with the door shut. You should always avoid confidential discussions with a client in common areas of the office, especially areas such as the reception area where other clients could overhear.

If you work for a law firm or other type of organization with a receptionist who is located in a common reception area, the receptionist must be aware of the need to keep client names and other information confidential. Callers should be announced quietly—out of earshot of anyone who may be waiting in the reception area.

Outside the Office.   Not all confidential meetings and conversations will take place in the office. There will always be the need to meet at a client's office, at the office of the opposing counsel, or even as a business lunch. Extra caution must always be used when discussing confidential matters outside of the office. Keep the use of names and specifics to a minimum when necessary.

Cellular Phones.   Cellular phones are usually considered to be private and secure. However, it is possible that cellular phone conversations can be overheard. If you are using a cellular phone for a confidential and sensitive conversation, it is advisable that you let the party you are speaking to know, so that the party will not say anything he or she does not want overheard. Confidentiality and cellular phones are discussed further in Chapter 10.

Facsimile and E-mail. Communications by facsimile (fax) and e-mail are accepted almost as a necessity in the modern law office. If you are operating the fax machine, you must always double check the telephone number being used. If you fax documents to the wrong number, they cannot be taken back. You may want to limit the use of the speed dial and redial features to give yourself time to think things through before the actual transmission of documents. Before you send a fax, you must picture in your mind the receiving fax machine. If your transmission is going to another office, will it go to a fax machine where it can be picked up by anyone who may be near the machine? If so, you may want to call ahead to see that the recipient is standing by, ready to receive your message. Many law firms and law departments include a cover sheet with their fax transmissions with a message indicating that the transmission is confidential and should be forwarded to the intended party immediately (Figure 3–4).

Many law firms use e-mail as a common way to communicate with each other in the office, with attorneys in other offices, and with clients. If you are ever in a position to transmit confidential client information by e-mail, you must use the proper security measures to ensure that the information does not land in the wrong hands. Always use a secure password and turn off your computer screen when you are not using your computer. Confidentiality and e-mail is discussed further in Chapter 10.

GARCIA AND WHITE
ATTORNEYS AT LAW
3499 Second Street
St. Paul, Minnesota 55101
Telephone: 612-483-4753 Facsimile: 612-483-4755

CONFIDENTIAL FACSIMILE TRANSMITTAL

DATE: _____ PAGES: _____ (including cover)

TO: _____

_____

SENDER: _____

COMPANY: _____

FAX: _____

COMMENTS: _____

_____

_____

CONFIDENTIALITY NOTICE: The information contained in this facsimile transmission is legally privileged and confidential, intended only for the use of the individual or entity named above. If the reader of this information is not the intended recipient, you are hereby notified that any dissemination, distribution or copying of this transmission is strictly prohibited. If you received this in error, please phone the sender or notify us immediately and return the original to us at the above address.

FIGURE 3–4
Facsimile Cover Sheet

Talking to the Press. This section may be more appropriately entitled "Not Talking to the Press." If you are contacted by a reporter requesting information on a particular client or case, your only response can be NO COMMENT! You can take a message and refer the call to the supervising attorney. You will probably not want to give out the attorney's name or phone number unless you have discussed the situation in advance. Never talk to the press concerning a client or a case without the permission of the supervising attorney.

Protecting Confidential Files and Documents. Protecting confidential files and documentation is just as important as protecting confidential conversations and messages. Files and confidential documents must always be kept in a secure location to prevent loss, theft, or the inadvertent breach of confidential information.

Securing Files After Hours. All client files should be locked in fireproof file cabinets at night to prevent loss by fire or theft or a breach of confidence. If there are no fireproof file cabinets within the attorney or paralegal offices, the files should be kept in a safe central location.

Keeping Confidential Information Out of Sight. Never leave confidential information in plain sight. If you meet with clients in your office, you must be certain that no confidential information is left lying about on your desk or cabinets. Also you must be certain that confidential documents are not visible on your computer screen. Be sure to take a quick look over your office before admitting a client or anyone else to your office to make sure that all confidential information is secure.

Shredding Confidential Materials When Necessary. Drafts of confidential documents and other information that is to be disposed of should be shredded whenever possible. Confidential information should not land in trash baskets that will eventually be emptied into a central location.

A Question of Ethics

You are reviewing the Answers to Interrogatories received on the *Burns v. Value Auto* case when you find something amiss on page 32. There is an extra page stuck in the document, upside down and backward. A yellow Post-it note on the extra page reads "Please mark 'Confidential'" and file in the Value Auto file." A quick glance at the extra page tells you that it is correspondence from Tim Jensen, the President of Value Auto to his attorney—the opposing counsel in the *Burns v. Value Auto* case. The correspondence was apparently stuck in among the documents unintentionally.

This is really intriguing; there may be something that could benefit your client in this letter. What do you do?

Answer and Discussion: The only thing you can do is fold the letter (without reading it), and put it in an envelope returning it to the opposing counsel. Consult with your supervising attorney to tell him or her what happened, then one of you should call the opposing counsel to let them know the letter is on its way back. When an attorney (or paralegal) inadvertently receives materials that appear to be confidential and not intended for him or her, the recipient should refrain from examining the materials, notify the sending attorney, and abide by his or her instructions.[25]

Double-Checking Everything that Leaves the Office. When you are sending information out of the office, especially if you are sending large volumes of documents to opposing counsel, such as a response to a request for a production of documents, you must always double check to see that nothing is inadvertently sent out of the office or sent to the wrong person. If necessary, review your correspondence and your secretary or assistant's outgoing mail, with the rules of confidentiality in mind.

Dealing with Outside Services. Exceptions to the ethical codes of conduct allow for the utilization of outside services such as billing services, photocopying services, and file storage services. Only the minimum information required should be given to these types of services. When using such outside services, you must be certain that you use a reliable service that employs individuals who are aware of the importance of confidentiality. Under certain circumstances, outside vendors may be requested to execute confidentiality agreements, promising their confidentiality.

CHAPTER SUMMARY

- With a few exceptions, attorneys and paralegals have an ethical duty to keep confidential information learned from and about the client during the course of representation.
- The rule of confidentiality begins with the client's first meeting with the attorney and lasts indefinitely.
- The attorney–client privilege is a privilege found in evidence law that governs the use of information in court proceedings.
- The attorney–client privilege protects communications made for the purpose of securing legal advice or assistance.
- The exact rules for confidentiality are prescribed by state law and by the code of ethics, which is binding on attorneys in each state.
- The attorney's ethical duty to confidentiality extends to the attorney's employees, especially paralegals.
- Confidential information may be divulged with the client's permission and when disclosure is implicitly authorized.
- In some instances confidential information may be divulged to prevent the commission of a crime.
- Confidential information may be disclosed to establish a claim or defense in a controversy between an attorney and client.
- Confidential information must be divulged to rectify or prevent a fraud on the court.
- Both of the national paralegal associations recognize the importance of client confidentiality and include provisions for paralegals to maintain client confidentiality in their codes of ethics.
- Confidential client information may usually be discussed with other attorneys and paralegals within the office. Client permission is usually required to release confidential information to attorneys outside of the office who may be consulted.
- Care must be taken that confidential conversations with or about a client are never overheard either within the office or outside of the office.
- Written confidential information that must be disposed of should be shredded.

SUMMARY QUESTIONS

1. Is it unethical for an attorney to divulge confidences of a client in a book *after* the attorney's representation has ceased?
2. Suppose your supervising attorney has just taken on representation of a new client who has been charged with the murder of the client's brother. Your supervising attorney gets him out on bail and two days later he comes into your office and confesses to the murder he has been charged with and says that he is about to go out and do in his sister, too. What is your ethical duty? What can you divulge and what can't you divulge assuming you work in a jurisdiction that follows the Model Rules in this regard?
3. You have just finished working on the Smith divorce when you get a call from someone identifying herself as Mr. Smith's new accountant. She is requesting copies of Mr. Smiths' income tax returns for the past three years, which you know are in the Smith file. Do you discuss Mr. Smith's divorce with his accountant? Do you send her copies of the income tax returns? How would you handle this request?
4. What action, if any, must an attorney take if she hears her client lie under oath while being questioned by the other attorney in a civil lawsuit?
5. What are an attorney's obligations for reporting cash receipts to the IRS?
6. Is an attorney prohibited from suing a client for attorneys' fees if it would mean divulging confidential information to prove the fees were earned?
7. What are the differences between the attorney–client privilege and the ethical duty to confidentiality?
8. What does it mean to say that paralegals are "subject to the principles of the attorney–client privilege"?
9. Where can a paralegal turn to have questions answered concerning what does and does not constitute a breach of confidentiality?
10. Is it permissible for a paralegal to release confidential information to a photocopying service to be copied and bound?

ENDNOTES

[1]ABA Model Rules of Professional Conduct, Rule 1.6(b)(1) (1996).

[2]Ibid., Rule 3.3

[3]ABA Model Code of Professional Responsibility, DR 4-101(A) (1986).

[4]ABA Comm. On Ethics and Professional Responsibility, Formal Op. 90-358 (1990).

[5]ABA Model Rules of Professional Conduct Rule 1.6 cmt. (1996).

[6]Swidler & Berline, et al. V. U.S., 118 S.Ct. 2081 (1998).

[7]Florida Bar Association Ethics Opinion 86-5 (1986).

[8]ABA Model Rules of Professional Conduct Rule 1.6 cmt. (1996).

[9]Ibid.

[10]Ibid.

[11]ABA Model Rules of Professional Conduct Rule 3.3(b) (1996).

[12]ABA Model Rules of Professional Conduct Rule 3.3(c) (1996).

[13]Minnesota v. Casby, 348 NW2d 736 (Minn. 1984).

[14]ABA Model Rules of Professional Conduct Rule 3.3 cmt. (1996).

[15]Ibid.

[16]Ibid.

[17]Nix v. Whiteside, 475 U.S. 157 (1986).

[18]Florida Bar Association Ethics Opinion 92-5, December 7, 1993.

[19]U.S. v. Zolin, 491 U.S. 554 (1989).

[20]Ballentines Legal Dictionary and Thesaurus, Lawyers Cooperative Publishing (1995).

[21]Hickman v. Taylor, 329 U.S. 495 (1947).

[22]Gold Standard v. American Resources, 805 P.2d 164 (Utah 1990).

[23]Goldberg v. United States, 425 U.S. 94 (1976).

[24]Upjohn Co. v. United States, 449 U.S. 383 (1981).

[25]ABA Comm. On Ethics and Professional Responsibility, Op. 92-368 (1992).

THE LITIGATION EXPLOSION

"... the best check on the excesses of litigation is not the rules of the profession or even judicial oversight but the values and character of individual lawyers. ..."

—Joseph G. Allegretti

Kaboom!! Was that a litigation explosion you just heard? It depends on who you ask. There is a public perception in the United States that we are in the middle of a litigation explosion. Many believe we have become too litigious and are too quick to rely on the courts to solve our problems. People perceive there is too much litigation, jury and court awards are too high, and there are just too many lawyers.

Many believe that the so-called litigation explosion has been caused by a glut of unethical lawyers who are looking to create business where solutions other than litigation would best serve the public. They are angry that the law has assumed an all-pervading role in our society and they sense that "enormous amounts of outright fraud are committed by lawyers."[i]

According to a *U.S. News and World Report* poll, fifty-six percent of those polled believe that lawyers use the system to protect the powerful and get rich, while only thirty-five percent believe lawyers play an important role in holding wrongdoers accountable.[ii]

It is not easy to determine the extent to the litigation explosion or, in fact, whether there actually is one. Groups most hurt by litigation, such as insurance companies and manufacturers, provide statistics indicating that the litigation explosion causes the country billions of dollars every year. Tort reform advocates say that the civil justice system drains our economy of at least $130 billion annually.[iii] However, this figure includes every insurance claim paid in the United States and the administrative costs of processing them.

Other groups, such as the Association of Trial Lawyers of America (ATLA) and consumer groups, argue that there is no litigation explosion. These groups point out that the number of tort filings have held steady or actually declined in recent years and that "most of the 10 million civil suits that are clogging the state courts each year are divorce cases and contract and property disputes." According to the ATLA, the real increase in litigation is due to businesses suing businesses, not consumers seeking compensation through personal injury litigation. Statistics provided by the ABA indicate that of the total caseload in state courts, only a very small percentage (approximately six percent) comprises personal injury tort claims. According to a study done by the Rand Corporation on compensation for accidental injuries in the United States, only ten percent of those injured ever used the court system to seek compensation for their injuries and, of those, only two percent actually filed a lawsuit.[iv]

One reason for the public perception of the litigation explosion is the award of seemingly astronomical awards in a few well-publicized cases, such as the McDonald's coffee award of $2.9 million, awarded to a woman who burned herself on a cup of McDonald's coffee. That award was later knocked down to $640,000 by the presiding judge. Asbestos litigation and the tobacco trials have also caught the public's attention with huge awards. While public perception may be that million-dollar awards are common, the average award in personal injury cases is actually $48,000.

Many high-profile cases include huge awards for punitive damages. Punitive damages are damages awarded over and above actual damages because of the wanton, reckless, or malicious nature of the wrong done by the plaintiff. Punitive damages bear no relation to the plaintiff's actual loss because their purpose is to make an example of the plaintiff to discourage others from engaging in the same kind of conduct in the future. However, only a small percentage of civil jury verdicts (less than four percent) involve punitive damages.

Whether the litigation explosion is real or not, there is a serious tort reform movement underway. The movement, not surprisingly, is being lead by those most affected, the insurance companies, manufacturers, and others who have been affected by the cost of litigation or insurance premiums.

Tort reform legislation has been introduced at the federal level and in several state courts. The aim of much of the litigation is as follows:

1. To put a cap on punitive damages
2. To require the loser of certain types of civil lawsuits to pay the legal costs of the winner
3. To limit certain medical malpractice awards
4. To curb joint liability awards that require any defendant with the financial means to pay the damages awarded against all defendants in a lawsuit

While tort reform proponents are lobbying their agendas at the state and federal level, the bar associations continue to combat those efforts and to work to improve the public's perception of the legal system and the role of attorneys. President Clinton recently stated "If I were a practicing member of the bar today, I would be working on ways to make the society less lawsuit-dominated [and seeking] more ways to solve problems without ultimately going to court."

---

[i] Lester Bickman of Cardozo School of Law in New York, quoted in *U.S. News and World Report*, January 30, 1995, p. 51.

[ii] How Lawyers Abuse the Law, *U.S. News and World Report*, January 30, 1995, p. 51.

[iii] Are Lawyers Burning America?, *Newsweek*, March 20, 1995, p. 32.

[iv] Hensler et al., *"Compensation for Accidental Injuries in the United States,"* Rand Corporation, Institute for Civil Justice (1991).

Chapter 4

Conflict of Interest

*"The greatest conflicts are not between two people
but between one person and himself."*

Garth Brooks

An Ethical Dilemma
Introduction
The General Rule
Conflict of Clients' Interests
Conflicting Interests of Current Clients
Civil Litigation Clients
Codefendants in Criminal Matters
Nonlitigation Clients
Clients with Competing Interests Unrelated to
the Representation
Conflicting Interests of Current and Former
Clients
Consenting to Representation
Attorney's Belief that Representation is
Consistent with Client's Interests
Consent Preceded by Consultation
Consent of All Affected Clients
Imputed Disqualification
Definition of Firm
Conflicts Brought On by Change in
Employment
Screening and Erecting Ethical Walls
Detecting Conflicts of Interest
The Organization as a Client
**Special Rules Concerning Government
Lawyers**

**Conflict of Client's Interests and Attorney's
Personal Interests**
Business Transactions
Information Relating to the Representation
Gifts to Lawyer
Literary or Media Rights
Financial Assistance to the Client
Fees Paid from a Source Other than Client
Settlements and Pleas on Behalf of Two or
More Clients
Potential Malpractice Claims
Related Lawyers
Interest in Cause of Action
The Attorney as a Witness
Attorney's Employees and Agents
Case and Discussion
From the Paralegal's Perspective
The NALA's Rules
The NFPA's Rules
Practical Considerations
A Question of Ethics
Case and Discussion

Chapter Summary

Summary Questions

An Ethical Dilemma

John Jacobson is an attorney for a small practice in a typical small town in the Midwest. His practice includes family law, estate and probate, and some minor criminal matters. One day Katherine Alexander, an old friend of the family, comes into the office to request Mr. Jacobson to draft her last will and testament. Mr. Jacobson readily agrees. He is somewhat surprised and flattered when Ms. Alexander indicates that she would like to leave him a rather large gift in her will. Ms. Alexander is his godmother and he has always been quite close to her. He usually calls her Aunt Katie. She has few living relatives, and none that she really associates with. Ms. Alexander is definitely of sound mind, and her wishes are clear. Mr. Jacobson drafts the will, having it duly witnessed and notarized in accordance with state law. Has he acted ethically?

Answer and Discussion: No. If Ms. Alexander were in fact Mr. Jacobson's aunt, there would be no problem. However, since Ms. Alexander is not related to Mr. Jacobson, and he is preparing a will for her in which he is left a substantial gift, he is in violation of the Model Rules. Model Rule 1.8(c) states that a "lawyer shall not prepare an instrument giving the lawyer or a person related to the lawyer . . . a testamentary gift, except where the client is related to the donee." In this case, Mr. Jacobson has done nothing to coerce Ms. Alexander into giving him the gift and it is clearly her desire to do so. However, upon Ms. Alexander's death at some time in the future, it may appear that Mr. Jacobson took unfair advantage of Ms. Alexander. Mr. Jacobson should refer Ms. Alexander to another attorney to prepare her will.

INTRODUCTION

Of the utmost importance in any attorney–client relationship are the duties of loyalty and confidentiality owed to the client by the attorney. An attorney must not represent a client unless he or she can do so with undivided loyalty. An attorney's loyalty must not be interfered with by the interest of other clients, the personal interests of the attorney, or the interests of third parties. When the interests of the client conflict with the interests of the attorney or other clients represented by the attorney, the situation is referred to as a **conflict of interest** (Figure 4–1). Rules for handling conflicts of interest and potential conflicts of interest are established at the state level in the code of ethics that apply to attorneys, and in case law.

An attorney's wrongful actions influenced by a conflict of interest can be grounds for civil malpractice suits. Courts have found that a lawyer's representation of an interest adverse to his client simultaneously or to a former client can constitute malpractice because such action is taken against the client's interests and constitutes the failure to exercise the knowledge, skill, and ability ordinarily possessed and exercised by lawyers.[1] Representing a client when an impermissible conflict of interest exists can also result in the loss of fees and clients, as well as reprimands and other sanctions meted out by the state disciplinary boards.

Not only attorneys are subject to ethical rules concerning conflicts of interest. It is possible for paralegals to become involved in conflicts as well. It is therefore very important that paralegals are familiar with the rules of ethics concerning conflicts of interest. This chapter begins with a look at the general rule of conflict of interest, certain types of conflicts, and the rules that permit

Conflict of interest
A real or seeming incompatibility between the interest of two of a lawyer's clients, such that the lawyer is disqualified from representing both clients if the dual representation adversely affects either client or if the clients do not consent. (*Black's Law Dictionary, Seventh Edition*)

> A conflict of interest can arise when . . .
>
> - The interests of two clients are directly adverse (simultaneous representation)
> - The interests of a client and a former client are materially adverse in a substantially related matter (successive representation)
> - The personal interests of the attorney or paralegal are adverse to the interest of a client
> - The business interests of the attorney or paralegal are adverse to the interest of a client

FIGURE 4-1
Conflicts of Interest

Imputed disqualification
Rule that disqualifies all of the members of a firm when one attorney is disqualified.

representation of clients notwithstanding conflicts. Because conflicts with one attorney or one paralegal have an impact on the entire law firm, the next section focuses on **imputed disqualification.** We then look at possible conflicts between an attorney's interest and the interests of the client and the effect of conflict of interest rules on the attorney's employees and agents. The second part of this chapter focuses on conflicts of interest from the paralegal's perspective, including the rules of the paralegal associations and practical considerations for avoiding conflicts of interest.

THE GENERAL RULE

The general rule is that "loyalty to a client prohibits undertaking representation directly adverse to that client without that client's consent."[2] Conflicts of interest most commonly arise under the following conditions:

1. When an attorney is asked to simultaneously represent two or more clients with conflicting interests
2. When an attorney is asked to successively represent the interests of a client whose interests conflict with the interests of a former client
3. When an attorney enters into certain personal business transactions that conflict with the interests of a client

If a conflict of interest will arise from representation of a new client, the attorney should decline that representation. If a conflict of interest arises during the representation of a client, the attorney usually must withdraw from representation.

An attorney with a conflict of interest who does not voluntarily withdraw may be disqualified by court order on motion brought by opposing counsel. A court-ordered disqualification can be used to remove an attorney who may have an unfair advantage gained through a breach of confidence or other violation of the rules of ethics.

The rules of ethics are drafted for attorneys. However, paralegals may be held to the same standards in many instances. In one case heard by the United States Court of International Trade, it was found that "Although the Model Rules are for lawyers, nonlawyers are also under an obligation not to compromise the legal representation of the clients of firms in which they work."[3]

A conflict of interest can arise without any actual wrongdoing on the part of the attorney. For example, it is possible for an attorney to represent two clients with marginally conflicting interests and still give each client the best possible representation. For that reason, under certain circumstances, it is possible for an attorney to handle representations notwithstanding a conflict of interest situation so long as all clients involved are consulted about the conflict and consent to the representation.

Where a conflict of interest exists, the actual wrongdoing occurs when the attorney betrays the trust of a client or former client and uses the situation to the unfair advantage of the attorney, a client, or a third party.

Canon 9 of the Model Code provides that an attorney should avoid even the *appearance* of **impropriety.** Prior to the Model Rules the appearance of impropriety was the usual determinant of a conflict of interest. If there was the *appearance* of a conflict of interest, there *was* a conflict of interest. In recent years courts have been looking more to the substance of the situation and attempting to prevent actual breaches of confidence and misconduct adverse to the client. Under the Model Rules, the appearance of impropriety is not a ground for disqualifying a lawyer from representing a party to a lawsuit (Figure 4–2).[4]

Impropriety
An act of misconduct. That which is socially unacceptable.

CONFLICT OF CLIENTS' INTERESTS

An attorney must at all times be careful not to represent two or more clients with conflicting interests. As established by Model Rule 1.7(a) and most codes of ethics, an attorney may not represent clients whose interests are directly adverse or where the representation of one client may be materially limited by the interests of another client, unless all affected clients properly consent to the representation. A conflict of interest may arise when the attorney takes on representation of a client whose interests conflict with the interests of a current client or with the interests of a former client.

Conflicting Interests of Current Clients

With few exceptions, simultaneous representation of multiple clients with conflicting interests is prohibited. Obviously, an attorney cannot represent both the plaintiff and defendant to the same lawsuit. However, simultaneous representation of multiple clients is rarely that simple. For example, suppose that the Jarvis Development Corporation comes to the Klein, Long, and Moore law firm requesting the representation of one of their attorneys, Bruce Nelson. Mr. Nelson would have to turn down that representation if he determines that another attorney in the firm represents the plaintiff in a lawsuit in which the Jarvis Development Corporation is named as one of the defendants.

	Model Rules		Model Code
Rule 1.7	General Rule	DR 5–101	Refusing Employment When the Interests of the Lawyer May Impair His Independent Professional Judgment
Rule 1.8	Concerning Prohibited Transactions	DR 5–102	Withdrawal as Counsel When the Lawyer Becomes a Witness
Rule 1.9	Concerning Former Clients	DR 5–103	Avoiding Acquisition of Interest in Litigation
Rule 1.10	Concerning Imputed Disqualification	DR 5–104	Limiting Business Relations with a Client
Rule 1.11	Concerning Government Lawyers	DR 5–105	Refusing to Accept or Continue Employment if the Interests of Another Client May Impair the Independent Professional Judgment of the Lawyer
Rule 1.12	Concerning Judges or Arbitrators	DR 5–106	Settling Similar Claims of Clients
Rule 1.13	Concerning Representation of Corporations	DR 5–107	Avoiding Influence by Others Than the Client
Rule 3.7	Lawyer as Witness		

FIGURE 4–2
Model Rules and Model Codes Concerning Conflicts of Interest

Civil Litigation Clients. A conflict of interest may exist if an attorney represents multiple clients whose interests differ in civil litigation. Attorneys must be cautious of representing more than one party in civil litigation, even if their interests initially appear to coincide. Throughout the course of litigation, it may become apparent that the interests of the parties conflict by way of incompatibility in positions against the opposing party or conflicting interests with regard to settling the matter. For example, it is inadvisable for a personal injury attorney to represent both the driver and passenger of an automobile for damages they sustained when their car was hit by another car whose driver ran a red light. Although it may appear at the outset of the case that the interests of the two clients coincide, it is possible that facts could come to light during the trial that would cause a conflict of their interests. What if the attorney learns through representation of the passenger client that the driver client had been drinking prior to the accident and may have been at least partially at fault?

Simultaneous representation of multiple clients may be acceptable if it is clear that the attorney may adequately represent the interests of each client, and each client consents after consultation in accordance with the applicable rules of ethics.

Codefendants in Criminal Matters. An attorney's loyalty must not be divided among his or her clients. For that reason, it is usually inadvisable for an attorney to represent more than one defendant in a criminal matter. "The potential for conflict of interest in representing multiple defendants in a criminal case is so grave that ordinarily a lawyer should decline to represent more than one codefendant."[5] Problems presenting a conflict of interest for the attorney may arise if the best defense of one client implicates another client. However, in instances where defense of multiple clients is clearly in the best interests of the defendants, and all clients properly consent after consultation, representation of **codefendants** may be permissible.

Codefendant
One of two or more defendants sued in the same litigation or charged with the same crime. Also termed *joint defendant.* *(Black's Law Dictionary, Seventh Edition)*

Nonlitigation Clients. An attorney may represent multiple clients in nonlitigation matters if the clients have a mutual interest and if the clients agree after consultation. It is not uncommon for a client to request his or her attorney to represent the client and another in the purchase and sale of a home, in documenting a loan between them, or in a similar type of transaction that they do not perceive to be adversarial. If the attorney has a longstanding relationship with one of the parties, and there are still unresolved issues between the parties, the attorney must decline such representation. The attorney cannot represent the best interests of both clients with undivided loyalty under such circumstances. If, however, the parties have already agreed on the terms of an agreement and simply need the attorney to document the transaction, it may be permissible. Other examples would be assisting two clients with the formation of a partnership or drafting an employment agreement. In this instance the attorney must carefully consider the potential for conflicting interests between the parties, and the clients must be made fully aware of the potential conflicts. Another example would be the representation of both a husband and wife in an amicable marriage dissolution. Under most circumstances, the attorney may represent *either* the husband or wife and advise the spouse to seek other representation.

Clients with Competing Interests Unrelated to the Representation. Generally an attorney may represent clients with adverse legal positions on different matters. However, if the outcome of one of the representations has the potential to adversely affect another client, the attorney must decline representation or withdraw. For example, it would probably not be considered a conflict of interest for an attorney to represent two competing car dealerships on general business matters. However, that same attorney may not represent one dealer if the dealer decides to sue the other for unfair competition.

CONFLICTING INTERESTS OF CURRENT AND FORMER CLIENTS

As with the ethical duty to client confidentiality, the attorney's duty of loyalty to the client begins with the initial meeting and outlasts the attorney's representation of the client. It is therefore possible for an attorney to have a conflict of interest involving a current or prospective client and a former client.

Rule 1.9 of the Model Rules, which has been closely followed by the drafters of the codes of ethics of many states, prevents an attorney from successively representing a client with adverse interests to a former client in the same or substantially related matter.

The rules regarding successive representation differ from those concerning the simultaneous representation of clients who may have adverse interests. Under Rule 1.7 concerning simultaneous representation, an attorney may not represent a client whose interests are *directly adverse* to another client, unless the attorney reasonably believes the representation will not adversely affect the other client and both clients consent. Rule 1.9 concerning former clients provides that an attorney must decline representation of a new client if the following three tests are met:

1. The new representation is materially adverse to the interests of a former client
2. The subject matter of the new representation is the same or substantially related to the representation of the former client
3. Confidential information was learned in the representation of the former client's interests that could be used to the disadvantage of the former client

To illustrate, suppose that an attorney has been requested to represent the surviving widow of an airplane crash victim in a wrongful death suit against the airline. However, the attorney had defended that same airline against a similar suit by a passenger who survived the same crash. The attorney would have to decline the representation because (1) the new representation (of the widow) is materially adverse to the interests of the former client (airline), (2) the subject matter (wrongful death due to airplane crash) is substantially similar to the subject matter of the previous representation, and (3) the attorney learned confidential information through his former representation of the airline that could be used to the airlines' disadvantage in the potential representation of the widow.

Attorneys may not oppose a former client in the *same or a substantially related matter*. However, it may be permissible for an attorney to oppose a former client in a different matter that is unrelated to the matter in which the attorney represented the former client. Such representation may be permissible so long as the attorney did not learn anything in representing the former client that may be used as a detriment to the former client. For example, prior defense of the airline in a personal injury suit stemming from an airplane crash would probably not preclude the attorney from opposing his former client (the airline) in a wrongful dismissal suit brought by a former employee—so long as the attorney learned nothing through prior representation that would constitute an unfair advantage in the second suit.

Even if it is established that the interests of a new client may be materially adverse to those of a former client, the attorney may take on the representation if all parties consent after consultation in accordance with the pertinent rules.

Consenting to Representation

Conflict of interest rules are designed to protect the client, but a fully informed client may consent to representation notwithstanding a conflict. If an attorney believes that representing a client would be in the best interests of a client, even though it may appear to be contrary to the rules concerning conflicts of interest, the attorney may, after consultation with the client, accept the consent of the client to representation.

It is ethical for a client to consent to representation by an attorney who may otherwise be considered to have a conflict of interest if the three following conditions are met:

1. The attorney must believe that his or her representation of the client is in the client's best interests
2. The client must consent to the representation after a full consultation reasonably sufficient to permit the client to appreciate the significance of the matter in question
3. All affected clients must consent in writing

Attorney's Belief that Representation is Consistent with Client's Interests. If a disinterested attorney would conclude that the client should not agree to representation by the attorney with the potential conflict of interest, the prospective attorney may not request the client to consent to representation notwithstanding the conflict.

Consent Preceded by Consultation. For proper consent to representation notwithstanding a conflict of interest, the client must consent after a consultation. Consultation, as defined by the Model Rules, is "communication of information reasonably sufficient to permit the client to appreciate the significance of the matter in question."[6]

The attorney has a special duty to the client to use independent judgment when assessing the facts surrounding the potential representation and conflict. The attorney must fully advise the clients of all circumstances surrounding the potential conflict and any foreseeable consequences. If the attorney would be required to divulge confidences in order to fully advise all parties, the attorney should not seek the consent. The attorney must not attempt to persuade the client to waive the attorney's disqualification and consent to the representation.

Consent of All Affected Clients. When more than one client is involved with a possible conflict, the issue must be resolved with regard to each client. Each of the affected clients must consent to the representation after consultation with the attorney, who must believe that his or her representation of all affected clients will not adversely affect any of them. Such consents should be obtained in writing signed by all affected parties.

IMPUTED DISQUALIFICATION

It is assumed that, in the practice of law, an attorney may share client confidences with others in the attorney's firm. For that reason, the general rule of imputed disqualification provides that all members of the firm are disqualified from representing a potential client if one member of the firm is disqualified because of a conflict of interest. This same general rule has been applied to paralegals as well. If a paralegal has a conflict of interest, the whole firm may be disqualified from representation of a client, unless proper measures are taken to rectify the situation.

In a 1998 case in Texas, a law firm representing one of the plaintiffs in a suit against a contraceptives company was disqualified on motion by the attorneys for the defendant shortly before trial when it was determined that a paralegal employee of the firm was previously employed by a distributor for the contraceptives company. Although the plaintiff attorneys argued that the paralegal did not learn any confidential information from her previous employment with the defendant, the court held that it must be presumed that confidences and secrets were imparted to a paralegal or legal assistant who has worked on a case. The court further found that "The risk that a person who has functioned as a legal assistant may disclose confidential information to a new employer under circumstances such as these is unacceptably high."[7]

Specific rules regarding imputed disqualification are set by each state in the code of ethics that attorneys must abide by. Rule 1.10 of the Model Rules states that no attorneys in a law firm shall knowingly represent a client when any one of the attorneys in the firm would be prohibited from doing so under the pertinent conflict of interest rules. The rule further provides for a waiver of the disqualification by the affected client.

Definition of Firm

Under the Model Rules, a **firm** "includes lawyers in a private firm, and lawyers in the legal department of a corporation or other organization, or in a legal services organization."

Attorneys who are sharing office space may be considered a firm for purposes of imputed disqualification rules, depending on the circumstances of the situation and whether confidential information is shared among the attorneys.

Firm
A group of lawyers formed for the purpose of practicing law, including lawyers in a private firm and lawyers in the legal department of a corporation or other organizations or in a legal services organization.

Conflicts Brought On by Change in Employment

Conflicts of interest involving the interests of two or more clients or a current and former client present a special concern for attorneys and paralegals who leave one law firm to join the practice of another law firm. With the mobile nature of today's workforce, opportunities for conflicts abound. A strict interpretation of the ethical rules provides that if any current client of the attorney or paralegal's new firm has interests directly adverse to any client of the attorney or paralegal's previous firm, a conflict of interest would exist, and the new firm would be required to withdraw from representing the client who provided the conflict.

Screening and Erecting Ethical Walls

Although not specifically addressed by the Model Rules, many jurisdictions have permitted an exception to the imputed disqualification rule where a **screening** process was properly implemented. Screening, also referred to as erecting an **ethical wall** or **Chinese wall,** refers to a policy within a law firm to *screen* or *shut out* a disqualified attorney within the firm from representation of the client presenting the conflict. Effective screening has been used, in some jurisdictions, to allow a law firm to represent a client where that representation would otherwise be disqualified due to prior representation of an adverse party by one attorney in the firm. An effective screen usually provides that the disqualified attorney:

1. Does not participate in the matter
2. Does not discuss the matter with any member of the firm
3. Represents through sworn testimony that he or she has not shared any confidential information with a member of the firm
4. Does not have access to any documentation concerning the matter
5. Does not share in any fees from the matter

Screening
A policy within a law firm to screen or shut out a disqualified attorney within the firm from representation of the client representing the conflict.
Ethical wall
Fictional wall erected around a lawyer or nonlawyer within a law firm to screen that individual from a particular client and information concerning a particular client's case when that particular lawyer or nonlawyer has a conflict of interest with that client.
Chinese wall
Same as ethical wall.

Screening can also be used to isolate a paralegal from a particular matter to avoid imputed disqualification. Screening, or erecting an ethical wall around a paralegal who may have a conflict due to prior employment, is typically a sufficient remedy to imputed disqualification of a paralegal's new employer.

Many law firms have written procedures for erecting an ethical wall. The process usually begins with a memorandum to all employees in the firm, or all employees associated with the client or files in question, notifying them of the ethical wall. Employees working on the affected files will be asked to keep all information on those files confidential from the attorney or paralegal with the conflict, and to restrict access to files and information available via the firm's computer network.

DETECTING CONFLICTS OF INTEREST

Law firms are getting larger and more specialized and are merging at an unprecedented rate. All of these factors make it crucial to have proper procedures in place for detecting conflicts of interest. For example, when a new file is opened in a law firm, a database search by client and adverse party is usually done to make sure there is no conflict (Figure 4–3). It is the responsibility of every attorney and paralegal to ensure that they do not unknowingly become involved in a conflict-of-interest situation that could prove inconvenient and costly to the client when discovered too far into the representation. "The lawyer should adopt reasonable procedures, appropriate for the size and type of firm and practice, to determine in both litigation and non-litigation matters the parties and issues involved and to determine whether there are actual or potential conflicts of interest."[8]

Consider the two following scenarios: In the first scenario, a well-established client of the law firm brings in a new litigation case concerning a property devel-

FIGURE 4–3
New Litigation Client Conflict of Interest Check Form

Client(s)' Name(s) _____

Date of Initial Contact _____

Supervising Attorney(s)_____

Assigned Paralegals _____

Type of Matter _____

Parties Involved:

Names of All Plaintiffs or Potential Plaintiffs (include all maiden and corporate names where appropriate):

_____
_____
_____
_____

Names of All Known Attorneys and Law Firms Associated with Plaintiffs:

_____
_____
_____

Names of All Defendants or Potential Defendants (include all maiden and corporate names where appropriate):

_____
_____
_____

opment project gone wrong. The firm does a conflict-of-interest check and realizes immediately that one of the firm's attorneys was formerly in-house counsel for one of the potential defendant in the matter. The responsible attorney immediately tells the firm's client that the firm will be unable to represent the client on this particular matter. The client is understanding and seeks other counsel for this matter.

In the second scenario, the conflict goes undetected until two weeks before the trial, when the opposing counsel files a motion to disqualify the firm. The supervising attorney must talk to the client and admit that the conflict was not detected. For the firm to withdraw at this point will be a great hardship to the client, and the firm may lose all of the client's future business.

THE ORGANIZATION AS A CLIENT

An attorney representing a corporation or other business organization has a duty of loyalty to the organization itself and must act to protect the interests of the organization. The attorney may not represent officers, directors, or others associated with the firm if the interests of the individual conflict with the interests of the organization.

If an attorney becomes aware of actions being taken by officers, directors, agents, or others that are harmful to the organization the attorney represents, the attorney must act according to prescribed ethical rules to protect the organization. Rule 1.13(b) of the Model Rules provides that the measures to be taken by the attorney may include:

1. Asking reconsideration of the matter
2. Advising that a separate legal opinion on the matter be sought for presentation to appropriate authority in the organization
3. Referring the matter to higher authority in the organization, including, if warranted by the seriousness of the matter, referral to the highest authority that can act in behalf of the organization as determined by applicable law

Any of these actions taken by an attorney for the organization can have an impact on the entire organization and thus must not be taken lightly. Any measures the attorney chooses to take should be taken "to minimize disruption of the organization and the risk of revealing information relating to the representation to persons outside the organization."[9]

SPECIAL RULES CONCERNING GOVERNMENT LAWYERS

Attorneys who represent government agencies must generally abide by the rules of ethics that apply to attorneys in private practice. In addition, some special rules apply—especially to those attorneys who leave government employment for private practice.

Attorneys who work for government agencies become very familiar with the policies and procedures of their governmental employers. Those same attorneys often take their specialized knowledge with them and use it in private practice. Although government attorneys owe the same duty of loyalty and confidentiality to their client (the government agency that employs them), much of the information learned during their representation is not considered confidential, and it is not improper for an attorney to disclose that information during a subsequent representation of a client.

An attorney who leaves a government position for private practice must be certain to never use confidential information learned through government employment to the unfair advantage of a client. Information may be considered confidential government information if:

1. It is not otherwise available to the public
2. It was obtained under governmental authority
3. At the time the conflict rule is applied, the government is prohibited by law to disclose the information to the public
4. It is otherwise qualified for protection by the attorney–client privilege

CONFLICT OF CLIENT'S INTERESTS AND ATTORNEY'S PERSONAL INTERESTS

The attorney must not have any interests that would adversely affect the interests of a client, although the possibility of a conflict does not, in itself, preclude representation. "The critical questions are the likelihood that a conflict will eventuate and, if it does, whether it will materially interfere with the lawyer's independent professional judgment in considering alternatives or foreclose courses of action that reasonably should be pursued on behalf of the client."[10]

Rule 1.8 of the Model Rules provides for ten types of transactions that may cause a conflict of interest because of the attorney–client relationship. Those types of transactions include:

1. Entering into certain business transactions
2. Using information relating to the representation to the disadvantage of the client
3. Preparing instruments giving the attorney or person close to the attorney a gift from the client, except where the client is related
4. Making or negotiating an agreement giving the attorney literary or media rights regarding the representation—prior to the conclusion of the representation
5. Providing certain types of financial assistance to the client
6. Accepting compensation for representing the client from someone other than the client
7. Making certain aggregate settlements of claims or aggregate plea bargains when representing multiple clients
8. Making certain agreements limiting the attorney's liability for malpractice
9. Representing a client in opposition to a client represented by a relative
10. Acquiring an interest in a cause of action or the subject of litigation in a matter relating to the attorney's representation of the client

Business Transactions

An attorney who chooses to transact personal business with a client must be very careful to not create a conflict of interest (or even the appearance of one). "A lawyer commits a breach of trust going to the very essence of the attorney-client relationship when he takes a position adverse to that of his client, or former client, in a business transaction."[11] Following are some of the considerations to be taken into account when attorneys and clients transact business together:

- The transaction must be fair and reasonable to the client
- The client must fully understand the terms of the transaction
- The client must be given the opportunity to seek independent counsel
- The client should consent in writing to the business transaction

For example, suppose a client consults with her attorney when her business runs into financial trouble. The client is contemplating the sale of the business, and her attorney decides that he would like to buy it. The attorney would definitely have a conflict of interest if he were to continue representing the client in seeing to its successful sale and purchase. If the client, after being fully consulted, decides that she would like to sell her business to the attorney, the client should immediately retain a new attorney to represent her interests in the transaction.

Information Relating to the Representation

Rule 1.8(b) states that an attorney "shall not use information relating to representation of a client to the disadvantage of the client unless the client consents after consultation, except as permitted or required by Rule 1.6 or Rule 3.3." This rule again emphasizes the importance of the proper treatment of confidential information learned by an attorney through representation of a client, and the attorney's duty of loyalty to the client. Attorneys have been found to be in violation of this rule by misusing the client's trust to their own advantage. For example, several courts have found attorneys to be in violation of this rule due to their engaging in sexual relations with a client the attorney has found to be vulnerable through representation of the client in divorce or similar matters.

Gifts to Lawyer

Attorneys may not draft wills or other instruments that grant a substantial gift from the client to the attorney, unless the attorney and client are related. This rule would prevent an unethical attorney from taking advantage of an elderly client with no living relatives, but would not prevent an attorney from drafting a last will and testament for his or her parents in which the attorney is named as a beneficiary. An attorney may accept a gift from a client if the transaction meets general standards of fairness.[12]

Literary or Media Rights

Rule 1.8(d) states that "Prior to the conclusion of representation of a client, a lawyer shall not make or negotiate an agreement giving the lawyer literary or media rights to a portrayal or account based in substantial part on information relating to the representation." An attorney is thereby prohibited from accepting literary rights or media rights as compensation for their representation from a client. If an attorney were allowed to sell literary or media rights based on his or her representation of a client prior to the conclusion of that representation, the attorney's personal financial interests may be influenced by the outcome of that representation. For example, it may be a more interesting story if the matter were to go through a lengthy trial, as opposed to an amicable settlement. This rule attempts to abolish any conflict of interest that may arise when the attorney's financial interests and the client's interests differ.

Financial Assistance to the Client

It is unethical for an attorney to encourage a client or potential client to initiate a lawsuit by enticing them with financial assistance. There are, however, two important exceptions to this rule.

The first exception allows an attorney to advance court costs and expenses of litigation. This is often done when the client is represented on a contingency basis. Under a contingency fee arrangement the attorney agrees to represent a client in return for a percentage (usually one third to one half) of the court award or settlement obtained for the client. If the attorney collects nothing for the client, the attorney receives no fee. Contingency fee arrangements are discussed in detail in Chapter 6.

The second exception allows attorneys to pay court costs and expenses for indigent clients. This may be done in connection with pro bono work performed on behalf of the attorney.

Fees Paid from a Source Other than Client

It is unethical for an attorney to accept payment of a client's fees from someone other than the client if the attorney allows the individual paying the fees to affect the attorney's professional judgment or the attorney–client relationship in any way. If an attorney accepts payment of legal fees from a source other than the client, the attorney must be sure that the source of the fee payment does not influence or jeopardize the attorney's representation of the client's best interests.

It is not uncommon for an attorney to be chosen and retained by an insurance company to represent an insured pursuant to the terms of an insurance policy. An attorney in this position must be cautious to always represent the interests of the insured (his actual client) and not the insurance company (the payer of the fee).

Settlements and Pleas on Behalf of Two or More Clients

An attorney must not accept a settlement or plea bargain on behalf of two or more clients as a "package deal" if it is not in the best interests of all affected clients, and unless the clients all agree after consultation.

Potential Malpractice Claims

When an attorney agrees to represent a client, the attorney may not ask the client to enter into an agreement whereby the client promises not to sue the attorney for malpractice for the representation if the outcome is not to the client's satisfaction. Further, if a client has a claim of malpractice against the attorney, the attorney should not settle with the client unless the client is represented by an independent counsel, or unless the attorney has informed the client of the advisability for the client to seek the advice of an independent counsel.

Related Lawyers

It is considered a conflict of interest for an attorney to represent a client in a matter when he or she is closely related to the opposing counsel, unless the client has been consulted and consents. For example, Adam Brown should not represent Chris in a lawsuit against Dennis who is represented by Adam's sister, Ellen Brown.

This disqualification of a related attorney is usually specific to the individual attorney and does not apply to the other attorneys in the disqualified attorney's firm, although an ethical wall must be erected around the attorney with a conflict.

Interest in Cause of Action

With few exceptions it is unethical for an attorney to acquire an interest in the client's cause of action or the subject matter of litigation. The longstanding rule against an attorney acquiring an interest in a client's litigation is designed to prevent conflicts that might impair the attorney's exercise of independent judgment on a client's behalf. However, attorneys may file a lien against property of the clients, including property that is the subject of litigation. Rules for filing an attorney's lien are usually established by state law. Another very common exception to this rule is the contingency fee arrangement.

THE ATTORNEY AS A WITNESS

A conflict of interest can arise when an attorney who is acting as an advocate in a trial also serves as a witness. Rule 3.7 of the ABA's Model Rules prohibits attorneys from representing a client in a matter where the attorney is likely to be called as a witness. The Model Code also prohibits attorneys from accepting representation of a client if that representation involves contemplated or pending litigation that the attorney knows will result in the attorney, or an attorney in the same law firm, being called as a witness.

"The rules prevent situations in which others might think the lawyer, as witness is distorting the truth for his client or is enhancing his own credibility as advocate by virtue of having taken an oath as witness, as well as the uneasy situation that arises when an opposing counsel must impeach on cross-examination another lawyer–adversary."[13]

There are several exceptions to these rules. The representation may be acceptable under the following conditions:

- If the testimony will relate solely to an uncontested matter.
- If the testimony will relate solely to a matter of formality and there is no reason to believe that substantial evidence will be offered in opposition to the testimony.
- If the testimony will relate solely to the nature and value of legal services rendered in the case by the lawyer or his firm to the client.
- As to any matter, if refusal would work a substantial hardship on the client because of the distinctive value of the lawyer or his firm as counsel in the particular case.[14]

According to the Model Code "[t]he roles of an advocate and of a witness are inconsistent; the function of an advocate is to advance or argue the cause of another, while that of a witness is to state facts objectively."[15]

ATTORNEY'S EMPLOYEES AND AGENTS

It is the attorney's duty to ensure the ethical conduct of agents and nonlawyer employees, including paralegals. Pursuant to Rule 5.3 of the ABA Model Rules and corresponding state rules of ethics, supervising attorneys have a duty to ensure that nonlawyers" conduct is compatible with the professional obligations of lawyers.

Attorneys are responsible for seeing to it that their employees and agents do not have a conflict of interest. In instances where nonlawyer employees may be in a position to have a conflict of interest due to a change in employment, the responsible attorneys must see to it that the employee is screened from the client's file and information.

Guideline 7 of the ABA Model Guidelines for the Utilization of Legal Assistant Services follows:

> Guideline 7: A lawyer should take reasonable measures to prevent conflicts of interest resulting from a legal assistant's other employment or interests insofar as such other employment or interests would present a conflict of interest if it were that of the lawyer.

CASE AND DISCUSSION

The following case involves a motion to disqualify a law firm due to a possible conflict of interest involving one of its attorneys and her former client. Although the court found that the interests of the attorney's current client were adverse to the interests of her former client, it also found that the representation was not substantially related to the subject matter of the former representation and that no pertinent confidential information was learned through the representation of the former client.

Dennis MARTEN, Plaintiff,

v.

YELLOW FREIGHT SYSTEM, INC., Defendant.

Civ. A. No. 96-2013-GTV.

United States District Court, D. Kansas.

Sept. 5, 1996.

Gail M. Hudek, Paul F. Pautler, Jr., Kimberly A. Jones, Hudek & Associates, P.C., Kansas City, MO, for plaintiff.

Robert W. McKinley, Tedrick Addison Housh, III, Swanson, Midgley, Gangwere, Kitchin & McLarney, LLC, Kansas City, MO, for defendant.

MEMORANDUM AND ORDER
VAN BEBBER, DISTRICT JUDGE:

*1 This matter is before the court on defendant's motion to disqualify plaintiff's counsel pursuant to the Model Rules of Professional Conduct as adopted by the Kansas Supreme Court. 1995 Kan.Ct.R.Ann. Rule 226. Plaintiff has responded and opposes defendant's motion. Following a hearing before the court and after careful consideration of the evidence and arguments in this case, the court concludes that defendant's motion is denied for the reasons explained in this order.

In the motion to disqualify, defendant claims that plaintiff's lead counsel, Gail Hudek ("Hudek"), formerly represented defendant in employment matters during her association with the law firm of Blackwell, Sanders, Metheny & Lombardi ("Blackwell"). It is defendant's contention that the issues raised in the instant action are "substantially related" to the matters involved in Hudek's prior representation of defendant. Consequently, defendant requests that the court disqualify Hudek under Rule 1.9 of the Model Rules of Professional Conduct ("Model Rules"). Defendant also moves the court to disqualify Hudek's law firm, Hudek & Associates, under the imputed disqualification requirement of Model Rule 1.10.

I. FACTUAL BACKGROUND

The court finds the following facts:

1. Plaintiff's counsel is Hudek & Associates. Gail Hudek serves as lead counsel for plaintiff. From 1983 to 1993, Hudek practiced law with the firm of Blackwell, Sanders, Metheny & Lombardi ("Blackwell"). Defendant employed Blackwell to handle its legal affairs.
2. During her tenure at Blackwell, Hudek specialized in labor and employment law. While participating in client market-ing for the firm, Hudek met defendant's Equal Employment Opportunity Coordinator, Val Eitzman. After learning of Hudek's area of expertise, Eitzman recommended Hudek to defendant's Manager of Employee Relations, William Marden. Eitzman suggested that defendant engage Hudek to conduct a seminar for defendant's human resource personnel on employment discrimination and affirmative action law.
3. After meeting with Hudek in early 1990, Marden requested that Hudek direct a training seminar for defendant's human resource personnel. Hudek assented and her contemporaneous time records reflect that she spent approximately twenty-eight hours working on this project for defendant. In her preparation for the training seminar, Hudek was not privy to defendant's existing Affirmative Action or Equal Employment Opportunity policies.
4. Hudek conducted the training seminar for defendant's human resource department field managers in June 1990. The seminar focused on the general parameters of affirmative action law, and it was similar to the affirmative action program that Hudek has delivered over three hundred times. . . .
5. Upon completion of the training seminar assignment, Hudek performed no additional legal work for defendant. . . .

In this action, plaintiff claims that defendant violated Title VII of the Civil Rights Act of 1964. Plaintiff also makes various state law claims. Based on Hudek's prior representation in conducting the training seminar, defendant filed the current motion to disqualify plaintiff's counsel.

II. DISCUSSION

It is well-established in the Tenth Circuit that " 'the control of attorneys' conduct in trial litigation is within the supervisory powers of the trial judge,' and is thus a matter of judicial discretion." . . . Pursuant to D.Kan. Rule 83.6.1, "The Code of Professional Responsibility and the Model Rules of Professional Conduct ("Model Rules") as adopted by the Supreme Court of Kansas" govern the standards of conduct for attorneys practicing in this court. The Kansas Supreme Court has adopted the Model Rules. 1996 Kan.Ct.R.Anno. Rule 226. Thus, the Model Rules, and Kansas case law construing them, control this action. . . .

In its motion, defendant moves for disqualification of Hudek under Model Rule 1.9(a) and the imputed disqualification of Hudek & Associates under Model Rule 1.10(b). Defendant's burden under Model Rule 1.9(a) is to show that:

(1) an actual attorney–client relationship existed between the moving party and the opposing counsel;

(2) the present litigation involves a matter that is "substantially related" to the subject of the movant's prior representation; and

(3) the interests of the opposing counsel's present client are materially adverse to the movant. . . .

If disqualification is sought solely under Model Rule 1.9(a), the movant's satisfaction of its burden gives rise to an irrebuttable presumption. Under this presumption, an inference arises that defendant disclosed material and confidential information to plaintiff's counsel during the prior representation that requires counsel's disqualification. In the instant action, it is undisputed that the interests of Hudek's current client are adverse to the interest of her former client. Thus, the court's inquiry focuses on whether the instant action is "substantially related" to the subject matter of Hudek's prior representation of defendant and whether Hudek acquired material, confidential information during that representation. . . .

Here, defendant fails to satisfy its burden that Hudek's prior representation of defendant is substantially related to the subject matter of the instant action. Hudek's legal representation of de-

fendant focused solely on providing a training seminar. The seminar, which dealt with the then current law regarding affirmative action and employment discrimination, was conducted more than six years ago. Hudek expended approximately twenty-eight hours in preparing and conducting the seminar.

In reconstructing the scope of Hudek's prior representation of defendant, the court finds that defendant disclosed no confidential information to Hudek. Additionally, Hudek's prior representation of defendant is not substantially related to the issues present in the instant action. The court concludes that disqualification of plaintiff's counsel in this case is unwarranted.

IT IS, THEREFORE, BY THE COURT ORDERED that defendant's motion to disqualify plaintiff's counsel is denied.

. . .

IT IS SO ORDERED.

FROM THE PARALEGAL'S PERSPECTIVE

As a paralegal, you must be aware of and abide by the ethical rules concerning conflicts of interest that govern attorneys. Your personal interests must not conflict with those of a client of an attorney you are assisting. In addition, you must not be put in the position of assisting a client who has an interest adverse to a client of your current or former employer. If you work for a law firm or legal department in a traditional role under the supervision of an attorney, you usually need only be concerned with potential conflicts between clients of your current employer and any former employers. A paralegal in a nontraditional role who assists clients without the supervision of an attorney will be responsible for ensuring that there are no conflicts of interest involving current clients and current and former clients— in much the same way that attorneys are. Courts have held that paralegals should be held to the same standards as attorneys, although, if such a conflict does exist, it is usually a sufficient remedy to screen the paralegal from involvement with that client and all confidential information relating to that client.

If you are ever involved in a conflict-of-interest situation, chances are it will be due to a change of employers. Under the imputed disqualification rule, a paralegal accepting a position in a new firm could disqualify the firm from representing a client if that client has interests adverse to a client of the paralegal's previous firm. The court expressed the following opinion in *Williams v. TransWorld Airlines*[16]:

> If information provided by a client in confidence to an attorney for the purpose of obtaining legal advice could be used against the client because a member of the attorney's non-lawyer support staff left the attorney's employment, it would have devastating effect both on the free flow of information between client and attorney and on the cost and qualify of the legal services rendered by an attorney. Every departing secretary, investigator, or paralegal would be free to impart confidential information to the opposition without effective restraint. The only practical way to assure that this will not happen and to preserve public trust in the scrupulous administration of justice is to subject these "agents" of lawyers to the same disability lawyers have when they have legal employment with confidential information.

To disqualify an entire law firm from representing a client because a paralegal has a conflict of interest stemming from prior employment could restrict the mobility and employability of a paralegal who has worked for a large litigation firm. The ABA and the courts have recognized this as being unnecessarily restrictive to paralegals, and has recommended that "any restrictions on the nonlawyer's employment should be held to the minimum necessary to protect confidentiality of client information."[17] The ABA recommends the following procedures:

> A law firm that employs a nonlawyer who formerly was employed by another firm may continue representing clients whose interests conflict with the interests of clients of the former employer on whose matters the nonlawyer has worked, as long as the employing firm screens the nonlawyer from information about or participating in matters involving those clients and strictly adheres to the screening process described in this opinion and as long as no information relating to the representation of the clients of the former employer is revealed by the nonlawyer to any person in the employing firm. In addition, the nonlawyer's former employer must admonish the nonlawyer against revelation of information relating to the representation of clients of the former employer.[18]

The NALA's Rules

The NALA's Code of Ethics and Professional Responsibility does not specifically address conflicts of interest for the paralegal. However, Canon 8 states that "A legal assistant must do all other things incidental, necessary, or expedient for the attainment of the ethics and responsibilities as defined by statute or rule of court."

The NFPA's Rules

The NFPA addresses conflicts of interest in Canon 1.6 of its Code of Ethics and Professional Responsibility Model, which provides that paralegals shall avoid conflicts of interest and disclose any possible conflicts to their employers and clients, or prospective employers and clients. Several ethical considerations provide more guidance for this canon (Figure 4–4). The full text of the Model Code of Ethics and Professional Responsibility is found in Appendix D.

The NFPA has given the opinion that if it is determined that a conflict of interest exists, the paralegal is prohibited from participating in or conducting work on the matter and an ethical wall must be implemented and maintained. The NFPA further lists the following steps to erect and adhere to the ethical wall:

1. Prohibit the paralegal from having any connection with the matter.
2. Ban discussions with or the transfer of documents to or from the paralegal.
3. Restrict access to files.

- On your first day of employment (if it has not been done during the interview process), ask the supervising attorney or other appropriate person for a list of legal cases or matters that the firm or employer is handling. Review that list to identify the names of clients, parties in litigation, acquaintances, friends, or family members that you recognize.
- Compare your list of all legal cases or matters on which you have worked against the new employer's list. If you work in litigation, also review the names of attorneys representing the various parties.
- Advise the employer of any matters in which you suspect you may have a conflict of interest. Provide only enough information about the matter for the employer (or a firm or corporation conflicts committee) to determine whether there is a conflict of interest. Usually, the client or matter name is sufficient to assess this.
- As new clients and legal matters come into the office, or if new parties are added to cases already underway, check their names against your list as described above.
- Despite your best efforts, a matter or client in which you have a possible conflict of interest may slip through. If this happens, bring it to the attorney's attention as soon as you become aware of it.
- Maintain your list of matters on which you work throughout your paralegal career.

From The NFPA Web site **www.paralegals.org.**

FIGURE 4–4

How to Identify a Possible Conflict of Interest

4. Educate all members of the firm, corporation, or entity as to the separation of the paralegal (both organizationally and physically) from the pending matter.[19]

Practical Considerations

The consequences of an undisclosed conflict of interest involving a paralegal and a client of the law firm employer can be devastating to the client, the supervising attorney, the law firm, and the paralegal. If, as a paralegal, you have any question concerning a possible conflict of interest you may be involved in, you must report it to your supervising attorney immediately.

Here are some steps you can take to be certain that you are not involved improperly in a conflict-of-interest situation:

1. Keep a current list of client names and the matters on all files on which you work. This may be as simple as keeping copies of your billing records.

2. When you leave your position in a law firm, take a list of the clients on whose files you have worked and the matters to compare with any files you may be assigned to in the future. This list should be kept confidential. The only information to be disclosed from this list would be the name of a former client whose file you have worked on (or opposing party) if a conflict of interest arises.

3. Keep current with your firm's conflict-of-interest procedures. Law firms commonly circulate weekly lists of new clients and new matters that the firm is representing. This list should be checked against your current list of clients and any lists from previous employers.

4. If your firm takes on a client with whom you have a personal interest, either a financial interest or a personal relationship, that information should be reported to the supervising attorney as soon as possible.

5. If you ever even suspect that you may possibly be involved in a conflict-of-interest situation, report it to your supervising attorney or other appropriate individual in your law firm or law department immediately!

A Question of Ethics

Sandy Meyers had just begun her first week at her new job as a litigation paralegal, with the firm of Wendell & Jacobson, when she was confronted by a problem. She was assigned to work on the *Ace Manufacturing v. Diamond Supply* file, a case name that she recognized from her last job. At her previous position, her employer represented Ace Manufacturing. Sandy was not directly involved with the case, although she did help out one of the other paralegals at her last firm by summarizing a few depositions. Wendell & Jacobson represents Diamond Supply, and Sandy has been asked to oversee the entire litigation process. Sandy has a feeling that this might be considered a conflict of interest, but she isn't really sure. She is still on probation at her new job and doesn't want to rock the boat. Should she tell her new employer of her past involvement with the file?

Answer and Discussion: Yes, definitely! Even the appearance of conflict of interest such as this could cause severe problems for Sandy's new employers. At the least, they would be embarrassed if they knew nothing of Sandy's prior involvement and her former employer called them on it. At worst, Sandy's actions could be cause for an action by the state bar association's ethics committee. Her actions could also cause them to lose their client.

CASE AND DISCUSSION

The following case in Connecticut demonstrates how screening can be effectively used to avoid imputed disqualification of an entire law firm when a paralegal has a conflict of interest.

Sharon DEVINE et al.

v.

Malcolm BEINFIELD, M.D.

No. CV 930131721S.

Superior Court of Connecticut.

July 18, 1997.

MEMORANDUM OF DECISION RE:

MOTION TO DISQUALIFY (# 149)

KARAZIN.

This motion seeks to disqualify the law firm of Silver, Golub and Teitell from this case based on the hiring of Sue West a former paralegal at Rosenblum and Filan by Silver, Golub and Teitell.

The parties have agreed to a set of stipulated facts which are attached hereto and are made part of this decision. It is clear to this court that the law firm will be disqualified if: (1) the non-lawyer has revealed confidential information about former clients to any person in the new firm. (The facts stipulate that this has not happened since employment has not begun) and (2) The non-lawyer must be "screened" from access to and involvement with information and matters involving all clients of the former firm, including an admonition to the non-lawyer of the critical obligation to protect the interest of the former client.

This court is satisfied that an ethical wall has been built around the paralegal Sue West. In the Memorandum In Opposition To The Motion For Disqualification, there is an affidavit of Ernest F. Teitell a partner in the law firm of Silver, Golub and Teitell. In that affidavit there is laid out in thirteen consecutive paragraphs all of the procedures that will be followed to create the ethical wall for this paralegal. The court attaches that affidavit hereto as part of this decision. In addition, the affidavit of Susan West consisting of twelve numbered paragraphs is attached hereto.

The court is satisfied that Sue West has not provided any confidential information or any information about any previous Rosenblum client or case to Silver and Golub. That there has been set up effective screening procedures and other administrative procedures to ensure that Sue West will not be working on any Rosenblum cases. Furthermore, at the time of the hearing she had not begun employment.

The court is satisfied that there is adequate screening. The court does not subscribe to the argument that as a matter of law screening would be ineffective when a non-lawyer switches employment to "the other side." The ABA opinions indicate a law firm can set up appropriate screening and administrative procedures to prevent the non-lawyer from working on the other side of those common cases and disclosing confidential information.

The court is satisfied that a strong showing of adequate and detailed procedures will be set up and utilized in matters concern-ing Sue West at the law firm of Silver, Golub and Teitell, as it relates to Rosenblum cases.

Accordingly, the Motion To Disqualify is denied.

. . .

Affidavit

I, Ernest F. Teitell, being duly sworn, depose and state:

1. I am an attorney admitted to the practice of law in the State of Connecticut.
2. I am over 18 years of age and I understand the obligation of an oath.
3. I am a partner in the law firm of Silver Golub & Teitell in Stamford, Connecticut.
4. I interviewed Susan West when she responded to a classified ad in the Stamford Advocate for a paralegal.
5. Ms. West has been offered a position as a paralegal by Silver Golub & Teitell. However, her employment is being forestalled pending resolution of defendant's Motion to Disqualify in this matter.
6. At my first meeting with Ms. West, I indicated to her that I was aware that Silver Golub & Teitell and Rosenblum & Filan handled cases in common and that she could not divulge any information about any Rosenblum & Filan client or case in any of our meetings or discussions.
7. Ms. West was also interviewed briefly by Jonathan Mannina, an associate with Silver Golub & Teitell.
8. In addition, Ms. West was interviewed by my legal assistant, Jule Bowers.
9. At no time did Ms. West discuss any Rosenblum & Filan cases or clients or provide any Silver Golub & Teitell employee or representative with confidential information or other information about Rosenblum & Filan cases or clients.
10. I also made it clear to Ms. West that at no time could she ever divulge any information about any case or client of Rosenblum & Filan or impart any confidential information to anyone at Silver Golub & Teitell. Ms. West agreed to this condition.
11. Silver Golub & Teitell offered Ms. West a position as a paralegal with the firm, although she has yet to begin employment.
12. It is our intention to institute the following administrative procedures prior to Ms. West's beginning employment with the firm:
    a. Sue West will not work on or have access to any existing files jointly handled by Silver Golub & Teitell and Rosenblum & Filan.
    b. Sue West will not work on any future files Silver Golub & Teitell have with Rosenblum & Filan once those files have been identified as being handled by Rosenblum & Filan.

c. That all files jointly handled by Silver Golub & Teitell and Rosenblum & Filan will be flagged and segregated into separate filing cabinets.

d. That no employee or representative of Silver Golub & Teitell will speak with or about to Sue West any of the files or matters that are represented by Rosenblum & Filan.

e. That formal written procedures encompassing conditions 1-4 above will be distributed to all Silver Golub & Teitell employees.

f. That Sue West will not speak to anyone at Silver Golub & Teitell about any matters that occurred at Rosenblum & Filan, including, but not limited to the following:

   i. any of the matters and/or cases she worked on and/or received knowledge about while employed at Rosenblum & Filan;

   ii. any information about any client of Rosenblum & Filan;

   iii. any information about the internal workings of Rosenblum & Filan;

   iv. any information obtained about any expert witnesses that were retained by Rosenblum & Filan.

g. That all of these conditions will be put in writing and will be agreed to and signed by Sue West and Silver Golub & Teitell.

13. Silver Golub & Teitell has sufficient other paralegals and personnel to accommodate the necessary work on cases common to Silver Golub & Teitell and Rosenblum & Filan.

By:
ERNEST F. TEITELL
SILVER GOLUB & TEITELL
[Address and Certification Omitted]

CHAPTER SUMMARY

- When the interests of the client conflict with the interests of the attorney or other clients represented by the attorney, the situation is referred to as a conflict of interest.
- Loyalty to a client prohibits undertaking representation directly adverse to the interests of a client without that client's consent.
- Paralegals may be held to the same standards as attorneys concerning conflicts of interest.
- An attorney may not represent a client with interests materially adverse to those of a former client in the same or substantially related matter unless the former client consents after consultation.
- Under the rule of imputed disqualification, members of a law firm are disqualified if one member of the firm is disqualified to represent a client due to a conflict of interest.
- Under certain circumstances, imputed disqualification can be avoided if an ethical wall is erected around the attorney or paralegal with the conflict of interest.
- An attorney must not have any personal or business interests that conflict with the interests of a client.
- An attorney may enter into a business transaction with a client only if every safeguard is taken to ensure that the transaction is fair and reasonable to the client.
- An attorney must not use confidential information learned through representation of a client to the client's disadvantage.
- It is an attorney's duty to ensure the ethical conduct of paralegals and to prevent conflicts of interest arising from the paralegal's other employment or interests.
- When paralegals find themselves in a conflict-of-interest situation, it is most often due to a change of employers.

SUMMARY QUESTIONS

1. What are the sources of rules concerning conflict of interest that apply to attorneys? What are the sources of rules for paralegals?
2. Is it possible for an attorney to represent two clients with adverse interests?

3. Suppose that Allan wants to sell his home to Betty and she wants to buy it at a reasonable price. They are not sure how much the property is worth or how to document the transaction, so they contact Charles, Allan's attorney and ask him to represent them both to find a fair price and draft the necessary documents. Can Charles represent both Allan and Betty?

4. Suppose that Darlene wants to sell her home to Edward. They have researched the market and agreed that the home is worth $200,000. Edward has agreed to get his own financing and pay Darlene in cash. However, neither Darlene nor Edward are certain about the documentation required and exactly what needs to be filed at the county level, so they contact Fiona to represent both of them to prepare the documentation. Can she represent both clients?

5. Suppose that you are a paralegal with the firm of Green and Hansen, a large law firm in a metropolitan area. As you are reviewing the list of new clients, you see that your firm has initiated a lawsuit on behalf of a client, Isaac, against Jensen Sporting Goods. Your wife is one of the three shareholders of Jensen Sporting Goods. Do you have a conflict? What should you do?

6. Suppose that Kevin has just come in to your law firm to request representation. Kevin has been injured in an automobile accident due to brake failure just two weeks after he had new brakes installed at Larry's Auto Shop. Three years ago, your firm defended Larry in such a case. Can your firm represent Kevin?

7. Assume the same facts above, except that Kevin's brakes were fixed at Mack's Auto Shop and Larry's Auto Shop was your former client. Can your firm represent Kevin?

8. Suppose that your law firm Nelson & Opperman has been sought out for representation by Paul for his pending marriage dissolution. One of the attorney's in your firm recently left the firm of Quinn and Robbins—the firm that currently represents Paul's wife in their pending divorce. Can Nelson & Opperman take on representation of Paul if a different attorney handles the matter?

9. Can Sarah represent a client in a case against Tim, who is represented by Sarah's husband?

10. Is it permissible for an attorney to draft wills for her parents, even if her parents have left her a gift in their wills?

END NOTES

[1]Apple v. Hall, 412 N.E. 2d 114 (Ind. App. 1980).

[2]ABA Model Rules of Professional Conduct Rule 1.7 cmt. (1996).

[3]Makita Corp. v. U.S. 819 F.Supp. 1099 (CIT 1993).

[4]Waters v. Kemp, 845 F.2d 260 (1988).

[5]ABA Model Rules of Professional Conduct Rule 1.7 cmt. (1996).

[6]ABA Model Rules of Professional Conduct, Terminology (1996).

[7]In Re AMERICAN HOME PRODUCTS CORPORATION, 985 S.W. 2d 68 (Tx. 1998).

[8]ABA Model Rules of Professional Conduct Rule 1.7 cmt. (1996).

[9]ABA Model Rules of Professional Conduct Rule 1.13(b).

[10]ABA Model Rules of Professional Conduct Rule 1.7 cmt. (1996).

[11]Bell v. Clark, 653 N.W.2d (Ind. App. 1995).

[12]ABA Model Rules of Professional Conduct Rule 1.7 cmt. (1996).

[13]In re Am. Cable Publications, Inc., 768 F.2d 1194 (10th Cir. 1985).

[14]ABA Model Code of Professional Responsibility, DR 5-101.

[15]ABA Model Code of Professional Responsibility, EC 5-9 (1983).

[16]Williams v. Trans World Airlines, 588 F.Supp. 1037 (W.D.Mo. 1984).

[17]ABA Comm. On Ethics and Professional Responsibility, Informal Op. 88-1526 (1988).

[18]Ibid.

[19]NFPA Informal Ethics and Disciplinary Opinion No. 95-3. (1995).

THE RIGHT TO EFFECTIVE COUNSEL AND THE ETHICAL CHALLENGES OF PUBLIC DEFENDERS

Imagine that you have been accused of murder. If convicted you could be executed. You have been waiting in jail for several months and have had only two brief meetings with a court-appointed public defender. Finally you have your day in court. Your attorney, who looks rather exhausted, stands up and says:

"Your Honor, I request a continuance in this matter. Due to my overburdened caseload I have not had time to prepare adequately, and I do not feel I could represent this client competently at this time."

The Judge bangs the gavel. "Denied! You will proceed." So begins your journey to justice. . . .

Unfortunately, the above scenario is not far from reality. Public defenders in many areas have overwhelming caseloads that leave them little time to prepare adequately for many cases. Judges too often are faced with a crowded court calendar that leaves them little room for flexibility.

Any indigent who is a defendant in a criminal prosecution has the right to have counsel appointed to assist in his or her defense.[i] The defendant's rights include the right to "effective assistance of counsel."[ii]

Under law, and under the rules of ethics, attorneys must provide competent representation, with adequate skill and knowledge. Attorneys must spend the time and resources necessary to provide their clients with competent representation.

In reality, public defenders often meet their clients only shortly before they are to appear in court. These court-appointed attorneys may be handling as many as seventy felonies at one time, along with several other pending matters. They may not have adequate time to conduct proper investigations or prepare their cases. The workload of many public defenders makes it increasingly difficult to fulfill their ethical duty to provide competent representation.

The "war on crime" in the United States has had a significant impact on the criminal justice system in the United States. Arrests are on the rise. Although public sentiment approves of increased spending on police forces and prisons, funding for defense of indigent defendants has in many cases remained stagnant or even decreased. In many areas, inadequate funding for legal representation of indigents has left too few attorneys in the public defenders offices to offer what some believe is adequate representation of all clients.

In 1991 the ABA adopted standards for the maximum conceivable caseload that an attorney can manage. Those standards included a maximum of 150 felonies per attorney per year. The increasing need for representation of indigent defendants has made that standard just a dream in many busy offices. In a California case where the effectiveness of counsel issue was raised, the public defender had admitted in court that she had a caseload of approximately 2,000 cases per year. This public defender actually collapsed in court a few months after the conviction of the petitioner in the case and shortly thereafter resigned from the public defender's office, stating that she was "actually doing the defendants more harm by just presenting a live body than if they had no representation at all. "[iii]

Attorneys who work for public defender's offices face tough ethical dilemmas daily. They are constantly forced to make tough choices. On the one hand they have an ethical duty to provide each of their clients with competent representation. They must investigate their cases, be thoroughly prepared, and communicate with their clients as prescribed by the pertinent rules of ethics. If they fail to do so, they can face disciplinary charges from the state bar association or even, in many states, be sued for legal malpractice.

On the other hand, the number of clients assigned to them may make it nearly physically impossible to meet with all their clients, investigate each case, and keep communications to the levels that they feel comfortable with. At times, judges are reluctant to grant relief in the form of continuances because they are under pressure to push an unreasonably high number of cases through their courts every day. As noted by the court in one case where the defendant's constitutional guarantee of right to counsel was questioned, "Not even a lawyer with an S on his chest could effectively handle this docket!"[iv]

What can be done to alleviate the problem? Everyone involved agrees that additional funding for public defender's offices is top priority. Barring that, other suggestions have been made that the quality of the public defense should be monitored by the courts, or that additional training of public defenders may be beneficial. While there has been little consensus on how to deal with the problem, there is little doubt that something needs to be done about any situation that systematically threatens the ethical standards of even the most conscientious public defenders.

---

[i] Gideon v. Wainwright, 372 U.S. 335 (1963).
[ii] Strickland v. Washington, 466 U.S. 668 (1984).
[iii] Cooper v. Fitzharris, 551 F.2d 1162 (9th Circ. Ct. of App. 1977).
[iv] State v. Peart, 621 So. 2d 780 (La. 1993).

Chapter 5

Competent, Diligent, and Zealous Representation of the Client

"The true test of character is not how much we know how to do, but how we behave when we don't know what to do."

John Holt

An Ethical Dilemma
Introduction
Competent Representation Defined
    Legal Knowledge
        Self Education
    Skill
        Document Drafting
        Research and Analytical Skills
        Office Management
Case and Discussion
    Thoroughness and Preparation
        Investigation and Research
Accepting or Declining Representation
    Specialization
Maintaining Competence
Basic Rules Concerning Diligent Representation of Client
    Procrastination and Failure to Act in a Timely Manner
    Communication with Clients
Case and Discussion

Zealous Representation
    Providing Zealous Representation
    Remaining Within the Bounds of the Law
From the Paralegal's Perspective
Paralegal Competence and Diligence
A Question of Ethics
    Organization and Management Skills
    Communication Skills
    Analytical Skills
    Computer Skills
    Legal Research and Investigation Skills
    Interpersonal Skills
Standards for Paralegal Competence
    The NFPA's Recognition of Competence
    The NALA's Recognition of Competence
Maintaining Competence

Chapter Summary

Summary Questions

An Ethical Dilemma

Virginia Gerber is an attorney who has been in solo practice for fifteen years. Her caseload consists mainly of family law and personal injury cases. In 1995, Hanna Stein and her granddaughter brought a case to her. Hanna had been involved in an accident at the retirement home where she lives. Hannah was injured due to what she and her granddaughter believe to be the negligent behavior of one of the employees of the nursing home who let her wheelchair fall down two flights of stairs. Hanna's injuries are substantial, and it appears that the retirement home is at fault. Hanna's granddaughter wants to be sure that her grandmother is not taken advantage of and that a competent attorney sees to her case. However, she lives in a distant state and she must leave town and get back to her own life. She doesn't have time to stay and oversee the process for her elderly grandmother, who tends to be a bit confused and forgetful.

Virginia takes on the case and begins making preliminary inquiries. She is hoping to get an offer of reasonable settlement from the retirement home without having to file an action on behalf of Hanna. Virginia asks her legal assistant to mark on the office calendar the last possible date to file suit on Hanna's behalf to comply with the **statute of limitations.**

In the following months, Virginia's own life changes drastically. Her assistant leaves, and Virginia is without help for some time. Then, out of the blue, she is handed a case involving two wrongful deaths that could be worth millions to the victims' families (and Virginia). Virginia can't find the calendar her assistant used to keep, so she begins a new one marked with important dates relevant to her new case.

It has been quite some time since Virginia has contacted the retirement home where Hanna lives, and after a few attempts to contact Virginia, Hanna's granddaughter has given up. By the time Virginia has settled her new lawsuit involving the wrongful deaths and she has picked up Hanna's file again, the statute of limitations has run out. Virginia contacts the retirement home, but they are no longer interested in talking settlement. Has Virginia acted unethically here? Was it Hanna's (or her granddaughter's) responsibility to follow up with Virginia?

Answer and discussion: Yes, Virginia has acted unethically. Virginia has a duty to act with reasonable diligence and promptness in representing all of her clients. Virginia's failure to act diligently and promptly on behalf of Hanna may have cost Hanna a fair settlement of her case. It was not the responsibility of Hanna or her granddaughter to track the statute of limitations of Hanna's case; it was Virginia's.

INTRODUCTION

Attorneys must represent their clients with competence and diligence. Competent representation requires attorneys to have the legal knowledge, skill, thoroughness, and preparation reasonably necessary for representation.

Diligent representation requires attorneys to pursue matters on behalf of their clients with commitment and dedication. Attorneys must pursue each client's

Statute of limitations
Statutes of the federal government and various states setting maximum time periods during which certain actions can be brought or rights enforced. After the time period set out in the applicable statute of limitations has run, no legal action can be brought, regardless of whether any cause of action ever existed.

matter despite any obstruction or personal inconvenience to the attorney, with zeal, through whatever legal and ethical means appropriate, without procrastination.

Attorneys who do not provide competent and diligent representation of their clients are violating the codes of ethics that apply to them and may be subject to disciplinary action. In addition, they may be liable for legal malpractice if a disgruntled client brings a civil lawsuit against the attorney.

As a paralegal you will be assisting attorneys to provide their clients with competent and diligent representation. As part of the legal representation team, you must be aware of the standards for competence and diligence applied to attorneys. You must have an understanding not only of what zealous representation means but also the legal and ethical limits of zealous representation. All paralegals have an ethical duty to perform their work competently and to assist attorneys in providing competent and diligent representation to their clients.

This chapter begins by defining exactly what is meant by the terms **competent** and **diligent**, and discussing the standards that must be met by attorneys. The first part of the chapter concludes with a look at the attorney's ethical duty of zealousness and what is required of attorneys to provide zealous representation. The second part of the chapter looks at competence and diligence from the paralegal's perspective and the knowledge and skills a paralegal must possess to be considered competent. The chapter concludes with a look at standards for measuring paralegal competence.

COMPETENT REPRESENTATION DEFINED

Rule 1.1 of the ABA Model Rules states that competent representation requires the following at a level reasonably necessary for representation:

1. Legal knowledge
2. Skill
3. Thoroughness
4. Preparation

The standard of competence that must be provided by attorneys is the skill and knowledge normally possessed by other attorneys in good standing, undertaking similar matters (Figure 5–1). In most instances, attorneys are held to the proficiency of a general practitioner. However, under certain circumstances, expertise in a particular field of law may be required.

Legal Knowledge

Attorneys must have the requisite knowledge and skill in any matter in which they represent a client. That knowledge must include an understanding of legal principles applicable to each matter in which the attorney undertakes representation. "A lawyer is expected to be familiar with well-settled principles of law applicable to a client's needs."[1]

Competence
A basic or minimal ability to do something; qualification, especially to testify (competence of a witness). *(Black's Law Dictionary, Seventh Edition)*

Diligence
A continual effort to accomplish something. Care; caution; the attention and care required from a person in a given situation. *(Black's Law Dictionary, Seventh Edition)*

Model Rule 1.1
A lawyer shall provide competent representation to a client. Competent representation requires the legal knowledge, skill, thoroughness, and preparation reasonably necessary for the representation.

CPR Canon 6
A lawyer should represent a client competently.

FIGURE 5–1

Model Rule 1.1 and CPR Canon 6

In addition to possessing knowledge of basic legal principles, competent attorneys must have an understanding of the court rules and court procedures that apply to every matter that they undertake, and the knowledge required to conduct the research necessary to provide clients with competent representation. Courts have found that attorneys must "discover those additional rules of law which, although not commonly known, may be readily found by standard research techniques."[2]

Factors taken into consideration in determining the requisite knowledge and skill include the relative complexity and specialized nature of the matter, the lawyer's general experience, and the lawyer's training and experience in the field in question.[3]

Self-Education. All attorneys, especially newer attorneys, are from time to time presented with potential representation of clients concerning legal matters of which they have little or no knowledge and no experience. Although occasionally a lack of experience requires new attorneys to associate with a more-experienced attorney or decline representation of a client, newer attorneys with little or no experience can usually represent a client competently. To compensate for their inexperience and lack of knowledge, they must research and educate themselves diligently to the point that they can advise their clients and represent them competently.

Skill

A unique set of skills is required of attorneys in their representation of clients (Figure 5–2). Some of the specific skills attorneys must possess to competently represent a client include document drafting skills, the ability to analyze precedent and evaluate evidence, and the management and supervisory skills necessary to manage their practice of law and supervise employees.

Document Drafting. Competent attorneys must be skilled in drafting pleadings and other legal documents. So important are the attorney's writing skills and ability to draft legal documents that the inability to do so is considered a lack of competent representation. In one Minnesota case, an attorney was publicly reprimanded and ordered to complete continuing education courses as specified by the court when the court determined that "his repeated filing of documents rendered unintelligible by numerous spelling, grammatical, and typographical errors were sufficiently serious that they amounted to incompetent representation."[4]

In a case in Illinois, the court found that the attorney "lacked the fundamental skill of drafting pleadings and briefs, and although his deficiencies were remediable, respondent was incompetent to practice law and to represent clients."[5]

Research and Analytical Skills. Attorneys must have the legal research and analysis skills necessary to provide their clients with competent representation. It is assumed that "competent handling of a particular matter includes inquiry into

---

- Legal document drafting
- Legal research skills
- Analytical skills
- Office and time management skills
- Supervisory skills

FIGURE 5–2

Skills Required of Competent Attorneys

and analysis of the factual and legal elements of the problem and use of methods and procedures meeting the standards of competent practitioners."[6]

Office Management. Attorneys must possess the office management skills requisite to serving their clients in a competent manner. Office management skills include accurate calendaring, billing, filing, recordkeeping, and supervision of office staff.

One of the most common reasons for complaints against attorneys involves lapsed statutes of limitations. Statutes of limitations are the state and federal laws that set a limit on the time period during which a lawsuit may be brought. The time period begins when the cause of action begins. For example, suppose that a new client comes into your office concerning a possible personal injury lawsuit involving a motorcycle accident. The accident occurred five years ago, but the client was severely injured and is still receiving treatment. The lawsuit must be brought before the statute of limitations for this type of matter (usually no more than six years from the date of the accident), or your client will lose his or her right to bring any type of legal action against the responsible party. Maintaining a calendar system that alerts the responsible attorney to upcoming deadlines for filing and statutes of limitations on all matters and cases for which an attorney is responsible is of the utmost importance. An improperly kept calendar can result in missed court dates and missed filing dates that may mean a total dismissal of a client's claim.

Although calendaring and numerous other tasks may be assigned to paralegals or other office staff, the responsible attorney must maintain adequate supervision to the extent necessary to provide clients with competent representation.

CASE AND DISCUSSION

A lack of office management skills can result in incompetent representation of a client and disciplinary action against the attorney. The following case is a proceeding to review a disciplinary board recommendation for attorney suspension for negligence. The action was a result, in part, of the attorney's poor staff supervision and failure to establish an internal calendaring system to record litigation deadlines.

LOU SANCHEZ, PETITIONER
v.
THE STATE BAR OF CALIFORNIA, RESPONDENT
L.A. 30625
Supreme Court of California
In Bank.
Nov. 10, 1976.

BY THE COURT
This is a proceeding to review a recommendation of the Disciplinary Board of the State Bar that petitioner be suspended from the practice of law for three months. Petitioner was admitted to practice law in California in 1961 and has no prior disciplinary record. . . .
JARAMILLO MATTER (COUNT I)
On or about November 14, 1967, petitioner's office was retained to represent Mr. Victor Jaramillo in a personal injury matter. Jaramillo paid petitioner $300. Petitioner had earlier defended Jaramillo in a criminal matter that resulted in a dismissal. Jaramillo claimed to have been mistreated when arrested by the police, and a civil complaint for damages was filed against the City of San Diego. The action was dismissed for failure to serve summons within three years.

Petitioner testified that he had not seen Jaramillo following the conclusion of the criminal matter and did not know that a civil complaint had been filed by his office until notified by the State Bar that Jaramillo had complained against him. After the file was found in the 'dead files,' petitioner apologized to Jaramillo and accepted responsibility for the dismissal. He offered to repay him $300, which Jaramillo refused because he had filed a malpractice action against him.

Petitioner testified that he did not know who prepared the complaint; that he did not prepare it; that the signature thereon was not his; and that his name was signed by an employee who was not authorized to practice law. He was a sole practitioner and the only employees were a law student and secretaries, none of whom was authorized to sign his name to any documents.
ALFARO MATTER (COUNT II)
Mrs. Anna Alfaro paid petitioner $210 to represent her in a personal injury action, and a complaint was filed July 27, 1967. The only services performed by petitioner were the preparation of interrogatories, appearing with Mrs. Alfaro at a deposition in 1968, and the filing of an at-issue memorandum on August 13, 1971. He signed neither the complaint nor the at-issue memorandum. On September 22, 1972, the action was dismissed for failure to bring it to trial within five years.

About a year before the five-year statute expired, petitioner instructed his secretary to prepare a motion for an early trial setting. She did not do so until shortly before the expiration date when she prepared the motion, a declaration in support thereof, and points and authorities. She signed petitioner's name to the documents and arranged for an attorney who sometimes made appearances for petitioner to attend the hearing. She did not tell petitioner that the motion was denied.

Petitioner's secretary falsely informed Mrs. Alfaro that trial had been set for September 7, 1972. When Mrs. Alfaro telephoned petitioner on September 6 to confirm the trial date, petitioner informed her that there was no trial set for the 7th. He did not check the file, and it did not occur to him that the five-year statute had already run. It was not until sometime in January 1973 when Mrs. Alfaro made further inquiry that petitioner discovered the action had been dismissed. He accepted responsibility for the dismissal and offered to pay her $400.

The local committee found and concluded that on both counts petitioner was grossly negligent in permitting circumstances to exist by which employees not authorized to practice law could sign his name to legal documents. In the Alfaro matter he was grossly negligent in failing to establish any internal calendaring system to record deadlines with regard to litigation and failing to reveal to his client on September 6, 1972, that the five-year statute had run. The committee recommended 30 days' suspension. The disciplinary board approved the committee's findings and by a vote of 11 to 3 recommended 3 months' suspension. . . .

. . . In the Alfaro matter, petitioner does not dispute the finding of gross negligence in allowing pleadings to be signed by an office employee not authorized to practice law. He concedes that he was negligent in not following through to determine whether his instructions to prepare the motion for an early trial setting were followed, but argues that the latter was not gross negligence because of his secretary's failure to inform him that the motion had been denied. As in the Jaramillo matter, petitioner is responsible for the supervision of his staff. Reasonable attention on his part would have disclosed the improprieties. . . . Apart from his secretary's misconduct, petitioner knew in mid-1971 that the Alfaro case was in danger of dismissal under the five-year statute. Yet when Mrs. Alfaro telephoned him on September 6, 1972, regarding a trial date, it did not occur to him that the statute had already run. Had he looked at the file he would have discovered that the motion for an early trial setting had been denied. Instead he did nothing further until Mrs. Alfaro again phoned early in 1973, at which time he pulled the file and discovered the action had been dismissed. . . .

It is ordered that petitioner be suspended for 3 months, the order to be effective 30 days after the filing of this opinion. It is further ordered that within one year from the effective date of this order, petitioner pass the Professional Responsibility Examination.

Thoroughness and Preparation

For an attorney to provide competent representation to a client, the attorney must be thorough and prepared. The attorney must undertake necessary investigation of the facts of each case, and the attorney must research the law pertaining to each case as necessary. Failure to handle a matter on behalf of a client without *preparation adequate in the circumstances* can lead to serious consequences for both the client and the attorney.

In a disciplinary proceeding in Colorado, an attorney was disbarred for several infractions, including attending a hearing in a dissolution case with her only preparation being in the car on the way to the courthouse. The attorney in this case was found to be handling a legal matter without adequate preparation in violation of ABA Model Rule 1.1.[7]

Investigation and Research. Being adequately prepared and thorough includes an attorney's responsibilities to investigate the facts of each matter and research the applicable law. "An attorney owes his client the duty of diligent investigation and research."[8]

Attorneys have a duty to thoroughly investigate the applicable facts and circumstances surrounding each particular matter to the degree necessary for preparing the case or otherwise advising the client. Part of an attorney's investigation of a matter will include obtaining relevant information from the client—and verifying that information when circumstances warrant. Attorneys must give every matter they handle the required attention and preparation, including inquiry into and analysis of the factual and legal elements of the problem. The amount of preparation required depends on the complexity of the matter and what is at stake.

Attorneys cannot know every aspect of the law, even in those areas in which they specialize. Attorneys must research the pertinent law in each case as necessary to provide competent representation. Although attorneys are not expected to be infallible, they must conduct the measure of research sufficient to allow their clients to make informed decisions.[9]

> Even with respect to an unsettled area of the law, ". . . an attorney assumes an obligation to his client to undertake reasonable research in an effort to ascertain relevant legal principles and to make an informed decision as to a course of conduct based upon an intelligent assessment of the problem."[10]

ACCEPTING OR DECLINING REPRESENTATION

When an attorney is presented with a case that requires legal knowledge or skill he or she does not possess, the attorney has three options. The attorney may associate with, or consult, an attorney with known competence in that area, make a commitment to self-education, or turn down the representation. For example, a personal injury attorney who is offered a case involving copyright or trademark issues would probably seek the assistance of an intellectual property attorney, unless he or she was willing to commit several hours to self-education with regard to intellectual property law. If the attorney is not associated with an intellectual property attorney and does not want to commit to the time it would take to gain the required knowledge, then the attorney must turn down the case.

Whichever route an attorney decides to take in compensating for a lack of competence in a certain area of law, the action must be clearly communicated to the client in writing. Especially if an attorney determines that he or she cannot accept representation of a potential client, the attorney must notify the potential client in writing as soon as possible. If an attorney decides to consult with an outside specialist in the relevant area of law concerning a client's case, the client should be notified and consulted concerning the details of the professional relationship.

Specialization

Because of the complexity of modern law, most attorneys specialize in one or more areas of law. Because it is difficult for attorneys to be knowledgeable and competent in areas outside of their specialty, they often refer such business to specialists. For example, it is not uncommon for attorneys who specialize in family law to refer divorcing clients who have complicated income tax questions to tax attorneys.

Attorneys may even be *required* to refer certain types of business to specialists when they lack the necessary competency. In a 1979 California case, an attorney who set up a defective **irrevocable trust** for a client's three sons was subsequently sued for legal malpractice. The court held that a general practitioner has a duty to refer a client to a specialist under certain circumstances or to meet the standard of care of a specialist.[11]

While specialists have always existed in the practice of law in the United States, only in recent years have these specialists been recognized by certification. As of the end of 1996, there were over 21,000 specialty certificates issued to attorneys in the United States.[12] To obtain the Certified Specialist designation, attorneys must meet with the requirements of the certifying board, which usually include acquiring a determined amount of experience in the area and passing a written examination. Attorneys may be certified as specialists by state-sponsored certification plans or by private organizations that offer certification programs that are accredited by the ABA. Currently the states of Arizona, California, Florida, Louisiana, Minnesota, New Jersey, New Mexico, North Carolina, South Carolina, and Texas offer state-sponsored certification plans (Figure 5–3). The ABA Accred-

Irrevocable trust
A trust that cannot be terminated by the settlor once it is created. In most states, a trust will be deemed irrevocable unless the settlor specifies otherwise. *(Black's Law Dictionary, Seventh Edition)*

State-Sponsored Certification Plans offer certification of specialists directly in various fields of law to lawyers licensed in their state.

State	Certifications Available
Arizona	Bankruptcy; Criminal; Domestic Relations; Injury and Wrongful Death; Real Estate; Tax; Workers' Compensation
California	Appellate; Personal and Small Business Bankruptcy; Criminal Law; Domestic Relations–Family; Estate Planning, Trust and Probate; Immigration and Nationality; Taxation; Workers' Compensation
Florida	Admiralty and Maritime; Appellate Practice; Aviation; Business Litigation; City, County and Local Government; Civil Trial; Criminal; Health; Immigration and Naturalization; Marital and Family; Real Estate; Tax, Wills, Trusts and Estates; Workers' Compensation
Louisiana	Business Bankruptcy; Consumer Bankruptcy; Estate Planning and Administration; Family Law; Tax Law
Minnesota	Civil Trial, Real Property
New Jersey	Civil Trial; Criminal Trial; Matrimonial; Workers' Compensation
New Mexico	Appellate Practice; Bankruptcy Law; Civil Trial; Criminal Trial; Estate Planning, Trusts and Probate; Family Law; Natural Resources; Personal Injury Trial; Real Estate Law; Taxation; Workers' Compensation
North Carolina	Bankruptcy Law; Criminal Law; Estate Planning and Probate Law; Family Law; Real Property Law
South Carolina	Bankruptcy and Debtor–Creditor Law; Employment and Labor Law; Estate Planning and Probate Law; Family Law; Taxation
Texas	Administrative; Business Bankruptcy; Consumer Bankruptcy; Civil Appellate; Civil Trial; Commercial Real Estate; Consumer; Criminal; Estate Planning and Probate; Family; Farm and Ranch Real Estate; Immigration and Nationality; Labor and Employment; Oil, Gas, and Mineral; Personal Injury Trial; Residential Real Estate; Tax

State-Sponsored Plans to Accredit Private Certifiers approve certification programs offered by state bar sections and other organizations to lawyers in their state.

State	Certifications Available
Alabama	Accounting Professional Liability, Civil Trial Advocacy, Criminal Trial Advocacy, Business Bankruptcy, Creditors' Rights, Consumer Bankruptcy, Elder Law, Legal Professional Liability, Medical Professional Liability.
Connecticut	Business Bankruptcy, Civil Trial, Consumer Bankruptcy, Criminal Trial.
Georgia	Civil Trial Advocacy, Criminal Trial Advocacy
Idaho	Accounting Professional Liability, Business Bankruptcy, Civil Trial Advocacy, Consumer Bankruptcy, Creditors' Rights, Criminal Trial Advocacy, Elder Law, Legal Professional Liability, Medical Professional Liability, Workers' Compensation.
Indiana	Civil Trial Advocacy, Criminal Trial Advocacy
Maine	Accounting Professional Liability, Civil Trial Advocacy, Criminal Trial Advocacy, Business Bankruptcy, Consumer Bankruptcy, Creditors' Rights, Elder Law, Estate Planning, Legal Professional Liability, Medical Professional Liability.
Pennsylvania	Business Bankruptcy, Civil Trial Advocacy, Consumer Bankruptcy, Criminal Trial Advocacy.
Tennessee	Accounting Professional Liability, Business Bankruptcy, Civil Trial Advocacy, Consumer Bankruptcy, Creditors' Rights, Criminal Trial Advocacy, Elder Law, Estate Planning, Legal Professional Liability, Medical Professional Liability.

FIGURE 5–3
Specialty Certification Plans

ited Certification Programs include certification in business and consumer bankruptcy, accounting, legal and medical professional liability, elder law, estate planning, and civil and criminal trial advocacy.

MAINTAINING COMPETENCE

To ensure an attorney's continued competence; attorneys are required to continually educate themselves to keep abreast of new developments. "To maintain the requisite knowledge and skill, a lawyer should engage in continuing study and education."[13] Continuing Legal Education (CLE) courses are offered throughout the country to help attorneys maintain their competence and expertise in most every area of law. A majority of the state bar associations now requires that attorneys complete a certain number of hours of education through approved CLE courses.

BASIC RULES CONCERNING DILIGENT REPRESENTATION OF CLIENT

Attorneys must represent their clients with reasonable diligence. An attorney who has the required legal knowledge and skill does not offer adequate representation of a client if the attorney demonstrates a lack of diligence or promptness. Comments to the Model Rules indicate that "A lawyer should pursue a matter on behalf of a client despite opposition, obstruction or personal inconvenience to the lawyer, and may take whatever lawful and ethical measures are required to vindicate a client's cause or endeavor."[14] Attorneys must avoid procrastination when acting on a client's behalf and they must keep current in their communications with their clients.

The obligation to act diligently encompasses providing services within a reasonable time, prompt attendance to legal matters with which one is entrusted, and a commitment to achieve the clients' lawful objectives.

Procrastination, neglect, forgetfulness, or lack of reasonable efficiency can each result in discipline and liability for malpractice.

Procrastination and Failure to Act in a Timely Manner

Although almost all of us are guilty of procrastinating in our personal lives, procrastination in the practice of law can have serious consequences. Failure to act on behalf of a client in a timely manner is one of the most frequent causes of legal malpractice suits. An attorney's procrastination, in addition to being a source of irritation to the client, can lead to missed deadlines resulting in the termination of legal rights and remedies of the client.

Communication with Clients

Attorneys must effectively communicate with their clients as to the status of the matters that are being handled for them. Failure on the part of an attorney to communicate with a client's inquiries can result in discipline for lack of diligence.

CASE AND DISCUSSION

Attorneys may give several reasons for procrastinating. In the following case, one of the reasons the attorney procrastinated on several estate and probate matters was that he lacked the necessary competence to take action. He was unsure of how to proceed, so he did nothing—thereby compounding the problem.

Committee on Professional Ethics and Conduct
of the Iowa State Bar Association, Complaintant,

v.

Carroll King BATSCHELET, Respondent
No. 86-1716
Supreme Court of Iowa
March 18,1987.

In August of 1986 the Committee on Professional Ethics and Conduct of the Iowa State Bar Association (committee) charged respondent Carroll King Batschelet with professional misconduct in his representation of several executors and administrators. In addition, the committee alleged that respondent had not cooperated with the disciplinary authorities investigating his conduct. The Grievance Commission (commission) found that respondent had violated several provisions of the Iowa Code of Professional Responsibility for Lawyers and recommended in its report a six-month suspension of respondent's license to practice law. That report is now before us for review and final disposition. . . . We agree with commission's findings and recommendation. We suspend respondent's license to practice law indefinitely, with no possibility of reinstatement for six months from the date of this decision. . . .

I. INATTENTION TO LEGAL WORK.

Respondent admitted in responding to the committee's discovery requests and again at trial, that he had received notice of probate delinquencies in twenty estates and one conservatorship that he had opened. Respondent was the designated attorney in those probate matters which date back to as early as 1972. All but four of those estates remained open at the time of the hearing before the commission. Respondent had been delinquent in performing his responsibilities on at least one occasion while handling each of those twenty-one files; in one probate estate he had received eighteen separate delinquency notices.

At the hearing respondent attempted in several ways to explain his inattentiveness to these probate matters. Although he attributed the delay in several instances to difficulty in getting necessary information and the insufficiency of estate funds, he conceded that most of the estates remained open simply because he had not taken the time to complete and close them. . . .

Respondent suggested that in more than one situation uncertainty about the applicable law caused him to be dilatory in closing an estate. He acknowledged, however, that he had neither sought help from other attorneys nor requested that the court consider granting temporary relief from the problems which triggered the delinquency notices. Questioned about his failure to cure the delinquencies, respondent gave a candid though entirely unsatisfactory answer: I guess the idea never came to mind honestly. I thought I would try to do better as time would go by.

Procrastination was apparently the fundamental disease that infected respondent's practice, as revealed in his closing statement to the commission:

I would like to visit with the Commission just a little bit to say maybe how we get here, but I try day by day just to do whatever has to be done the most that day. I'm sure that's how the delay happens on these things. People come in, and they have to have the abstract continued or examined or deed prepared and that sort of thing. Obviously, why, then goes the estate proceedings do suffer because they can wait another day, and that goes from day-to-day too long.

The public in general and respondent's clients in particular were entitled to diligent handling of these probate files, not postponement to "another day" while other clients were accommodated.

In Committee on Professional Ethics & Conduct v. Bitter, 279 N.W. 2d 521 (Iowa 1979), we explained the options available to lawyers who find themselves unable to keep up their work: (1) they can "decline additional legal matters if accepting them would result in neglecting pending matters"; (2) they can "seek assistance"; or (3) they can "disengage . . . from these lingering matters and allow another lawyer to complete them." . . . Unfortunately respondent failed to heed those suggestions, apparently because his reach exceeded his grasp. Respondent insisted on continuing as the only attorney performing probate work for his friends and relatives even though he continually failed to perform the work in a prompt and satisfactory manner. . . .

III. DISPOSITION.

We agree with the commission's recommendation that respondent's license to practice law in Iowa should be suspended indefinitely with no possibility of reinstatement for six months from the date of the filing of this opinion. Any application for reinstatement shall be governed by court rule 118.13, . . .

LICENSE SUSPENDED.

Attorneys must share with clients all pertinent facts required to enable the client to make the best decision possible during negotiations with other parties. Attorneys must communicate to clients:

1. All serious proposals by opposing counsel
2. A review of all important provisions of proposed offer or settlement
3. A description of communications regarding the proposal received from opposing counsel
4. Details of any offers for a plea bargain
5. Any other information that may be needed by the client to make the best decision

Competence and diligence are closely related, and a lack of competence can often lead to a lack of diligence. For example, in *People v. Pooley,* 774 P2d 239 (Colo. 1989), a Colorado attorney was suspended from practice for ninety days for his incompetence and lack of diligence. In this case the attorney took on representation of clients in a medical malpractice case. The attorney lacked the requisite competence to represent a medical malpractice suit and failed to consult with a medical malpractice specialist. To make matters worse, the attorney's lack of diligence led to poor communication with the clients and the lapse of the statute of limitations on the client's potential claim before anything was done.

ZEALOUS REPRESENTATION

The word *zeal* means "eager and ardent interest in the pursuit of something."[15] *Zealous* representation is characterized by enthusiasm and fervent dedication on the part of the attorney. It requires attorneys to do everything legally and ethically possible to gain an acquittal for a defendant.[16] Canon 7 of the Code of Professional Responsibility reads as follows:

Canon 7
A lawyer should represent a client zealously within the bounds of the law.

Zealous representation is closely related to diligent representation, in that attorneys must pursue a matter on behalf of a client to their utmost ability, despite opposition, obstruction, or personal inconvenience to the lawyer, and may take whatever lawful and ethical measures are required to vindicate a client's cause or endeavor. There is no rule in the Model Rules that specifically requires zealous representation; however, the comments to Rule 1.3 requiring diligence and promptness indicate that "A lawyer should act with commitment and dedication to the interests of the client and with zeal in advocacy upon the client's behalf."

Providing Zealous Representation

The disciplinary rules to Canon 7 give more particulars regarding what zealous representation includes, and they give examples of what is not considered to be within the bounds of the law. Specifically, DR 7–101 provides that an attorney shall:

1. Seek the lawful objectives of clients through reasonably available means permitted by law and the disciplinary rules
2. Carry out an employment contract to provide legal services without withdrawing pursuant to the pertinent disciplinary rules
3. Not prejudice or damage clients during the course of the professional relationship except as required by the pertinent disciplinary rules.

Remaining Within the Bounds of the Law

Zealous representation of a client must remain within the bounds of the law. The attorney's ethical duty is to do everything *legally* and *ethically* permitted to pursue a client's interest. Attorneys must at all times be careful not to cross the line to illegal or unethical behavior in pursuing their clients' interests (Figure 5–4).

Rule	Applicable Disciplinary Rules Or Model Rules
Attorneys must not file unwarranted, frivolous suits or claims or take other actions merely to harass or maliciously injure others.	Model Rule 3.1 Disciplinary Rule 7–102(A)(1) & (2)
A lawyer shall not knowingly make a false statement of material fact or law to a tribunal.	Model Rule 3.3(a)(1) Disciplinary Rule 7–102(A)(4) & (5)
A lawyer shall not knowingly fail to disclose a material fact to a tribunal when disclosure is necessary to avoid assisting a criminal or fraudulent act by the client.	Model Rule 3.3(a)(2) Disciplinary Rule 7–102(A)(3) Disciplinary Rule 7–102(B)(1)
A lawyer shall not knowingly fail to disclose to the tribunal legal authority in the controlling jurisdiction known to the lawyer to be directly adverse to the position of the client and not disclosed by opposing counsel.	Model Rule 3.3(a)(3) Disciplinary Rule 7–106(B)(1)
A lawyer shall not offer evidence the lawyer knows to be false.	Model Rule 3.3(a)(4) Disciplinary Rule 7–102(A)(7) Disciplinary Rule 7–102(B)(1)
In an ex parte proceeding, a lawyer shall inform the tribunal of all material facts known to the lawyer which will enable the tribunal to make an informed decision, whether or not the facts are adverse.	Model Rule 3.3(d)
In representing a client, a lawyer shall not communicate about the subject of the representation with a person the lawyer knows to be represented by another lawyer in the matter, unless the lawyer has the consent of the other lawyer or is authorized by law to do so.	Model Rule 4.2 Disciplinary Rule 7–104(A)(1)
A lawyer shall not communicate ex parte with a judge, juror, prospective juror or other official by means prohibited by law	Model Rule 3.5 Disciplinary Rule 7–106, 7–108, 7–109, 7–110
A lawyer shall not unlawfully obstruct another party's access to evidence or unlawfully alter, destroy or conceal evidence or counsel another to do so.	Model Rule 3.4(a) Disciplinary Rule 7–104(A)(4) & (5) Disciplinary Rule 7–109(A) & (B)
A lawyer shall not falsify evidence or counsel or assist a witness to testify falsely or offer an illegal inducement to a witness.	Model Rule 3.4(b) Disciplinary Rule 7–102(A)(4) & (5) Disciplinary Rule 7–102(A)(6) Disciplinary Rule 7–109(A) & (B)
A lawyer shall not knowingly disobey an obligation under the rules of the court or tribunal.	Model Rule 3.4(c) Disciplinary Rule 7–106(A) Disciplinary Rule 7–106(C)(5) & (7)
A lawyer shall not make frivolous discovery requests or fail to make reasonably diligent efforts to comply with a legally proper discovery request by opposing party in pretrial procedure.	Model Rule 3.4(d) Disciplinary Rule 7–106(A) Disciplinary Rule 7–106(C)(7)

FIGURE 5–4
Rules Limiting Zealous Representation

There are numerous rules concerning actions considered to be unethical or outside the bounds of the law in the representation of clients. These rules are set forth in several of the Model Rules, disciplinary rules to the Model Code, and the rules of ethics adopted by each state. Following are some of the more important rules for keeping zealous representation within the bounds of the law:

1. **Attorneys must not file unwarranted, frivolous suits or claims or take other actions merely to harass or maliciously injure others.** Although it is important that attorneys use the legal process to the full benefit of their clients, it is also important that they do not abuse the legal process by filing lawsuits and other types of legal claims that are unwarranted, frivolous, or without merit merely to harass others. This rule is designed to prevent courts from getting clogged with suits that do not merit the time of the legal system but are merely designed to harass.

2. **Attorneys have a duty of candor.** The attorney's duty of candor toward the tribunal means that the attorney must not conceal information legally required to be disclosed, and the attorney must not use or create perjured testimony or false evidence or make false statements of law or fact. The attorney must not assist his or her client in any illegal or fraudulent activity or engage in any such activity. One aspect of this rule provides that an attorney must disclose to the tribunal controlling legal authority—even if it is adverse to his or her client. For example, suppose that an attorney is defending a corporation in a suit brought by shareholders. She researches her position very carefully and finds a published case that is right on point with the case at hand. The case was heard in a higher court in the same jurisdiction and its outcome was in direct opposition to the corporation's current case. If the attorneys for the shareholders do not uncover this case and argue its applicability in the current case, the attorney for the corporation has an ethical duty to present that information to the court.

Ex parte
On or from one party only, usually without notice to or argument from the adverse party (the judge conducted the hearing ex parte). *(Black's Law Dictionary, Seventh Edition)*

3. **Attorneys must not communicate directly with an adverse party, judges, or jurors.** The rules concerning **ex parte** communications prohibit attorneys from having any direct communication with an adverse party who is represented by an attorney. All communication with an individual who has an interest adverse to a client in a pending legal matter must be through the adverse party's counsel, unless the counsel grants permission.

4. **Threatening criminal prosecution.** Attorneys must never threaten criminal charges solely to gain advantage in a civil matter. For example, it would be unethical for an attorney who has been retained to collect on a bad debt to threaten the debtor with criminal prosecution for writing bad checks unless the debtor pays his client immediately.

5. **Trial conduct and publicity.** Attorneys must abide by all legal and ethical rules concerning trial conduct and publicity. There are several specific rules concerning proper conduct for court appearances and the proper handling of publicity before, during, and after a trial that attorneys must be aware of and follow. These rules are set forth in the pertinent rules of ethics as well as in the rules of the courts.

6. **Contact with witnesses.** Any contact attorneys have with witnesses or potential witnesses to a legal matter is strictly regulated by rules of ethics and court rules that the attorney must be aware of and comply with.

FROM THE PARALEGAL'S PERSPECTIVE

PARALEGAL COMPETENCE AND DILIGENCE

As part of the legal services team, paralegals must provide competent and diligent services to the attorneys they work for and, ultimately, to the client. As a paralegal, you must be certain you have the requisite knowledge and skill to perform the tasks that have been assigned to you. If you do not possess such skill, you must work to educate yourself, ask for help, or both. It is important that you do not misrepresent the level of your knowledge and skill. To do so can have serious consequences to you, the attorneys you work for, and the clients they represent.

Paralegals must be diligent in the completion of their assignments. Attorneys will rely on your ability, skills, and diligence to get work done thoroughly and on time.

Interrogatory

A written question (usually in a set of questions) submitted to an opposing party in a lawsuit as part of discovery. *(Black's Law Dictionary, Seventh Edition)*

A Question of Ethics

You have finally landed the job you want—you are a litigation paralegal for one of the major law firms in town. You are assisting one of the busiest partners in the firm, as well as two of his associates.

Before Randall Cummings, the partner you report to, leaves town for Germany for three weeks, he gives you brief instructions to prepare **interrogatories** on a medical malpractice suit he is working on and have them served on the opposing counsel. The trial date is coming up on this case, and you know it is a priority for Mr. Cummings. Although you have represented to Mr. Cummings that you are experienced in all facets of litigation, in fact you have never worked on a medical malpractice suit and you are unsure of the applicable rules and procedures to be followed. There are interrogatories in several other files that you could use for guidance, and the applicable court rules are online and in hard copy in the library. You could ask for help, but you are reluctant to let on how little you know. The other two attorneys you work for have seen Mr. Cummings' upcoming absence as a time to clear their desks of pending projects—much of that work has been delegated to you, and things are starting to snowball. . . . Mr. Cummings will be gone for three weeks and no one will ask about the interrogatories until he gets back, so perhaps you could just set these aside and work on them later. . . . What should you do?

Answer and Discussion: As a paralegal, you must be competent and diligent. This means that you must have the requisite knowledge and skill to complete your assignments, and they must be done promptly to the best of your ability. You really have several options here. First, you probably do not have the competence required to complete your assignment without some assistance or self-education. If time permits, you can educate yourself with regard to the pertinent rules of discovery regarding interrogatories. Background knowledge of the rules, in addition to forms previously followed in your office, could give you the competence and confidence you need to prepare a draft of the interrogatories. You may ask another paralegal in your department to review the interrogatories first if you are unsure of your work. Then, you will want to ask one of the other attorneys you work for to review and sign the documents.

What you must not do is set the work aside and forget about it. Procrastination on the part of a paralegal can be just as destructive as procrastination on the part of an attorney.

A competent paralegal has a basic knowledge of the American legal system and possesses skill in the following areas:

- Organization and management
- Communication
- Analytical
- Computer
- Legal research and investigation
- Interpersonal

Organization and Management Skills

Both attorneys and paralegals must have excellent organizational skills to provide clients with competent, diligent representation. According to a recent survey, calendaring deadlines was the third most common responsibility assigned to the paralegals who responded. Case management was the sixth most commonly assigned task.[17] By tracking important court dates and other deadlines and assisting with accurate timekeeping and recordkeeping, you will help to ensure that the attorneys you report to comply with the rules of ethics regarding competent, diligent representation of clients.

Communication Skills

As a paralegal, you must have excellent communication skills when communicating with attorneys, clients, and other individuals. You must have the basic communication skills, including good grammar and vocabulary, and you must be able to communicate effectively in person and in writing.

Your in-person communication will include meeting with and speaking to attorneys, your co-workers, and possibly clients. It is very important that clients receive personal attention and have their questions answered within a reasonable time period. Attorneys do not always have time to answer phone calls and correspondence and meet with clients when the clients desire. As a paralegal, you may serve as the communication link between the attorney and his or her clients.

According to a recent survey, eighty percent of paralegals participate in attorney/client meetings at least occasionally. For that reason, it is imperative that you have effective personal communication skills. You must have the ability to communicate clearly, concisely, and politely. And your nonverbal communication must match your spoken words.

Paralegals must be able to communicate effectively in writing. Drafting correspondence and pleadings are among the tasks most often assigned to paralegals. Paralegals spend more of their time drafting correspondence than any other single task.[18]

Attorneys have an ethical duty to keep clients informed about the status of their legal matters, to promptly reply to requests for information, and to explain legal matters to clients to the extent necessary to permit them to make informed decisions. As a paralegal, your assistance to the attorneys you work for and your communications with clients can ensure that clients receive competent, diligent legal services.

Analytical Skills

Competent paralegals must have the analytical skills necessary to analyze and summarize legal documents. As a paralegal, you will often be responsible for analyzing a given set of facts and summarizing them for the attorneys you work for or for clients. You may also need analytical skill for legal analysis—applying the law to a given set of facts. Your analytical skills will help to provide the attorneys you work for with the information they need to provide competent, diligent legal services to their clients.

Computer Skills

Competent paralegals are computer literate and skilled in several computer applications. According to a 1999 survey, almost ninety-nine percent of responding paralegals are using computers daily.[19] As a paralegal, you may need to use several computer applications daily. Some of the more frequently used computer applications include word processing, legal research, and billing and timekeeping (Figure 5–5).

Legal Research and Investigation Skills

Attorneys have an ethical duty to be diligent in their research and investigation on each legal matter they handle. As a paralegal, you will probably be given research and investigation assignments on a regular basis. Your assignments will provide the attorneys you work for with information that may be critical to the competent representation of their clients. The legal research you conduct may include research done by computer and by telephone. It may also include checking a simple procedure in a handbook or manual. Understanding the basics of legal research is of the utmost importance to every paralegal.

To offer clients competent and diligent services, the legal team must thoroughly investigate the facts of a legal matter, as well as the law. The term *investigate* means to inquire; to look into; to make an investigation. When the term is taken literally, much of any paralegal work involves investigating. Whether you are searching for witnesses and evidence for a trial or trying to locate the registered office of a corporation, you must have excellent investigative skills.

Interpersonal Skills

As a competent paralegal, you must possess the interpersonal skills required to successfully interact with those you come into contact with. As part of the legal team you must have effective team-building skills, and you must be able to communicate, empathize, and interact with individuals with diverse backgrounds and education. Your interpersonal skills must also include the interviewing skills necessary to conduct thorough investigations in litigation matters.

STANDARDS FOR PARALEGAL COMPETENCE

Paralegal competence is a sensitive issue with many paralegals because there are no universally accepted standards. With virtually no mandatory education

1. Billing and timekeeping
2. Internet legal and factual research
3. Word processing
4. Westlaw or Lexis legal research
5. E-mail communication
6. Spreadsheet applications
7. Database design and searching

FIGURE 5–5
Computer Applications Most Frequently Used by Paralegals

The ABA's Definition
A legal assistant or paralegal is a person, qualified by education, training or work experience . . . who performs specifically delegated substantive legal work for which a lawyer is responsible.

The National Association of Legal Assistants' Definition
. . . Through formal education, training and experience, legal assistants have knowledge and expertise regarding the legal system and substantive and procedural law which qualify them to do work of a legal nature under the supervision of an attorney.

The National Federation of Paralegal Association's Definition
. . . A person qualified through education, training or work experience to perform substantive legal work that requires knowledge of legal concepts and is customarily but not exclusively performed by a lawyer . . . .

FIGURE 5–6

Paralegal Competence as Addressed in the Definitions of the Terms Paralegal *and* Legal Assistant

requirements for the profession, paralegals are leery of uneducated and incompetent paralegals who misrepresent themselves and work against the professional image of the entire profession.

Both of the national paralegal associations have been working to combat this problem—by requiring a certain level of competence in their codes of ethics and by providing tests to identify competent paralegals and give them credibility (Figure 5–6).

The NFPA's Recognition of Competence

Section 1.1 of the NFPA's Model Code of Ethics and Professional Responsibility, and the accompanying ethical considerations, outline the NFPA's definition of competence:

1.1   A Paralegal Shall Achieve and Maintain a High Level of Competence

EC–1.1(a)   A paralegal shall achieve competency through education, training, and work experience.

EC–1.1(b)   A paralegal shall participate in continuing education in order to keep informed of current legal, technical and general developments.

EC–1.1(c)   A paralegal shall perform all assignments promptly and efficiently.

The NFPA recommends paralegals prove their competence by passing the Paralegal Advanced Competency Exam (PACE). PACE is a two-tiered exam that may be taken by experienced paralegals who meet certain education requirements to "validate experience and job skills, establish credentials and confirm their value to the legal industry."[20] Tier I of the exam tests critical thinking skills and problem-solving abilities, including general legal and ethical questions. Tier II tests the knowledge of the paralegal in specific legal practice areas. The NFPA's stated purposes of PACE are as follows:

- To provide the groundwork for expanding paralegal roles and responsibilities
- To provide the public and legal community with a mechanism to gauge the competency of the experienced paralegal
- To be used in states considering regulation of experienced paralegals

The pace exam may only be taken by paralegals who have two years of work experience. Education requirements for taking the PACE are as follows:

Tier 1 Requirements

- a minimum of four (4) years' work experience as a paralegal if application is made within the global grandparenting period (through December 31, 2000) **OR**
- a bachelor's degree and completion of a paralegal program within an institutionally accredited school (which may be embodied in the bachelor's degree), **and** a minimum of two years' work experience as a paralegal

Tier II Requirements

- successful completion of the first tier, **AND** one of the following
- a minimum of six (6) years' work experience as a paralegal, if application is made within the global grandparenting period (through December 31, 2000), **OR**
- a bachelor's degree, and completion of a paralegal program within an institutionally accredited school (which may be embodied in the bachelor's degree), **and** a minimum of four years' experience as a paralegal

The NALA's Recognition of Competence

Canon 6 of the NALA's Code of Ethics and Professional Responsibility addresses paralegal competence as follows:

Canon 6
A legal assistant must strive to maintain integrity and a high degree of competency through education and training with respect to professional responsibility, local rules and practice, and through continuing education in substantive areas of law to better assist the legal profession in fulfilling its duty to provide legal service.

The NALA also promotes standards for paralegal competence in its NALA Model Standards and Guidelines for Utilization of Legal Assistants. The Model Standards portion of that document reads as follows:

Standards
A legal assistant should meet certain minimum qualifications. The following standards may be used to determine an individual's qualifications as a legal assistant:

1. Successful completion of the Certified Legal Assistant certifying (CLA) examination of the National Association of Legal Assistants;
2. Graduation from an ABA approved program of study for legal assistants;
3. Graduation from a course of study for legal assistants which is institutionally accredited but not ABA approved, and which requires not less than the equivalent of 60 semester hours of classroom study;
4. Graduation from a course of study for legal assistants, other than those set forth in (2) and (3) above, plus not less than six months of in-house training as a legal assistant.
5. A baccalaureate degree in any field, plus not less than six months in-house training as a legal assistant;
6. A minimum of three years of law-related experience under the supervision of an attorney, including at least six months of in-house training as a legal assistant; or
7. Two years of in-house training as a legal assistant.

The NALA encourages paralegals to take the Certified Legal Assistant examination to obtain a CLA designation as evidence of their competence.

Requirements for CLA designation include successful completion of a two-day comprehensive examination based on federal law and procedure covering communications, ethics, human relations and interviewing techniques, judgment and analytical ability, legal research, and legal terminology. In addition, the test covers substantive areas of law, including the American legal system, administrative law, bankruptcy law, business organizations/corporate law, contracts, family law, criminal law and procedure, litigation, probate and estate planning, and real estate. Paralegals taking the test are tested on the American legal system and four of the foregoing areas of substantive law. The NALA offers certification to paralegals who pass the examinations. Specialty certification is also available in the areas of bankruptcy, civil litigation, corporations/business law, criminal law and procedure, intellectual property, estate planning and probate, and real estate for students who pass additional testing requirements in those areas. Specialty certification specific to the states of California, Florida, and Louisiana is also available.

MAINTAINING COMPETENCE

Changes in the law and in the legal environment require paralegals to work to maintain their competence—usually through continuing legal education. Although there are no mandatory requirements for continuing legal education at this time, both of the national paralegal associations strongly recommend continuing education. A minimum number of hours of continuing legal education is required to maintain the registered paralegal status (for paralegals who pass the PACE exam) and the CLA credential (for paralegals who pass the Certified Legal Assistant exam).

It has never been easier for paralegals to maintain competence in their profession. Although new laws are being adopted at a rapid rate and the legal environment is constantly changing, there are numerous continuing legal education (CLE) options available—even to busy paralegals. The national, state, and local paralegal associations, as well as private organizations, offer CLE courses. Paralegals are also invited to attend many CLE opportunities that are designed for attorneys. CLE courses can be taken by attending seminars, by watching seminars on videos, by listening to audio tapes, and more frequently over the Internet.

CHAPTER SUMMARY

- Attorneys have an ethical duty to provide their clients with competent, diligent, and zealous representation.
- Competent representation requires the attorney to have legal knowledge, skill, thoroughness, and preparation all at a level reasonably necessary for representation.
- Attorneys lacking the requisite level of knowledge can seek assistance of an expert or more experienced attorney, educate himself or herself as necessary, or decline the representation.
- Attorneys must undertake the necessary level of investigation and legal research to competently represent their clients.
- Attorneys maintain their competence through continuing legal education (CLE) courses.
- Attorneys must provide their clients with diligent representation by providing services within a reasonable time, attending promptly to legal matters, and making a commitment to achieving the client's legal objectives.
- Attorneys have an ethical duty to communicate to clients all pertinent facts required to enable the client to make the best possible decisions.
- Zealous representation requires attorneys to do everything legally and ethically possible to gain an acquittal for a defendant or otherwise promote their client's claims.

- A competent paralegal has a basic knowledge of the American legal system and possesses organization and management, communication, analytical, computer, legal research, and investigative and interpersonal skills.
- There are no mandatory requirements or standards for paralegal competence at this time.
- Both of the national paralegal associations have set standards and guidelines for paralegal competence.
- The NFPA recommends that paralegals prove their competence by passing the Paralegal Advanced Competency Exam (PACE).
- The NALA recommends that paralegals evidence their competence by passing the Certified Legal Assistant exam (CLA).

SUMMARY QUESTIONS

1. What is meant by competent representation?
2. What is meant by diligent representation?
3. Suppose a recent law school graduate has just gone into practice as a sole practitioner. She is presented with a potential divorce case, but she has no experience in marriage dissolutions and very little personal knowledge. Under what conditions can she accept the representation?
4. Explain how an attorney's or paralegal's procrastination in the practice of law can have serious consequences to the client.
5. What actions can an attorney take to remain diligent if his or her workload becomes too heavy?
6. What does zealous representation entail?
7. Mark is representing Karen in a divorce proceeding. He knows that he must do everything possible to win custody of the couple's children for his client. He feels that maybe if he could just talk to her husband, without the husband's lawyer present, he could make the husband see reason and agree to giving his client custody. Is this permissible? Why or why not?
8. Janice is taking a deposition of Rob, the driver of a car who injured her client in a personal injury suit. Although Janice has witnesses who claim they saw Rob drinking prior to the accident, Rob denies drinking, or that he was intoxicated at the time his car collided with Jan's client's car. Janice tells Rob "if you don't admit to your intoxication and your fault at the time of the accident, I am going to talk to my friend, District Attorney Samuelson, about bringing criminal DUI charges against you." Is this permissible? Why or why not?
9. What education requirements must an individual fulfill to be a competent paralegal?
10. What skills should a paralegal possess to be competent?
11. What functions do the Certified Legal Assistant and Registered Paralegal designations perform with regard to paralegal competency?

ENDNOTES

[1]People ex rel. Goldberg v. Gordon, 607 P2d 995 (Colo. 1980).

[2]Baird v. Pace, 752 P2d 507 (Ariz. 1987).

[3]Comments to Rule 1.1, ABA Model Rules of Professional Conduct.

[4]In Re Hawkins, 502 N.W.2d 770 (Minn. 1993).

[5]In Re Hogan, 490 N.E. 2d 1280 (Ill. 1986).

[6]Comment [5] to Rule 1.1 of the Model Rules of Professional Conduct.

[7]People v. Felker, 770 P.2d 402 (Colo. 1989).

[8]Muse v. St. Paul Fire and Marine Insurance Company, 328 So. 2d 698 (La. App. 1st Cir. 1976).

[9]Collas v. Garnick, 624 a.2D 120 (Pa. 1993).

[10]Smith v. Lewis, 530 P.2d 589 (Cal. 1975).

[11]Horne v. Peckham, 97 Cal.App.3d 404 (1979).

[12]ABA Standing Committee on Specialization, www.abanet.org (December 1998).

[13]Comment [6] to Rule 1.1 of ABA Model Rules of Professional Conduct.

[14]Comment [1] to Rule 1.3 of ABA Model Rules of Professional Conduct.

[15]*The Merriam Webster Dictionary,* Merriam-Webster (1995).

[16]Rule 29(a), DR 7-101, Rules of the Supreme Court.

[17]1997 National Utilization and Compensation Survey Report, National Association of Legal Assistants (1997).

[18]Ibid.

[19]Legal Assistant Today Technology Survey 1999, Legal Assistant Today, March/April 1999, p. 55.

[20]The Paralegal Partner in Progress, from the NFPA's Web site at www.paralegals.org (March 1998).

CONTINGENT FEE CONTROVERSY

In 1998, the Minneapolis law firm of Robins, Kaplan, Miller & Ciresi earned approximately $560 million for its part in the settlement of the Minnesota tobacco litigation. That same year, a group of attorneys representing Florida, Mississippi, and Texas was awarded $8.2 billion for its part in the tobacco company settlement with those states.[i] In recent years, a few select law firms have been earning contingent fees in the hundreds of millions of dollars for their representation of plaintiffs in the tobacco trials, as well as the asbestos, breast implant, and Dalcon shield cases. Several individual attorneys have received contingent fees in the tens of millions.

The huge fees earned by attorneys in high-profile civil cases have brought contingent fee representation to the attention of the media and the public. Does contingent fee representation afford access to our legal system to those who could not otherwise afford it? Or does it encourage frivolous lawsuits and unreasonable verdicts while lining the pockets of wealthy, unethical attorneys? Unfortunately, the answer is probably *both*.

When an attorney represents a client on a contingent fee basis, the attorney agrees to represent the client in a particular matter and to accept as his or her fees a percentage (usually twenty-five to fifty percent) of any amount recovered by the client. If the client recovers nothing on the action, the attorney receives no fees. Typically the client agrees to pay for any costs associated with the litigation, regardless of the outcome. Either the client can pay the expenses as the suit progresses or the attorney or law firm may finance the litigation. Contingent fees are expressly permitted under the Model Rules of Professional Conduct and the rules of ethics in most jurisdictions.

Several opponents to the use of contingent fees in civil litigation have voiced their concerns that contingent fee arrangements are unfair and unjustly enrich a few unscrupulous lawyers. They suggest that much of the mass tort litigation is actually motivated by huge legal fees, rather than the compensation of injured plaintiffs. They believe contingent fee arrangements encourage lawsuits without merit and increase the volume of litigation in this country, causing the public a hardship in the form of increased insurance premiums, higher medical costs, increased prices on certain products, and overloaded court systems.

Proponents of the contingent fee arrangement point out that it provides access to the courts by individuals who may not otherwise be able to hire an attorney and finance a lawsuit, even when they have a just claim. In fact, clients who hire attorneys on a contingent fee basis often have very valid cases involving wrongful death and injuries, product liability, unlawful terminations, and sexual harassment. Many of these individuals would never get their day in court—or even be taken seriously by the wrongdoer in the case— if not for the contingency fee arrangement. As stated in the comments to the Model Rules, and EC 2-20 of the Model Code, "Contingency fee arrangements . . . often . . . provide the only practical means by which [one party] can economically afford, finance, and obtain the services of a competent lawyer . . . and successful prosecution of the claim produces a res out of which the fee can be paid."

Recent publicity has fueled a movement in several states to legislate limits on attorneys' fees and the use of contingent fee agreements. Many proposals have been brought forth for dealing with the perceived problem. Probably the most common method of doing so is to put a cap on the percentage of recovery that attorneys can collect as their fee. This has been done in many states, especially with regard to medical malpractice cases. Opponents to much of the proposed legislation claim that it would give attorneys an incentive to settle cases as early as possible. They claim that the reduced attorney's fees that would be allowed would not be enough to cover an attorney's expenses to take a case all the way through trial. The result under this scenario would be that the proposed legislation may unclog the courts, but that plaintiffs would not get a fair settlement of their cases.

Other legislation attempts to mandate compensation of attorneys based on the amount of time they spend on a case and the value they add to the client's outcome. For example, a case that is settled within a short time period would result in a lesser percentage of the settlement being paid to the attorney than if the case were to go to trial. Opponents to this type of legislation claim that it would, in fact, cause a conflict of interest for the attorney, who may be better off not encouraging an early settlement of the case for his client. The end result could be an increase in the number of cases that go to trial.

Many members of the bar are in favor of self-regulation. They point out that Model Rule 1.5 provides that legal fees should be *reasonable,* and attorneys should not charge in excess of what is considered to be a reasonable fee. They believe that any contingent fee charged should take into consideration the amount of time and effort expended by the attorney, the risk taken by the attorney, and the benefit to the client. The attorney has an ethical duty to discuss the contingent fee arrangement in detail with the client and estimate the amount of risk and time the attorney will take. This full disclosure should give clients a better bargaining position before entering into a contingent fee agreement.

Part of the problem, of course, with mandating reasonable contingent fees is defining *reasonable.* For example, in the Minnesota tobacco trial, the attorneys agreed to a contingency fee of approximately seven percent of the settlement gained for their client. Even though the firm had financed approximately four million dollars in costs during the trial, expended thousands of hours in attorney and paralegal time, and assumed monumental risk, the firm agreed to reduce their agreed-upon twenty-five percent contingency fee to seven percent as part of the settlement package. The result of this *reasonable* fee was $560 million for the 60-partner law firm.

---

[i] Meier, Barry, and Richard A. Oppel, Jr., States' Big Suits Against Industry Bring Battle on Contingent Fees, *New York Times,* October 15, 1999.

Chapter 6

The Ethics of Legal Fees and Financial Matters

*Any business arrangement that is not profitable
to the other person will in the end prove unprofitable
for you. The bargain that yields mutual satisfaction
is the only one that is apt to be repeated.*

B. C. Forbes

An Ethical Dilemma
Introduction
Client Trust Accounts
   Funds that Must Be Held in Trust
   IOLTA Accounts
   Client Trust Accounts
   Required Recordkeeping
   Commingling of Funds
   Misappropriation of Client Funds
Legal Fees and Billing
   Reasonable Fees
      Time and Labor
      Preclusion from Other Employment
      Customary Fee
      Results Obtained
      Time Limitations
      Nature and Length of the Professional Relationship
      Experience, Reputation, and Ability of the Attorney
      Contingent Fees

Payment of Fees
   General Retainer
   Special Retainer
   Flat Fee
Contingent Fees
   Impermissible Contingent Fees
Fee Agreements
Fee Disputes
Division of Fees with Others
Case and Discussion
From the Paralegal's Perspective
Trust Accounting
A Question of Ethics
Paralegals and Billing
Paralegal Fee Recoverability
   Recent Case Law Concerning Legal Fees for Paralegals
Fee Splitting with Attorneys
Case and Discussion

Chapter Summary

Summary Questions

An Ethical Dilemma

Jim Robertson is a sole practitioner with a general practice focusing on family law and personal injury, and he has a problem. As a newer attorney with a recently established practice, his cash flow is somewhat irregular. Today is payday for the three individuals on his staff and he has just learned that there is not enough cash in the business account to cover payroll. He can go to the bank for another short-term loan, but he is afraid that they may lose confidence in him. He could ask his staff to wait for a few days, but he doesn't believe that's fair to them and he doesn't want them to worry about their jobs.

Business is not all that bad for Mr. Robertson. He is expecting a very large settlement on one of his personal injury cases next week, of which he will receive one third as a contingency fee. In addition, he has over $20,000 in advance fees in the client trust account for fees he will be earning on family law matters. . . . Robertson gets an idea—surely he could borrow the $5,000 from the client trust account necessary to make payroll and pay it back after the personal injury settlement next week. The money in the trust account will eventually be paid to the firm for fees, anyway. It would not be stealing; it would just be a loan. Is there a problem with Robertson's solution?

Answer and Discussion: Yes, definitely! The money in the trust account belongs to Mr. Robertson's clients and must not be used for his personal or business expenses. Mr. Robertson is acting as a fiduciary in safeguarding the funds in the client trust account, and to remove any of that money before it is earned and properly accounted for is considered a misappropriation of funds and can be grounds for attorney disciplinary action—possibly even disbarment.

INTRODUCTION

Fiduciary duty
A duty to act for someone else's benefit, while subordinating one's personal interests to that of the other person. It is the highest standard of duty implied by the law.

Any time attorneys and clients are concerned with a mutual financial matter, attorneys must use the utmost care to follow the pertinent rules of ethics—many of which are designed to protect the client. With regard to safekeeping of a client's funds and trust accounting, the attorney has a **fiduciary duty** to the client. When it comes to assessing fees for legal services and billing clients, attorneys must deal fairly with the client—taking into consideration their unequal positions.

The rules of ethics of each state include very specific rules for financial dealings between attorneys and their clients. The rules of ethics prescribe guidelines for safekeeping a client's property, establishing reasonable fees for legal services, fee agreements, and fee-splitting arrangements. Regardless of these safeguards, a high proportion of ethical complaints against attorneys concern financial matters, either mishandling of monies held by attorneys on behalf of clients or excessive or unfair billing.

This chapter explores the rules of ethics governing financial dealings between attorneys and their clients, especially the safekeeping of client funds, requirements for client trust accounting, and fees for legal services. The second part of this chapter focuses on these same issues from the paralegal's perspectives, and takes a look at the recoverability of paralegal fees.

CLIENT TRUST ACCOUNTS

When attorneys receive money or property that belongs to clients or third parties, the attorney must act as a fiduciary for the owner of the money or property. The attorney's fiduciary duty includes confidentiality, honesty and good faith, the duty to keep the client informed with regard to any disbursements of funds, and the duty of safekeeping. Any funds that belong to the client, or in which the client has an interest, must be held in trust for the client in a specially designated client trust account. The purpose of holding money in a separate client trust account is to prevent the danger of losing a client's money when it is commingled with the money of the attorney or the law practice. As a fiduciary, the attorney has an obligation to:

1. Segregate the funds
2. Safeguard the funds
3. Notify the client (or third party owner of the funds) of any disbursement of the funds
4. Accurately keep records of the account
5. Deliver the funds to the client or appropriate third party when entitled
6. Render an accounting when asked to by the client or the third party[1]

Model Rule 1.15(a) addresses client trust accounts as follows:

Rule 1.15
Safekeeping Property
    (a) A lawyer shall hold property of clients or third persons that is in a lawyer's possession in connection with a representation separate from the lawyer's own property. Funds shall be kept in a separate account maintained in the state where the lawyer's office is situated, or elsewhere with the consent of the client or third person. Other property shall be identified as such and appropriately safeguarded. Complete records of such account funds and other property shall be kept by the lawyer and shall be preserved for a period of five years after termination of the representation.

Some of the most frequent types of complaints concerning attorneys are mishandling and mismanagement of client funds. One reason for this is that attorneys are not always aware of all the rules that must be followed. Another reason is that the prescribed trust accounting procedures are details that many attorneys do not give priority to and tend to overlook when they get busy. Inconvenience and practical problems with establishing and maintaining client trust accounts is no excuse for noncompliance for the ethical rules requiring their use. State bar associations and other legal organizations have published an abundance of information on the mechanics of properly opening and maintaining trust accounts and complying with all rules in that regard. It is the attorney's responsibility to know the rules applicable in each jurisdiction in which he or she practices and to follow those rules carefully.

Funds that Must be Held in Trust

The practice of many attorneys requires them from time to time to hold funds belonging to their clients or to third parties. Following are some examples of the types of funds that must be held in a client trust account:

1. Advance payment of legal fees and costs
2. Client funds that may be used in the event of a settlement of a lawsuit
3. Personal injury settlement checks
4. Payments of child support or alimony by a client or for the benefit of a client

5. Funds for real estate closings
6. Client funds to pay income taxes
7. Estate funds held during the probate process
8. Funds associated with merger or acquisition closings

In some jurisdictions, all fees received in advance of the work completed must be held in a client trust account. In *Iowa Supreme Court Board of Professional Ethics and Conduct v. Apland*, 577 NW2d 50 (Iowa 1998), the court held that all advance fee payments must be held in a client trust account. The court reasoned that keeping all advance fees in a client trust account (1) preserves the client's funds from the attorneys' creditors, (2) prevents possible misappropriation by the attorney, and (3) enables the client to realistically dispute the fee where the funds are already in the attorney's possession.

As the fees are earned, the client is billed and the money is transferred from the client's trust account to the attorneys' general account. Attorneys should notify clients in writing when they are disbursing money from their client trust accounts for payment of fees. The notification should include the time, amount, and purpose of the withdrawal, as well as a complete accounting of the client trust account. Courts, including the Supreme Court of Iowa, which stated its position as follows, have approved this safekeeping:

> We think such rule not only protects lawyers from potentially unethical conduct but it also protects the client's interests. We hold that lawyers accepting advance fee payments must notify their clients in writing of the time, amount, and purpose of any withdrawal of the fee together with a complete accounting. No withdrawal of any part of the fee shall occur until the lawyer has rendered some services. Suffice it to say that the prudent lawyer will reduce an advance fee payment agreement to writing, spelling out its purpose, at what intervals the lawyer may withdraw a portion of the fee, and at what intervals the lawyer will render an accounting.[2]

Part of the reason that advance fees must be held in a client trust account is to ensure that the funds are there should the client be entitled to a refund of fees. Legal fees are generally refundable to the client if the anticipated legal services are not performed or if the attorney is otherwise discharged from service.

IOLTA Accounts

IOLTA

Interest on Lawyers' Trust Accounts. Type of trust account designed for the pooling of funds of several clients when those funds individually are too small to earn significant interest. Interest earned on IOLTA accounts is donated to nonprofit organizations that work to deliver legal services to low-income individuals.

When client funds entrusted to attorneys are in a small amount to be held for a short period of time, attorneys may be required to hold the money in an IOLTA account. **IOLTA** (Interest On Lawyers Trust Account) accounts are a special type of trust account designed for the pooling of the funds of several clients when those funds individually are too small to generate the interest income required for the administrative costs associated with setting up a separate account. Attorneys pool all such funds together by depositing them in an IOLTA account, thus creating a large enough sum to earn interest. Any interest earned on IOLTA accounts is donated to nonprofit organizations that have as their primary purpose the delivery of legal services to low-income individuals. The principal in such accounts remains the property of the individual clients.

Prior to the early 1980s, small amounts of client funds that were to be held for a short time were held in non–interest-bearing accounts. In the early 1980s, federal law made interest-bearing checking, including client trust accounts, permissible. However, the fees associated with establishing separate interest-bearing client trust accounts for clients with smaller deposits were rarely covered by the minimal interest earned on the accounts. There was no net income to the client.

In the 1980s, the Florida Bar Association initiated a creative solution to this problem—the IOLTA Account (Interest on Lawyer's Trust Account). All 50 states and the District of Columbia have IOLTA programs. Use of IOLTA accounts under established guidelines is mandatory in most states. These programs generate an estimated $100 million per year in interest—which is used to provide legal services for the indigent and disadvantaged.

The future of the IOLTA account became uncertain in 1998 when the U.S. Supreme Court issued an opinion in *Phillips v. Washington Legal Fund,* 118 S.Ct. 1925 (1998), declaring that interest generated by IOLTA accounts is the property of the client. The opinion was issued in a lawsuit brought by the Washington Legal Fund, which argued that IOLTA accounts violate the First and Fifth Amendment rights of clients.

The First Amendment argument is that IOLTA accounts violate the freedoms granted under the First Amendment to the Constitution of the United States because the interest generated by the client funds may be used to promote charitable purposes not philosophically supported by the clients.

The Fifth Amendment provides that private property shall not be taken for public use without just compensation. Attorneys for the Washington Legal Fund, an advocate of personal property rights, argued that the IOLTA accounts violate the constitutional rights of clients to the ownership of the interest earned on their funds—even though there would be no interest generated if not for the IOLTA account.

The Supreme Court did not address the First Amendment issue in the *Phillips* case. In a five to four decision the court ruled only that the interest held in IOLTA accounts is the property of the client. It did not decide that the IOLTA accounts unlawfully take the property of the client without just compensation. These questions may be decided in the state courts, along with the future of the IOLTA account. The IOLTA accounts have many strong supporters, and so far the *Phillips* decision has had little practical affect on their use, although the state of Missouri did temporarily suspend use of the IOLTA accounts until the matter is finally decided.

Client Trust Accounts

Non-IOLTA client trust accounts are designed to hold larger sums of money for longer periods of time. Some non-IOLTA client trust accounts do not earn interest, or if they do, it is paid to the client. If the sum and the length of time are such that the funds could earn significant interest, the attorney may have the fiduciary responsibility to invest the funds in an interest-bearing client trust account. If this is done, the interest belongs to the client or the third party who owns the funds. For significant amounts that will be held for a significant amount of time, attorneys may set up separate bank accounts for each client. If the number of clients requiring this type of account makes this impractical, the attorney may set up one general client trust bank account and account for each client's funds, and accrued interest, separately (Figure 6-1).

Required Recordkeeping

Attorneys must keep exact and proper books and records of all funds held in trust. The code of ethics in some jurisdictions provides specific instructions for how the

IOLTA Accounts	Non-IOLTA Client Trust Accounts
• For smaller sums that do not have the potential to earn a significant amount of interest	• For larger amounts of cash
• For funds that are to be held short-term	• For funds that may be held for a significant period of time
• Interest earned on the funds held is paid to a nonprofit organization established to assist with providing legal services to the poor	• If any interest is earned, it becomes the property of the client, or the third party who owns the principal sum being held in trust

FIGURE 6-1

IOLTA Trust Accounts vs. Client Trust Accounts

funds must be accounted for and which type of records must be kept. Records must be kept in the state in which the attorney's office is located, unless otherwise agreed to by the client, and they must be kept for the prescribed number of years after the account is closed (typically five).

Commingling of Funds

The only funds that may be deposited in any type of client trust accounts are funds in which the client has an interest; attorneys may not deposit any of their own personal funds or general business funds into client trust accounts. To mix an attorney's funds with client funds so that the funds lose their individual ownership identity is considered **commingling of funds.** In some jurisdictions it is permissible for an attorney to deposit his or her own funds as necessary to pay any banking fees or administrative expenses associated with the administration of the client trust account.

Misappropriation of Client Funds

Improper use of client funds by an attorney for any unauthorized purpose is considered **misappropriation.** This includes not only **conversion,** or stealing the funds, but also unauthorized temporary use for the attorney's personal benefit. Misappropriation may occur when the attorney pays the funds of one client to another client, if the attorney keeps unearned advance fee, or if the client's funds are used for the personal purposes of the attorney.

Often, attorney disciplinary actions result not from the outright theft of client funds by an attorney, but when attorneys *borrow* client funds with the intention of repaying them at a later date. Even if the funds are fully repaid, the attorney has still misappropriated them. Courts have held that "a lawyer's subjective intent, whether it be to borrow or to steal, is irrelevant to the determination of the appropriate discipline in a misappropriation case."[3]

Misappropriation of a client's funds is a very serious breach of ethics that typically results in disbarment of the attorney and often in criminal prosecution. The need to maintain public confidence in the bar has caused the bar associations and the courts to deal quite severely with attorneys who misappropriate client funds. As stated by the District of Columbia Court of Appeals, "in virtually all cases of misappropriation, disbarment will be the only appropriate sanction unless it appears that the misconduct resulted from nothing more than simple negligence."[4]

LEGAL FEES AND BILLING

Attorneys have an ethical duty to bill their clients fairly and receive no excessive or unfair payment from their clients. They must not use coercion to extract or increase fees at any point during the representation.

When attorneys contract with their clients, they bear the burden of showing the utmost good faith and complete disclosure on their part, and the full understanding of all the facts and their legal consequences on the clients' part, as well as the demonstrable fairness of the agreement reached.[5] There is a decided inequality in bargaining positions between the attorney and the client (who may be unaware of his or her legal rights) that must be taken into consideration by attorneys when negotiating legal fees. Attorneys owe their clients the "obligation to deal fairly and in good faith when negotiating a fee when ultimately charging and collecting the fee."[6]

Commingling of funds
Act of an attorney or other fiduciary in mingling funds of the client or owner of the funds with his or her own funds so that the funds lose their individual ownership identity.

Misappropriation
The application of another's property or money dishonestly to one's own use. (Black's Law Dictionary, Seventh Edition)

Conversion
Wrongful control over the property of another that violates the owner's title to, or rights in, the property.

Reasonable Fees

Attorneys' fees must be reasonable. Several factors are considered when determining the reasonableness of attorneys' fees, including the time and labor involved, the difficulty of the questions involved, and the skill required to perfor
the legal service properly. Reasonableness also depends on the fee customari
charged in the locality for similar legal services, the time limitations imposed on
the attorney, and several other matters set forth in Rule 1.5 of the Rules of Professional Responsibility (Figure 6-2).

Time and Labor.   One of the more important factors in determining the reasonableness of attorneys' fee is the time and labor required of the attorney and
the attorneys' firm. The time and labor will depend, in large part, on the novelty
and difficulty of the question at hand. For example, if a client raises a legal issue
that the attorney, and possibly even the courts, have never addressed before, it
will take much more time, and more highly skilled time, than the pursuit of a
routine legal matter similar to that handled by the attorney before.

The level of skill required to perform the legal services also determines the
reasonableness of the fees charged. For example, the level of skill required to draft
a simple will is much less than that required to draft a will that includes trusts and
more complex situations. An attorney can delegate the drafting of a simple will to
a paralegal, who will prepare the document based on the client's personal facts
and available forms. The attorney will then review the completed document. To
draft a will with trusts involved requires a higher level of skill to advise the client
on complex tax matters, to draft the trusts precisely within the wills, and to
choose the correct format to fit the client's particular desires. Much more attorney involvement and possibly some legal research will be required. It is reasonable to charge a higher fee for work requiring a higher level of skill.

Preclusion from Other Employment.   Whether an attorney's representation of a client precludes the attorney from accepting other employment will
have an impact on the reasonableness of the fee charged. At times, an attorney
may be presented with a legal matter or representation that will preclude him or
her from accepting other employment. When this is the case, it is reasonable that
the attorney be fairly compensated for foregoing other representations.

Customary Fee.   When the reasonableness of a fee is considered, it will be
taken into account what fee is typically charged for a similar matter in the locality

---

Model Rules 1.5(a)
  (a) A lawyer's fee shall be reasonable. The factors to be considered in determining the rea-
      sonableness of a fee include the following:
      (1) the time and labor required, the novelty and difficulty of the questions involved, and
          the skill requisite to perform the legal service properly;
      (2) the likelihood, if apparent to the client, that the acceptance of the particular employ-
          ment will preclude other employment by the lawyer;
      (3) the fee customarily charged in the locality for similar legal services;
      (4) the amount involved and the results obtained;
      (5) the time limitations imposed by the client or the circumstances
      (6) the nature and length of the professional relationship with the client;
      (7) the experience, reputation, and ability of the lawyer or lawyers performing the ser-
          vices; and
      (8) whether the fee is fixed or contingent

FIGURE 6-2

Model Rule 1.5(A):
Reasonableness Of Attorneys'
Fees

for similar services. Fees vary from region to region, and attorneys are allowed to bill whatever is customary within their areas.

Results Obtained. When an attorney achieves exemplary results for a client, this can be taken into consideration when determining the reasonableness of the fee. For example, the recent tobacco litigation in Minnesota earned one Minnesota law firm in excess of $500 million. While this may seem to be an outrageous sum, taking into consideration the time and resources spent by the firm, the risk taken on the case, and the fact that the firm won over $6 billion for its clients, many believed it was reasonable, and the fee was awarded. This was a contingent fee of approximately seven percent of the award (compared with the customary twenty-five to fifty percent).

Although a higher rate of attorney's fees may be reasonable when the attorney is able to reach beneficial results for the client, the attorney may not justify a higher fee just because the client has the ability to pay it. Courts have found that "A client's ability to pay cannot justify a charge in excess of the value of that service."[7]

Time Limitations. The time limitations placed on legal services by a client can have an effect on the reasonableness of the attorneys' fees. For example, suppose the president of a corporation presents her attorney with a proposed multimillion dollar merger in November and declares that she wants it to be a *done deal* by the end of the year. Such a request would mean that the attorney may have to hire additional help, put other matters on hold, and work days, nights, and weekends to get the transaction completed on time. It would be reasonable for the attorney to charge above-average fees under these strict time constraints.

Nature and Length of the Professional Relationship. The nature and length of the professional relationship between the attorney and client can also have a bearing on the reasonableness of the attorneys' fees. For example, compare the representation of an established corporate client in a civil suit with the one-time representation of an out-of-town corporation. When it comes to representing the established client, the law firm may already have pertinent corporate documents on hand. The attorneys and law firm staff will know who to contact at the corporation for the information they need, and they will have established procedures for coordinating litigation. In representing the out-of-town corporation, a significant amount of time may be spent just getting to know the corporation, the pertinent individuals at the corporation, and how to approach the situation. Much more time will be spent transporting documentation and information between the corporation and the law firm and communicating with the new client. It is reasonable that the law firm should charge the out-of-town corporation more than the established client for similar representation.

Experience, Reputation, and Ability of the Attorney. It is reasonable for experienced attorneys with an excellent reputation to expect more for their time than newer attorneys of lesser ability.

Contingent Fees. A **contingent fee** that calculates to more than the attorney's usual per hour rate is usually considered reasonable because the attorney is taking a risk that the client will not collect anything, and thereby the attorney will not get paid. In addition, attorneys working on a contingent basis may be required to put in a significant amount of time before they ever see any fee from their clients.

A contingent fee may be found to be unreasonable in the event that a relatively small amount of work is done on the case or if the case does not involve any

Contingent fee
A fee charged for a lawyer's services only if the lawsuit is successful or is favorably settled out of court. Contingent fees are usually calculated as a percentage of the client's net recovery (such as 25% of the recovery if the case is settled, and 33% if the case is won at trial). Also termed contingency fee, contingency. (Black's Law Dictionary, Seventh Edition)

real risk to the attorney. It may also be found to be unreasonable if it is grossly disproportionate to the fees charged by other attorneys in the area.[8]

Payment of Fees

There are numerous options available for the payment of legal fees, including flat fee, contingent fee, and general and special retainers. The method of payment chosen will depend on several circumstances, including the type of services rendered, the past relationship between the attorney and the client, the financial circumstances of the client, and the estimated length of time the rendering of the services will take.

Perhaps the most important aspect of the payment of fees is that there is a clear understanding between the attorney and the client as to how fees will be billed, how payment will be made, what services will be rendered for the fees, which costs and expenses incurred during the representation will be included in the fee, and which will be billed additionally. This agreement should be in writing. As the legal work for the client proceeds, often one or more of the agreed-upon circumstances will change. Any changes in expected billing, payment, or expected services rendered should be discussed and further agreed upon in writing between the attorney and the client, and this should be discussed from the outset of the relationship.

General Retainer.

When a client hires an attorney to represent him or her, the client is said to have retained the attorney. A **general retainer** refers to the situation in which a client hires an attorney for a specific length of time, rather than for a specific project. During the time the attorney is under general retainer, the attorney may not accept any representation that may be contrary to the interests of the client who has retained the attorney. The attorney agrees to make legal services available to the client during the general retainer period. The attorney may bill additional amounts for special projects taken on during the general retainer term, per agreement with the client. The general retainer is not considered advance payment; rather it is considered to be earned when paid.

For example, a corporation may have a law firm on general retainer on an annual basis to answer general legal questions that arise during the year. The officers and managers of the corporation would be free to call their attorneys during the year with legal questions without worrying about additional legal expenses. However, if the corporation becomes involved in a significant lawsuit during the year, the corporation would enter into another agreement with the law firm for representation on this particular matter. An additional agreement regarding payment of fees for this lawsuit would have to be entered into.

Special Retainer.

A special retainer refers to employment of an attorney for a specific case or legal project. For example, when a client and attorney enter into an agreement whereby the attorney agrees to represent a client in a divorce proceeding, regardless of the arrangements that are made for payment of the attorneys' fees, the attorney is on a special retainer.

A special retainer is a prepayment to the attorney prior to performance of the legal services. In most circumstances, the special retainer must be retained in trust for the client until the fees are earned. If the representation ends before the attorney earns the entire special retainer, a refund of the unearned fee must be made to the client. Nonrefundable fee agreements, which allow an attorney to keep an advance payment whether or not the agreed-upon services are performed, are considered in most instances to be unethical because they interfere with the client's right to terminate his or her agreement with the attorney at will.

General retainer
Fee paid to an attorney or law firm to retain their services for a specific amount of time. During that time period, the attorney and law firm may not accept any conflicting employment.

Flat Fee. Attorneys can be hired to perform certain legal services on a flat fee basis. This means that the client will not be billed by hour, but rather by the service performed regardless of the time it takes. Bankruptcy proceedings, simple wills, and divorces are services that are often performed on a flat-fee basis. For example, attorneys who specialize in estate planning may tell clients at the first meeting that they will prepare simple wills for $250. The $250 will include all of their services rendered in connection with the will.

Contingent Fees

Contingent fees arrangements, whereby the attorney will receive a portion of the settlement obtained on behalf of the client, are usually considered to be reasonable and ethical (Figure 6-3). Contingent fee arrangements allow individuals to retain attorneys without having to invest heavily in attorneys' fees before they collect anything. Contingent fee arrangements may offer access to the legal system to those who may otherwise not be able to afford it.

The attorneys of *Law Firm* hereby agree to act as your counsel to represent you in connection with all claims for compensation and damages relating to the personal injuries received from the automobile accident which occurred on July 20, 2000.

Client hereby agrees to pay compensation to *Law Firm* for legal services as follows:

1. In the event of recovery of any sums of money on my *(Client's)* claims by way of settlement prior to institution of legal proceedings in a Court of Law, *Law Firm* shall receive 25% of the gross sum recovered as its fee.
2. In the event of recovery at any time after legal proceedings have been instituted with the court, *Law Firm* shall receive 30% of all gross sums recovered as its fee.
3. In the event of recovery at any time after an appeal to a higher court, *Law Firm* shall receive 35% of all gross sums recovered as its fee.

Law Firm agrees to advance all necessary and reasonable costs for preparing and presenting any claim or litigation covered by this agreement. A statement for costs advanced by the law firm on client's behalf will be submitted to client periodically, and *Client* agrees to pay the same out of the proceeds of *Client's* share of any recovery in this matter. If *Client* recovers nothing in this matter, or does not recover an amount sufficient to pay the costs and expenses incurred by *Law Firm* on its behalf, *Client* understands and agrees that he shall still be liable for the payment of said costs and expenses within 30 days of receipt of the final bill for said costs and expenses.

Costs and expenses for which *Client* will be responsible may include, but are not limited to:

- Filing fees
- Expert fees
- Expert witness fees
- Investigators
- Court reporters and deposition costs
- Long-distance telephone calls
- Computerized research costs
- Travel

We have read and discussed the foregoing agreement on this _____ day of February, 2001, and agree to the terms therein.

LAW FIRM

By:_____

Client

_____

FIGURE 6-3

Contingency Fee Retainer Agreement

A contingent fee of twenty-five to fifty percent of the total amount collected on behalf of the client is customary. The drawback to attorneys accepting representation on a contingent fee basis is that if the attorney collects nothing for the client, the attorney receives no compensation for his or her time.

Contingent fee arrangements must be fully explained to the client and contingent fee agreements should be made in writing.

Impermissible Contingent Fees. Subsection (d) of Rule 1.5 of the Model Rules of Professional Conduct and provisions of the codes of ethics of most states prohibit contingent fee arrangements based on securing a divorce or upon the amount of alimony, support, or property settlement in a domestic relations case. Subsection (d) also prohibits attorneys from charging a contingent fee in a criminal matter. Contingent fees in domestic relations cases are prohibited because they may discourage reconciliation between divorcing parties. Contingent fees are prohibited in criminal matters because they cause a potential conflict of interest for the attorney who may not get paid if his or her client makes a plea bargain or accepts some other type of arrangement that may be in the client's best interest.

FEE AGREEMENTS

Whenever an attorney takes on a new representation of a client, the attorney must discuss the new fee arrangement with the client and obtain the client's agreement for payment—preferably in writing.

Model Rule 1.5(b) provides that "when the lawyer has not regularly represented the client, the basis or rate of the fee shall be communicated to the client, preferably in writing, before or within a reasonable time after commencing the representation."

New clients should have the firm's billing procedures clearly explained to them. They should understand whether they will be billed on an hourly basis, a flat fee, or a contingent fee basis. If the client will be billed on an hourly basis, the attorney should explain to the client the billing rates of various individuals who will be working on the client's file, including paralegals. In addition, it should be clearly communicated to the client that there may be additional charges for reimbursement to the firm for expenses incurred by the firm during the course of the representation.

New clients are typically asked to enter into a written fee agreement that includes information discussed concerning the basis for the billing and the client's obligation to pay. A written fee agreement reduces the likelihood of a misunderstanding that could lead to a dispute concerning fees (Figure 6-4).

FEE DISPUTES

Unfortunately, at times disputes concerning attorneys' fees lead to court actions. Most often these are actions brought by the attorney to enforce payment of fees. If the client has not paid a bill for legal fees, it may be because the client believes the fees were unreasonable. The courts have the final authority to approve attorneys' fees. As a part of their inherent authority to regulate the practice of law, the court has the power to decide on the reasonableness of attorneys' fees, even if the attorney and client have entered into a written fee agreement.

Often fee disputes arise when the client believes that he or she has not received the services being billed. The attorney must be able to prove that the proper, competent services were rendered, resulting in a reasonable fee. An

Contract to Employ Law Firm

I, Grace Martin, of 123 Main Street, Hometown, California, referred to in this agreement as client, agree to retain Stein & Jones Law Firm, of Hometown, California, referred to in this agreement as the firm, in connection with the dissolution of my marriage to James Martin and all matters related thereto.

Section One: Initial Retainer

The firm acknowledges receipt of Five Hundred Dollars ($500.00) as an initial retainer in this matter and, in consideration of that payment, agrees to provide legal service in connection with this matter. The initial retainer paid shall be applied against actual legal services performed for the client and for costs and expenses incurred.

Section Two: Hourly Rates

The client and the firm agree that the retainer paid by client shall be applied against the legal services actually performed for the client by the firm, which services shall be charged at the following standard hourly rates:

(1) Partners: $160–$180 Dollars.
(2) Associates: $125–$140 Dollars.
(3) Paralegal: $45–$80 Dollars.

Section Three: Final Bill

The client and the firm agree that the final bill to be rendered by the firm shall, in addition to reflecting the time expended, take into account any factors prescribed by the State Bar of the State of California to be considered as guides when determining the reasonableness of fees for legal services, such as the following:

(1) The time and labor required, the novelty and difficulty of the questions involved, and the skill requisite to perform the legal service properly.
(2) The fee customarily charged in the locality for similar legal services.
(3) The amount involved and the results obtained.
(4) The time limitations imposed by the client or by the circumstances.
(5) The nature and length of the professional relationship with the client.
(6) The experience, reputation, and ability of the lawyer or lawyers performing the services.

Section Four: Interim Billings

Interim billings may be submitted to the client from time to time in the event the time charges of the firm exceed the initial retainer. All interim billings shall be due and payable on receipt unless otherwise stated. Failure to pay interim billings promptly will permit the firm after notice to the client to terminate its representation of the client. It is understood that the hourly time charges include but are not limited to: court appearances; telephone conferences; office conferences; legal research; depositions; review of file materials and documents sent or received; preparation for trials, hearings, and conferences; drafting of pleadings or instruments; and office memoranda and correspondence.

Section Five: Out-of-Pocket Disbursements

The client agrees to assume and pay for all out-of-pocket disbursements incurred in connection with this matter. These shall include filing fees, witness fees, travel, sheriff's and constable's fees, expenses of depositions, investigative expenses, and other incidental expenses. The firm agrees to obtain the client's prior approval before incurring any disbursement in excess of One Hundred Dollars ($100.00).

Section Six: Refund to Client

In the even that, upon either the completion of the matter or the termination of the firm's representation of the client, the total cost of the legal services performed by the firm shall be less than the amount of any retainer paid by the client, the balance shall be refunded to the client by the firm.

Section Seven: Miscellaneous

In some cases, the court awards counsel fees to one party and orders the other party to pay the amount awarded. This is solely in the discretion of the court and cannot be relied on with certainty. Also, in some cases if there is a settlement agreed to by both parties to avoid a contested trial, the settlement agreement may provide that one of the parties will contribute an agreed amount toward the other party's legal expenses. In the initial stages of a case it is impossible to predict whether either of the above situations will materialize, and therefore no representation is made in this agreement that any contribution by the other party will be obtained toward the client's legal expenses. In the event, however, that one of such contributions is obtained for the benefit of the client, the amount in question will be credited against the firm's final bill to the client.

Dated: _____

Client:

_____
Grace Martin

STEIN & JONES LAW FIRM

By: _____
William Stein

FIGURE 6-4
Sample Fee Agreement

attorney will not be allowed to recover fees if the attorney demonstrated incompetence, negligence, or divided loyalty toward the client.

An attorney will be barred from collecting his or her fee if:

1. The attorney fails to represent the client with undivided fidelity.
2. The attorney's negligence or incompetence adversely affects the client.
3. The attorney represents parties with opposing interests and conceals that fact from those parties.
4. The attorney prematurely abandons a client's cause and has no justification for doing so.
5. The attorney's responsibilities under contract with the client are not met.
6. The attorney's agreement with the client for representation is induced by fraud or undue influence.

DIVISION OF FEES WITH OTHERS

Referral fees and agreements between attorneys to share fees are usually acceptable, so long as the client is fully informed (and agrees to the arrangement), and so long as the particular agreement is permitted by the rules of ethics in the pertinent jurisdiction.

Failure to fully inform the client, and obtain the client's approval, concerning a proposed fee-splitting agreement can cause the agreement to fail. According to the Supreme Court of Minnesota,

> Each client has a right to choose the attorney that he/she prefers and to be knowledgeable about the specifics of his/her case, especially those terms regarding the payment of fees. To allow attorneys to proceed with fee-splitting arrangements without the client's written agreement or knowledge would put the client at a severe disadvantage in the lawyer-client relationship.[9]

Attorneys are prohibited from sharing fees with nonlawyers (except under special circumstances) and forming a partnership with a nonlawyer if any of the partnership's activities include the practice of law. The intention of these rules is to protect the attorney's professional independence of judgment. The concern of the drafters of these rules is that if attorneys share fees with nonlawyers, there is the risk that the attorney's actions will be controlled by the nonlawyer, who may place his or her interests before the interests of the client.

Rule 5.4(c) of the Model Rules states that a lawyer shall not let a person who recommends, employs, or pays the lawyer to render legal services for another to direct or regulate the lawyer's professional judgment in rendering legal services.

Rule 5.4(a) prohibits lawyers or a law firm from sharing fees with nonlawyers, except under the following conditions:

1. Payments may be made over a reasonable period of time, pursuant to agreement, to the estate or one or more specified individuals after an attorney's death. For example, attorneys who form a partnership may include in their agreement that the spouse, children, or estate of a partner who dies while the partnership is still active, may receive the partners' share of income for a period of two years, or until the partnership is dissolved.
2. An attorney who purchases the practice of a deceased, disabled, or disappeared lawyer may pay the estate or other representative of that lawyer the agreed-upon price.
3. Nonlawyers may participate in a compensation or retirement plan of a lawyer or law firm, even if that plan is based in whole or in part on a profit-sharing basis. For example, a law firm may make contributions to a retirement plan based on a formula that equals ten percent of the gross profits of the law firm per year, even though a portion of that amount will be received by nonlawyers.

Moral turpitude
Conduct that is contrary to justice, honesty, or morality. In the area of legal ethics, offenses involving moral turpitude-such as fraud or breach of trust-traditionally make a person unfit to practice law. Also termed moral depravity. (Black's Law Dictionary, Seventh Edition)

Mitigating circumstances
A fact or situation that does not justify or excuse a wrongful act or offense but that reduces the degree of culpability and thus may reduce the damages (in a civil case) or the punishment (in a criminal case). (Black's Law Dictionary, Seventh Edition)

The rule against sharing fees with nonlawyers is currently under scrutiny by the legal community. The complexities of doing business in the twenty-first century have led many to believe that it is time to change the rule. For example, individuals who need advice with both financial and legal matters are often forced to consult with two unrelated firms—a law firm and an accounting firm. Many point out the advantages that allowing multidisciplinary practice could offer to clients, who could have all of their financial, tax, accounting, and legal services met by a coordinated group of professionals.

A growing number of professional service firms, such as large accounting firms, have several attorneys on staff and offer services traditionally offered only by law firms. The ABA Commission on Multidisciplinary Practice is studying the extent to which professional service firms operated by nonlawyers are providing legal services to the public, and the advisability of changing the rules to allow for partnerships and fee sharing between attorneys and professionals from different disciplines.

CASE AND DISCUSSION

In the following disciplinary proceeding, the Supreme Court of California found the petitioner had broken several of the rules of ethics examined so far in this text, including the rule against commingling funds and the rule against fee splitting with nonattorneys.

Franklin Bell GASSMAN, Petitioner,
v.
The STATE BAR of California, Respondent.
L.A. 30582.
Supreme Court of California.
Sept. 24, 1976.

BY THE COURT.

We review a recommendation of the Disciplinary Board (the Board) of the State Bar that petitioner be suspended from the practice of law for two years on conditions of probation, including actual suspension for the first six months.

Petitioner was admitted to practice in 1962 and has no prior disciplinary record. He was charged with the violation of his oath and duties as an attorney . . . , the willful violation of rule 9 of the Rules of Professional Conduct of the State Bar (present rule 8–101, commingling of clients' funds), and the commission of acts involving **moral turpitude** and dishonesty. . . .

This proceeding is based upon a series of events following the death of Violet Powaukee, who was killed in an automobile accident and survived by her three minor children. In January 1971, petitioner was retained by Judy Jones, Mrs. Powaukee's sister, to probate the Powaukee estate. Although petitioner filed for and obtained letters of administration, and published a notice to creditors, thereafter he took no further action in the estate. . . . In a related matter, petitioner had also been retained by Tillie Mericle, the children's grandmother, to establish a guardianship for the minors. Once again, although he filed for and obtained letters of guardianship, and a support allowance for the minors, petitioner thereafter neglected to file either the requisite inventory or accounting.

Petitioner was also retained to prosecute a civil action against the driver of the other vehicle on behalf of the estate and the two Powaukee children injured in the collision. The action was settled in favor of the estate for $15,000, and in favor of the chil-

dren for $13,500. The estate's settlement check was given to petitioner in August 1971, and was deposited in a commercial account in petitioner's sole name at Security Pacific National Bank. Thereafter, from time to time, these funds were used for the payment of his own office expenses.

Between July 1970 and February 1973, petitioner employed Walter Graham as secretary, bookkeeper, and paralegal assistant. Graham was compensated by receiving 20 percent of petitioner's legal fee in those cases in which Graham participated. Many of the checks drawn on the above-mentioned commercial account were signed by Graham using petitioner's signature without authorization; four such checks were rejected for insufficient funds.

Based on the foregoing evidence, the Board found that petitioner willfully failed to establish and maintain the Security Pacific account as a client trust account and failed to maintain in a separate client's trust account the client's portion of the $15,000 settlement received for the estate; that petitioner knowingly delegated to Graham, without adequate supervision, the responsibility of maintaining a client trust account, . . . ; that petitioner willfully abandoned his client, Judy Jones, with regard to action required to be taken in the estate of Violet Powaukee, deceased; . . . ; that petitioner willfully abandoned his client, Tillie Mericle, with regard to the action required to be taken in the guardianship of the Powaukee children; and that petitioner engaged in an illegal fee-splitting agreement relating to fees earned from legal work done with Walter Graham, a person not admitted to the State Bar.

Petitioner contends that the evidence is insufficient to sustain the findings that he acted willfully with respect to the above matters, and that the discipline recommended by the Board is excessive; it is petitioner's position that this court should impose the lesser discipline recommended by the local committee. . . .

Petitioner finally contends that the Board's recommendation of six months' actual suspension is excessive and that the local committee's one-month actual suspension recommendation is '. . . more than adequate to serve the ends of justice. . . .' Six months' actual suspension for the various acts of misconduct involved in the present case, including a willful violation of rule 9, is clearly not excessive and, indeed, as we explain below, is inadequate in the light of our prior holdings that a willful violation of rule 9 alone warrants a maximum of three years' suspension.[10]

The record here reveals an attorney who has failed to render adequate services to a number of related clients, in a number of separate proceedings, for a period of over four years. During this time, petitioner mismanaged thousands of dollars of his clients' funds. Some of his clients' monies inured to petitioner's benefit, in that the Security Pacific account was used to pay a portion of petitioner's office expenses.

While such trust fund mismanagement is a very serious offense by itself, the record demonstrates further areas of petitioner's misconduct, including failure to provide promised legal services and making false representations to his clients. Finally petitioner admits his participation in an illegal fee-splitting agreement with nonattorney Graham.

We have imposed severe discipline in prior cases where, as here, an attorney's failure to render services is combined with misrepresentation and failure to communicate with the client. . . . Moreover, prior cases involving similar offenses (commingling clients' funds and committing acts involving moral turpitude in violation of attorney's oath and duties) by attorneys with no previous disciplinary record suggest that as much as one-year actual suspension is an appropriate sanction.[11]

Furthermore, we note that despite petitioner's motive in so doing, his participation in an illegal fee-splitting arrangement with Graham posed serious danger to the best interests of his clients, and warrants discipline in and of itself. 'Prohibited fee-splitting between lawyer and layman . . . poses the possibility of control by the lay person, interested in his own profit rather than the client's fate" . . . That very possibility has been realized here.

Petitioner asks us to consider, in mitigation, the serious emotional stress under which he was laboring from early 1971 to mid-1972 due to marital problems, child custody battles, and the sudden death of a close friend and former partner. While serious personal problems may be considered in mitigation . . . , petitioner's difficulties provide no explanation for his continued serious misconduct over a three-year period after his substantial recovery from any emotional problems in mid-1972.

After careful consideration of all the **mitigating circumstances** invoked by petitioner, we conclude that the recommended discipline of six months' actual suspension is inadequate. It is ordered that petitioner be suspended from the practice of law for two years with execution stayed and petitioner placed on probation for that period upon the conditions of probation recommended by the Board, except that the period of actual suspension be one year, and that he pass the Professional Responsibility Examination within one year after the effective date of this order. . . .

FROM THE PARALEGAL'S PERSPECTIVE

Attorneys have the ultimate ethical responsibility for most financial matters, including billing and handling client funds. This does not mean, however, that the paralegal profession does not affect, or is unaffected by, the ethical rules concerning billing and other financial matters. Quite the opposite is true. Because clients are generally billed for the time paralegals spend working on their files, paralegals must be familiar with the rules of ethics concerning billing and fee splitting. In addition, because paralegals are often responsible for the bookkeeping and recordkeeping associated with accounting for client funds, it is imperative that they are familiar with the ethical rules applicable to attorneys concerning client funds, as well as the rules for bookkeeping and record keeping of client funds.

TRUST ACCOUNTING

Paralegals are often responsible for trust accounting functions. As a paralegal, you may find that your work on probate, real estate, personal injury, or other types of files requires you to set up and maintain trust accounts to hold and distribute funds on behalf of clients. For example, if you are working on a probate file, distributions from the estate may be run through a trust account.

Any attorney who delegates work involving trust accounting to you will have the ultimate responsibility for the funds and for overseeing the proper accounting of the funds. An attorney's duty to preserve clients' funds is nondelegable. However, as a paralegal, you must be aware of the ethical rules for handling client funds. You can help ensure that the responsible attorney complies with ethical rules concerning supervision by providing periodic reports concerning any trust accounting matters to the responsible attorney and by having all books readily accessible to him or her (Figure 6-5).

Following is a sample ledger that may be used to account for client trust funds.

Transaction Date	Client Name and Number	Activity (Deposit or Withdrawal)	Source of Deposit or Payee	Purpose	Amount	Balance

FIGURE 6-5
Client Trust Account Ledger

Some of the tasks that you may be assigned with regard to client trust accounts include:

1. Notifying clients of any disbursements or withdrawals from the trust accounts
2. Preparing statements of the accounts for clients, to be approved by the supervising attorney
3. Reconciling monthly bank statements to trust account registers and calculating interest

A Question of Ethics

Paola Sanchez is a legal immigrant from Monterey, Mexico. She has been in the United States most of her life and is married to a U.S. citizen. Paola is a paralegal for a Houston, Texas, law firm that specializes in immigration law. Paola's paralegal education, dedication, and her ability to speak both English and Spanish fluently have made her a real asset to the firm. Recently, Paola's cousin Maria immigrated to the United States from Mexico. Paola's law firm assisted Maria with her immigration and all her related legal needs. Paola was proud of the fine job her law firm did for her cousin and that she was able to bring some business to her law firm. Paola personally thanked one of the partners of the firm for helping her cousin. He responded by saying that it was a pleasure and that if she had any other friends or relatives who were in need of immigration assistance, the firm would give Paola a bonus of 10% of the fees the firm earns for each client she brings in to the firm. Paola is excited about the prospect—not only could she help certain of her relatives, but she can earn a substantial bonus on a continuing basis. Is there a problem here?

Answer and Discussion: Yes, definitely. It is unethical for attorneys to share legal fees with nonattorneys. Although it may seem harmless for paralegals to be paid on a commission basis, or to receive bonuses based on client fees received, both situations are considered to be fee-splitting and are prohibited by the rules of ethics. If you are in a situation where your employer offers to pay you on such a basis, you must make sure that it is permissible under the rules of ethics in the jurisdiction in which you are working.

4. Keeping trust account journal current
5. Preparing deposits and writing checks from account (for attorney's signature)

PARALEGALS AND BILLING

If you are a traditional paralegal working for a law firm, chances are your employer will bill clients based on time spent by attorneys and paralegals on each client's file. Attorneys and paralegals have set billing rates, and clients are billed accordingly. Billing rates are usually based on the market, the paralegal's experience, and level of expertise. One recent survey indicated that the average top paralegal billing rate charged by law firms was $105 per hour, and the average low paralegal billing rate was $58.[12] However, newer paralegals who are performing more routine work with less responsibility may see their time billed for as low as $25, while very experienced paralegals, with a high level of expertise in a certain area, may find their time billed as high as $250. It is very important to a law firm's bottom line that every individual with billing authority, including paralegals, closely track their **billable hours** and meet their set requirements for annual billable hours.

It will be the ethical responsibility of the attorneys in your firm to determine a fair and reasonable amount to bill each client, based on several factors, including your time spent on the file. It will be your ethical responsibility to keep accurate time records, reflecting the amount of time spent on each client's file and the work done for that client. If you work in a corporate legal department, you may also be required to track your time carefully so that the legal expenses associated with the legal department can be allocated to the appropriate corporate project and/or department within the corporation.

Paralegals who work in law firms are required to closely account for their time spent on client matters and work a requisite number of billable hours. Billable hours are hours and fractions of hours that are spent working on a client's file that will later be billed to that client. In addition to their billable hours, paralegals are usually assigned several administrative responsibilities that are considered nonbillable. Nonbillable time includes time spent on training and interviewing, continuing education, marketing, form file maintenance, billing, miscellaneous administrative matters, pro bono work, and personal matters.

Pressure can be high, especially in large law firms, for paralegals to meet their annual billable hour goals. Your raise, bonus, and possibly continued employment can depend on it. According to one recent survey, the average number of hours billed by paralegals in 1997 was 1,413, or approximately six and one-half hours per working day with two weeks vacation per year.[13] You must always remember to be meticulous with your timekeeping, and (most importantly) to be honest. Do not let billing pressures compromise your ethics (Figure 6-6).

Billable hours
Hours billed to client for legal services performed by each attorney, paralegal, or other timekeeper.

PARALEGAL FEE RECOVERABILITY

It is not uncommon in matters that are litigated for attorneys' fees to be awarded to the prevailing party. Attorneys' fees may be awarded to the prevailing party, and the losing party required to pay, if the award of attorneys' fees is approved by statute or prior agreement or if it is deemed lawful and equitable by the court. If the court awards attorneys' fees, the court generally must approve the amount of fees. "In addition to establishing entitlement to attorney fees, the party requesting them must also establish they are reasonable."[14]

The legal fees awarded by courts include the attorney's fees for his or her time, plus certain allowable costs. Most, but not all, courts have allowed legal fees

FIGURE 6-6

Tips for Timekeeping

1. Most firms require that you track your time in six-minute intervals (one-tenth of an hour).
2. Budget your time carefully starting with a determination of your annual billable hour requirements.
3. Don't forget to allow time for vacations and holidays.
4. Keep copies of all time sheets.
5. Don't procrastinate when it comes to recording your time—you will be surprised how much you may forget after several interruptions.
6. Record all of your billable hours. If you have spent too much time on a certain matter, that is for the billing attorney to decide.
7. Always be honest.
8. Manage your time carefully.

that include fees for paralegal time. There is still a certain amount of controversy surrounding the collection of legal fees for paralegal time spent on behalf of a client, and some courts have disallowed the recovery of fees for paralegal time.

Both state and federal statutes address the awarding of legal fees to the prevailing party under certain circumstances. Five federal statutes and several state statutes specifically provide for the award of paralegal fees as well. These statutes acknowledge the importance of the paralegal to providing affordable legal services (Figure 6-7).

Missouri v. Jenkins, 491 U.S. 274 (1989) was the landmark case concerning paralegal fee recovery. In this case, the prevailing plaintiffs in a school desegregation case sought recovery of their attorneys' fees, which included paralegal time. The U.S. Supreme Court approved the fees charged for paralegal time at market rates. The court held that "By encouraging the use of lower cost paralegals rather than attorneys wherever possible, permitting market-rate billing of paralegal hours encourages cost-effective delivery of legal services and, by reducing the spiraling cost of civil rights litigation, furthers the policies underlying civil rights statutes."[15]

Paralegal fees are usually found to be recoverable so long as the work performed by the paralegal is considered legal in nature, the work performed by the paralegal is supervised by an attorney, the time spent by the paralegal on the particular matter in question is clearly documented, the paralegal is considered by the court to be qualified by education and experience, and the paralegal fees charged are charged at the prevailing market rate in the area. Many courts have approved the recovery of paralegal fees in recognition of the contribution of paralegals in controlling the cost of legal services.

The petitioner for the award of attorney's fees has the burden of establishing that the time expended by paralegals is time for which recovery of attorney's fees is appropriate. "The party seeking fees has the burden in the trial court to represent sufficiently specific evidence of his entitlement."[16] This is typically done by providing the court with detailed time records—making it imperative that you keep accurate and detailed records of all of your billable time.

FIGURE 6-7

Federal Statutes Allowing the Award of Paralegal Fees

- Civil Rights Attorney's Fee Award Act of 1976 (42 U.S.C.S. Sec. 1988)
- The Federal Bankruptcy Law (11 U.S.C.S. 330)
- The Employee Retirement Income Security Act of 1974 (29 U.S.C.S. 1001)
- The Sherman Anti-Trust Act and Clayton Act (15 U.S.C.S.)
- The Surface Mining Control and Reclamation Act of 1977 (30 U.S.C.S. 1270)

In some recent court cases involving the reasonableness of attorneys' fees, courts have held that work that could have effectively been done by a law firm's paralegal could not be billed at the hourly billing rate of a partner. Decisions such as this emphasize the importance in utilizing paralegals to keep client fees reasonable.

In 1995 the NFPA adopted a model act concerning the inclusion of paralegal fees wherever the term *attorneys' fees* are used throughout state statutes. According to the NFPA, "If state and federal statues and court rules contain a provision permitting an award of attorney fees for paralegal services at market rates, statutory interpretation by the courts may be more likely to include fees for paralegal services in an award of attorney fees."[17] The model act defines the term *paralegal* and is designed to reduce the inconsistent treatment among the states and the courts concerning the inclusion of fees for paralegal services in the award of attorneys' fees (Figure 6-8).

Recent Case Law Concerning Legal Fees for Paralegals

The following sample of court cases addressing the award of fees for paralegal services indicates the inconsistent treatment of paralegal fees among the courts. For the latest developments in case law concerning paralegal fee recovery, check the companion Web site to this text at **www.westlegalstudies.com.**

In *Depenthal v. Falstaff Brewing Corporation,* a 1980 action concerning the award of attorneys' fees to attorneys in a suit for violations of the Employee

---

[INSERT STATE]

[INSERT STATE/FEDERAL LEGISLATIVE BODY NAME]

[INSERT SESSION NO. AND YEAR]

A BILL FOR AN ACT to amend the [INSERT STATE] [INSERT EITHER "CODE" OR "COURT RULES"] concerning the following provisions, [INSERT APPROPRIATE REFERENCE]

Be it enacted by the [INSERT STATE/FEDERAL L
EGISLATIVE BODY NAME] of the [INSERT STATE]:

SECTION [INSERT APPROPRIATE REFERENCE] IS ADDED TO THE [INSERT STATE] [INSERT EITHER "CODE" OR "COURT RULES"] AS A NEW SECTION TO READ AS FOLLOWS: [INSERT APPROPRIATE SECTION REFERENCE]. AS USED IN THE SECTION, "PARALEGAL" MEANS "
A person, qualified through education, training or work experience, to perform substantive legal work that requires knowledge of legal concepts and is customarily, but not exclusively, performed by a lawyer. This person may be retained or employed by a lawyer, law office, governmental agency or other entity or may be authorized by administrative, statutory or court authority to perform this work." The terms "paralegal" and "legal assistant" are interchangeable and used synonymously.

Any and all references in the [INSERT STATE] [INSERT EITHER "CODE" OR "COURT RULES"] to attorney's fees shall include paralegal's fees.

In any action or decision in which attorneys' fees are to be determined or awarded by the court, the court shall consider, among other things, the time and labor of any paralegal who contribute or perform nonclerical, legally substantive tasks that in the absence of the paralegal would be performed by the attorney. The award of such fees shall be based on the nature, the extent, and the value of such services, the time spent on such services, and cost of comparable services. The award of such fees shall be based on the hourly rate charged to the consumer of the legal services.

Effective date: _____

Reprinted with permission of the National Federation of Paralegal Associations.

FIGURE 6–8
Model Act for Paralegal Fee Recovery

Retirement Income Security Act (ERISA), the court found that the attorneys who successfully prosecuted the suit were entitled to an award of attorneys' fees, including compensation for work done by paralegals on the cases. The court stated that "Were this work not done by paralegals and interns, the time of attorneys would have been necessary."[18]

In *Bill Rivers Trailers, Inc. v. Miller,*[19] a 1986 case heard before the District Court of Appeal of Florida, First District, the court found that the trial court erred in awarding "attorney fees" for the time of a legal assistant employed by the plaintiff's attorneys, stating that the applicable statute covers only the award of fees for legal services rendered by an attorney authorized to practice law.

In *United States of America v. The Boeing Company,* 747 F.Supp. 319 (E.D. Vir. 1990), the United States District Court approved an award of attorney's fees and costs, including paralegal fees, pursuant to the Equal Access to Justice Act. The court disagreed with the U.S. Government (the Plaintiff in the action) that the $50 hourly rate for the paralegals was excessive and should be compensated at the rate the law firm pays the paralegals. The court held that paralegal time should be awarded at the market rate billed to clients.

In *Dayco v. McLane,* a 1997 Florida workers' compensation claim, the court of appeals held that the lower court erred in awarding a fee for paralegal time because the paralegal's time included time spent faxing transmission and numerous telephone conferences and the claimant failed to demonstrate that the paralegal time was nonclerical.[20]

In 1997, in *Ferguson v. FDIC,* the United States District Court in Texas held that "like federal law, Texas law holds that paralegal fees are recoverable as attorney's fees to the extent that the paralegal performs work traditionally done by an attorney. Otherwise, paralegal expenses are unrecoverable overhead expenses."[21]

In *Hines v. Hines,* a 1997 case wherein a man sued his former wife for breach of fiduciary duty and fraud concerning the buyout of his minority interest in the parties' corporation, the Supreme Court of Idaho found that "paralegal services clearly are not contemplated as awardable attorney's fees or costs under" the applicable statute.[22]

In *Perez v. Eagle,* a 1997 case, the prevailing plaintiffs moved for an award of attorney's fees, paralegal fees, and costs pursuant to the pertinent statute. The New York District Court reduced the paralegal fees from the requested $110 per hour to a "market rate" of $25 per hour, stating that the plaintiff did not give the court supporting documentation for a $110 per hour rate.[23]

In *Cleveland Area Board of Realtors v. City of Euclid,* 965 F.Supp.1017 (1997), the Ohio court held that "Paralegal time, like attorney time, is measured in comparison to market rate, if prevailing practice in area is to bill paralegal time separately at market rates."

In the 1998 case *McGreevy v. Oregon Mutual Insurance Company,* the Court of Appeals of Washington held that paralegals fees may be properly requested as part of an attorney's fee award, but that the request should include the paralegal's qualifications, work performed, and hours worked.[24]

In *Shell Oil Company v. Meyer,* a 1998 Indiana Toxic Tort case, the court held that paralegal fees were recoverable, stating that "When one considers that attorneys utilize paralegals to perform tasks which might otherwise have to be accomplished by a lawyer with a higher billing rate, recovery for a paralegal's fees is hardly unreasonable."[25]

FEE SPLITTING WITH ATTORNEYS

Rule 5.4 of the Model Rules of Professional Conduct, which prohibits sharing legal fees with nonlawyers, includes paralegals in that definition. It is considered unethical for attorneys to split legal fees with paralegals. This rule is intended to prevent solicitation of clients by paralegals and to avoid encouraging the unauthorized practice of law by paralegals. You may participate in a retirement or profit-sharing plan established by your employer, but you must be wary of any arrangement that involves a percentage of legal fees collected or any bonuses for bringing in new clients to the firm. Both of these situations have been found to be unethical. In a case heard before the Supreme Court of California, an attorney was disciplined for entering into a fee-splitting arrangement with a paralegal in his employ who was paid a set percentage on cases in which the paralegal was involved. The attorney involved was suspended from practice for two years for violation of the fee-splitting rule and other rules of ethics.[28]

CASE AND DISCUSSION

The following case discuses in detail the circumstances under which costs for services performed by nonlawyer personnel (paralegals in this instance) may be recovered under Washington law.

ABSHER CONSTRUCTION COMPANY, a Washington corporation;
Chapman Mechanical, Inc., a Washington corporation;
and Emerald Aire, Inc., a
Washington corporation, Appellants,
v.
KENT SCHOOL DISTRICT NO. 415, Respondent.
No. 33489-1-I.
Court of Appeals of Washington,
Division 1.
Nov. 20, 1995.
As Modified May 3, 1996.

PER CURIAM.

Kent School No. 415 (Kent) has requested an attorney fee award which includes payment for the time of non-lawyer personnel. We hold that such time may be compensable as part of an attorney fee award and set out guidelines for determining when such fees are appropriate. We find, however, that the total amount requested by Kent is not reasonable under the circumstances of this case and therefore award a lesser amount.

The appellants sued Kent for amounts they claimed were owing under a public works contract, approximately $205,000. Kent won on summary judgment and was awarded $34,648.86 in fees and costs. Kent also prevailed on appeal and now seeks an additional $36,911.54 in fees and costs. The basis for the award is RCW 39.04.240.

The fee request includes time for the following individuals:

(1) A partner in practice for 20 years billed 104.2 hours at $225.00 per hour ($23,445);

(2) A fourth-year associate billed 53.1 hours at $130.00 per hour ($6,903);

(3) A sixth-year associate billed 4.5 hours at $155.00 per hour ($697.50);

(4) A legal assistant billed 39.5 hours at $67.00 per hour ($2,646.50);

(5) A legal editor billed 4 hours at $62.00 per hour ($248); and

(6) A legal clerk billed 8.5 hours at $35.00 per hour ($297.50).

The latter three are not attorneys.

No case in Washington specifically addresses whether the time of non-lawyer personnel may be included in an attorney fee award.[26]

We find persuasive the reasoning of the Arizona court in Continental Townhouses East Unit One Ass'n v. Brockbank.[27] Properly employed and supervised non-lawyer personnel can decrease litigation expense. Lawyers should not be forced to perform legal tasks solely so that their time may be compensable in an attorney fee award.

The question then becomes what sort of work performed by non-lawyer personnel is compensable. Regardless of the name given to the category of person who performs the work, we believe, as did the Arizona court, that the definition of legal assistant formulated by the American Bar Association Standing Committee on Legal Assistants provides appropriate guidance. Under that definition:

A legal assistant is a person, qualified through education, training, or work experience, who is employed or retained by a lawyer, law office, governmental agency, or other entity in a capacity or function which involves a performance, under the ultimate direction and supervision of an attorney, of specifically delegated substantive legal work, which work, for the most part, requires a sufficient knowledge of legal concepts that, absent such assistant, the attorney would perform the task.

The following criteria will be relevant in determining whether such services should be compensated: (1) the services performed by the non-lawyer personnel must be legal in nature; (2) the performance of these services must be supervised by an attorney; (3) the qualifications of the person performing the services must be specified in the request for fees in sufficient detail to demonstrate that the person is qualified by virtue of education, training, or work experience to perform substantive legal work; (4) the nature of the services performed must be specified in the request for fees in order to allow the reviewing court to determine that the services performed were legal rather than clerical; (5) as with attorney time, the amount of time expended must be set forth and must be reasonable; and (6) the amount charged must reflect reasonable community standards for charges by that category of personnel. . . .

Employing these criteria, we allow only part of the fees requested for the legal assistant's services. He has requested compensation for preparing pleadings for duplication, preparing and delivering copies, requesting copies, and obtaining and delivering a docket sheet. We do not view this time as work which falls within these guidelines. We do allow an award for time spent preparing the briefs and related work. In computing the time we allow for him, we will assume, absent any other evidence in the record, that the hourly rate of $67.00 is reasonable for this type of work. We allow an award of $2,110.50 for 31.5 hours. We allow the recovery of fees for the time claimed by the legal editor for verifying citations and quotations. We disallow the time claimed for the legal clerk, which appears to consist primarily of obtaining copies of pleadings and organizing working copies of the pleadings. . . .

In sum, we conclude that the fees of non-lawyer personnel may be properly requested as part of an attorney fee award. In this case, applying the factors and considerations listed above, we award $23,055.50 plus $1,633.74 as a reasonable attorney fee on appeal, together with $134.65 costs on appeal.

CHAPTER SUMMARY

- Attorneys have a fiduciary duty to clients and third parties with regard to the safekeeping of funds belonging to the client or third party.
- Any funds that an attorney holds for a client or third party must be kept in a separate client trust account.
- The attorney's funds must not be commingled with the client's funds; they must be kept separate.
- Advance fees must be kept in trust until they are earned.
- IOLTA accounts are client trust accounts for relatively small deposits of funds that will not be held for a significant period of time. Interest earned on IOLTA accounts is paid to a special nonprofit organization that promotes access to legal services for everyone.
- Improper use of client funds for any unauthorized purpose is considered a misappropriation of funds.
- Attorney's fees must be reasonable based on the attorney's time and labor, preclusion from other employment, customary fee, results obtained, time limitations, nature and length of the professional relationship, experience, reputation, and ability of the attorney, and whether the fee is a contingent fee.
- Contingent fees are fees earned by an attorney based on a percentage of the award the attorney can obtain for the client. If the client collects nothing, the attorney is not compensated for his or her time.
- Fee agreements should be detailed, should be discussed thoroughly with clients, and should be in writing.
- Attorneys are prohibited from splitting fees with nonattorneys under most circumstances.
- Paralegal fees are usually recoverable, but not in every instance and in every jurisdiction.
- Paralegals must not enter into fee-splitting agreements with attorneys.

SUMMARY QUESTIONS

1. Suppose that an attorney is representing a client on the sale of a piece of real estate. During the course of the representation, the attorney receives funds from the buyer of the property to hold until the closing. To whom does the attorney owe a fiduciary duty?
2. What are the attorney's obligations with regard to the safekeeping of a client's funds?
3. Janet Jenson, an attorney, receives $500 as a general retainer from the Acme Doorknob Company. Must this amount be held in trust?

4. Suppose that the $500 Janet receives is a special retainer as advance payment for the incorporation of a subsidiary in a neighboring state. Must this amount be held in trust?

5. As a paralegal, can you accept full responsibility for opening and maintaining a trust account, including signing the checks?

6. What is an IOLTA account and how does it differ from a non-IOLTA account?

7. Is it unethical for an attorney to borrow funds from a client's trust account to pay office expenses?

8. Is it permissible for a paralegal to be paid on an incentive basis based on a percentage of fees paid by any new clients he or she brings in to the firm?

9. What are the factors taken into account, under rule 1.5(a) when considering the reasonableness of legal fees?

10. Why may a contingent fee be considered reasonable when the amount may be significantly larger than the amount the client would be billed if billed on an hourly basis?

ENDNOTES

[1]*ABA/BNA Lawyers' Manual on Professional Conduct,* Client Funds and Property (1998).

[2]*Iowa Supreme Court Board of Professional Ethics and Conduct v. Apland,* 577 N.W. 2d 50 (Iowa 1998).

[3]*In Re Warhaftig,* 524 A2d 398 (N.J. 1987).

[4]*In Re Micheel,* 610 A2d 231 (D.C. 1992).

[5]*Bounogias v. Peters,* 198 N.E. 2d 142 (Ill. App. 2d. 1964).

[6]*Morse v. Espeland,* 696 P.2d 429 (Mont. 1985).

[7]*Drake v. Becker,* 303 N.E. 2d 212 (Ill. App. 3d 1973).

[8]*Teche Bank & Trust Co. v. J.B. Willis,* 631 So. 2d 644 (La. Ct. App. 1994).

[9]*Christensen v. Eggen,* 577 N.W.2d 221 (Minn. 1998).

[10]Bus. & Prof.Code, s 6077; Greenbaum v. State Bar (1976) 15 Cal.3d 893, 905, 126 Cal.Rptr. 785, 544 P.2d 921.

[11]*Brody v. State Bar* (1974) 11 Cal.3d 347, 350-351, 113 Cal.Rptr. 371, 521 P.2d 107, and citations herein.

[12]Smith, Larry, Of Counsel 700 Data . . . Paralegal Hiring, Billing Rate Increases or Moderate in Strong but Steady Market, *Of Counsel,* September 1, 1997.

[13]*Law Firm Partnership and Benefits Report,* Billing Rates and Hours Up, But Profits Mainly Flat (August 1998), citing Altman and Weil 1998 Annual Survey of 483 responding law firms.

[14]*McGreevy v. Oregon Mutual Insurance Company,* 951 P.2d 798 (Wash. Ct. of App., Div. 3 1998).

[15]*Quoting Cameo Convalescent Center, Inc. v. Senn,* 105 S.Ct. 780 (1985).

[16]*In Re Marriage of Nasir J. Ahmad and Carolyn A. Ahmad,* 555 N.E. 2d 439 (Ill. 1990).

[17]*Comments of the NFPA on the June, 1995 Report of the ABA Commission on practice—Exhibit A*

[18]*Dependahl v. Falstaff Brewing Corporation,* 496 F. Supp. 215 (E.D. Mo. 1980).

[19]*Bill Rivers Trailers, Inc. v. Miller,* 489 So. 2d 1139 (Fla. 1986).

[20]*Dayco v. McLane,* 690 So. 2d 654 (Dist. Ct. of App. Fla., 1st Dist 1997).

[21]*Ferguson v. FDIC,* 1997 WL 279885 (N.D. Tex. 1997).

[22]*Hines v. Hines,* 934 P.2d 20 (Idaho 1997).

[23]*Perez v. Eagle,* 1997 WL 458787 (S.D.N.Y. 1997).

[24]*McGreevy v.Oregon Mutual Insurance Company,* 951 P.2d 798 (Ct. of App. Of Wash., Div. 3 1998).

[25]*Shell Oil Company v. Meyer,* 684 N.E.2d 504 (Ind. Ct. App. 1998).

[26]In *Boeing Co. v. Sierracin Corp.,* 108 Wash.2d 38, 64-65, 738 P.2d 665 (1987), the court upheld a fee award that included "clerk time," but the issue presented here was not discussed.

[27]*Continental Townhouses East Unit One Ass'n v. Brockbank,* 152 Ariz. 537, 733 P.2d 1120, 73 A.L.R.4th 921 (1986).

[28]*Gassman v. State Bar,* 553 P.2d 1147 (Cal. 1976).

THE RACIST WHO WANTS TO BE A LAWYER

Matthew Hale is a white supremacist who thinks all nonwhite Americans should be deported. He is a self-proclaimed racist and a bigot who has passed the Illinois Bar examination and wants to be an attorney. He wants to be "an advocate for white people in the courtroom."

To be a licensed attorney in the State of Illinois, one must have a law degree, pass the Illinois State Bar examination, and receive approval from the Illinois Board of Admissions to the Bar Character and Fitness Committee. Hale received his law degree from Southern Illinois University in May 1998, and subsequently passed his bar exam. Although Hale met with the first two requirements for bar admission, the Committee on Character and Fitness rejected him. Hale's appeals have resulted in three separate rejections by Illinois Bar Committees, the final rejection being received by Hale on July 1, 1999. In their opinion, the committee members found that Hale's extreme views would not allow him to follow the Supreme Court's Rules of Professional Conduct.

For a young man (late twenties at the time of publication), Hale has a long and public history as a racist. As a young boy in East Peoria, Hale was fascinated with the Nazis and formed a "Little Reich" group at school. In high school, and later at college, Hale attended "white power" rallies.

In the early 1990s, when attending Bradley University, Hale led the American White Supremacist Party in Peoria. After he lost a Peoria city council race, Hale reorganized the nearly defunct Church of the Creator, of which he is now a minister and the leader. Hale describes the church, which has no actual, physical building, as a "dynamic, religious organization that seeks to insure the survival, advancement and expansion of the white race." Reverend Hale claims the Church of the Creator has approximately 7,000 followers.

According to information published on its Web site, the main objective of the Church of the Creator is "The Survival, Expansion and Advancement of the White Race." Among the Church's beliefs is a statement that "the most deadly enemies of the White Race are first of all the Jews, and secondarily, all the other mud races who are competing for food and living space on this limited planet." The course the Church of the Creator has chosen is "to keep our own race pure and expand until we finally inhabit all the good lands of this planet."

Members of the Church of the Creator have been indicted on race-related crimes in more than one instance. One member has been sentenced to life in prison for killing an African-American sailor in Florida. Four other members were indicted for holding up a Miami video store, acting on the group's belief that all media outlets are controlled by Jews. Most notably, former church member Benjamin Nathaniel Smith went on a three-day shooting rampage aimed at African-Americans, Jews, and Asians during the Fourth of July weekend in 1999, killing African-American Ricky Byrdsong, a former Northwestern University basketball coach, and a Korean-American Indiana University student, Won Joon Yoon. Nine others were injured in Illinois and Indiana. Smith's shooting spree ended when he shot himself while being pursued by the police.

Smith was not only a follower of the church but also a friend of Matthew Hale's who actually testified on Hale's behalf before a hearing board reconsidering the Fitness Committee's decision to reject Hale's application to the Illinois Bar. Smith's shooting spree began just hours after Hale's news conference announcing that the hearing board had denied him.

After Smith's Fourth of July weekend shooting spree, Attorney General Janet Reno announced that the Justice Department would be reviewing all aspects of the shootings in Illinois and Indiana, including Smith's connection to the World Church of the Creator and whether it's creator Matthew Hale, incited Smith to act. Hale was questioned by members of a task force dealing with the shooting spree shortly after it occurred. Hale's problems don't end there. Two of the Orthodox Jew victims who were shot at by Smith have filed a civil lawsuit, naming Hale as one of the defendants. The shooting victims are seeking damages for physical and mental injuries sustained during the shooting. The documents filed in the lawsuit assert that Smith was acting as Hale's agent during his shooting spree.

Hale claims that he does not support violence and has no control over the actions of the members of the church, although he admitted that the denial of his Illinois Bar admittance may have triggered Smith's shooting spree. According to Hale, "There wouldn't be anyone dead in my opinion if we had a society that let people truly speak their minds. I can't say what motivated him, but I strongly believe it was the denial of my law license and the fact that he was arrested for trying to speak his mind."[i] Smith had previously been arrested for littering in Indiana—an incident stemming from his distribution of World Church of the Creator hate literature.

Although much public comment has been made concerning Hale's unpopular and hateful views, initially he received a surprising amount of support from staunch supporters of the First Amendment right to freedom of speech. Some support for this self-proclaimed bigot, who displays swastikas on the wall in his home office, came from some very unlikely sources, including a Jewish attorney and national civil rights organizations.

Reverend Hale, who is a self-proclaimed anti-Semite, turned to an unlikely ally to assist him with his fight against the Illinois State Bar Association—Jewish lawyer Alan Dershowitz (of O.J. Simpson case fame). Hale retorts "He's a great attorney, but I won't change my views. I'm an anti-Semite. I freely say it. I recognize we are involved in a crucial struggle, and I'll utilize whatever means are necessary."

Although Dershowitz finds Hale's views "utterly reprehensible and despicable," he doesn't believe anyone should be denied admission to the bar based on their views. "Character committees should not become thought police," says Dershowitz. "It's not the content of the thoughts I'm defending, it's the freedom of everybody to express their views and to become lawyers."

Because Dershowitz supported Hale's First Amendment Rights he considered taking Hale's case. However, Dershowitz's plans changed after the 1999 shooting spree by Benjamin Smith and his connection to the Hale. "I don't think this case is any longer a pure First Amendment case," Dershowitz said. "I think he has condoned violence. . . . We know he spoke to this man Smith hours before the rampage."

After Hale's initial rejection by the Illinois Bar Fitness Committee, the Anti-Defamation League (ADL), a worldwide group founded in 1913 to fight anti-Semitism through programs and services that counteract hatred, prejudice, and bigotry, issued a press release concerning the Illinois Board of

Admissions rejection of Matthew Hale. In its release the ADL stated its belief that "Matt Hale's moral compass is seriously defective. Exposing him and condemning his views are consistent with ADL's mandate to combat prejudice and discrimination." However, in the same press release, the ADL stated that denying Hale a license to practice because of his views sets a dangerous precedent. The ADL agreed with the dissenter on the Illinois panel who wrote that the "advocacy of beliefs, no matter how repugnant to current law, cannot be the basis for denial of certification to an applicant who will subscribe to his oath as an attorney."

Several editorials have been printed in newspapers in Illinois and throughout the Midwest denouncing Hale and the World Church of the Creator while also calling for a protection to his First Amendment rights. Most of those in favor of admitting Hale to the Illinois Bar despise his views, but they believe that he should not be discriminated against because of them. They point out that until 1960 communists could be refused admission to the bar because of their views. Those who favor allowing Hale to practice law fear that to reject him because of his personal views sets a dangerous precedence. According to Jay Miller, director of the Illinois Chapter of the American Civil Liberties Union, "He hasn't committed any felony. He's talked and written. You can't deprive someone the right to practice law because of their political views."

Widespread support for Hale's First Amendment rights may be lost, however, if it is determined that he did incite violence by encouraging Benjamin Smith's shooting spree or by failing to prevent it if he had prior knowledge of Smith's plans.

In late July 1999, Hale filed documents with the Illinois State Supreme Court, continuing his mission to be admitted to practice law in Illinois. He was reportedly optimistic about his chances of being admitted.

Excerpts from Opinion of the Illinois Bar Committee on Character and Fitness Panel:

> Under any civilized standards of decency, the incitement of racial hatred for the ultimate purpose of depriving selected groups of their legal rights shows a gross deficiency in moral character, particularly for lawyers who have a special responsibility to uphold the rule of law for all persons. If the civilized world had no experience with Hitler, Matthew Hale might be dismissed as a harmless 'crackpot.' However, history teaches a different lesson.

---

[i] Spree Shooter, Would-Be Lawyer Shared Racist Goal, Chicago Daily Law Bulletin, July 6, 1999.

Chapter 7

Maintaining Integrity and Public Respect for the Legal Profession

No man can ever be a truly great lawyer,
who is not in every sense of the word a good man . . .

G. Sharswood, *Professional Ethics* (1844)

An Ethical Dilemma
Introduction
Bar Admission
Disciplinary Matters
Misconduct
   Criminal Acts
   Dishonesty, Fraud, Deceit, or Misrepresentation
   Conduct Prejudicial to the Administration of
      Justice
   Stated or Implied Ability to Influence Improp-
      erly a Government Agency or Official
   Assisting Judge or Judicial Officer in Violation
      of Rules of Judicial Conduct
Reporting Misconduct
   Conduct that Must be Reported
   Preserving Client Confidences
   Failure to Report Misconduct
   Reporting Judicial Misconduct

Case and Discussion
Pro Bono Service
   Pro Bono Opportunities
From the Paralegal's Perspective
A Question of Ethics
Maintaining the Integrity of the Profession
Paralegal Misconduct
The Paralegal's Duty to Report Misconduct
   Reporting Paralegal Misconduct
   Reporting Attorney Misconduct
Pro Bono for Paralegals

Chapter Summary

Summary Questions

An Ethical Dilemma

Megan Brown has always been a good and conscientious attorney. She has never had any complaints filed against her, and her clients and the people in the community generally like and respect her. However, Megan has been plagued with financial problems due to a secret gambling addiction. Megan falsified her income tax returns for three consecutive years to avoid paying taxes she couldn't afford. Despite her legal savvy, Megan has been caught. She feels that her legal problems with the IRS have in no way affected her practice of law, nor should they impede her ability to practice in the future. Is Megan right? Is she in violation of the rules of legal ethics?

Answer and Discussion: Unfortunately for Megan, her falsification of income tax returns, although not directly related to her practice of law, will probably be considered to be a violation of the rules of ethics in her state. Fraudulent behavior of an attorney, even if not related to the practice of law, reflects poorly on the legal profession and is considered cause for disciplinary action against the attorney—possibly even disbarment. In 1974 the Court of Appeals of Maryland ordered that former Vice President Spiro Agnew should be disbarred for willfully and knowingly filing a false income tax return.

INTRODUCTION

Judges, attorneys, paralegals, and everyone working within the legal profession have a duty to maintain the integrity and public respect for the legal profession. This includes following the applicable rules of ethics, remaining honest and always staying within the law, and reporting any serious incidents of misconduct by attorneys or other legal professionals. Legal professionals must also strive to improve the legal system and offer assistance wherever possible, especially in offering their services pro bono.

The rules of ethics discussed in this chapter are rules designed to maintain the integrity of the legal profession. These rules concern bar admissions and disciplinary matters, misconduct, and reporting professional misconduct. Also discussed in this chapter is another issue that affects the integrity of the profession—**pro bono** work.

The second part of this chapter examines many of the same issues from the paralegal's perspective, beginning with a look at recommendations by the paralegal associations for maintaining integrity and public respect for the paralegal profession and the legal profession in general. Next, the focus will be on **misconduct** within the profession, and a paralegal's ethical duty to report misconduct of attorneys and other paralegals. The chapter concludes with a look at pro bono opportunities for paralegals.

Pro bono
[Latin *pro bono publico* "for the public good"] Being or involving uncompensated legal services performed especially for the public good (took the case pro bono; 50 hours of pro bono work each year). *(Black's Law Dictionary, Seventh Edition)*
Misconduct
A dereliction of duty; unlawful or improper behavior. *(Black's Law Dictionary, Seventh Edition)*

BAR ADMISSION

Before an attorney can practice law, he or she must be licensed and admitted to the bar of the jurisdiction in which the attorney wishes to practice. The state bar associations, judiciary, and legislatures work to ensure the integrity of the legal profession by setting competence and moral character standards for bar applicants. The bar associations also review and approve bar applications.

Each applicant to the bar must file a written request for admission to the bar with the appropriate authority in each jurisdiction in which he or she wishes to be admitted. The request must be accompanied by an affidavit of the applicant that includes the applicant's age, residence, and time and place of study and degree, or admission and period of practice in other states, together with the affidavits of at least two citizens of the community in which the application is made. Such other information as may be requested by each state must also be furnished.

The applicant must respond completely and truthfully to each question asked on the application and in any subsequent hearings or other proceedings held in connection with the application process. Falsifying an application for bar admission may result in failure to be admitted to the bar or later disbarment. In *People v. Culpepper,* the attorney-respondent was disbarred after it was determined that he had falsified his college records to obtain admission into law school and then again lied in his application to the bar. The Supreme Court of Colorado found that the respondent's conduct was "contrary to the high standards of honesty, justice and morality required for lawyers. . . ."[1]

Certification of the applicant's good moral character is required as a prerequisite for admission to the bar in every state. The burden is on the applicant to furnish the committee with evidence of his or her good moral character and general fitness to practice law.[2] Good moral character is a requirement to protect the public and to protect the bar's image and the image of the profession. It is believed better to prevent future problems caused by the immoral applicant's irresponsibility by denying admission, than to seek to remedy the problem after it occurs and the attorney victimizes a client.

Determining whether an applicant has *good moral character* can be problematic. A series of questions, determined to give guidance to the admission review board, is included in the application. Some of the *red flags* on applications that may be considered an indication of a lack of good moral character include:

- Misconduct in employment
- Acts involving dishonesty, fraud, deceit, or misrepresentation
- Abuse of legal process
- Neglect of financial responsibilities
- Neglect of professional obligations
- Violation of an order of a court, including child support orders
- Evidence of mental or emotional instability
- Evidence of drug or alcohol dependence or abuse
- Denial of admission to the bar in another jurisdiction on character and fitness grounds
- Disciplinary action by a lawyer disciplinary agency or other professional disciplinary agency of any jurisdiction

Any character traits considered in denying admission to a bar applicant must have a rational connection to the applicant's present fitness to practice law and must relate to the state's legitimate interest in protecting prospective clients and the system of justice. In Minnesota, the Board of Law Examiners rejected the application of an individual who filed bankruptcy shortly after his graduation from law school—a decision that was supported by the Supreme Court of Minnesota. It was the board's opinion that the applicant did not make every effort possible to pay his creditors, but rather that he filed bankruptcy merely to avoid his obligation to repay his student loans. According to the court,

> A flagrant disregard of this repayment responsibility by the loan recipient indicates to us a lack of moral commitment to the rights of other students and particularly the rights of creditors. Such flagrant financial irresponsibility reflects adversely on an applicant's ability to manage financial matters and reflects adversely on his

commitment to the rights of others, thereby reflecting adversely on his fitness for the practice of law. It is appropriate to prevent problems from such irresponsibility by denying admission, rather than to seek remedy to the problem after it occurs and victimizes a client.[3]

Any attorney who knowingly submits a false affidavit in support of an application to the bar by another is subject to disciplinary action.

DISCIPLINARY MATTERS

The legal disciplinary system is designed to safeguard the public and maintain the integrity of the legal profession.[4] The disciplinary system is intended to maintain the integrity of the bar in the eyes of the public. "The purpose of a bar disciplinary proceeding is not to punish the attorney but to vindicate in the eyes of the public the overall reputation of the Bar."[5] Attorneys have a duty of candor to any disciplinary board with jurisdiction, as well as the duty to cooperate fully with any disciplinary proceeding. The failure to respond truthfully and fully in connection with a disciplinary proceeding constitutes a violation of the rules of ethics. An attorney's false and misleading information to bar authorities constitutes a separate basis for discipline.[6]

Attorneys who do not cooperate with disciplinary boards, including not filing responses when requested to and not appearing at scheduled meetings and hearings, are subject to disciplinary action by the board, including suspension or disbarment. At times an attorney's failure to respond may be considered an admission to the ethical violation in question.

> . . . In order to expedite the investigation of an ethics complaint by the Bar, an attorney's failure to respond to a request for information concerning allegations of ethical violations within a reasonable time will constitute an admission to those allegations for the purposes of the disciplinary proceeding.[7]

When a serious charge has been brought by a disciplinary agency against an attorney, the attorney must respond, cooperate, and answer any questions put forth by the board in their investigation. Under certain circumstances, an attorney can claim the Fifth Amendment privilege and refuse to answer certain questions that may incriminate him or her. However, when this is done, the disciplinary agency may impose appropriate sanctions based on the evidence presented.

MISCONDUCT

The legal profession is largely self-governing. This means that attorneys are responsible for establishing ethical guidelines for members of their profession to follow. They are also responsible for policing their profession and handling misconduct among its members. To maintain the integrity and respect of the profession, there must be a system for reporting the misconduct of attorneys when they breach the established codes of ethics and for disciplining attorneys when necessary. Each state has established rules and guidelines for reporting the misconduct of an attorney—by disgruntled clients, as well as others in the legal profession. States also have established procedures for handling complaints.

An attorney's first professional obligation is to obey the rules of professional ethics of the jurisdictions in which the lawyer is licensed to practice. Any violation of the rules, or assistance to another in violating the rules, is considered misconduct. Rule 8.4 of the Model Rules of Professional Conduct, which is followed closely by most states, is designed to cover any behavior that diminishes respect for the legal profession and is not covered elsewhere. It overlaps most other rules of the Model Rules of Ethics, and any violation of another rule means automatic violation of Rule 8.4, which follows:

Rule 8.4 Misconduct
It is professional misconduct for a lawyer to:
(a) violate or attempt to violate the Rules of Professional Conduct, knowingly assist or induce another to do so, or do so through the acts of another;
(b) commit a criminal act that reflects adversely on the lawyer's honesty, trustworthiness or fitness as a lawyer in other respects;
(c) engage in conduct involving dishonesty, fraud, deceit or misrepresentation;
(d) engage in conduct that is prejudicial to the administration of justice;
(e) state or imply an ability to influence improperly a government agency or official; or
(f) knowingly assist a judge or judicial officer in conduct that is a violation of applicable rules of judicial conduct or other law.

Criminal Acts

Attorneys may be disciplined for criminal conduct unrelated to their practice of law. The reasoning behind this rule is that to allow attorneys to break the law without discipline from the bar association leads to loss of respect for the legal profession itself.

Although attorneys are personally responsible for all crimes committed by them, they are only professionally answerable for offenses that indicate a lack of those characteristics relevant to law practice. The commission of crimes, especially those dealing with dishonesty, fraud, deceit, misrepresentation, or others that adversely affect the attorney's fitness to practice law, may be punished by law and by the bar association or other disciplinary agency. "Although a lawyer is personally answerable to the entire criminal law, a lawyer should be professionally answerable only for offenses that indicate lack of those characteristics relevant to law practice."[8] For example, in *In re Glover-Towne,* the court found that bribery was grounds for automatic disbarment.

Sexual misconduct also falls under this rule. According to the ABA Committee on Ethics and Professional Responsibility,

A sexual relationship between lawyer and client may involve unfair exploitation of the lawyer's fiduciary position, and/or significantly impair a lawyer's ability to represent the client competently, and therefore may violate both the Model Rules of Professional Conduct and the Model Code of Professional Responsibility.[9]

Traditionally, the test for determining which criminal acts constituted misconduct under the attorney's code of ethics was moral turpitude. Illegal conduct involving moral turpitude was considered misconduct under the Model Code of Professional Responsibility, and that term is still used in some jurisdictions. Moral turpitude has been defined in many ways, but generally, it includes "act of baseness, vileness, or the depravity in private and social duties which man owes to his fellow man."[10] The term *moral turpitude* is not used in the Model Rules and the code of ethics in most states because of its lack of specificity to the fitness for the practice of law. Generally, any illegal conduct that reflects adversely on an attorney's fitness to practice law will be considered grounds for disciplinary action that may result in disbarment or some lesser sanction.

Dishonesty, Fraud, Deceit, or Misrepresentation

"Dishonest conduct by an attorney with his own client goes to the very core of a lawyer's fitness to practice law."[11] Dishonesty, fraud, deceit, and misrepresentation are prohibited by Section 8.4 of the Model Rules. Similar prohibitions exist in several other rules already discussed in this text, including rules concerning financial matters, conflicts of interest, confidentiality, and the attorney's duty to clients, as well as in the codes of ethics of each jurisdiction.

Because public confidence is so vital to the legal profession, and public confidence is easily shaken by the dishonest actions of attorneys, the state disciplinary boards tend to come down hard on attorneys who have been dishonest with their clients or with the courts. As stated by the Mississippi Supreme Court, "This Court will not hesitate to impose substantial sanctions upon an attorney for any act that evinces want of personal honesty and integrity or renders such attorney unworthy of public confidence."[12]

Conduct Prejudicial to the Administration of Justice

Attorneys must not engage in any conduct that could be considered prejudicial to the administration of justice. Violation of this broad rule often involves litigation and court proceedings, although it may be applied in a wide variety of contexts. Some examples of violations of this rule include obstructing the discovery process, lying to the court to cover error, appearing in court while intoxicated, and filing false and fraudulent pleadings.

Stated or Implied Ability to Influence Improperly a Government Agency or Official

Even the suggestion that one may be able to improperly influence, or bribe, a government or judicial official is a violation of the rules of ethics. An attorney may not suggest that he or she can obtain results through improper government influence or political power. In one case in Indiana, an attorney was disbarred for several violations, including representing to his client that he was a close friend of the Chief Justice of the Supreme Court and that his friendship would influence a successful outcome of the client's case.[13]

Assisting Judge or Judicial Officer in Violation of Rules of Judicial Conduct

Any action taken by an attorney to assist a judge or judicial officer to violate any of the rules of judicial conduct that apply to judges and judicial officers is considered unethical and in violation of Model Rule 8.4.

Rules concerning misconduct vary somewhat among the different jurisdictions. However, violation of the state's code of ethics, serious criminal conduct, dishonesty, prejudicing the administration of justice, bribery, and assisting a judge in violating rules applicable to him or her are all usually actions considered to be misconduct.

REPORTING MISCONDUCT

Because the legal profession is a self-governing profession responsible for policing itself, it is mandatory that attorneys report misconduct by their fellow attorneys to the state bar disciplinary agency, a peer review agency, or other proper authority as designated by the pertinent rules of ethics. Rule 8.3(a) of the Model Rules specifically states that an attorney who has knowledge of another attorney's violation of the Rules of Professional Conduct shall inform the appropriate professional authority.

For example, suppose that attorney Marvin Terry is working on a personal injury lawsuit, representing the defendant. The plaintiff's attorney, Clint James, is constantly calling Mr. Terry's client on the telephone. Even after Mr. Terry has specifically told Mr. James that all contact with his client should be made through him, Mr. James continues to contact Mr. Terry's client, trying to get him to make admissions over the telephone. Under these circumstances, Mr. James' behavior is clearly misconduct, and Mr. Terry has a duty to maintain the integrity of the legal profession by reporting his behavior to the proper authority.

> Rule 8.3 Reporting Professional Misconduct
> (a) A lawyer having knowledge that another lawyer has committed a violation of the Rules of Professional Conduct that raises a substantial question as to that lawyer's honesty, trustworthiness or fitness as a lawyer in other respects, shall inform the appropriate professional authority.

Conduct that Must be Reported

Attorneys are not required to report all types of misconduct they witness, but they are required to report the following types of violations:

1. Violations that the attorney has knowledge of.
2. Violations that raise a substantial question as to the other attorney's honesty, trustworthiness, or fitness as a lawyer in other respects.
3. Violations that are not protected by the rules of confidentiality.

The knowledge that the attorney has must be real. While it does not require the attorney to have all knowledge necessary to prosecute the matter, it does require that the attorney's knowledge of the misconduct amount to more than simple rumor or suspicion. To report all rumors or suspicion would mean harassment to attorneys who may be victims of unfair gossip.

Attorneys are only required to report serious misconduct. The attorney's duty to report misconduct is limited to actions that "a self-regulating profession must vigorously endeavor to prevent"[14] (Figure 7-1).

Preserving Client Confidences

Preserving client confidences is so important that an attorney is prohibited from reporting misconduct if doing so would breach a duty of client confidentiality. The information protected under client confidentiality is very broad and, at times, the attorney may be required to get permission from any client involved in the misconduct before reporting it.

Failure to Report Misconduct

Although rarely pursued, an attorney's failure to report misconduct is in itself misconduct. In one case before the Illinois Supreme Court, an attorney was suspended from practice for one year for failing to report the serious misconduct of another attorney of which he had knowledge.[15]

Although it is not expressly prohibited under the Model Rules, threatening another attorney with filing a disciplinary complaint against him or her to gain

---

FIGURE 7-1

When an Attorney Must Report Misconduct

Attorneys have an obligation to report misconduct when:
1. The attorney has knowledge of the misconduct
2. The attorney's knowledge is not protected as a confidence or secret
3. The conduct violated a disciplinary rule
4. The violation raises a substantial question as to honesty, trustworthiness, or fitness to practice law

an advantage in a civil suit is improper.[16] If the misconduct falls under the above criteria, the attorney is *required* to report misconduct. The reporting attorney does not have the option of whether or not to report the alleged misconduct.

Reporting Judicial Misconduct

Judges also have the ethical duty to report attorney misconduct to the proper disciplinary board, and attorneys are responsible for reporting judicial misconduct to the proper authority. The type of judicial misconduct that must be reported is limited to violations that raise a substantial question as to the judge's fitness for office.

Few attorneys enjoy the thought of "turning in" a fellow attorney for disciplinary action, especially when the attorney is an acquaintance, a co-worker, or even a superior. However, the importance of doing so is evident. Courts have held that an attorney has the duty to report the misconduct of his or her partners or associates. Strict enforcement of the rules requiring reporting misconduct actually takes some of the burden off of attorneys who are struggling with the question of whether to report misconduct. Honest self-regulation is necessary to maintain the integrity of the profession.

CASE AND DISCUSSION

In the following case before the Illinois Supreme Court, the attorney respondent was suspended from practice of law for one year for failing to report the misconduct of another attorney.

In re James H. HIMMEL, Attorney, Respondent.
No. 65946.
Supreme Court of Illinois.
Sept. 22, 1988.

This is a disciplinary proceeding against respondent, James H. Himmel. . . .

We will briefly review the facts, which essentially involve three individuals: respondent, James H. Himmel, licensed to practice law in Illinois on November 6, 1975; his client, Tammy Forsberg, . . . and her former attorney, John R. Casey.

The complaint alleges that respondent had knowledge of John Casey's conversion of Forsberg's funds and respondent failed to inform the Commission of this misconduct. The facts are as follows.

In October 1978, Tammy Forsberg was injured in a motorcycle accident. In June 1980, she retained John R. Casey to represent her in any personal injury or property damage claim resulting from the accident. Sometime in 1981, Casey negotiated a settlement of $35,000 on Forsberg's behalf. Pursuant to an agreement between Forsberg and Casey, one-third of any monies received would be paid to Casey as his attorney fee. In March 1981, Casey received the $35,000 settlement check, endorsed it, and deposited the check into his client trust fund account. Subsequently, Casey converted the funds.

Between 1981 and 1983, Forsberg unsuccessfully attempted to collect her $23,233.34 share of the settlement proceeds.

In March 1983, Forsberg retained respondent to collect her money and agreed to pay him one-third of any funds recovered above $23,233.34. Respondent investigated the matter and dis-

covered that Casey had misappropriated the settlement funds. In April 1983, respondent drafted an agreement in which Casey would pay Forsberg $75,000 in settlement of any claim she might have against him for the misappropriated funds. By the terms of the agreement, Forsberg agreed not to initiate any criminal, civil, or attorney disciplinary action against Casey. This agreement was executed on April 11, 1983. Respondent stood to gain $17,000 or more if Casey honored the agreement. In February 1985, respondent filed suit against Casey for breaching the agreement, and a $100,000 judgment was entered against Casey. If Casey had satisfied the judgment, respondent's share would have been approximately $25,588.

The complaint stated that at no time did respondent inform the Commission of Casey's misconduct. According to the Administrator, respondent's first contact with the Commission was in response to the Commission's inquiry regarding the lawsuit against Casey.

In April 1985, the Administrator filed a petition to have Casey suspended from practicing law because of his conversion of client funds and his conduct involving moral turpitude in matters unrelated to Forsberg's claim. Casey was subsequently disbarred on consent on November 5, 1985.

A hearing on the complaint against the present respondent was held before the Hearing Board of the Commission on June 3, 1986. In its report, the Hearing Board noted that the evidence was not in dispute. The evidence supported the allegations in the complaint and provided additional facts as follows.

Before retaining respondent, Forsberg collected $5,000 from Casey. After being retained, respondent made inquiries regarding Casey's conversion, contacting the insurance company that issued the settlement check, its attorney, Forsberg, her mother, her fiancé and Casey. Forsberg told respondent that she simply wanted her money back and specifically instructed respondent to take no other action. Because of respondent's efforts, Forsberg collected another $10,400 from Casey. Respondent received no fee in this case.

The Hearing Board found that respondent received unprivileged information that Casey converted Forsberg's funds, and that respondent failed to relate the information to the Commission in violation of Rule 1-103(a) of the Code.... the Hearing Board recommended a private reprimand.

... The Review Board's report stated that the client had contacted the Commission prior to retaining respondent and, therefore, the Commission did have knowledge of the alleged misconduct. Further, the Review Board noted that respondent respected the client's wishes regarding not pursuing a claim with the Commission. Accordingly, the Review Board recommended that the complaint be dismissed.

The Administrator now raises three issues for review: (1) whether the Review Board erred in concluding that respondent's client had informed the Commission of misconduct by her former attorney; (2) whether the Review Board erred in concluding that respondent had not violated Rule 1-103(a); and (3) whether the proven misconduct warrants at least a censure. . . .

Our analysis of this issue begins with a reading of the applicable disciplinary rules. Rule 1-103(a) of the Code states:

"(a) A lawyer possessing unprivileged knowledge of a violation of Rule 1- 102(a)(3) or (4) shall report such knowledge to a tribunal or other authority empowered to investigate or act upon such violation." 107 Ill.2d R. 1-103(a).

Rule 1-102 of the Code states:

"(a) A lawyer shall not
  (1) violate a disciplinary rule;
  (2) circumvent a disciplinary rule through actions of another;
  (3) engage in illegal conduct involving moral turpitude;
  (4) engage in conduct involving dishonesty, fraud, deceit, or misrepresentation; or
  (5) engage in conduct that is prejudicial to the administration of justice." 107 Ill.2d R. 1-102.

These rules essentially track the language of the American Bar Association Model Code of Professional Responsibility, upon which the Illinois Code was modeled. . . . Thus, if the present respondent's conduct did violate the rule on reporting misconduct, imposition of discipline for such a breach of duty is mandated.

The question whether the information that respondent possessed was protected by the attorney-client privilege, and thus exempt from the reporting rule, requires application of this court's definition of the privilege. . . . We agree with the Administrator's argument that the communication regarding Casey's conduct does not meet this definition. . . .

Though respondent repeatedly asserts that his failure to report was motivated not by financial gain but by the request of his client, we do not deem such an argument relevant in this case. This court has stated that discipline may be appropriate even if no dishonest motive for the misconduct exists. . . . In addition, we have held that client approval of an attorney's action does not immunize an attorney from disciplinary action. . . . Respondent does not argue that Casey's conversion of Forsberg's funds was not illegal conduct involving moral turpitude under Rule 1-102(a)(3) or conduct involving dishonesty, fraud, deceit, or misrepresentation under Rule 1- 102(a)(4). (107 Ill.2d Rules 1-102(a)(3), (a)(4).) It is clear that conversion of client funds is, indeed, conduct involving moral turpitude. . . .We conclude, then, that respondent possessed unprivileged knowledge of Casey's conversion of client funds, which is illegal conduct involving moral turpitude, and that respondent failed in his duty to report such misconduct to the Commission. Because no defense exists, we agree with the Hearing Board's finding that respondent has violated Rule 1- 103(a) and must be disciplined.

The third issue concerns the appropriate quantum of discipline to be imposed in this case. . . .

This failure to report resulted in interference with the Commission's investigation of Casey, and thus with the administration of justice. Perhaps some members of the public would have been spared from Casey's misconduct had respondent reported the information as soon as he knew of Casey's conversions of client funds. We are particularly disturbed by the fact that respondent chose to draft a settlement agreement with Casey rather than report his misconduct. As the Administrator has stated, by this conduct, both respondent and his client ran afoul of the Criminal Code's prohibition against compounding a crime. . . . Both respondent and his client stood to gain financially by agreeing not to prosecute or report Casey for conversion. According to the settlement agreement, respondent would have received $17,000 or more as his fee. If Casey had satisfied the judgment entered against him for failure to honor the settlement agreement, respondent would have collected approximately $25,588.

We have held that fairness dictates consideration of mitigating factors in disciplinary cases. . . . However, these considerations do not outweigh the serious nature of respondent's failure to report Casey, the resulting interference with the Commission's investigation of Casey, and respondent's ill-advised choice to settle with Casey rather than report his misconduct.

Accordingly, it is ordered that respondent be suspended from the practice of law for one year. Respondent suspended.

PRO BONO SERVICE

Access to the legal system for all Americans is something members of the legal community aspire to. Attorneys contribute to this ideal by providing pro bono services. The term pro bono is used to describe the legal services performed free of charge [*for the good*] to the public and society. Attorneys have an ethical duty to volunteer their time by providing legal services to the poor and to charitable organizations. The codes of ethics in most jurisdictions state that attorneys should aspire to render pro bono services by rendering a certain number of hours of pro bono services per year to:

1. Persons of limited means
2. Charitable, religious, civic, community, governmental, and educational organizations that address the needs of persons of limited means

In addition, attorney are encouraged to provide their services at no fee or substantially reduced fees to individuals or organizations that have a goal of protecting civil rights; civil liberties or public rights; or charitable, religious, civic, community, governmental, and educational organizations. Attorneys are also encouraged to participate in activities to improve the law, the legal system, or the legal profession, and to contribute financial support to organizations that provide legal services to persons of limited means.

Rules concerning pro bono activities are aspirational. That means that attorneys should strive to achieve these goals, but the rules are not enforceable. The Model Rules of Professional Conduct clearly state that attorneys should contribute at least 50 hours of service each year to pro bono activities, but this rule is not enforceable by disciplinary action. Most states have adopted rules similar to the model rules; however, some have set different requirements for minimum hours. Florida, for example, has suggested 20 hours per year or a $250 contribution to a legal aid organization.

Pro Bono Opportunities

Numerous opportunities exist for attorneys to provide their services pro bono. The codes of ethics of some states indicate that the bulk of an attorney's pro bono services should be rendered to the poor or to organizations designed primarily to address the needs of the poor. Attorneys can usually register with their state bar association or the state or local court authorities to be included on a list of attorneys who will provide their services pro bono.

In several jurisdictions, attorneys are selected more or less at random by the courts and requested to serve as attorneys for indigents on criminal matters. These attorneys are usually paid some remuneration, although it is usually minimal. In addition, attorneys who serve indigents in this manner are usually reimbursed by the state for any expenses they incur due to their representation.

The ABA Center for Pro Bono offers assistance to attorneys in developing and supporting effective pro bono legal services in civil matters as part of the profession's "effort to ensure access to legal representation and the American system of justice." The 1997/98 Pro Bono Directory of Pro Bono Programs included more than 800 pro bono programs across the country.

From time to time the suggestion is brought forth that pro bono services be required of attorneys and that a certain number of hours be made mandatory. So far, this suggestion has met with much resistance. Opponents to mandatory pro bono service argue that it is unconstitutional to enforce voluntary service of one's time, and that the rule would place too big a burden on certain attorneys. In some jurisdictions, attorneys are subject to mandatory reporting of their pro bono service each year when they pay their annual dues to the bar association.

**FROM THE
PARALEGAL'S
PERSPECTIVE**

Although attorneys are responsible, in many instances, for the ethical conduct of the paralegals they supervise, paralegals must follow their own set of ethical guidelines and rules and do their part to maintain the integrity of the legal profession in general and the paralegal profession in particular. As a paralegal you must be certain your actions maintain, and build on, the integrity and public perception of the paralegal profession. You must avoid any form of misconduct and report serious misconduct you witness to the appropriate authorities. You must also do your part to make our legal system assessable to everyone, including those who cannot afford to pay for legal services.

A Question of Ethics

Suppose you are a paralegal in the corporate department of a law firm in your hometown. You have just finished working on a huge merger deal. You and your co-worker, Diane, another paralegal, have made a significant contribution to the successful closing of the deal, and you are working on the final documentation and billing.

You are filing away copies of the final bill when you notice Diane has considerably more billable time on the file than you do. You know that's not correct. You have worked side-by-side with Diane and, in fact, you are sure you put in more time on the file than she did. When you ask Diane about it, she just shrugs and says something about needing billable hours to reach her quota for the year. "With a bill this size, no one will notice if I add a few hours." Her padding the bill has actually amounted to more than $2,000. Your supervising attorney, Sharon, has signed off on the bill already, and the bill will leave the office by the end of the week. What, if anything, should you do?

Answer and Discussion: This is a really tough situation. You have several options here. The easy way out is to do nothing. Legally you are probably not required to. However, padding a bill is wrong. It is dishonest, unethical, and an attempt to cheat your client out of an additional $2,000. If you are a member of the NFPA, your code of ethics *requires* you to report such behavior. If you have a good working relationship with Diane, you may want to talk to her and try to urge her to talk to her supervising attorney and claim a mistake in her timekeeping. If this isn't possible, you may want to talk to your supervising attorney, Sharon, and explain the situation to her. She can then take what further action may be needed.

MAINTAINING THE INTEGRITY OF THE PARALEGAL PROFESSION

Every working paralegal has a responsibility to all members of the paralegal profession. You are responsible for conducting yourself in a professional and ethical manner, especially because much of the public and a fair portion of the legal community do not know what to expect from paralegals. Every paralegal represents the entire paralegal profession with his or her behavior.

You can help to maintain the integrity of the profession by always acting in a professional manner and by following the code of ethics of any paralegal association to which you belong. Because your supervising attorneys are responsible for your ethical behavior, you must conduct yourself in a manner that will never cause your supervising attorneys to violate their codes of ethics.

NFPA Model Code of Ethics and Professional Responsibility

1.3   A PARALEGAL SHALL MAINTAIN A HIGH STANDARD OF PROFESSIONAL CONDUCT

Ethical Considerations

EC-1.3(a)   A paralegal shall refrain from engaging in any conduct that offends the dignity and decorum of proceedings before a court or other adjudicatory body and shall be respectful of all rules and procedures.

PARALEGAL MISCONDUCT

Paralegal misconduct occurs whenever a paralegal violates any applicable code of ethics. Paralegal misconduct is defined as "the knowing or unknowing commission of an act that is in direct violation of those Canons and Ethical Considerations of any and all applicable codes and/or rules of conduct."[17] This definition includes any violation of the applicable paralegal codes of ethics (the code of ethics adopted by any paralegal association to which the paralegal belongs), as well as the pertinent sections of the code of ethics binding on the attorneys in the jurisdiction in which the paralegal is working.

Although the NALA does not specifically address misconduct in its Code of Ethics and Professional Responsibility or Model Standards and Guidelines, Canon 8 of the NALA Code of Ethics does state that "A legal assistant must do all other things incidental, necessary, or expedient to the attainment of the ethics and responsibilities as defined by statute or rule of court." Further, Canon 9 of the code states that "A legal assistant's conduct is guided by bar associations' codes of professional responsibility and rules of professional conduct."

THE PARALEGAL'S DUTY TO REPORT MISCONDUCT

To maintain the integrity of the legal profession in general and the paralegal profession in particular, you have an ethical duty to report certain serious misconduct, of both paralegals and attorneys, to the proper authorities.

Reporting Paralegal Misconduct

As members of the legal service team, it is important for paralegals to police themselves in order to continue to grow and gain respectability. As a paralegal, you have an ethical duty to report the misconduct of other paralegals under certain circumstances. This concept is supported in the code of ethics of both national associations, as well as the codes of local associations.

Exactly what type of paralegal misconduct must be reported to authorities often remains a judgment call on behalf of the paralegal. It is clearly your ethical duty to report the misconduct of other paralegals when that misconduct may be harmful to clients, employers, or the paralegal profession as a whole, especially when that misconduct is continuing. Some types of behavior that may require reporting include the unauthorized practice of law by a paralegal, improper contact with an opposing party or witnesses in litigation by a paralegal, unfair timekeeping, theft or misappropriation of a client's funds, or other fraudulent or dishonest acts in violation of the code of ethics of paralegals or attorneys.

The NFPA Model Code of Ethics and Professional Responsibility requires reporting of the following types of paralegal misconduct:

1. Any action of another legal professional that clearly demonstrates fraud, deceit, dishonesty, or misrepresentation
2. Dishonest or fraudulent acts by any person pertaining to the handling of the funds, securities, or other assets of a client

If you have witnessed unethical behavior by another paralegal, you may be required to report that behavior under the code of ethics of the paralegal association you belong to. The Model Code of Ethics and Professional Responsibility of the NFPA describes several different types of unethical paralegal behavior that must be reported and states further that "Failure to report such knowledge is in itself misconduct and shall be treated as such under these rules" (Figure 7-2).

If you are ever required to report misconduct of an attorney or paralegal outside of your law firm or legal department, you must remember client confidences and be sure you never break any rules of client confidentiality.

If you have witnessed unethical behavior by a paralegal, and you have determined that you are required to report the behavior, you must next decide to whom that behavior should be reported. Unlike attorneys, paralegals have several options in this area. At times, it may be most appropriate to report the behavior to your supervising attorney. If your supervising attorney is also responsible for supervising the paralegal you suspect of misconduct, you must remember that he or she could be held responsible for that paralegal's misconduct. The circumstances may also warrant reporting the misconduct to your paralegal manager or to an ethics committee within your law firm or corporate legal department. At other times the behavior and circumstances may require you to go to the paralegal association, local or state bar association, or even to the prosecutor's office.

Who you report misconduct to will depend on the type of misconduct and the circumstances surrounding it. For example, if you witness a co-worker paralegal stealing funds from a client trust account and falsifying documents to cover it up, you definitely must report this behavior. The conduct should be reported to your supervising attorney or an ethics committee within your law firm or corporate legal department, depending on your employer's policy.

If you witness misconduct by a paralegal from another law firm, your actions will be different. For example, if you are working on a civil litigation matter and you have knowledge that a paralegal for the opposition has destroyed documents that your law firm has requested in discovery, you will need to take action. First, talk to your supervising attorney. Your supervising attorney may decide the paralegal's supervising attorney should be reported for disciplinary action—either for conspiring with the paralegal to destroy the documents, or for lack of supervision.

As discussed previously in this text, enforcing ethical paralegal behavior is somewhat more problematic than enforcing the codes of ethics for attorneys.

FIGURE 7-2
Excerpts From the NFPA Model Code of Ethics and Professional Responsibility

EC-1.2(f) A paralegal shall advise the proper authority of non-confidential knowledge of any dishonest or fraudulent acts by any person pertaining to the handling of the funds, securities or other assets of a client. The authority to whom the report is made shall depend on the nature and circumstances of the possible misconduct, (e.g., ethics committees of law firms, corporations and/or paralegal associations, local or state bar associations, local prosecutors, administrative agencies, etc.). Failure to report such knowledge is in itself misconduct and shall be treated as such under these rules.

(From NFPA Model Code of Ethics and Professional Responsibility.)

Although you may subscribe to a code of ethics of the paralegal association you belong to, there is no paralegal association that has authority over you, and no court of law that has jurisdiction over the ethics of paralegals, unless there is criminal activity involved.

The NFPA recognizes this dilemma and also recognizes the necessity for enforcement of its Code of Ethics and Professional Responsibility. In 1997 the NFPA drafted Model Guidelines for the Enforcement of the Model Code of Ethics and Professional Responsibility. These guidelines, which may be adopted by paralegal associations, provide for the creation of a disciplinary committee and set forth procedures for reporting alleged violations of the Model Code and disciplinary rules. Under the Model Guidelines for Enforcement, paralegals who witness misconduct can report that misconduct confidentially to a disciplinary committee. The disciplinary committee then investigates the complaint and takes such further action as may be required. The report of misconduct can be made to the committee anonymously under certain circumstances. Currently, no paralegal is obliged to belong to the NFPA or to any paralegal association. However, in the event that paralegals are regulated in the future, either by licensing, certification, or registration, the Model Disciplinary Rules may serve as a model that will be adopted by any paralegal regulation board or agency for enforcing the adopted code of ethics for paralegals. The NFPA Guidelines for the Enforcement of the Model Code of Ethics and Professional Responsibility can be found as part of Appendix D.

If you have knowledge of paralegal misconduct that you feel you must report, be sure to check with your state or local paralegal association to see if they have adopted such procedures.

Reporting Attorney Misconduct

One of the most difficult ethical dilemmas paralegals may encounter is discovering unethical behavior by the attorneys they work for. Suppose you witness one of the attorneys you work for shredding documents that have been requested by the opposing counsel in a civil lawsuit, or that you discover him or her borrowing money from a client trust account. Reporting unethical behavior could mean the loss of status or employment with the firm. Is it unethical to remain silent? Yes. Paralegals have an ethical duty to report misconduct of attorneys. The code of ethics for attorneys in nearly every jurisdiction requires attorneys to report misconduct by other attorneys, and this duty then extends to paralegals.

There are measures short of reporting an attorney to the state's professional authority that you can take if you witness unethical behavior by your attorney employer. Depending on your relationship, you may want to discuss the behavior with the attorney who appears to be acting unethically. Are there circumstances you are unaware of? Possibly the action is not, in fact, unethical. If it becomes clear after addressing the attorney that the actions are unethical and/or illegal, perhaps the matter can be handled by others within the firm. You may believe it is more appropriate to bring the matter to the attention of the appropriate individual or committee within the law firm. If this still does not produce positive results, the attorney should be reported to the ethics committee of the state bar association.

To date there have been no cases involving a paralegal's duty to report unethical or illegal behavior. However, it remains clear that if questioned by a court or an ethics committee of the state bar, you have a duty to report the full truth concerning any actions you have knowledge of. Any time you are involved in testifying or reporting unethical attorney behavior, you must use extreme caution not to divulge confidential client information.

If you find yourself in a serious ethical dilemma that may require reporting an attorney, you may want to seek independent legal advice on the proper steps to take. Your paralegal association may also be able to help (Figure 7-3).

FIGURE 7-3

*What You Can Do If You
Witness Misconduct*

- Talk to the paralegal or attorney you suspect of misconduct—perhaps you have misunderstood what you witnessed.
- Consult your office policy—does your office have a policy for reporting unethical behavior?
- Talk to your supervising attorney about it.
- Talk to your paralegal manager or office manager about it.
- Report the misconduct to your office ethics committee.
- Report the misconduct to your paralegal association (if the suspected individual is a paralegal).
- Report the misconduct to the bar association disciplinary agency (if the suspected individual is an attorney).

PRO BONO FOR PARALEGALS

Pro bono work is not only an ethical duty for paralegals but also an opportunity. Many paralegals report that the pro bono work they have done has been the most rewarding work of their careers.

The ABA, both national paralegal associations, and most local associations promote pro bono work for paralegals. As a paralegal, you can independently volunteer your services for tasks that do not constitute the *practice of law.* You can also work with attorneys as part of a legal team to provide pro bono services. According to the ABA, more than three million hours of legal services are donated annually as pro bono work.[18]

Many law firms and corporate legal departments have pro bono committees that set the standards for pro bono participation by attorneys and paralegals of their firms, and they encourage a certain amount of pro bono work on firm time. They recognize that active pro bono programs in the law firm provide unique experience and training to the attorneys and paralegals in the firm and that pro bono work can enhance the reputation of the firm in the community.

Although paralegals must not partake in activities that can be considered the practice of law, there are numerous ways in which paralegals are uniquely qualified to assist those in need. Some of the ways paralegals can offer their pro bono services include:

- Working as advocates for victims of abuse and domestic violence
- Acting as an advocate for children within the court system or administrative agencies (e.g., working with children who are limited by medically determined physical or mental conditions to see that the families of these children receive the SSI benefits they are due from the Social Security Administration)
- Assisting at legal aid clinics that strive to meet the legal needs of the poor, including assistance with divorces, bankruptcies, and landlord-tenant disputes
- Working in homeless shelters and legal clinics for the homeless
- Assisting with the drafting of wills and other estate-planning documents for indigent sick and elderly people
- Assisting with the legal work performed for nonprofit organizations
- Educating children regarding law-related careers
- Mentoring children and young adults in their communities

While you are helping others, you will also be helping yourself. Many pro bono programs offer free training to paralegals—training that may be valuable throughout your career.

If you want to volunteer your time for a good cause, there is no shortage of opportunities or resources. Most state and local paralegal associations have pro bono committees that work to match paralegal volunteers with pro bono opportunities. Your school, employer, and the state bar association may also assist in finding the right opportunity for you.

For more information, contact:

The National Federation of Paralegal Associations Pro Bono Committee
http://www.paralegals.org/probono/home.html

American Bar Association Center for Pro Bono (312) 988-5769
http://www.abanet.org/legalserv/probono.html

CHAPTER SUMMARY

- Bar applicants have a duty of candor when applying for admission to the bar, and attorneys have a duty of candor when involved in any disciplinary proceeding.
- An applicant's good moral character is required as a prerequisite to admission to the bar.
- Any violation of the pertinent rules of ethics by an attorney is considered misconduct.
- Commission of certain crimes, even crimes unrelated to an attorney's profession, is considered misconduct and grounds for disbarment or other discipline if the crime reflects adversely on the attorney's honesty, trustworthiness, or fitness as an attorney.
- Attorneys have a duty to report the unethical conduct of other attorneys if they have knowledge of that conduct, if that conduct raises a substantial question as to the attorney's fitness as an attorney, and if that information is not protected by rules concerning client confidentiality.
- Rule 6.1 of the Model Rules of Professional Conduct provides that attorneys should aspire to render at least fifty hours of pro bono service per year.
- Paralegal misconduct occurs when a paralegal violates rules of the applicable codes of ethics.
- Paralegals have an ethical duty to report certain types of misconduct of other paralegals and attorneys.

SUMMARY QUESTIONS

1. What are the possible consequences to someone who lies on his or her application to the bar?
2. Why is it so important for attorneys to report the misconduct of other attorneys?
3. Under what conditions is an attorney obligated to report misconduct of another attorney?
4. Suppose you find out the sole practitioner you work for has been writing checks out of the client trust account to cover the office rent for the month, then paying it back. What would you do? Would you report the behavior? What if you found out that same attorney was systematically stealing money from the trust account of an elderly client of the firm and falsifying the accounting?
5. If an attorney runs a red light or speeds, is this considered to be misconduct? What if an attorney is arrested for domestic abuse?
6. How is the paralegal's duty to report misconduct different from an attorney's duty to report misconduct?

ENDNOTES

[1]*People v. Culpepper,* 645 P.2d 5 (Co. 1982).

[2]*In re Martin-Trigona,* 302 N.E. 2d 68 (Ill. 1973).

[3]*Application of Gahan for Admission to the Bar of Minnesota,* 279 NW2d 826 (1979).

[4]*In ree Russell Vernon Guilford,* 505 N.E. 2d 342 (Ill. 1987).

[5]*Levi v. Mississippi Bar,* 436 So.2d 781 (Miss. 1983).

[6]*The Florida Bar v. Vaughn,* 608 So. 2d 18 (Fla. 1992).

[7]*The Committee on Legal Ethics of the West Virginia State Bar v. Martin,* 419 S.E. 2d 4 (W. Va. Sup. Ct. of App. 1992).

[8]Comment to *Annotated Model Rules of Professional Conduct,* American Bar Association (1999).

[9]ABA Comm. on Ethics and Professional Responsibility, Formal Op. 92-364 (1992).

[10]Notes to Disciplinary Rules, DR 1-102(A)(3), *Model Code of Professional Responsibility.*

[11]*Reid v. Mississippi State Bar,* 586 So. 2d 786 (Miss. 1991).

[12]*Foote v. Mississippi State Bar Association,* 517 So. 2d 561 (Miss. 1987).

[13]*In re Dahlberg,* 611 N.E. 2d 641 (Ind. 1993).

[14]Comment to Rule 8.3, *Annotated Model Rules of Professional Conduct,* American Bar Association (1999).

[15]*In re Himmel,* 533 N.E. 2d 790 (Ill. 1988)

[16]*ABA Formal Op. 94-383.*

[17]*NFPA Model Guidelines for the Enforcement of the Model Code of Ethics and Professional Responsibility* (1997).

[18]Leader of the Pro Bono Pack, *ABA Journal,* October 1997.

YOU'VE COME A LONG WAY BABY?

You need only turn on the television or open the pages of your favorite magazine. A voluptuous, thirsty, bikini-clad blonde on the beach wants to sell you a soft drink. A gorgeous brunette in a slinky evening gown wants to sell you your next luxury car. A redhead with an incredible, voluminous mane of hair wants to sell you her favorite shampoo. An attractive, enticing woman with long blond hair, lounging across a desk in a miniskirt, wants to sell you— *legal services?* Anyone in the advertising business will tell you that sex sells. It sells soft drinks, automobiles, and shampoo. And, at least according to Rosalie Osias, a member of the bar in Great Neck, New York, sex sells legal services.

Rosalie Osias is an attorney who specializes in the mortgage-banking field, a field that, she claims, is totally male dominated. Rosalie's controversial advertising is meant to draw attention—and it does. One full-page advertisement ran in 1995 showed Ms. Osias lying prone across her desk with her feet kicked up behind her in black spike heels; her long blonde hair fanning a law book in front of her. The photo's caption read: *Does this law firm have a reputation? You bet it does!!!*

Another ad shows Rosalie in a leather miniskirt, sitting astride a motorcycle. The caption reads: *We will ride anything to get to your closing on time.*

A third ad shows Rosalie lying on her side holding onto a golf club. The caption indicates that her firm doesn't play golf, they're too busy closing loans.

Rosalie's advertising led to a battle of the sexes with other real estate attorneys. One male real estate attorney responded by placing his own ad, showing himself partially clad in the shower. The caption read: *I don't look as good as you know who, but I can do great closings!*

Rosalie says her advertising campaign was designed to help her break into a completely male-dominated industry. She decided to use her "assets as a woman and how I look to generate an interest and make men stop and talk about me." Men have stopped to talk about Rosalie, and they have started to hire her. Rosalie's business has been booming since she began her advertising campaign. The number of banks Rosalie represents at mortgage closings has gone from five to approximately forty.

Rosalie's suggestive advertisement has also caught her plenty of unwelcome attention, including the attention of the local bar. The ABA, as well as the state and local bar associations, have always advocated dignity for any advertising by attorneys. The president of the Nassau County Bar called Rosalie's advertising "a disgrace that degrades the legal profession." Feminists across the country have spoken out against Rosalie, her ads, and her controversial point of view.

The Tenth Judicial District's Grievance Committee initiated action against Rosalie in 1995 when the provocative advertisements first appeared in print. The bar concluded that, although they found Ms. Osias's ads "unseemly," they could find no legal basis for filing a complaint against her.

In her press release, Rosalie called the decision not to file a complaint against her "a vote for sanity for those of us in the legal profession." Further, Ms. Osias said that the decision "sends a signal to all of my colleagues that creativity in marketing your business is not against the law." Rosalie believes she has advanced First Amendment rights for all attorneys and opened the door to a new type of advertising. Rosalie has declared a victory, claiming that "lawyers can now use plenty of cleavage and leg in advertising."

Rosalie Osias is not one to stay out of the public eye for long. Ms. Osias has appeared on television talk shows, expressing her rather controversial position that women should be encouraged to use their sexuality to get ahead in the workplace. In 1998 Ms. Osias formed a foundation that provided the initial contribution of $10,000 to fund the Monica Lewinsky Defense Fund, claiming that Monica Lewinsky has become the "most betrayed individual since Joan of Arc" and that she needs assistance to pay her millions of dollars of legal fees.

Chapter 8

Advertising and Solicitation

*I'm not an ambulance chaser because
I'm usually there before the ambulance.*

Melvin Belli, a.k.a. "The King of Torts"

An Ethical Dilemma
Introduction
Advertising Acceptance
Supreme Court Decisions Allowing Advertising
 The Bates Decision
 In Re R.M.J.
Current Rules Regulating and Restricting Advertising
False and Misleading Advertising
 Misrepresentation and Misleading Advertising
 Unjustified Expectations
 Comparison
 Fees
 Dignity in Advertising
Case and Discussion
Advertising Media
Advertising Records and Reporting
Specialization
Advertising Costs and Referral Fees
Law Firm Names and Letterhead

Solicitation
 Solicitation Letters
 Solicitation Not for Profit
 Solicitation of Friends, Family Members, and Prior Clients
A Question of Ethics
 Federal Class Actions
 Prepaid or Group Legal Services Plan
From the Paralegal's Perspective
Paralegal Advertising
 Traditional Paralegals
  Letterhead
  Business Cards
  Advertisements
  CLA and RP Designations
 Freelance Paralegals
 Independent Paralegals
Solicitation
Case and Discussion

Chapter Summary

Summary Questions

An Ethical Dilemma

When a small commuter plane recently went down in Florida, attorney Sam Kelsey wanted to help. Mr. Kelsey had extensive experience in representing the families of plane crash victims. He also had a strong belief that the representatives of the airline and the airline's insurance carrier would act quickly to reach settlements with the families of the passengers killed in the crash, thereby taking advantage of their shock and grief. Mr. Kelsey wanted to give fair representation to these families. He wanted to reach those individuals as early as possible so they would not be taken advantage of. Mr. Kelsey waited two weeks after the crash and then sent letters to the families of the victims offering his services. Has he offered a needed service or acted unethically?

Answer and Discussion: Mr. Kelsey has acted unethically. Pursuant to the Aviation Disaster Family Assistance Act of 1996,[1] attorneys are prohibited from making any "unsolicited communication concerning a potential action for personal injury or wrongful death" for 30 days following the date of an airline crash.

INTRODUCTION

Not too many years ago, advertisement of legal services by attorneys was considered unprofessional and unethical and thus was strictly prohibited. Obviously, as demonstrated by the television, newspaper, and other sources of advertisements that are prevalent today, this is no longer the case.

However, advertising and soliciting by attorneys is strictly regulated by the code of ethics of each state. To thwart "ambulance chasers," the aggressive in-person solicitation of individual clients by both attorneys and paralegals is still prohibited.

This chapter examines the rules of ethics concerning advertising and solicitation. The second part of this chapter focuses on the topic from the paralegal's perspective and takes a look at the rules for including information about paralegals in law firm advertising and permissible advertising by freelance and independent paralegals.

ADVERTISING ACCEPTANCE

Advertising legal services benefits members of the legal community in increased clientele and revenues, but it also benefits the community. The public's need to be informed about available attorneys, their services, and their prices for services is a very strong argument in favor of advertising. For the public to benefit, the advertising must be informative, truthful, and not misleading.

The first advertising permitted was very limited in scope and media. Over time, restrictions on advertising content and the form of media that can be used have been liberalized. In every instance, the change was first brought about by the challenge of a state rule leading to a decision by the U.S. Supreme Court. U.S. Supreme Court decisions have lead the way to freedom to advertise, followed by corresponding changes to the ABA's Model Code or Model Rules, and the codes of ethics of each of the states. The state codes of ethics cannot be in conflict with decisions of the U.S. Supreme Court. If they are, they are subject to being challenged and overturned by the state courts or the U.S. Supreme Court.

Advertising has become crucial to many attorneys to remain competitive in the legal community, and it has become a big business. Attorney marketing expenses grew to $5.5 million per week in 1995,[2] and law firm marketing has become a whole new industry.

SUPREME COURT DECISIONS ALLOWING ADVERTISING

Although many attorneys remember when advertising was considered unethical and absolutely prohibited, this wasn't always the case. Attorney advertising was acceptable during the nineteenth century. In fact, Abraham Lincoln advertised his services in newspapers, along with the bankers and other professionals of the day. However, by 1908, when the first ABA Canons of Professional Ethics were adopted, the opinion of most members of the bar had changed, and advertising of any kind was prohibited. The prohibition on attorney advertising was in effect until the *Bates* decision in 1977.

The Bates Decision

The prohibition on attorney and law firm advertising was lifted with the 1977 Supreme Court decision of *Bates v. State Bar of Arizona,* 433 U.S. 350 (1977). The Bates case began in Arizona, where two attorneys placed an advertisement in the *Arizona Republic,* a daily newspaper circulated in Phoenix. The advertisement stated that the attorneys offered "legal services at very reasonable fees" and listed their fees for certain services. This advertisement was in violation of Arizona DR 2-101(B), incorporated into the Rules of the Supreme Court of Arizona. This rule specifically stated that attorneys may not *publicize* themselves through newspaper or magazine advertisements, radio or television announcements, display advertisements in the city or telephone directories, or other means of commercial publicity . . .[3] The Supreme Court of Arizona imposed sanctions on the two attorneys, who then challenged the constitutionality of the total ban on attorney advertising and appealed to the U.S. Supreme Court.

The Supreme Court of the United States deemed attorney advertising to be commercial speech and applied First Amendment protection (Figure 8–1). The Court affirmed an attorney's constitutional right to advertise legal services. All states were forced to follow suit.

The Bates opinion also acknowledged the states' rights to regulate and restrict attorney advertising, so long as it was within the guidelines established by the court. In his Bates opinion, Justice Blackmun listed some of the permitted regulations that may be established by the states, including restricting false and misleading advertising and claims about the quality of legal services.

The ABA responded by adopting conservative amendments to the Model Code of Professional Responsibility in 1978. The amendment to the Model Code listed twenty-five categories of information that could be included in advertising by attorneys and law firms. The Model Code was followed by most states in this regard.

AMENDMENT I
Congress shall make no law respecting an establishment of religion, or prohibiting the free exercise thereof; or abridging the freedom of speech, or of the press; or the right of the people peaceably to assemble, and to petition the Government for a redress of grievances.

FIGURE 8–1
First Amendment to the Constitution of the United States of America

In Re R.M.J.

In 1980 the United States Supreme Court again heard a case concerning advertising by attorneys and law firms. In this case, *In re R.M.J.,* a Missouri attorney appealed an order of the Missouri Supreme Court disbarring him for violating the state's rules concerning attorney advertising. The attorney challenged the restrictiveness of Rule 4 of the Missouri Supreme Court, which dictated specific permissible language for attorney advertising and restricted mailing of law firm announcement cards to a select group of individuals. This rule was typical of the rules adopted by several states immediately following the Bates decision. The U.S. Supreme Court discussed the following three violations that the attorney was disbarred for:

1. In a Yellow Pages advertising the attorney listed his areas of practice in language that was not prescribed by Rule 4. Rule 4 of the Missouri Supreme Court prescribed exact language that was permissible for advertising areas of practice. The Missouri Court did not contend that the attorney's choice of words was misleading, rather that they were not those prescribed by Missouri rules.
2. The attorney listed the courts and states in which he was admitted to practice. This information was also not prescribed under the Missouri rules.
3. The attorney mailed announcement cards announcing his new practice to persons other than *lawyers, clients, former clients, personal friends, and relatives* in violation of the Missouri rules.

The U.S. Supreme Court found that the Missouri rules were too restrictive and they reversed the judgment of the Supreme Court of Missouri. In his opinion, Justice Powell stated:

> . . . We emphasize, as we have throughout the opinion, that the States retain the authority to regulate advertising that is inherently misleading or that has proved to be misleading in practice. There may be other substantial state interests as well that will support carefully drawn restrictions. But although the States may regulate commercial speech, the First and Fourteenth Amendments require that they do so with care and in a manner no more extensive than reasonably necessary to further substantial interests. The absolute prohibition on appellant's speech, in the absence of a finding that his speech was misleading, does not meet these requirements.

The Supreme Court has made several decisions concerning attorney advertising and solicitation since the Bates decision—many of which are discussed in this chapter. In every instance the court has had to weigh the interests of several competing groups. On the one hand are the public's need for information and the attorneys' First Amendment rights to freedom of speech. On the other hand are the bar's desire to maintain public respect and dignity and the right of the states to protect their consumers. These considerations will undoubtedly continue to be paramount in any future decisions concerning attorney advertising and soliciting (Figure 8–2).

CURRENT RULES REGULATING AND RESTRICTING ADVERTISING

The many U.S. Supreme Court decisions have lead to several revisions first to the Model Code and then, more recently, to the Model Rules of Professional Conduct and the codes of ethics of the individual states. The Model Rules adopted by the ABA in 1983 do not dictate the type of information that can be included in attorney and law firm advertising, but rather prohibit false or misleading communications.

1908	The American Bar Association's ABA Canons of Professional Ethics prohibited attorney advertising of any kind.
1977	The U.S. Supreme Court lifted the total ban on attorney advertising in its Bates decision. The court found that attorney advertising was protected under the First Amendment as commercial speech. Weighing the interest of the individual states and the interests of the attorneys, the court found that states could not place a total ban on attorney advertising but could restrict it.
1978	The ABA amended its Model Code of Professional Responsibility to conform to the Bates decision. The amendment listed twenty-five categories of information that could be included in advertising by attorneys and law firms.
1978	In *Ohralik v. Ohio State Bar*, the Supreme Court upheld a ban on in-person solicitation, indicating that the same First Amendment protections that applied to attorney advertising did not apply to in-person solicitation.
1978	The U.S. Supreme Court decision in *In Re Primus* provided that in-person solicitation may be permitted under certain circumstances when the attorney's motive is political or ideological. The court ruled that when the motive behind the solicitation is political expression, the First Amendment is applied much more broadly than if the motive is purely commercial.
1980	The U.S. Supreme Court handed down a decision in the *In Re RMJ* case that emphasized the limits of the states' authority to restrict attorney advertising. The court affirmed the states' right to restrict misleading advertising and other types of advertising contrary to substantial state interests. However, the court ruled that the First and Fourteenth Amendments require that states restrict attorney advertising with care and in a manner no more extensive than reasonably necessary to further substantial interests.
1983	The Model Rules of Professional Conduct are adopted by the ABA. Unlike the prior Model Code, the Model Rules do not dictate the information that may be contained in attorney advertising, but provide that advertising must not be false or misleading.
1988	The U.S. Supreme Court ruled that a Kentucky rule prohibiting all targeted direct-mail solicitation by attorney's for pecuniary gain was unconstitutional, and that states may not categorically prohibit attorneys from soliciting business by sending truthful and nondeceptive letters to potential clients known to face particular legal problems.
1989	The Model Rules of Professional Conduct are amended to provide for restricted direct-mail solicitation by attorneys.
1990	The Supreme Court ruled on *Peel v. Attorney Registration and Disciplinary Commission of Illinois*, holding that, consistent with the First Amendment, states may not categorically prohibit attorneys from advertising their certifications as specialists by bona fide organizations.
1995	The NFPA issued Ethics Opinion 95–6 indicating that it is ethical for freelance paralegals, also known as contract paralegals, to advertise their services, so long as several conditions listed in the opinion are met.
1995	In *Florida Bar v. Went For It*, the Supreme Court upheld a rule of the Florida Bar mandating a thirty-day waiting period after an accident or disaster before a solicitation letter can be sent to the victims of the accident.

FIGURE 8–2
Timeline of Attorney Advertising

Most state rules now follow the general provisions of the Model Rules (Figure 8–3). However, there is still a lot of variance among the specific provisions of the state's codes of ethics concerning advertising and solicitation. The rules of ethics addressing advertising generally include:

- Prohibition of false and misleading advertising
- Requirements for recordkeeping of advertisements
- Restrictions on advertising areas of practice

> **Rule 7.1 Communications Concerning a Lawyer's Services**
> A lawyer shall not make a false or misleading communication about the lawyer or the lawyer's services. A communication is false or misleading if it:
> (a) contains a material misrepresentation of fact or law, or omits a fact necessary to make the statement considered as a whole not materially misleading;
> (b) is likely to create an unjustified expectation about results the lawyer can achieve, or states or implies that the lawyer can achieve results by means that violate the Rules of Professional Conduct or other law; or
> (c) compares the lawyer's services with other lawyers' services, unless the comparison can be factually substantiated.

- Restrictions on the payment of referral fees
- Restrictions on solicitation of potential clients by mail
- Restrictions on in-person solicitation of potential clients

FALSE AND MISLEADING ADVERTISING

Since the Bates decision, the individual states may not prohibit advertising by attorneys and law firms in general; however, they do have the right to regulate that advertising. The Supreme Court has held that "Truthful advertising related to lawful activities is entitled to the protections of the First Amendment. But when the particular content or method of the advertising suggests that it is inherently misleading or when experience has proved that in fact such advertising is subject to abuse, the states may impose appropriate restrictions."[4]

The rules of all jurisdictions provide that advertising must not be false or misleading. The Model Rules provide three types of advertising communication that is considered misleading, including:

1. Advertising containing a material misrepresentation of fact or law or omitting a fact necessary to make the statement considered as a whole not materially misleading
2. Advertising likely to create unjustified expectations about results an attorney can achieve, or that implies the attorney can achieve results by unethical or illegal means
3. Advertising comparing the services of two or more attorneys or law firms, unless the comparison can be factually substantiated

Misrepresentation and Misleading Advertising

Advertising that contains material misrepresentation of fact or law is relatively easy to determine because it deals with concrete information and statements that are usually easily proved or disproved. Misleading advertising, on the other hand, is somewhat more difficult to define. What is considered misleading, as opposed to informative, can be subjective, and the definition varies among the states. For example, although it is not an untrue statement, in the RMJ case it was found misleading to advertise that an attorney is a member of the U.S. Supreme Court Bar because the general public is unfamiliar with requirements of admission.[5]

Unjustified Expectations

Advertising is considered false and misleading if it causes the recipient of the material to have unjustified expectations. If the advertising material would cause the recipient to have the expectation of a favorable verdict (when this is not realistic) unrealistic expectations are created. Advertisements concerning results obtained on behalf of other clients, such as winning favorable verdicts or collecting large settlements, may fall under this category because it may cause the potential client to expect the same or a similar outcome.

Comparison

Advertising that compares the skill or quality of legal services rendered by one attorney with the skills and legal services rendered by another may be misleading and is generally prohibited. However, factual statements such as "the largest law firm in the city" may be permissible.

Fees

Advertised statements concerning fees charged by attorneys are generally acceptable, provided they are not false or misleading. For example, it is not inherently misleading to indicate that fees or prices charged for "routine" legal services.[6] It is also permissible to say that legal services are offered at "very reasonable prices" if the prices charged are within the low range of prices for similar services commonly charged in the attorney's geographical area.[7] However, advertising claiming that no fee will be charged unless the client recovers damages has been considered misleading unless the advertisement includes a statement that the client will be responsible for costs and expenses of litigation (when that is the case).[8] Advertisements for fixed fees for certain representations, where there are hidden costs, are also considered misleading.

Dignity in Advertising

Most members of the legal profession would agree that truly tasteless and undignified advertising is embarrassing and reflects poorly on the entire legal community. At one time, the codes of ethics of most jurisdictions contained statements indicating that all advertising must be dignified. However, "good taste" and "dignity" in advertising are purely subjective terms and impossible to regulate, and those provisions have now been mostly eliminated.

DR 2-102 of the ABA's Model Code included a requirement that communications about legal services be dignified. This requirement was not continued in the Model Rules.

CASE AND DISCUSSION

In the following case, the attorney broke several disciplinary rules of the former Code of Professional Responsibility and several rules of the current Rules of Professional Conduct concerning advertising. The attorney's Yellow Pages advertising was found to be false and misleading. In addition, the attorney was operating an unauthorized for-profit lawyer referral business.

The PEOPLE of the State of Colorado, Complainant,

v.

Robert H. CARPENTER, Attorney-Respondent.

No. 95SA86.

Supreme Court of Colorado,

En Banc.

April 24, 1995.

PER CURIAM.

In this lawyer discipline proceeding, the respondent[1] and the assistant disciplinary counsel executed a stipulation, agreement, and conditional admission of misconduct. . . . An inquiry panel of the Supreme Court Grievance Committee approved the stipulation, and recommended that the respondent be publicly censured. We accept the conditional admission and the recommendation of the inquiry panel.

---

[1] The respondent was admitted to the bar of this court on December 11, 1981, is registered as an attorney upon the official records of this court, and is accordingly subject to the jurisdiction of this court and its grievance committee in these proceedings. C.R.C.P. 241.1(b).

I

According to the stipulation, beginning in November 1990, the respondent placed an advertisement in the Metro Denver U S WEST Yellow Pages under the name of "An Able Attorney Referral, Inc." The advertisement continued to run up to and including the 1993/1994 U S WEST Yellow Pages. The parties stipulated that the advertisement contained false, misleading, deceptive, or unfair statements, including:

a. It implied that a number of lawyers were available to prospective clients in at least thirteen specified fields of practice, when in fact there was a maximum of five lawyers available at any given time, and most of the time there were fewer than five attorneys available in substantially fewer fields of expertise than those represented in the advertisement.

b. Notwithstanding the fields listed in the advertisement, there were never any referral lawyers available in certain of the specified fields, including estates, wills and trusts, real estate, securities and tax, trials and appeals, workers' compensation, business, and contracts.

c. Although respondent represented that he conducted business as "An Able Attorney Referral, Inc.," there was no properly incorporated or duly organized entity with the name "An Able Attorney Referral, Inc."

d. The respondent charged the other lawyers involved $50 to $75 a month for referral business.

e. The respondent operated a for-profit lawyer referral service not operated, sponsored, or approved by any bar association, contrary to DR 2-103(D).

The respondent admitted that his conduct also violated DR 1-102(A)(4) (a lawyer shall not engage in conduct involving dishonesty, fraud, deceit, or misrepresentation); and DR 2-101(A) (a lawyer shall not use any form of advertising, solicitation or publicity containing a false, fraudulent, misleading, deceptive, or unfair statement or claim). On and after January 1, 1993, the effective date of the Rules of Professional Conduct, respondent violated R.P.C. 7.1 (a lawyer shall not make a false or misleading communication about the lawyer or the lawyer's services), and R.P.C. 8.4(c) (a lawyer shall not engage in conduct involving dishonesty, fraud, deceit, or misrepresentation).

The assistant disciplinary counsel indicates that the respondent terminated the referral service after the initial request for investigation in this proceeding was filed.

II

. . . The respondent's conduct involved dishonesty and misrepresentation, and, in conjunction with his prior discipline, forecloses a private sanction. . . . We therefore accept the conditional admission and the recommendation of the inquiry panel.

III

It is hereby ordered that Robert H. Carpenter be publicly censured. It is further ordered that the respondent pay the costs of this proceeding in the amount of $178.62 to the Supreme Court Grievance Committee, 600 Seventeenth Street, Suite 920-S, Denver, Colorado 80202, within thirty days after the announcement of this opinion.

ADVERTISING MEDIA

Most current advertising rules focus on content rather than the media used for disseminating the information. Therefore, those rules apply to all types of printed advertising, as well as to television and the Internet.

Initially, television advertising was prohibited in most jurisdictions. However, television has become one of the most prevalent forms of communication, and its power to reach the public is unequaled by other forms of media. Because it is the primary source of information for many people of low to moderate income, and especially to those who are illiterate, bans on television advertising have been found to be too restrictive and have been overturned. As stated by the Supreme Court of Connecticut,

> A total ban on advertising through the electronic media would not only exceed the state's legitimate interest in protecting potential consumers, but its overinclusiveness would also keep a great deal of information from consumers, thereby hindering their ability to make an informed choice.[9]

Currently, attorneys and law firms use several types of media to communicate their advertising, including newspaper and periodical advertising; Yellow Pages advertising; billboards; newsletters; television; radio; and, with increasing frequency, Web sites and banner advertising on the Internet. Yellow Pages advertising is the most frequently used type of advertising. Recently, much attention has been focused on advertising over the Internet, which introduces several new issues to the topic. Focus will be given to advertising over the Internet in Chapter 10.

- Yellow Pages ads
- Attorney and law firm directories
- Seminars and other speaking engagements
- Newspaper and periodical advertisements
- Television advertisements
- Sponsoring community events
- Web sites and advertising on the Internet
- Firm brochures
- Newsletters sent to clients and potential clients
- Hire publicist to prepare press releases concerning the law firm

FIGURE 8–4

How Law Firms Market Their Services

Whatever the media used to communicate the attorney's message, the message must comply with all rules concerning advertising, including rules prohibiting false or misleading advertising (Figure 8–4).

ADVERTISING RECORDS AND REPORTING

Under Model Rule 7.2, copies of all advertising, including a record of the content and use of the advertising, must be kept for two years. Advertising need not be approved prior to dissemination and it need not be submitted to the bar association. This is contrary to the rules of several states, which require copies of all advertising by attorneys and law firms to be submitted to a committee of the bar association prior to, or simultaneous with, its release to the public. This requirement is not included in the Model Rules because, according to the comments to the Model Rules, "Such a requirement would be burdensome and expensive relative to its possible benefits, and may be of doubtful constitutionality."

The rules of most states require all attorney advertising to be labeled *Advertising* or *Advertising Material.* This is to avoid any confusion on the part of the public who may mistake attorney advertising for some other type of document that may require their attention or *require* them to contact the lawyer or law firm in question.

In addition, all advertisements must include the name of at least one attorney responsible for its content.

SPECIALIZATION

Attorneys who specialize in one or a few fields of law find it beneficial to so indicate in their advertising materials. Because the main purpose of advertising is to attract business, they want to be sure to attract the right kind of business. Attorneys are generally permitted to indicate in advertising and other communications areas of law in which they specialize. If an attorney practices only in certain fields, he or she may say so. It is generally permitted for an attorney to use the word *specialist* or to indicate that he or she "practices a specialty." The words *specialist* and *specialty* must not be used in a way that could be misleading.

Use of language concerning an attorney's certification in a specialty is generally restricted by the state codes of ethics. Prior to 1990, attorneys were prohibited from advertising their certifications as specialists in specific areas of law. The recognized exceptions to this rule were for attorneys who specialized in patent law or admiralty law, two fields of law that were certified by recognized federal agencies.

Prohibition on advertising attorney certifications as specialists was banned by a decision of the Supreme Court in 1990.[10] In that case, *Peel v. Attorney Registration and Disciplinary Commission of Illinois,* disciplinary proceedings were brought against an attorney who included a truthful statement on his letterhead that he was certified as a trial specialist by the National Board of Trial Specialists (contrary to the Rules of Illinois). The case was appealed to the U.S. Supreme Court, which held that, consistent with the First Amendment, states may not categorically prohibit attorneys from advertising their certifications as specialists by bona fide organizations.

Any advertising or communication concerning an attorney's fields of law must not be misleading. In a recent case before the Ohio Supreme Court, an attorney was publicly reprimanded for indicating that he was "specializing in" medical malpractice when, in fact, the attorney had little experience in the field and could not reasonably be considered a specialist.[11]

Rule 7.4 of the Model Rules concerning fields of practice specifically permits attorneys to state they have been recognized or certified as a specialist in a particular field of law if:

- They are admitted to engage in patent practice before the United States Patent and Trademark Office
- They are engaged in Admiralty practice
- They are certified in a field of law by a regulatory authority (in states where there is a regulatory authority granting certification)

The Model Rules provide that in states where there is no procedure for certification of specialties or for approval of organizations granting certification, attorneys may communicate the fact that they are certified as specialists in a field of law by a named organization, so long as they state in that communication that there is no procedure in the jurisdiction for approving certifying organizations, unless the certifying organization is approved by the ABA.

Some states allow attorneys to state that their practices are limited to or concentrated in particular fields. These rules allow attorneys to describe their practices without implying a formal recognition of a certification or specialization in a field of law.

ADVERTISING COSTS AND REFERRAL FEES

An attorney is allowed to pay for permitted advertising and to pay fees to not-for-profit lawyer referral agencies. Otherwise, most types of referral fees are considered unethical and prohibited under the codes of ethics in most jurisdictions. Fees paid to lay people for referring a friend or acquaintance, and fees paid to others for soliciting business on their behalf, are generally prohibited.

Certain types of not-for-profit lawyer referral agencies specialize in assisting members of the public in finding an appropriate attorney, and attorneys are permitted to pay them a customary fee for their services.

LAW FIRM NAMES AND LETTERHEAD

Attorneys must choose the names of their law firms carefully so that they are not misleading. The name should clearly indicate what type of entity the firm is— whether it is a **sole proprietorship**, a **partnership**, a **professional corporation**, a **professional limited liability company**, or some other type of entity. The name of the firm may include the name of any practicing attorneys of the firm and the names of any deceased partners. The name of the firm may also be a trade name if it is not misleading and does not imply a connection to a government entity.

Attorneys must be careful that the name of their firm does not imply a partnership where none exists. For example, if Simons and Jacobson are two attorneys

Sole proprietorship
Ownership by one person, as opposed to ownership by more than one person, ownership by a corporation, ownership by a partnership, etc.

Partnership
An undertaking of two or more persons to carry on, as co-owners, a business or other enterprise for profit; an agreement between or among two or more persons to put their money, labor, and skill into commerce or business, and to divide the profit in agreed-upon proportions.

Professional corporation
Type of corporation that may be formed in most states by those rendering personal services to the public of a type that requires a license or other legal authorization.

Professional limited liability company
Entity, similar to a professional corporation, that allows limited liability and partnership taxation status to its members, who must be professionals.

who merely share office space, they may not use the name Simons & Jacobson for marketing purposes. To do so would be misleading and may cause Simons to be liable for any malpractice of Jacobson and Jacobson to be liable for Simons.

Letterhead is considered a form of public communication, and the letterhead of attorneys and law firms must not be misleading. Letterhead must conform to the Rule 7.1 concerning false and misleading information. In addition, letterhead, business cards, and law firm announcements must comply with state ethics rules.

If any nonlawyers are included on law firm letterhead, the status of the nonlawyer must be clearly indicated. Not every jurisdiction allows the use of nonlawyers' names on letterhead.

SOLICITATION

Although the rules and views expressed by the bar and the courts concerning advertising have changed dramatically since 1977, the general prohibition on in-person solicitation remains.

The U.S. Supreme Court has supported this ban on solicitation for decades. In 1978, the Supreme Court upheld a ban on in-person solicitation, indicating that the state's interest in protecting the public by preventing "those aspects of solicitation that induce fraud, undue influence, intimidation, overreaching, and other forms of vexatious conduct"[12]. . . took priority over the attorney's interest in communication. In *Ohralik v. Ohio State Bar,* the Supreme Court held that the same First Amendment protections that applied to attorney advertising did not apply to in-person solicitation, stating:

> Unlike a public advertisement, which simply provides information and leaves the recipient free to act upon it or not, in-person solicitation may exert pressure and often demands an immediate response, without providing an opportunity for comparison or reflection.

Rule 7.3 of the Model Rules of Professional Conduct prohibits in-person and telephone solicitation of potential clients with individuals the attorney has no family or prior professional relationship when financial gain is a significant motive for the attorney.

Solicitation of clients is prohibited to protect the public because the potential for abuse is considered great. It is generally agreed that in-person and telephone solicitation of a potential client puts too much pressure on that individual, who may be experiencing extreme stress, loss, or grief. The comments to Model Rule 7.3 justifies this ban on in-person solicitation as follows:

> The prospective client, who may already feel overwhelmed by the circumstances giving rise to the need for legal services, may find it difficult fully to evaluate all available alternatives with reasoned judgment and appropriate self-interest in the face of the lawyer's presence and insistence upon being retained immediately. The situation is fraught with the possibility of undue influence, intimidation, and over-reaching.

There are a few recognized exceptions to the prohibition on solicitation. Solicitation of individuals by mail is generally acceptable, although regulated by the states. In-person solicitation may also be permitted if the attorney's purpose behind the solicitation is not financial, or if the solicitation is done in connection with a class-action suit.

Solicitation Letters

Letters sent to a target group of individuals known to need legal services is permissible advertising. In *Shapero v. Kentucky Bar Association,*[13] a case that came before the U.S. Supreme Court in 1988, the court ruled that a Kentucky rule prohibiting all targeted direct-mail solicitation by attorneys for pecuniary gain was unconstitutional. The court held that states may not categorically prohibit attorneys from soliciting business by sending truthful and nondeceptive letters to potential clients known to face particular legal problems.[14]

Solicitation letters are viewed in a different light than in-person or live telephone solicitation for the following reasons:

- The recipient of a targeted solicitation letter is not faced with the coercive presence of an attorney.
- The recipient of a targeted solicitation letter, unlike someone who is faced with in-person solicitation, need not give an on the spot yes or no answer. The recipient is allowed time to consider all options.
- The recipient of a targeted solicitation letter always has the option of ignoring the letter and throwing it away.
- Where copies of targeted solicitation letters are submitted to a state agency for approval either prior to, or when, the letter is sent out, they can be scrutinized for fraudulent or misleading statements, unlike statements made during an in-person solicitation.
- The contents of written communications concerning an attorney's proposed services are documented with copies and there can be no question as to exactly what was communicated to the potential client.

Under Rule 7.3, any form of solicitation, whether in person, live telephone, written, telephone, or recorded telephone, is prohibited if the prospective client has made it known to the attorney that he or she desires not to be solicited,[15] or if the solicitation involves coercion, duress, or harassment.

The solicitation letter is strictly regulated by state rules. One state rule, recently challenged in the U.S. Supreme Court, is a Florida Bar rule that prohibits attorneys from using direct mail to solicit personal injury or wrongful death clients for thirty days after the accident. In *Florida Bar v. Went For It,*[16] the court upheld the thirty-day waiting period rule because (1) the bar has a substantial interest in protecting the privacy and tranquillity of personal injury victims; (2) a study presented by the bar shows that the Florida public views direct mail solicitations immediately following an accident to be intrusive on their privacy; and (3) the rule is sufficiently narrow in scope.

Following are some of the types of restrictions that may be placed on written solicitations:

- Attorneys may be required to observe a thirty-day waiting period following an accident or disaster before sending targeted direct mail to victims or their relatives
- All mailings to potential clients must be labeled as *Advertising* or *Advertising Material* on the envelope and on the communication itself
- The solicitation letter must not involve duress, coercion, or harassment
- No solicitation letter may be sent to a prospective client who has made it known to the attorney that he or she does not want to be solicited by the attorney

Solicitation Not for Profit

In-person solicitation is generally banned when the attorney's financial gain is a significant motive. However, in-person solicitation may be permitted under certain circumstances when the attorney's motive is political or ideological. When the motive behind the solicitation is political expression, the First Amendment is applied much more broadly than if the motive is purely commercial. In *In Re*

Primus,[17] a case heard before the U.S. Supreme Court in 1978, at issue was the reprimand of a South Carolina attorney for violating the rules of South Carolina regarding solicitation of clients. The attorney in this case, who was representing the local branch of the American Civil Liberties Union (ACLU), spoke to a group of African-American women who had allegedly been sterilized as a condition of their continued receipt of public medical assistance. The attorney advised the women of their legal rights and later informed one of the women by letter that free legal assistance was available from the ACLU. The Supreme Court held that solicitation of possible litigants by the attorney for a nonprofit organization that engages in litigation as a form of political expression and political association constitutes expressive and associational conduct entitled to First Amendment protection that may be regulated only with narrow specificity.

Solicitation of Friends, Family Members, and Prior Clients

There is a general exception to the rules on solicitation of potential clients when the potential client is an acquaintance, family member, or a prior client. It is believed that individuals who are acquainted with the attorney will not be subject to potential abuses that strangers may be subject to. A family member or an acquaintance is also more likely to be familiar with the competence and qualifications of the attorney and will be in a better position to make an informed decision as to the attorney's ability to meet his or her needs.

Federal Class Actions

Direct contact with individuals who are potential clients in a federal class action is generally permitted under the Federal Rules of Civil Procedure.

Prepaid or Group Legal Services Plan

Prepaid legal service plans are offered as a benefit to employees. Participants in these plans typically pay premiums to cover certain legal services that may be required in the future. It is generally found to be acceptable for attorneys to solicit the business of such plans. The reason behind this is that the attorneys are not soliciting individuals who will become their clients. They are not soliciting individuals who have been injured, are distressed, or in immediate need of legal services. Rather they are soliciting the individuals who will administer the plan.

PARALEGAL ADVERTISING

FROM THE PARALEGAL'S PERSPECTIVE

Paralegals are involved in advertising and soliciting in several ways. As a paralegal, you must be aware of the rules of ethics concerning advertising and soliciting that will relate to your work. If you work as a traditional paralegal, you will need to know your state's rules concerning the inclusion of paralegals on letterhead and advertising. It is also possible that you may be involved in various marketing efforts by your firm. You must also know how to avoid impermissible solicitation on behalf of the attorneys you work for. If you work as a freelance paralegal or independent paralegal, you must be aware of rules concerning advertising that could directly affect your business. The rest of this chapter will focus on the issues concerning advertising and solicitation that directly affect paralegals. However, you must remember always to proceed with caution, because these rules vary significantly between states and are frequently revised (Figure 8–5).

- Refer friends and relatives to your law firm—when appropriate and NOT for compensation
- Become active in your paralegal association
- Network
- Assist with law firm marketing plans and help with placement of advertising
- Encourage the attorneys and management of your firm to sponsor worthwhile community events in which you are involved

FIGURE 8–5

What You Can Do to Promote Your Law Firm

Traditional Paralegals

Letterhead. The names of paralegals are often included on law firm letterhead. Most jurisdictions, but not all, permit this so long as the paralegal's title is clearly indicated by his or her name. Some jurisdictions, however, have issued opinions stating that the very use of a paralegal's name on letterhead is misleading and causes the potential for public confusion and potential for the paralegal to engage in the unauthorized practice of law.

The reasoning behind the general acceptability for listing paralegals on law firm letterhead with their titles is that it is useful information that may help to clear up any misunderstandings that clients may have as to who they are dealing with at the law firm.

ABA Informal Op. 89-1527 provides that "the listing of nonlawyer support personnel on lawyers' letterheads is not prohibited by these or any other Rules so long as the listing is not false or misleading."

A Question of Ethics

Suppose you have just started your first paralegal position at a small general practice law firm. The firm consists of five attorneys, two part-time law clerks, two secretaries, and one receptionist. You are the first paralegal the firm has hired. On your first day your supervising attorney approaches you and asks that you call the stationery supplier and the telephone directory sales representative. Your supervising attorney wants you to have your own business cards, have your name added to the firm letterhead, and to have your name added to the firm's Yellow Pages advertisement.

You are flattered that they want to include you, and so soon, but you are unsure as to how to proceed. Is it ethical to have the firm use your name in such a way?

Answer and Discussion: Probably, but you must do your research to be sure. Most jurisdictions allow the names of paralegals to be included on law firm letterhead and on firm business cards. Your name can probably also be included in the telephone directory advertisement. You must do your research to be sure your proposed actions are permissible within your jurisdiction. If it is acceptable to use your name in such a manner, you must remember that everywhere your name appears, your title must be included so as not to mislead the public into mistaking you for an attorney. Also, you must be sure that any advertisement that includes your name is not false or misleading.

As a paralegal, you must be sure that you use law firm letterhead only for law firm business. Any correspondence on law firm letterhead indicates that it is done with the authority of the law firm. Even if your name is on the letterhead, you must be careful to never use law firm letterhead for personal correspondence.

Business Cards.   If you work as a traditional paralegal, your employer will most likely furnish you with business cards with your name, title, and the firm or corporation name of your employer. You must be sure that any business card you use indicates your nonlawyer status.

Advertisements.   ABA Informal Opinion 89-1527 provides that the names and titles of paralegals may be included in written advertisements "provided the designation is not likely to mislead those who see it into thinking that the nonlawyers who are listed are lawyers or exercise control over lawyers in the firm."

CLA and RP Designations.   In addition to including your paralegal title on any letterhead, business cards, or advertising that includes your name, you may also wish to include your Certified Legal Assistant (CLA) or Registered Paralegal (RP) designation. To date there have been no challenges to this practice.

NFPA Model Code of Ethics and Professional Responsibility, Canon 6: A Paralegal's Title Shall Be Fully Disclosed:

EC-6.1 A paralegal's title shall clearly indicate the individual's status and shall be disclosed in all business and professional communications to avoid misunderstandings and misconceptions about the paralegal's role and responsibilities.

EC-6.2 A paralegal's title shall be included if the paralegal's name appears on business cards, letterhead, brochures, directories, and advertisements.

Freelance Paralegals

Freelance paralegals depend on the business of attorneys for their livelihood. Although word of mouth is often used to communicate the availability of a freelance paralegal's services, many freelance paralegals would not have work without effective advertising. According to the NFPA, the right of freelance paralegals to solicit attorneys, the consumers of their services, outweighs the state's right to restrict freelance paralegals' rights to advertise.[18] In 1995, the NFPA issued Ethics Opinion 95–6, indicating that it is ethical for freelance paralegals, also known as contract paralegals, to advertise their services, with several conditions:

- Freelance paralegals should be sure their advertising is aimed at attorneys, who will be responsible for their work, not to the public
- Any advertising by a paralegal should clearly indicate the nonattorney status of the paralegal
- Any advertising by a freelance paralegal should in no way indicate that the freelance paralegal offers legal advice or services to the public
- Paralegal advertising should comply with attorney advertising guidelines and code of ethics in the pertinent jurisdictions
- Paralegal advertising must not be false or misleading in any manner
- Paralegal advertising should include the paralegal's name, address, and phone number

- Paralegal advertising should avoid statements that may infer the nature or success of results that may be obtained
- Advertising concerning a freelance paralegal should avoid comparisons to other paralegals

As stated by the NFPA, the overall consideration in promoting freelance paralegals should include maintaining and preserving the dignity of and proper decorum in the legal profession.

Independent Paralegals

Independent paralegals can advertise any legal services they can provide without engaging in the unauthorized practice of law. The advertisements used by independent paralegals must make it clear that the services being offered are being performed by a paralegal (not a lawyer) and do not include giving legal advice or other activities considered to be the practice of law. If independent paralegals do advertise their services, they must be sure that their advertisements are not false or misleading. Exactly what can be advertised in each state varies, as does the definitions of the term *unauthorized practice of law* and the activities that may be performed by independent paralegals who do not work under the supervision of an attorney.

In one case heard before the Supreme Court of South Carolina, an independent paralegal's advertisement describing himself as a paralegal was found to be misleading and was not entitled to First Amendment protection because, as defined in South Carolina, paralegals work under the supervision of attorneys, and the defendant did not.[19] The court in that case found that "to legitimately provide services as a paralegal, one must work in conjunction with a licensed attorney. Robinson's advertisement as a paralegal is false since his work product is admittedly not subject to the supervision of a licensed attorney."

SOLICITATION

Attorneys are generally prohibited from engaging paralegals to solicit clients for them. If you work for a law firm as a traditional paralegal, you must not solicit business on behalf of your supervising attorney or law firm in contravention to the codes of ethics in place for attorneys in your jurisdiction. "Solicitation, whether in person or by hired proxy, is misconduct warranting appropriate discipline."[20] It is unethical for attorneys to violate their codes of ethics through the actions of others. Therefore, if the circumstances dictate that it is not permissible for the attorney to solicit potential clients under the circumstances, it is not permissible for you to do so on their behalf.

Also, you must avoid any situation in which you are paid referral fees or otherwise compensated for bringing business to your supervising attorney or law firm. Payment of referral fees to lay persons is generally prohibited under Model Rule 7.2(c) and similar rules under the codes of ethics in most states. The rules do not prohibit you from referring acquaintances to your supervising attorney or any attorney you are acquainted with. Rather, they prevent you from doing so for money.

CASE AND DISCUSSION

The following case is an attorney disciplinary action involving in-person solicitation by a paralegal. The proceedings were brought against the supervising attorney for failure to supervise his paralegal adequately and for improper solicitation through an agent. Although many of the facts in the case were clear, the Supreme Court of Idaho found that the strict burden of "clear and undoubted preponderance" or "clear and convincing" evidence standard was not met, and the recommendations of the Professional Conduct Board for suspension of the attorney were not adopted.

In the Matter of Gordon W. JENKINS, attorney at law,
IDAHO STATE BAR, Plaintiff,
v.
Gordon W. JENKINS, Defendant.
No. 18646, Supreme Court of Idaho,
Boise, November 1990 Term.
Aug. 7, 1991.

This attorney disciplinary action is before the Court to consider the findings and recommendation of the Idaho State Bar to impose sanctions on Gordon W. Jenkins, an attorney licensed to practice law in this state, because of actions and conduct of a legal assistant in his employ. . . .

I.
FACTS

The three remaining counts of the complaint filed against Jenkins charge him with violation of two sections of the Idaho Rules of Professional Conduct. In Counts I, II and V Jenkins is charged with solicitation of prospective clients by an agent or employee in violation of Rules 5.3(b)(1) and Rule 7.3 of the Rules of Professional Conduct.

A legal assistant employed by Jenkins' law firm by the name of Francis Landeros is a key figure in the events giving rise to these proceedings. Prior to her employment with Jenkins' law firm as a legal assistant, Landeros was involved in providing social services to members of the Hispanic community in east Idaho. When the funding for that program ceased, Landeros obtained employment with Jenkins' law firm as a legal assistant.

The hearing committee found, and the majority members of the Board accepted, that Gordon Jenkins ". . . hired Landeros because of her close contacts with the Mexican community and for the sole purpose of bringing in new clients to the firm in the areas of personal injury, workmen's compensation, and immigration." It is in this setting that we review the two incidents involving contact of prospective clients by Landeros. . . .

A. THE MARTINEZ INCIDENT—COUNTS I AND II.

On November 29, 1986, Robert Martinez was killed in a motor vehicle accident. Sometime after the fatal accident and prior to December 21, 1986, Landeros contacted Robert's parents, Joe and Mary Martinez, requesting to come to their home and visit with them about their son's death. The record is conflicting as to the nature of Landeros' personal visit to the Martinez home. Mary Martinez testified that she did not want to talk with Landeros and purposely left home at the time of the scheduled appointment because her hus-band told her Landeros desired to talk with them about suing the owners of the car in which their son was riding at the time of his death. Landeros testified that she was a close friend of the Martinez family and only went to their home to express her condolences.

The hearing committee found that when Mrs. Martinez returned home, Landeros was still in their house visiting with Mr. Martinez about suing the owners of the automobile. The record indicates that Landeros told the Martinez family that Jenkins was the best lawyer in the firm and that he had sent her out to their home to ". . . see what she could do to help the family." The record indicates that while at their home, Landeros and Mrs. Martinez embraced, cried and prayed together. Following their meeting Landeros left several of Jenkins' business cards with Mr. and Mrs. Martinez. Several days after the December 21, 1986 meeting, Landeros telephoned Mrs. Martinez to inquire whether they had decided to hire an attorney. Subsequently a complaint against Jenkins was filed with the Idaho State Bar.

B. THE BARRETT INCIDENT—COUNT V.

In January, 1986, Eileen Barrett was injured in an automobile accident. Mrs. Barrett had been negotiating with an insurance company in an attempt to settle her claim. Barrett's sister, fearing that she might settle for too little compensation, contacted Landeros and requested that she contact Barrett and provide her with legal counsel. Landeros placed several telephone calls to Barrett at her home and place of employment to inquire of the nature of her injuries and indicated that her employer, Gordon Jenkins, could assist her as he had other clients with automobile accident injury claims. Mrs. Barrett agreed to meet with Jenkins. At the conclusion of their consultation appointment Jenkins proposed that Barrett sign several medical consent release forms for convenience purposes even though she had not agreed to formally retain his services. Jenkins advised Barrett that he would destroy the signed release forms if she did not desire to retain him as her attorney.

Mrs. Barrett subsequently obtained the services of another attorney who requested the return of her paperwork. Jenkins returned the documents and in a cover letter advised Barrett's new counsel that even though he had started an investigation into the claim no costs had been incurred and none of the signed releases had been used to obtain medical information. Subsequently, a complaint was filed against Jenkins with the Idaho State Bar for the Barrett incident.

II.
APPLICABLE RULES OF PROFESSIONAL CONDUCT

The Idaho State Bar charges Jenkins with violation of Rules 5.3(b)(1) and 7.3 of the Idaho Rules of Professional Conduct.

Rule 5.3 provides:

Rule 5.3 Responsibilities Regarding Non-lawyer Assistants

With respect to a nonlawyer employed or retained by or associated with a lawyer:

(a) a partner in a law firm shall make reasonable efforts to ensure that the firm has in effect measures giving reasonable assurance that the person's conduct is compatible with the professional obligations of the lawyer;

(b) a lawyer shall be responsible for conduct of such a person that would be a violation of the rules of professional conduct if engaged in by a lawyer if:

(1) the lawyer orders or, with the knowledge of the specific conduct, ratifies the conduct involved; or

(2) the lawyer is a partner in the law firm in which the person is employed, or has direct supervisory authority over the person, and knows of the conduct at a time when its consequences can be avoided or mitigated but fails to take reasonable remedial action.

Rule 7.3 provides:[2]

A lawyer may not solicit professional employment from a prospective client with whom the lawyer has no family or prior professional relationship, by mail, in-person or otherwise, when a significant motive for the lawyer's doing so is the lawyer's pecuniary gain. The term "solicit" includes contact in person, by telephone or telegraph, by letter or other writing, or by other communication directed to a specific recipient, but does not include letters addressed or advertising circulars distributed generally to persons not known to need legal services of the kind provided by the lawyer in a particular matter, but who are so situated that they might in general find such services useful.

It is with the above rules of professional conduct in mind that we review the disciplinary action before us. . . .

IV.

As a preliminary observation, there is no question or doubt that the conduct of Landeros in the Martinez incident constituted blatant solicitation of professional employment from a prospective client clearly in violation of Rule 7.3(a) of the Idaho Rules of Professional Conduct. However, the precise issue presented to us is not whether Landeros' conduct was unethical solicitation, which we deem it to be, but rather as expressly required under Rule 5.3(b)(1) the issue is whether Jenkins "ordered" the conduct, or "with knowledge of the specific conduct involved" ratified the conduct of Landeros. . . .

After carefully analyzing and scrutinizing the entire record before us we are satisfied that if the burden of proof was a preponderance or greater weight of the evidence standard, we would also conclude and find that Jenkins knew or should of known of Landeros' conduct. However when applying the strict burden of "clear and undoubted preponderance" or "clear and convincing" evidence standard, we cannot defer to the findings made by the Board on either the Martinez incident or the Barrett incident. . . .

With respect to the Martinez matter, there is no evidence that Mr. Jenkins ever knew, prior to the initiation of these proceedings, that Francis Landeros did anything but offer the Martinez family her condolences after their son's death. . . .

While one might characterize Francis Landeros as a loose cannon rolling around the deck of Jenkins' law office, the overwhelming evidence established a firm policy, supported by frequent staff meetings, aimed at educating Mr. Jenkins' non-lawyer staff about impermissible in-person solicitations. This program is precisely the kind of action a lawyer must take to assure himself that the impermissible conduct itself, as well as the consequences of an in-person solicitation can be avoided or mitigated.

With respect to the Eileen Barrett matter, there is no evidence that Mr. Jenkins ever knew of Francis Landeros' repeated phone calls to Ms. Barrett for the purpose of soliciting her as a client for Jenkins' law office and Mr. Jenkins. . . .

The circumstantial evidence necessary to prove Mr. Jenkins' complicity in the Martinez and Barrett solicitations does not rise to the level of clear and convincing evidence necessary to support the imposition of sanctions by the Idaho State Bar and Idaho Supreme Court. . . .

---

[2] The above Rule 7.3 was rescinded and replaced on March 15, 1990.

CHAPTER SUMMARY

- Attorney and law firm advertising must be permitted under the code of ethics of each state. However, the states have the authority to restrict that advertising under certain conditions.
- Under most circumstances, in-person solicitation is considered unethical and prohibited by the code of ethics of each state.
- Most changes in the model codes and the state codes of ethics concerning advertising have been brought about by U.S. Supreme Court decisions.
- In the 1977 Bates decision, the U.S. Supreme Court deemed attorney advertising to be commercial speech and entitled to limited First Amendment protection. The court also affirmed the right of the states to restrict attorney advertising, especially where false and misleading advertising is concerned.
- Attorneys currently advertise through numerous types of media, including newspaper and periodical advertisements, mailed announcements, television and radio advertisements, and Web sites and advertisements over the Internet.
- Current rules restricting attorney advertising focus on the content rather than the media. All states prohibit advertising that may be false or misleading.
- Attorneys are required to comply with state regulations concerning advertising recordkeeping. Under the Model Rules of Professional Conduct, copies of all

advertisements, and information concerning the placement of such advertisement, must be kept for a minimum of two years.

- Attorney advertising, including targeted mailings, usually must be labeled *advertising*.
- It is generally unethical for an attorney to pay a lay person for referrals.
- In-person solicitation of a potential client is generally prohibited unless the attorney's motive is not monetary; the potential client is a friend, family member, or prior client; or the solicitation is in connection with a federal class action as permitted by federal rules.
- Paralegal names and titles may be included on law firm letterhead, on business cards, and in law firm advertising in most jurisdictions.
- Paralegals may advertise to their potential customers (attorneys), so long as they follow the general rules prohibiting false and misleading advertising.
- Independent paralegals may advertise any of the services they can legally provide in their jurisdictions. Their advertisements must not be misleading, and they must make it clear that the independent paralegal is not offering legal advice or any other services that would constitute the practice of law.

SUMMARY QUESTIONS

1. Why was attorney advertising banned prior to 1977?
2. What was the significance of the Bates decision?
3. Suppose that you are a paralegal in a law firm specializing in litigation. If there was a highly publicized natural gas line explosion in which three people were killed and twelve were injured, could the attorneys in your firm contact the survivors and families of the survivors in person to offer their help? Could they send you?
4. Assume the same circumstances as in question number 3. Could the attorneys in your state send a solicitation letter to the families of the victims of the disaster? What, if any, restrictions are placed on such letters in your state?
5. Suppose your new employer, a divorce lawyer, pays you a $75 bonus for referring your sister and then offers you $50 for every new client you refer to the firm. Is this permissible?
6. Is it unethical for you to refer your sister to the attorney you work for if you do not receive any additional compensation?
7. What are the requirements for keeping copies of advertisements or submitting copies of advertisements before they are published in your state?
8. Why is in-person solicitation prohibited when solicitation by targeted mailings is not?
9. Consider the following advertisement. What impermissible items can you find in this advertisement?

> **BEST & BETTER LAW FIRM**
> **LOWEST PRICES IN TOWN**
> **Our prices are better than East and West Law Firm**
> **(and our attorneys are smarter)**
>
> Have you been in an accident???
> We will help you collect the settlement you deserve,
> with no cost to you if we don't win.
> Last year we won two verdicts in excess of $1 Million!!
>
> Call (789) 555-1234 for a free consultation.

10. What possible exceptions are there to the prohibition against in-person solicitation under the Model Rules?

ENDNOTES

[1]49 USCA s 1136 (1998).

[2]Marketing, Software, Court Developments, Bar Associations, *West Legal News,* October 26, 1995.

[3]*17A Ariz. Rev. Stat.,* p. 26 (Supp. 1976).

[4]*In the Matter of R.M.J.,* 455 U.S. 191 (1982).

[5]Ibid. [To be admitted to the Bar of the Supreme Court, the applicant must have been admitted to practice in the highest court of a state, commonwealth, territory, or possession, or of the District of Columbia for the three years immediately preceding the date of application and must have been free from any adverse disciplinary action whatsoever during that three-year period, and the applicant must appear to the court to be of good moral and professional character.]

[6]*Bates v. State Bar of Arizona,* 433 U.S. 350 (1977).

[7]Ibid.

[8]*Zauderer v. Office of Disciplinary Counsel of the Ohio Supreme Court,* 471 U.S. 626 (1985).

[9]*Grievance Committee for the Hartford-New Britain Judicial District v. Trantolo,* 470 A.2d 228 (Conn. 1984).

[10]*Peel v. Illinois Attorney Registration and Disciplinary Commission,* 496 U.S. 91 (1990).

[11]*Trumbull County Bar Association v. Joseph,* 569 N.E. 2d 883 (Ohio 1991).

[12]*Ohralik v. Ohio State Bar Ass'n,* 436 U.S. 447 (1978).

[13]*Shapero v. Kentucky Bar Association,* 486 U.S. 466 (1988).

[14]Ibid.

[15]*Model Rules of Professional Conduct,* Rule 7.3(b)(1).

[16]*Florida Bar v. Went For It,* 115 S.Ct. 2371 (1995).

[17]*In Re Primus,* 98 S.Ct. 1893 (1978).

[18]*National Federation of Paralegal Associations Ethics and Disciplinary Opinion No. 95—6 (1995).*

[19]*State v. Robinson,* 468 S.E. 2d 290 (S.C. 1996).

[20]*In the Matter of the Application for the Discipline of Normal Pearl,* 407 NW2d 678 (Minn. 1987).

SOMEBODY'S WATCHING YOU . . .

People are spying on Jane. Someone has been listening to her phone calls. Her private e-mail has been opened without her knowledge. Someone is monitoring her computer to see which Web sites she logs on to. Her every move is being followed by hidden surveillance cameras. Who is Jane? Is she a criminal, a thief, a spy? Who is spying on her? Is it the CIA, the FBI, the Mafia? No. Jane is just a clerical worker at your typical American business. She has done no wrong or committed any crime. The spy is her employer, and her employer's actions are not uncommon among employers in the United States.

Jane is a fictional character, of course, but the ethical issues raised by the invasion of employee privacy by employers are very real. Developments in electronics have made it easier than ever for employers to keep track of their workers. Is it ethical for employers to monitor an employee's phone calls, to read an employee's e-mails, or to install hidden cameras in the workplace? Whether it is ethical or not, many employers are taking advantage of new technology to monitor employees at work.

- More than twenty million employees are subject to electronic surveillance at work.[i]
- Employers eavesdrop on approximately five billion phone calls annually.[ii]
- Twenty million Americans are subject to computer monitoring by their employers.[iii]
- More than one third of the members of the American Management Association report taping employee phone conversation, videotaping employees, reviewing voice mail, and checking computer files and e-mail.[iv]

Electronic monitoring of employees takes many forms, including: reading employee e-mail, searching computer files, listening to employee telephone calls, listening to employee voice mail messages, and video camera surveillance. New technology is making possible new ways to monitor employees, including electronic badges that track the movement of employees within the building.

Employers who monitor their employees electronically give several reasons. Electronic monitoring allows employers to measure the quality and quantity of employees' work. Electronic monitoring may also help to curb illegal activity by employees, including employee theft and industrial espionage, both of which can cost large companies millions of dollars. Some employers have established video surveillance in employee restrooms and locker rooms to prevent illegal drug use and sales.

Employers feel an increasing pressure to monitor employees to curb lawsuits that may be brought against them for incidents that occur at the workplace, including sexual harassment, racial discrimination, and even assaults. One Wall Street brokerage firm was recently sued for racist jokes that were sent over the company's e-mail system. Employers who monitor their employees feel that their need to protect themselves outweighs the employees' right to privacy at work in most instances.

What are the effects of this employee monitoring on employees? Many employees feel dehumanized. They feel their privacy has been invaded, and they are angry. Employees feel violated when they discover video monitoring of their locker rooms and restrooms. Stress levels are also often high among employees who believe they are constantly being monitored and watched. The constant stress of electronic monitoring can lead to illness and high turnover of employees.

One measure that can be taken by businesses to protect themselves and improve employee relations is to develop and implement comprehensive employee privacy policies. Written employee privacy policies fully inform employees of any monitoring that is done and why it is done. Privacy policies should cover the employer's rights to monitor and the employee's rights to privacy with regard to computer files, e-mails, voice mail, electronic surveillance, and telephone calls. The policy should also cover other issues connected with employee privacy, such as drug testing and all information kept on employees, including insurance and medical records.

If you don't work for a company that has such a privacy policy, just remember that somebody may be watching you. . . .

i Dowd, Ann Reilly, Your Dollars: Protect Your Privacy, *Money*, Aug. 1, 1997, p. 104.
ii Ibid.
iii ACLU In Brief: Electronic Monitoring, **www.aclu.org**, March 20, 1999.
iv Who's Watching Now?..., *U.S. News & World Report*, Sept. 15, 1997, p. 56.

Chapter 9

Business Ethics for Everyone

"I don't believe unethical people get ahead in business. If ethics are poor at the top, that behavior is copied down through the organization."

Robert Noyce, inventor of the silicon chip

Introduction
The Importance of Business Ethics
Ethics for All Members of the Organization
Ethics Programs
    Ethics Policies
        Model Business Principles
    Code of Conduct
Specific Issues in Ethics
    Contributions to the Community
    Honesty

    Employee Thefts
    Diversity in the Workplace
    Sexual Harassment
Resolving Ethical Dilemmas
Chapter Summary
Summary Questions

INTRODUCTION

Business ethics
The study and evaluation of decision making by businesses according to moral concepts and judgments.

Ethics is the discipline dealing with what is good and bad and with moral duty and obligation. It is a set of moral principles or values that guides the decisions you make. **Business ethics** is defined as "the study and evaluation of decision making by businesses according to moral concepts and judgments."[1]

The focus so far in this text has been on legal ethics and the rules of ethics that apply to attorneys, paralegals, and others within the legal profession. The focus of this chapter is business ethics and the rules of ethics that apply to everyone in the work force, including paralegals. This chapter begins with a look at the importance of business ethics and what organizations can do to promote ethical behavior. Next, this chapter examines a few of the common issues in business ethics that are relevant to corporations, law firms, and other types of businesses. This chapter concludes with a look at ethical decision making and provides some tools to assist you in making right and ethical decisions.

THE IMPORTANCE OF BUSINESS ETHICS

In recent years, business ethics has received much public attention—scandals in the headlines have led to public awareness and demand for ethical business practices. An increasing number of business leaders are recognizing the importance of sound ethical policies within their organizations, and they are taking steps to encourage ethical behavior of management and employees at all levels of the organization.

Sound ethical practices can be crucial to the success of any business. Law firms must maintain their integrity and reputation in the community to continue to attract clients. Poor ethical practices in a law firm can create a poor reputation in the community and cause the firm to lose clients. For example, if a lawsuit was brought against a law firm for racial discrimination by some of its employees, members of the wronged racial or ethnic group would probably be very reluctant to engage the services of the firm.

Business leaders adopt sound ethical policies because it is the right thing to do and because it is in their own best interests to do so. Some specific reasons that organizations give for initiating ethics programs and encouraging good business ethics include:

- It is right and moral
- Ethics programs lessen legal liability in the form of lawsuits against the organization for malpractice, product liability, or violation of federal rules and regulations
- Society benefits from improved business ethics
- Ethics programs aid in decision making
- Ethics programs boost employee morale
- Ethics programs often result in better customer relations and improved public image

ETHICS FOR ALL MEMBERS OF THE ORGANIZATION

Every level of an organization must be committed to ethical behavior for the organization to have good business ethics. In a corporation, the policies are made at the organizational level, and managed and implemented by the management level and individual employees of an organization. In the law firm, the partners (or shareholders of a professional corporation) set the policy that is carried out by the firm's management and acted on by the firm's individual employees.

All levels of an organization may deal with different aspects of the same ethical issues. For example, where environmental ethics are at issue, at the corporate or organizational level, the heads of the corporation or organization must establish ethical guidelines for the environmental impact of their organization. They must weigh the shareholders' interests against any negative impact their organizations may have on the environment, both now and in the future. The management of the organization must be sure that their piece of the business—the factories and so on under their management—meet with corporate policy regarding environmental impact. They must also decide how to deal with any accidents or other incidents that could have a negative impact on the environment—Will they cover it up or clean it up? Workers must decide how they will comply with corporate and management directives concerning the environment. What will they do if their error causes an environmental mishap, or if they witness environmentally unsound policies in their workplace?

ETHICS PROGRAMS

Ethical behavior can be encouraged in many ways. Many businesses and law firms have implemented comprehensive ethics programs to ensure that all individuals within the organization know what ethical behavior the organization condones and what is expected of each individual.

Ethics programs may have several different components, including:

- An organization **mission statement** setting forth the organization's philosophy
- A written **ethics policy** setting forth standards for ethical behavior
- A written **code of conduct** that includes specific rules for ethical behavior by all employees
- An ethics committee to address questions concerning ethics within the organization
- Workshops and seminars to educate employees at all levels of the organization on proper ethical behavior

Ethics Policies

The organization's ethics policy states the principles of the organization and those that will guide the decision-making in the organization. The policy is approved by the owners or top management of the organization. The ethics policy may be part of the organization's mission statement, or it may be based on the organization's mission statement. Often, individuals from all levels of the organization are asked to contribute to the ethics policy. In a law firm, an ethics committee may be responsible for preparing an ethics policy that will complement the code of ethics that applies to all attorneys.

Johnson & Johnson is an organization highly respected for its business ethics. In 1982, management of Johnson & Johnson used its Credo to resolve the ethical dilemmas created by the Tylenol scare, when five people in the Chicago area died from ingesting poisoned Extra-Strength Tylenol. Johnson & Johnson decided to pull its product from the shelves, costing it millions in immediate revenue, but earning respect for the corporation from the business community and the public (Figure 9–1).

Mission statement
A statement formally adopted by an organization setting forth the organization's purpose and philosophy
Ethics policy
A policy adopted by an organization stating the ethical principles of the organization and standards for ethical behavior.
Code of conduct
A written set of rules prescribing ethical behavior for all employees of an organization in accordance with the ethics policy of the organization.

Our Credo

We believe our first responsibility is to the doctors, nurses and patients,
to mothers and fathers and all others who use our products and services.
In meeting their needs everything we do must be of high quality.
We must constantly strive to reduce our costs
in order to maintain reasonable prices.
Customers' orders must be serviced promptly and accurately.
Our suppliers and distributors must have an opportunity
to make a fair profit.

We are responsible to our employees,
the men and women who work with us throughout the world.
Everyone must be considered as an individual.
We must respect their dignity and recognize their merit.
They must have a sense of security in their jobs.
Compensation must be fair and adequate,
and working conditions clean, orderly and safe.
We must be mindful of ways to help our employees fulfill
their family responsibilities.
Employees must feel free to make suggestions and complaints.
There must be equal opportunity for employment, development
and advancement for those qualified.
We must provide competent management,
and their actions must be just and ethical.

We are responsible to the communities in which we live and work
and to the world community as well.
We must be good citizens — support good works and charities
and bear our fair share of taxes.
We must encourage civic improvements and better health and education.
We must maintain in good order
the property we are privileged to use,
protecting the environment and natural resources.

Our final responsibility is to our stockholders.
Business must make a sound profit.
We must experiment with new ideas.
Research must be carried on, innovative programs developed
and mistakes paid for.
New equipment must be purchased, new facilities provided
and new products launched.
Reserves must be created to provide for adverse times.
When we operate according to these principles,
the stockholders should realize a fair return.

Johnson & Johnson

FIGURE 9–1

Johnson & Johnson's Credo
Courtesy of Johnson &
Johnson.

Model Business Principles. In 1995 the U.S. Department of Commerce released the following statement of Model Business Principles for consideration by all business owners.*

Recognizing the positive role of U.S. business in upholding and promoting adherence to universal standards of human rights, the Administration encourages all businesses to adopt and implement voluntary codes of conduct for doing business around the world that cover at least the following areas:

1. Provision of a safe and healthy workplace.
2. Fair employment practices, including avoidance of child and forced labor and avoidance of discrimination based on race, gender, national origin or religious beliefs; and respect for the right of association and the right to organize and bargain collectively.
3. Responsible environmental protection and environmental practices.
4. Compliance with U.S. and local laws promoting good business practices, including laws prohibiting illicit payments and ensuring fair competition.
5. Maintenance, through leadership at all levels, of a corporate culture that respects free expression consistent with legitimate business concerns, and does not condone political coercion in the workplace; that encourages good corporate citizenship and makes a positive contribution to the communities in which the company operates; and where ethical conduct is recognized, valued and exemplified by all employees.

Code of Conduct

An ethics policy may include specific rules of ethics that all employees must abide by, or a set of rules for following the organization's ethics policy may be set forth in a separate code of conduct. The code of conduct adopted by any organization typically repeats the principles of the ethics policy and includes a set of rules for upholding the principles of the organization. These rules may address specific matters such as accepting gifts from clients or customers, reporting theft in the workplace, antidiscrimination rules, rules prohibiting sexual harassment, and procedures for reporting ethical misconduct.

SPECIFIC ISSUES IN ETHICS

Several issues regarding business ethics apply to everyone in the workplace. These issues affect the work environment and performance of all employees, regardless of the type of organization. Some specific issues that organizations, including law firms, must deal with include:

- Contributions to the community
- Safe work environments
- Fair and equitable work environments
- Prevention of sexual harassment
- Prevention of discrimination based on race, gender, sexual preferences, physical disabilities, religion
- Employee privacy
- Fair business practices
- Honesty among all members of the organization/firm
- Providing a family-friendly work environment
- Environmental conservation and preservation

---

* We do not claim copyright on the Model Business Principles, which is a publication of the U.S. Government.

- Workplace theft
- Whistleblowing

Community contributions, honesty, employee thefts, diversity, and sexual harassment in the workplace are examples of ethical issues of great importance to businesses and to law firms and that have received much attention in recent years. These are not the only ethics issues faced by businesses and law firms. Any issue that involves a moral choice by individuals in business or law firms may be a business ethics issue.

Contributions to the Community

As a part of their ethics policies, many organizations give priority to making a contribution to the communities in which they are located. Many businesses and law firms contribute to their communities by sponsoring educational programs, donating a portion of proceeds to local charities, sponsoring fundraising events for charities, and allowing employees time off during work to volunteer their time.

Employees of corporations and law firms are often encouraged to get involved in fundraising drives and other community projects, many of which the employer pays for. Also, many organizations will *match dollars* for employee contributions made to specified charities.

Organizations benefit from their contributions by improving their reputation and increasing their goodwill in the community. Many law firms that are reluctant to advertise in the manner that other businesses do increase their visibility and establish their reputation by being very involved in community charities and allowing their employees time off for performing volunteer work and providing their services pro bono.

Individual employees can contribute to their communities by participating in any fundraisers and volunteer programs sponsored by their organizations and law firms, and by making suggestions for additional community involvement.

Honesty

The mission statement or ethics policy of most organizations includes a statement about honesty. Unfortunately, these statements are often overlooked or not taken seriously. A recent study taken by Montclair State University reported that eighty-five percent of the individuals polled admitted to having lied in a work situation.[2]

It is not always easy to tell the truth, and at times you may be asked outright to lie. You may be asked to "tell him I'm not in the office" or "tell her we are almost done with the report." How you respond to such requests can have a significant impact on your career. Although your honest opinion of your supervisor's new hairstyle is not of the utmost importance, honesty in timekeeping and billing in a law firm, or reporting to shareholders and the Securities Exchange Commission, is vitally important.

Although the management in some law firms and businesses consider a small deviation from the truth to be expected in the workplace, at other firms and businesses, lying is not tolerated. Law firms and organizations with codes of conduct usually address honesty in aspirational terms, as a goal to be strived for. Honesty in the workplace can only be mandated from the top down and by example. The management and leadership of the law firm and organization must be honest with employees if they expect the employees to be honest.

Lying in the workplace can have serious consequences. Lying about having an assignment done can only lead to more problems, which are often detected. Lying on your timekeeping records amounts to stealing and can result in the loss of your job. Lying to clients, customers, or regulatory agencies reflects poorly on the entire organization and can also lead to the loss of your job, and even legal action against your organization or against you personally.

Employee Thefts

Theft and fraud by employees are ethical problems that hurt not only the employer but also clients and customers. According to the results of a survey by Pinkerton Security & Investigation Services of 137 security directors at Fortune 1000 companies, the biggest security threat faced by employers is employee theft.[3] The Association of Certified Fraud Examiners reports losses to organizations and businesses in the United States of more than $400 billion annually due to fraud and abuse.[4]

Law firms are not immune to theft and fraud. Small to medium-size firms, where costly controls are often not in place, face the biggest threat. There are numerous reports of law firm bookkeepers embezzling funds from their employers—sometimes for years without detection.

In addition to embezzlement of law firm funds, theft of office supplies and equipment is also a problem. In law firms it is often difficult to know where to draw the line. Is it okay to grab a handful of pens on your way out the door because you are low on them at home? What about equipment? Can you borrow a laptop from the office to do some personal work at home overnight? What if that work takes longer than expected and it becomes a week . . . a month, and no one has noticed it is missing? Is it okay to make a few personal copies on the photocopier? What about your son's fifty-page book report?

The ethics policy or mission statement of most companies makes a broad statement condemning theft of the organization's property. A good code of conduct may further define the terms *theft* and *the organization's property.* Possibly the most important way to prevent unethical acts by employees, including theft and embezzlement, is modeling from the leaders of the organization. Organization leaders, including law firm partners and shareholders, should set an example of honesty and respect for the organization or firm's property. When one bookkeeper who embezzled $285,000 from her law firm employer and then went on to embezzle from another employer was asked why she did it, she indicated that "I felt my boss was dishonest—I lost all respect for him."[5]

Diversity in the Workplace

More and more businesses, including law firms, are taking a proactive approach to dealing with diversity in the workplace. Never before has the workforce of the United States been more diverse. The number of new women and minority workers is increasing significantly, while the overall labor pool is shrinking. According to one report, women and minorities will make up sixty-two percent of the workforce by the year 2005.

People often think of race when diversity is discussed—and this is often the case, but not always. Diversity also involves several other differences among people, including religion, gender, sexual orientation, disabilities, and age. To be successful, businesses must address the diverse needs of all workers and the diverse needs of all clients or customers.

As the twenty-first century begins, business owners, attorneys, and all employers are finding it to their advantage to take a proactive approach to hiring a diverse workforce. Some of the advantages to having a diverse workforce include:

- It is the ethical thing to do
- Some federal agencies and large corporations give hiring preference to law firms that have a diverse workforce
- It improves the company or firm's public image and reputation

- A diverse workforce can better serve a diverse client or customer base
- Some diversity skills are very important in dealing with a diverse client base, especially bilingual and multicultural skills

Recognizing the importance of hiring a diverse workforce is only the first step. In an effort to utilize *all* members of their workforce to their fullest potential, employers are taking steps to deal with diversity in the workplace, including:

- Actively recruiting a qualified and diverse workforce
- Offering flexible work schedules to accommodate women who are mothers
- Recognizing holidays observed by ethnic minorities within the firm
- Making sure the business or law firm has an anti-discrimination policy in place, that it is well communicated among workers, and that violations of the policy are dealt with swiftly
- Monitoring promotions to make sure that all minority groups have equal opportunities for advancement
- Offering diversity education training and seminars

While several law firms are making a conscientious effort to hire and promote women and minorities, the overall statistics are disappointing. According to a 1997–1998 study by the National Association of Law Placement, minorities account for only 2.95 percent of law firm partners nationwide.[6]

To be your best in the diverse workplace, you must first examine your own attitudes and beliefs. Very few of us want to admit to having any prejudices against those who are different from us. Are you sensitive to the needs of those who are different than you? Have you taken the time to get to know co-workers from different racial or cultural groups? What unique challenges are faced by those in diverse groups where you work?

Sexual Harassment

Sexual harassment

As a type of employment discrimination, includes sexual advances, requests for sexual favors, and other verbal or physical conduct of a sexual nature in the course of employment prohibited by federal law (Title VII of 1964 Civil Rights Act) and commonly by state statutes.

Sexual harassment in the workplace is a real problem that has been around for decades, and it affects everyone. According to one survey of 8,523 workers, 56 percent claimed to have experienced sexual harassment. The workers surveyed were from both public and private organizations.[7] In a 1994 survey of human resource professionals, 65.1 percent of the respondents indicated that their departments had handled sexual harassment complaints.[8] The number of sexual harassment cases filed rose from 2,850 per year in 1986 to over 15,000 in 1995.[9] Unchecked sexual harassment in the workplace can lead to decreased productivity, increased absenteeism, and higher turnover.

Sexual harassment has technically been forbidden by law since the enactment of the Civil Rights Act of 1964. The sexual harassment lawsuit brought under Title VII of the 1964 Civil Rights Act, which prohibits discrimination on the basis of sex, was decided in 1976. The Equal Employment Opportunity Commission (EEOC) generally defines sexual harassment as "unwelcome sexual advances, requests for sexual favors, and other verbal or physical conduct of a sexual nature." Sexual harassment, as defined by the EEOC, may fall into two varieties, quid pro quo and hostile work environment.

Quid pro quo sexual harassment occurs when demands for sexual favors are made by a supervisor as a condition of getting or keeping a job or job benefit. Examples of quid pro quo sexual harassment include demanding sexual favors in exchange for raises, favorable reviews, assignments, or continued employment.

Hostile work environment sexual harassment occurs when co-workers or supervisors engage in unwelcome and inappropriate sexually based behavior, unreasonably interfering with work performance or rendering the workplace atmosphere intimidating, hostile, or offensive. A plaintiff in a hostile workplace sexual harassment suit must prove that the situation is of a nature that a reasonable person would consider it to be harassment. Elements of a hostile workplace constituting sexual harassment include verbal abuse of a sexual nature, repeated sexual jokes and language, flirtation and propositions; sexually degrading words used to describe a person; display of sexually suggestive materials in the workplace (such as pin ups, etc.); suggestive, insulting, or obscene comments or gestures; hugging, grabbing, kissing, or other unwanted touching.

All types of business organizations, including law firms, are taking action to combat sexual harassment and the expense and negative publicity associated with sexual harassment. Many organizations are taking some of the following recommended steps:

1. Prepare a comprehensive written policy condemning sexual harassment by any member of the organization
2. Distribute the policy to all employees of the organization and follow up with memos and face-to-face meetings where possible
3. Provide training for all employees (especially management) on avoiding sexual harassment
4. Handle any complaints quickly and fairly
5. Protect victims and witnesses from retaliation for reporting sexual harassment

Any policy regarding sexual harassment must include a strong statement of the organization's policy against sexual harassment and the following:

- A definition of sexual harassment that all employees can understand, possibly including examples
- Procedures to be followed for reporting any form of sexual harassment, including a choice of several individuals to whom the harassment can be reported
- Procedures for investigating sexual harassment claims
- Penalties for any employee found to be guilty of sexual harassment
- Assurances that any report of sexual harassment will be handled confidentially

When you take a position with any new employer, you must be familiar with that employer's sexual harassment policy. You must always be conscious of the rules so that you will never be guilty of perpetrating sexual harassment against a fellow employee, and so that you will know what to do if you are ever the victim of sexual harassment. For more information on sexual harassment, contact the Equal Employment Opportunity Commission at 1-800-669-4000 or see its Web site at **www.eeoc.gov.**

RESOLVING ETHICAL DILEMMAS

If every decision you had to make involved two options, one that was the *right* thing to do and one that was the *wrong* thing to do, ethics would be easy. Ethical questions such as *Should I steal or not?* Are easy. Too often, however, your options may both seem wrong or both seem right, and you will be forced to choose the best, although difficult, answer.

There are several models to assist you with ethical decision making. Most of these involve asking yourself a series of tough questions that involve self-examination, examination of the problem, and examination of your options. Some of the questions you may want to ask yourself include:

- What is the ethical problem?
- What facts must be considered?
- Who will be affected by this decision?

- What moral obligations do you have to each of the parties who will be affected?
- What are three possible courses of action?
- For each course of action
  - What is the best possible outcome?
  - What is the worst possible outcome?
  - Would anyone be harmed?
  - Which course of action would cause the most good for all affected parties?

Decision-Making Check List

Using the 1 thru 5 scale, evaluate your preferred alternative (including the preventative ethics component you have added) against the below listed seven tests. Circle the most appropriate answer. Then, total all answers and check the appropriate category on the Decision-Making Confidence Scale.

DECISION-MAKING TESTS   Not At All ———— Totally Yes

1. *Relevant Information Test:*
   Have I obtained as much information as possible to make   1   2   3   4   5
   an informed decision and action-plan for this situation?

2. *Involvement Test:*
   Have I involved as many as possible of those who have a   1   2   3   4   5
   right to have input into (or actual involvement in) making this
   decision and action-plan?

3. *Consequentialist Test:*
   Have I attempted to accommodate for the consequences of   1   2   3   4   5
   this decision and action-plan on any who could be significantly
   affected by it?

4. *Ethical Principles Test:*
   Does this decision and action-plan uphold the ethical principles   1   2   3   4   5
   that I think are relevant to this situation?

5. *Fairness Test:*
   If I were any one of the stakeholders in this situation, would I   1   2   3   4   5
   perceive this decision and action-plan to be fair, given all of
   the circumstances?

6. *Universality Test:*
   Would I want this decision and action-plan to become a   1   2   3   4   5
   "universal law" applicable to all in similar situations,
   including myself?

7. *Light-of-Day Test:*   Not Good——Extremely Good
   How would I feel and be regarded by others (including
   those closest to me) if the details of this decision and   1   2   3   4   5
   action-plan were disclosed for all to know

TOTAL OF ALL CIRCLED NUMBERS: _____

DECISION-MAKING CONFIDENCE SCALE: How confident can you be that you have done a good job of decision-making? [Check the category that corresponds with the total of all of your circled numbers.]

____ 29 – 35 VERY Confident   ____ 15 – 21 SOMEWHAT Confident

____ 22 – 28 QUITE Confident   ____ 7 – 14 NOT VERY Confident

[Consider these answers when determining your decision and action-plan.]

FIGURE 9–2

Ethical Decision Checklist
Reprinted with permission of
The Fulcrum Group.

After answering all of these questions, you may want to test your decision (or your options) with the help of a worksheet similar to the one shown in Figure 9–2.

Sometimes even decisions made with the best intentions can be the wrong choice. However, if you make an attempt to resolve your ethical dilemmas in a reasoned, well-thought-out manner, you will be sure that you have not made your decision for the *wrong* reason and that you have made your best effort to do the right thing (Figure 9–2).

CHAPTER SUMMARY

- Business ethics is the study and evaluation of decision making by businesses according to moral concepts and judgments.
- Decisions involving business ethics must be made at all levels of the organization.
- Organizations may adopt ethics programs that include a broad ethics policy, a code of conduct, training, and seminars on ethics for all employees.
- Organization leaders, including law firm partners, adopt ethics programs both because it is the morally right thing to do, and because it is good for business.
- The Model Business Principles, adopted by the U.S. Department of Commerce in 1995, recommend provision for the following broad principles in each organization's ethics policy: a safe and healthy workplace; fair employment practices avoiding discrimination, responsible environmental protection and environmental practices; compliance with all applicable laws promoting good business practices; and maintenance of a corporate culture that respects free expression and encourages good corporate citizenship.
- Some of the ethical issues that must be addressed by organizations are common to most types of organizations and law firms, including contributions to the community; safe work environments; sexual harassment prevention; prevention of discrimination; fair business practices; honesty in the workplace; theft in the workplace; and provision of a family-friendly work environment.
- Many ethics policies include contributing to the community by supporting charitable causes as one of the principles the organization abides by.
- Although most Americans admit to having lied in a work situation, many organizations value honesty very highly, and lying about a serious matter in the workplace can lead to discipline, loss of employment, and even civil and criminal legal action under certain circumstances.
- Employee thefts are one of the biggest security risks to the organization. Theft of workplace supplies and equipment must be strictly prohibited, and such prohibitions must be enforced from the top down to effectively prevent losses to the organization.
- The workforce in the United States is becoming increasingly diverse, with the number of minorities and women in the workforce growing at a rapid rate. For an organization to perform optimally, it must address the diverse needs of all workers.
- Sexual harassment has become a very real problem in our country, with over half of the women in the workforce reporting to have experienced sexual harassment at some point.
- Individuals at all levels of an organization are often faced with making tough ethical choices. Models for making ethical choices can be used to assist individuals (and groups) in making the right and ethical choices.

SUMMARY QUESTIONS

1. What are some reasons businesses, including law firms, are adopting ethics programs?
2. What are some common elements of ethics policies?

3. Choose a common ethics issue in the workplace and describe how each level of an organization may face different dilemmas concerning that same issue.
4. How is a code of ethics different from an ethics policy?
5. What are some ways that organizations contribute to the community? Can you give an example from your community? Why is community involvement especially important to law firms?
6. How can organizations encourage honesty in the workplace?
7. What can law firm management do to discourage sexual harassment?

ENDNOTES

[1]*The Columbia Encyclopedia, Fifth Edition.* New York: Columbia University Press, 1993.

[2]Study: Lying Common In Workplace, *United Press International,* February 3, 1999.

[3]Employee-Related Threats Top List of Corporate Security Concerns, Pinkerton Survey Reveals, *Business Wire,* February 18, 1998.

[4]Harrison, Rainie, Margaret Loftus, and Mark Madden, The State of Greed, *U.S. News & World Report,* June 17, 1996, p. 62.

[5]Parrott, Phillip, The Enemy Within: Employee Embezzlement and the Law Firm, *Colorado Lawyer,*

[6]Color-Coded Hurdle, *American Bar Association Journal,* February 1999.

[7]U.S. Merit Systems Protection Board, 1987.

[8]*1994 Society for Human Resource Management Survey.*

[9]Statistics kept by the Equal Employment Opportunity Commission.

ATTORNEYS AND PUBLIC IMAGE

"The first thing we do, let's kill all the lawyers."

—William Shakespeare

Lawyers, as a group, have often suffered from poor public image and a certain lack of popularity. In a 1999 Gallup Poll, measuring how the public views the honesty and ethics of people in certain fields, attorneys were ranked 37 out of 45 professions. Nurses were ranked number one—car salesmen came in last. 41% of the 1,013 adults responding to the survey indicated that they ranked the honesty and ethical standards of lawyers either low or very low.[i]

Several reasons have been suggested for this lack of respect and popularity, including the adversarial nature of our legal system, the increased and unprofessional advertising by some attorneys, the unethical behavior of a few attorneys, and the poor portrayal of attorneys by the media.

The American Bar Association and bar associations across the country are working to improve the public image of attorneys in several ways. They attempt to maintain the integrity of the bar by requiring bar applicants to pass character tests. They also adopt and enforce strict codes of ethics for attorneys. The bar associations encourage their members to participate in pro bono activities and to work toward providing access to the legal system to all. Law schools and bar associations educate attorneys and future attorneys about legal ethics and how to effectively deal with the media.

Attorneys may also be receiving help with their public image from an unexpected source—prime-time television The country loves courtroom drama and all drama involving lawyers. *Ally McBeal, The Practice, L.A. Law* and other popular television shows have recently been portraying attorneys in a new and generally favorable light. Television attorneys have come a long way from Perry Mason to Ally McBeal. Initially, television attorneys, especially Perry Mason, were portrayed as brilliant heroes. Perry Mason always represented innocent clients and won their cases with his superior skill and intelligence against incredible odds. Some felt this type of portrayal actually hurt the legal profession by giving the public unrealistic expectations of attorneys and the legal system.

The portrayal of the attorney during modern prime time is a bit more realistic. While it is not unusual to see attorneys portrayed as being cold, calculating, and greedy, most modern television attorneys are honest, ethical, and a bit eccentric. The attorneys on *L.A. Law, Law and Order,* and *The Practice* don't always represent the good guy. They don't always win. Often, the fictional attorneys on television must deal with some of the same ethical dilemmas that many real attorneys must face. The new prime-time courtroom dramas tend to portray attorneys as more human, possibly giving the public a bit more realistic view.

Some studies have shown that watching fictional characters on television is the primary way the public learns about attorneys. Many individuals have little or no personal experience with attorneys, so they relate to fictional attorneys from television. In a 1993 survey that asked participants to name the attorney they admire the most, Perry Mason and Matlock both ranked among the most popular attorneys in the country.[ii]

[i]Poll Releases, The Gallup Organization, November 16, 1999 (**www.gallup.com**).
[ii]Samborn, Randall, Who's Most Admired Lawyer?, *National Law Journal*, August 9, 1993.

Chapter 10

Ethics for the Twenty-First Century

"If you do not think about the future, you cannot have one."

John Gale

Introduction
Ethics 2000
Client Confidentiality and New Technology
  E-Mail
  Cellular Phones
The Internet and the Practice of Law
  Advertising and Solicitation on the Internet
  The Internet and the Unauthorized Practice of
   Law

From the Paralegal's Perspective
The Future of the Paralegal Profession
  Paralegal Regulation
  Regulation and the Unauthorized Practice of Law
  The Internet and the Unauthorized Practice of
   Law by Paralegals
Chapter Summary
Summary Questions

INTRODUCTION

Changes in the legal community and in the practice of law necessarily lead to changes in the rules of legal ethics. Some of these changes are brought about by changes of public opinion and public perception. Other changes are brought about by advances in technology and the makeup of the workforce. This chapter takes a look at some of the latest developments in ethics and some predictions for the future of legal ethics, beginning with a look at Ethics 2000, the ABA's program for updating its Model Rules into the twenty-first century. The focus of this chapter then turns to the rules of ethics concerning client confidentiality in light of new and developing technology. Next, this chapter examines some of the ethical issues raised by the ever-increasing use of the Internet and World Wide Web in the practice of law. The second part of this chapter deals with recent developments and future predictions on ethical issues of particular interest to paralegals, including the regulation of the paralegal profession, the unauthorized practice of law, and paralegal disciplinary matters. This chapter concludes with a look at ethical issues concerning emerging technology that may affect the paralegal profession.

ETHICS 2000

In 1997 the American Bar Association appointed a Commission on the Evaluation of the Rules of Professional Conduct (Ethics 2000) to perform a comprehensive study and review of the current Model Rules of Professional Conduct and make recommendations for changes.

According to former ABA President N. Lee Cooper, the Ethics 2000 Commission is necessary "in light of changes in the legal profession, such as the increased size and mobility of law firms, the proliferation of in-house counsel, the increase in specialization, and the impact of global communications and technology on the legal profession."[1]

Ethics 2000 is likely to produce a comprehensive report on the state of legal ethics and recommend several changes to the Model Rules of Professional Ethics in the year 2000. The findings of Ethics 2000 are sure to be the subject of significant discussion and debate that will lead to major revisions in the Model Rules and subsequent changes in the codes of ethics in most, if not all, states.

CLIENT CONFIDENTIALITY AND NEW TECHNOLOGY

When we think of an attorney imparting legal advice to a client, an image may come to mind of an attorney, dressed formally in a suit, leaning over her desk to talk face to face to her client. In reality, more attorney advice is being imparted from the attorney's home, car, golf course, or even computer. New technology has made the *virtual office* a near reality, but not without some serious ethical consequences.

Some of the most important rules of ethics involve the confidentiality of client information and the confidential nature of the attorney–client relationship. New technology means new methods of communication, and may mean the need for new rules of ethics concerning client confidentiality.

E-Mail

E-mail, a form of communication that did not even exist a few years ago, is quickly becoming one of the preferred means of communication by attorneys.

E-mail offers the advantages of speed of communication, efficiency, and cost effectiveness. In addition, e-mail can be sent to more than one party at a time, and the recipients can retrieve the communication from their computers at their convenience—they need not be at their computers when the communication is sent.

E-mail is mail that is transmitted electronically. Correspondence, documents, and entire computer files can be sent via e-mail. Electronic mail may be transmitted within an office or through a local area network (LAN). Electronic mail may also be sent outside the office via a commercial network such as America Online or MCI Mail, or over the Internet.

Attorneys are required to take reasonable measures to ensure client confidentiality in all communications. If reasonable precautions to keep communications confidential are not taken, the attorney–client privilege can be lost. Different forms of communication come with different risks. The confidentiality of e-mail has been at issue since its inception. The most common risks associated with e-mail communication are intentional interception at the sender's computer, the receiver's computer, or during transmission by hackers.

Intercepting e-mail communication is a crime under the Electronic Communication Privacy Act of 1986 and several state laws.

E-mail sent via the Internet is considered the least secure, with the greatest risk of interception because of the number of individuals with the ability to illegally intercept the transmission. E-mail sent on a local network is transmitted only on the network and is therefore more secure. For that reason, attorneys in corporate legal departments will often have a LAN established that includes their outside counsel.

Several state bars have issued opinions that specifically provide that the attorney–client privilege is not waived merely because the medium used for communication was e-mail and confirming that clients have a reasonable expectation that their e-mail communications will remain confidential. Some states provide that clients should be advised of the potential risks associated with e-mail communication, and others suggest that encryption be used for highly sensitive material. Encryption involves the use of special software that encodes the message at the point of sending and decodes it only at the intended receiver's computer. Encrypted messages that may be intercepted are indecipherable without the proper, private codes.

Following are some considerations for sending secure, confidential e-mail:

- Always double check the e-mail address you are using
- Clients should be advised of any potential risks associated with e-mail communications
- Encryption should be used for highly sensitive privileged and confidential communication
- Consider who may have access to the recipient's e-mail—for example, employers or system managers
- Check for compliance with state ethics opinions in the state of transmission
- Consider sending a test message before a confidential message is sent to a new client to be sure that the proper e-mail address is used

Cellular Phones

The convenience offered by cell phones has made them an increasingly popular means of communication. In 1996, there were approximately 135 million cell phone users worldwide.[2] Cell phones give attorneys who are on the road, or otherwise out of the office, the ability to contact clients and their offices at any time. In addition, cell phones make the attorney much more accessible to clients.

Cellular phones are less secure than traditional telephones, and the increasing use of cell phones has lead to a concern over client confidentiality. The bar associations of most states have issued opinions advising against confidential conversations with clients via cellular telephones, or at least providing that the attorney must caution the client concerning the possible risks of using a cellular telephone before the conversation begins.

Although the federal Electronic Communications Privacy Act[3] prohibits the intentional interception of cellular telephone calls, cellular telephone conversations can be overheard by scanning receivers. Digital technology, which is becoming more commonplace, greatly reduces the ability for outside interception of the call.

In the future, digital technology will probably become widespread, making cellular telephone usage as secure as traditional telephones and providing greater peace of mind to the attorney and client.

THE INTERNET AND THE PRACTICE OF LAW

Use of the Internet by attorneys for marketing, research, and e-mail has grown at an exponential rate since the early 1990s. 1998 surveys by the ABA Legal Technology Resource Center indicated that eighty percent of small law firms, and nearly all large law firms, offered Internet access to at least some of its members. In the future, we are likely to see access by even more small firms, and a growth in the number and type of applications used. The Internet, a large, international computer network linking millions of users around the world, is a unique medium that presents unique ethical issues. Many of these issues have yet to be resolved.

Advertising and Solicitation on the Internet

The current Model Rules were written to encompass all forms of advertising media; however, they were not written with the Internet in mind. Although common sense would dictate that the Model Rules and state codes of ethics should be applied to the Internet in the same manner as they are applied to any other form of media, it is not that simple. The Model Rules and the state codes of ethics do not address all issues raised by the use of the Internet for advertising and solicitation, and there is still much uncertainty.

Most attorney advertising on the Internet is in the form of home pages on the World Wide Web. In 1998, fifty-eight percent of large law firms indicated that they had a World Wide Web home page, and another seventeen percent indicated that they had pages in development.[4] Law firm home pages usually include the following:

1. A description of the law firm, including its history and information about members of the firm
2. Direct e-mail links to the attorneys and other individuals in the firm
3. Information about the practice areas of the firm, including jurisdictions the attorneys are licensed to practice in

In addition, several home pages include links to a bulletin board that allows the attorneys of the firm to answer legal questions from potential clients and links to other sites that may be of interest.

Other forms of marketing and solicitation on the Internet include the use of banner ads, directory listings, and participation in discussion groups.

Web sites are maintained to promote the law firm and attorneys. Therefore, Web sites and banner advertising done over the Internet must comply with the ethical rules for all advertising. However, Internet advertising presents several issues unique to the Internet and not addressed in the codes of ethics in most states. Some of those issues include:

- Which state rules apply to Web page advertising that may be viewed all over the world?
- Do the rules of ethics concerning solicitation apply to attorneys participating in Internet discussions?
- Is it ethical for law firm Web sites to include links to other sites?

The codes of ethics of each state provide that attorney advertising must not be false or misleading. However, as discussed in Chapter 8, the definition of false or misleading may be very different from state to state. If a New York law firm that has attorneys licensed to practice law in several states throughout the country has a Web site, which state rules must it abide by? Will the New York rules suffice if they are significantly more liberal than another state in which the law firm practices? One approach that some law firms have taken is to follow the rules of the strictest state in which attorneys of the law firm are licensed to practice. This issue has not been addressed by the ABA or the states as yet, but will most certainly be debated in the near future.

In addition to state rules prohibiting false and misleading advertising, rules requiring copies of all advertising to be kept for a certain period of time, or requiring copies of all advertising to be submitted to the state bar before publication, also are difficult to apply to Internet advertising. It is as yet unclear in several states exactly what needs to be submitted and when in cases of advertising that is done over the Internet. In a state requiring that copies of all advertising must be submitted to the state bar, does a law firm need to submit printed copies of its entire Web site every time a change is made to that site? Can states impose this requirement on law firms that are not located in their state and have no attorneys licensed in their state, merely because their law firm Web site or advertising is available in their state?

Most states have requirements concerning the labeling of any solicitation by mail be labeled as *Advertising*. Should this also be a requirement for advertising and solicitations made over the Internet?

Attorney involvement in live chats on the Internet may be considered a form of solicitation. Although attorneys may participate in a live chat over the Internet and offer their services to one or more individuals who receive the offer immediately, as yet it has not been determined whether this would be considered in-person solicitation.

The Internet and the Unauthorized Practice of Law

Involvement in discussion groups over the Internet also brings up another ethical issue—that of the unauthorized practice of law. It is generally held that giving legal advice is considered the practice of law. Because attorneys must be licensed in any jurisdiction in which they practice law, the question arises as to whether an attorney who gives advice over the Internet in an open chat or discussion group that may be read by participants in every state in the country is engaging in the unauthorized practice of law. Attorneys frequently give advice over the Internet with several disclaimers, including one stating in which jurisdictions they are licensed to practice law and that the information they provide is relevant only for those jurisdictions. It has not yet been determined whether this is sufficient to prevent the charge of the unauthorized practice of law.

The new and emerging technology does not have an exact fit with any rules of ethics currently in place. The next decade will surely see several revisions and additions to state codes of ethics to accommodate the Internet and other new technology.

FROM THE PARALEGAL'S PERSPECTIVE

Paralegals will be affected by any developments in legal ethics for attorneys. Paralegals use new technology (at least) as much as attorneys do. Because paralegals must abide by any rules of ethics concerning attorneys, they must keep current with changes to the rules of ethics brought on by Ethics 2000 and new technology.

In addition, changes within the paralegal profession itself will have an impact on the rules of ethics for paralegals. If regulation is adopted in your state, it will affect your ethical obligations in several ways.

THE FUTURE OF THE PARALEGAL PROFESSION

Several current trends in the paralegal professional will likely lead to changes that will raise ethical issues for paralegals. The most drastic changes will likely occur from regulation of the paralegal profession. The debate over regulation has been raging for decades and doesn't show any sign of immediate resolution. However, some form of regulation, at some point in the future, appears to be almost inevitable.

Paralegal Regulation

Paralegal regulation would have an impact on paralegal ethics in several ways. Paralegals would probably be bound by the code of ethics that applies to them. Although at the current time paralegal associations have no authority to enforce their codes of ethics, if paralegals must be licensed, the associations or an appointed state agency would have the leverage needed to discipline paralegals who violate the pertinent codes of ethics.

Requirements for paralegal training and paralegal competence would likely be a significant part of any regulation scheme. Paralegal competence would be defined and required.

If regulation were to take place, the regulation would likely be accompanied by further definition of what tasks may be performed by paralegals, and the *unauthorized practice of law* would be more clearly defined.

Regulation and the Unauthorized Practice of Law

As the level of paralegal responsibility increases, so does the paralegal's risk of being found guilty of the unauthorized practice of law. Well-trained paralegals are competently performing tasks that have been considered the unauthorized practice of law by other lay people. Legislation has been adopted in some states to exempt certain paralegals from specific provisions of unauthorized practice of law statutes.

The NFPA supports such legislation as a means to promote added responsibility for paralegals while protecting them from prosecution under unauthorized practice of law statutes. The NFPA has drafted model language for adoption by state legislatures to exempt paralegals from certain unauthorized practice of law statutes (Figure 10–1).

[Insert State]

[Insert State Legislative Body Name]

[Insert Session No. And Year]

A BILL FOR AN ACT to amend the [INSERT STATE] [INSERT EITHER "CODE" OR CORRECT REFERENCE TO STATE STATUTES]2 concerning [INSERT APPROPRIATE REFERENCE e.g. THE UNAUTHORIZED PRACTICE OF LAW or THE PRACTICE OF LAW].

Be it enacted by the [INSERT STATE LEGISLATIVE BODY NAME] of the State of [INSERT NAME OF STATE].

SECTION [INSERT APPROPRIATE REFERENCE TO SECTION OR SUBSECTION] is added to the [INSERT STATE NAME] [INSERT EITHER CODE OR APPROPRIATE REFERENCE TO STATE STATUTES] as a new section [INSERT SUBSECTION IF APPLICABLE] to read as follows:

[INSERT APPROPRIATE SECTION/SUBSECTION REFERENCE]

Exempted 3 from those individuals considered to be engaged in the unauthorized practice of law are paralegals, also known as legal assistants, defined as persons qualified through education, training or work experience, to perform substantive legal work that requires knowledge of legal concepts and is customarily, but not exclusively, performed by a lawyer. These persons may be retained or employed by a lawyer, law office, governmental agency, or other entity or may be authorized by administrative, statutory or court authority to perform such work. These persons may be performing substantive legal work with the supervision of or accountability to an attorney or pursuant to statute, administrative regulation and/or court authority or persons performing procedural work which requires knowledge of procedural concepts and does not render legal advice.

Effective date_____

_____

2 NOTE TO NFPA MEMBER: It is important to review the existing statute in its entirety to assess how the UPL issue is addressed in your state. It is important that this amendment be placed in all applicable sections or subsection.

3 NOTE TO NFPA MEMBER: In the event the existing statute already excepts or exempts specific individuals or entities from unauthorized practice of law, you will need to add the words FURTHER EXEMPTED or ALSO EXEMPTED.

FIGURE 10–1

Model For State Statute to Exempt Paralegals from Unauthorized Practice of Law Reprented with permission of the National Federation of Paralegal Associations.

Along with the desire to exempt paralegals from portions of the unauthorized practice of law statutes comes two specific problems for paralegals and the legal community:

1. How do you define the term *paralegal*?
2. What qualifications must an individual have to meet the definition of *paralegal*?

These questions have led a strong portion of the legal community to believe that it is time for paralegal regulation, either in the form of licensing for all paralegals or, at a minimum, for independent paralegals.

Paralegal regulation in the form of licensing, certification, and registration has been proposed from many sources, and legislation has been introduced in several states. Although regulation in your state may directly affect only independent paralegals, the dialogue and resulting legislation should give guidance to all paralegals as to exactly what activities are permissible and which will be considered the unauthorized practice of law in your state.

The Internet and the Unauthorized Practice of Law by Paralegals

Paralegals who communicate over the Internet must be careful that their communications do not constitute the unauthorized practice of law. Rules prohibiting paralegals from giving legal advice and opinions apply to any type of communication, including communication via the Internet. This rule can be construed to restrict the exchange of information and resources via the Internet between paralegals, a very common and fruitful use of the Internet technology. One way to clarify that your communication over the Internet is not legal advice is to include a disclaimer with your communication—especially communication that may be posted for multiple readers. A disclaimer indicating that the sender is a paralegal and the following information is not to be considered legal advice or a legal opinion would weigh in the paralegal's favor should the question of unauthorized practice of law ever be brought up.

Changes to the rules of ethics and changes within the paralegal profession itself will affect your ethical obligations in the future. It is important that you keep current with the latest issues in legal ethics that will affect you. For the latest developments in legal ethics in your state, keep in touch with your paralegal association and visit the companion Web site to this text at **www.westlegalstudies.com**.

CHAPTER SUMMARY

- The Commission on the Evaluation of the Rules of Professional Conduct (Ethics 2000) was appointed to study and review the current Model Rules of Professional Conduct and make recommendations for changes.
- Special consideration must be given to client confidentiality when using certain forms of communication, especially cellular phones and e-mail.
- Generally, attorneys must follow rules of ethics concerning advertising and solicitation for any Internet advertising they do. Certain issues concerning the ethical use of the Internet have not yet been addressed by the codes of ethics.
- Some type of regulation will probably affect most paralegals in the future.
- Paralegals who communicate over the Internet must be careful that their communications do not constitute the unauthorized practice of law.

SUMMARY QUESTIONS

1. What are some possible reasons for amending the Model Rules of Professional Conduct?
2. What is the likely affect of amendments to the Model Rules of Professional Conduct?
3. Suppose you see a posting on an Internet bulletin board from a friend of yours in another state, asking for advice on how to prepare a draft of a petition for a divorce. You do this type of work all the time at your job, and are very familiar with the requirements in your state. What can you do to help her? What precautions might you take?
4. Suppose that you receive an e-mail from a client asking for some confidential information from his or her file. What are your options for responding?
5. If an attorney is stuck in traffic on the way to pick up a client for a hearing, would it be appropriate for the attorney to call the client on his cellular phone to let her know he is on the way? What should the attorney do if the client wants to discuss her case over the telephone?

ENDNOTES

[1]*ABA Establishes "Ethics 2000" to Evaluate Legal Ethics,* ABA Press Release, July 24, 1997.

[2]Mika, Karin, Of Cell Phones and Electronic Mail: Disclosure of Confidential Information Under Disciplinary Rule 4-101 and Model Rule 1.6, *Notre Dame Journal of Law, Ethics and Public Policy,* 1999.

[3]18 USC 2511 (1).

[4]*1998 Large law Firm Technology Survey,* American Bar Association Legal Technology Resource Center (1998).

APPENDIX A

Missouri's Rules of Professional Conduct

Missouri is one state that has closely followed the Model Rules of Professional Conduct in adopting its own Rules of Professional Conduct. Most of the section titles and numbers of the Missouri Rules are identical to the corresponding sections of the Model Rules of Professional Conduct discussed throughout this text.

CLIENT-LAWYER RELATIONSHIP

Rule 1.1 Competence

A lawyer shall provide competent representation to a client. Competent representation requires the legal knowledge, skill, thoroughness and preparation reasonably necessary for the representation.

Rule 1.2 Scope of Representation

(a) A lawyer shall abide by a client's decisions concerning the objectives of representation, subject to paragraphs (c), (d) and (e), and shall consult with the client as to the means by which they are to be pursued. A lawyer shall abide by a client's decision whether to accept an offer of settlement of a matter. In a criminal case, the lawyer shall abide by the client's decision, after consultation with the lawyer, as to a plea to be entered, whether to waive jury trial and whether the client will testify.

(b) A lawyer's representation of a client, including representation by appointment, does not constitute an endorsement of the client's political, economic, social or moral views or activities.

(c) A lawyer may limit the objectives of the representation if the client consents after consultation.

(d) A lawyer shall not counsel a client to engage, or assist a client, in conduct that the lawyer knows is criminal or fraudulent, but a lawyer may discuss the legal consequences of any proposed course of conduct with a client and may counsel or assist a client to make a good faith effort to determine the validity, scope, meaning or application of the law.

(e) When a lawyer knows that a client expects assistance not permitted by the Rules of Professional Conduct or other law, the lawyer shall consult with the client regarding the relevant limitations on the lawyer's conduct.

Rule 1.3 Diligence

A lawyer shall act with reasonable diligence and promptness in representing a client.

Rule 1.4 Communication

(a) A lawyer shall keep a client reasonably informed about the status of a matter and promptly comply with reasonable requests for information.

(b) A lawyer shall explain a matter to the extent reasonably necessary to permit the client to make informed decisions regarding the representation.

Rule 1.5 Fees

(a) A lawyer's fee shall be reasonable. The factors to be considered in determining the reasonableness of a fee include the following:

(1) the time and labor required, the novelty and difficulty of the questions involved, and the skill requisite to perform the legal service properly;

(2) the likelihood, if apparent to the client, that the acceptance of the particular employment will preclude other employment by the lawyer;

(3) the fee customarily charged in the locality for similar legal services;

(4) the amount involved and the results obtained;

(5) the time limitations imposed by the client or by the circumstances;

(6) the nature and length of the professional relationship with the client;

(7) the experience, reputation, and ability of the lawyer or lawyers performing the services; and

(8) whether the fee is fixed or contingent.

(b) When the lawyer has not regularly represented the client, the basis or rate of the fee shall be communicated to the client, preferably in writing, before or within a reasonable time after commencing the representation.

(c) A fee may be contingent on the outcome of the matter for which the service is rendered, except in a matter in which a contingent fee is prohibited by paragraph (d) or other law. A contingent fee agreement shall be in writing and shall state the method by which the fee is to be determined, including the percentage or percentages that shall accrue to the lawyer in the event of settlement, trial or appeal, litigation and other expenses to be deducted from the recovery, and whether such expenses are to be deducted before or after the contingent fee is calculated.

Upon conclusion of a contingent fee matter, the lawyer shall provide the client with a written statement stating the outcome of the matter and, if there is a recovery, showing the remittance to the client and the method of its determination.

(d) A lawyer shall not enter into an arrangement for, charge, or collect:

(1) any fee in a domestic relations matter, the payment or amount of which is contingent upon the securing of a divorce or upon the amount of alimony or support, or property settlement in lieu thereof; or

(2) a contingent fee for representing a defendant in a criminal case.

(e) A division of a fee between lawyers who are not in the same firm may be made only if:

(1) the division is in proportion to the services performed by each lawyer or, by written agreement with the client, each lawyer assumes joint responsibility for the representation;

(2) the client is advised of and does not object to the participation of all the lawyers involved; and

(3) the total fee is reasonable.

Rule 1.6 Confidentiality of Information

(a) A lawyer shall not reveal information relating to representation of a client unless the client consents after consultation, except for disclosures that are impliedly authorized in order to carry out the representation, and except as stated in paragraph (b).

(b) A lawyer may reveal such information to the extent the lawyer reasonably believes necessary:

    (1) to prevent the client from committing a criminal act that the lawyer believes is likely to result in imminent death or substantial bodily harm; or

    (2) to establish a claim or defense on behalf of the lawyer in a controversy between the lawyer and the client, to establish a defense to a criminal charge or civil claim against the lawyer based upon conduct in which the client was involved, or to respond to allegations in any proceeding concerning the lawyer's representation of the client.

Rule 1.7 Conflict of Interest: General Rule

(a) A lawyer shall not represent a client if the representation of that client will be directly adverse to another client, unless:

    (1) the lawyer reasonably believes the representation will not adversely affect the relationship with the other client; and

    (2) each client consents after consultation.

(b) A lawyer shall not represent a client if the representation of that client may be materially limited by the lawyer's responsibilities to another client or to a third person, or by the lawyer's own interests, unless:

    (1) the lawyer reasonably believes the representation will not be adversely affected;

    (2) the client consents after consultation. When representation of multiple clients in a single matter is undertaken, the consultation shall include explanation of the implications of the common representation and the advantages and risks involved.

Rule 1.8 Conflict of Interest: Prohibited Transactions

(a) A lawyer shall not enter into a business transaction with a client or knowingly acquire an ownership, possessory, security or other pecuniary interest adverse to a client unless:

    (1) the transaction and terms on which the lawyer acquires the interest are fair and reasonable to the client and are fully disclosed and transmitted in writing to the client in a manner which can be reasonably understood by the client;

    (2) the client is given a reasonable opportunity to seek the advice of independent counsel in the transaction; and

    (3) the client consents in writing thereto.

(b) A lawyer shall not use information relating to representation of a client to the disadvantage of the client unless the client consents after consultation.

(c) A lawyer shall not prepare an instrument giving the lawyer or a person related to the lawyer as parent, child, sibling, or spouse any substantial gift from a client, including a testamentary gift, except where the client is related to the donee.

(d) Prior to the conclusion of representation of a client, a lawyer shall not make or negotiate an agreement giving the lawyer literary or media rights to a portrayal or account based in substantial part on information relating to the representation.

(e) A lawyer shall not provide financial assistance to a client in connection with pending or contemplated litigation, except that:

    (1) a lawyer may advance court costs and expenses of litigation, the repayment of which may be contingent on the outcome of the matter; and

    (2) a lawyer representing an indigent client may pay court costs and expenses of litigation on behalf of the client.

(f) A lawyer shall not accept compensation for representing a client from one other than the client unless:

    (1) the client consents after consultation;

    (2) there is no interference with the lawyer's independence of professional judgment or with the client-lawyer relationship; and

    (3) information relating to representation of a client is protected as required by Rule 1.6.

(g) A lawyer who represents two or more clients shall not participate in making an aggregate settlement of the claims of or against the clients, or in a criminal case an aggregated agreement as to guilty or nolo contendere pleas, unless each client consents after consultation, including disclosure of the existence and nature of all the claims or pleas involved and of the participation of each person in the settlement.

(h) A lawyer shall not make an agreement prospectively limiting the lawyer's liability to a client for malpractice unless permitted by law and the client is independently represented in making the agreement, or settle a claim for such liability with an unrepresented client or former client without first advising that person in writing that independent representation is appropriate in connection therewith.

(i) A lawyer related to another lawyer as parent, child, sibling or spouse shall not represent a client in a representation directly adverse to a person who the lawyer knows is represented by the other lawyer except upon consent by the client after consultation regarding the relationship.

(j) A lawyer shall not acquire a proprietary interest in the cause of action or subject matter of litigation the lawyer is conducting for a client, except that the lawyer may:

    (1) acquire a lien granted by law to secure the lawyer's fee or expenses; and

    (2) contract with a client for a reasonable contingent fee in a civil case.

Rule 1.9 Conflict of Interest: Former Client

A lawyer who has formerly represented a client in a matter shall not thereafter:

(a) represent another person in the same or a substantially related matter in which that person's interests are materially adverse to the interests of the former client unless the former client consents after consultation; or

(b) use information relating to the representation to the disadvantage of the former client except as Rule 1.6 would permit with respect to a client or when the information has become generally known

Rule 1.10 Imputed Disqualification: General Rule

(a) While lawyers are associated in a firm, none of them shall knowingly represent a client when any one of them practicing alone would be prohibited from doing so by Rules 1.7, 1.8(c), 1.9 or 2.2.

(b) When a lawyer becomes associated with a firm, the firm may not knowingly represent a person in the same or a substantially related matter in which that lawyer, or a firm with which the lawyer was associated, had previously represented a client whose interests are materially adverse to that person and about whom the lawyer had acquired information protected by Rules 1.6 and 1.9(b) that is material to the matter.

(c) When a lawyer has terminated an association with a firm, the firm is not prohibited from thereafter representing a person with interests materially adverse to those of a client represented by the formerly associated lawyer unless:

    (1) the matter is the same or substantially related to that in which the formerly associated lawyer represented the client; and

    (2) any lawyer remaining in the firm has information protected by Rules 1.6 and 1.9(b) that is material to the matter.

(d) A disqualification prescribed by this Rule may be waived by the affected client under the conditions stated in Rule 1.7.

Rule 1.11 Successive Government and Private Employment

(a) Except as law may otherwise expressly permit, a lawyer shall not represent a private client in connection with a matter in which the lawyer participated personally and substantially as a public officer or employee, unless the appropriate government agency consents after consultation. No lawyer in a firm with which that lawyer is associated may knowingly undertake or continue representation in such a matter unless:

    (1) the disqualified lawyer is screened from any participation in the matter and is apportioned no part of the fee therefrom; and

    (2) written notice is promptly given to the appropriate government agency to enable it to ascertain compliance with the provisions of this Rule.

(b) Except as law may otherwise expressly permit, a lawyer having information that the lawyer knows is confidential government information about a person acquired when the lawyer was a public officer or employee, may not represent a private client whose interests are adverse to that person in a matter in which the information could be used to the material disadvantage of that person. A firm with which that lawyer is associated may undertake or continue representation in the matter only if the disqualified lawyer is screened from any participation in the matter and is apportioned no part of the fee therefrom.

(c) Except as law may otherwise expressly permit, a lawyer serving as a public officer or employee shall not:

    (1) participate in a matter in which the lawyer participated personally and substantially while in private practice or nongovernmental employment, unless under applicable law no one is, or by lawful delegation may be, authorized to act in the lawyer's stead in the matter; or

    (2) negotiate for private employment with any person who is involved as a party or as attorney for a party in a matter in which the lawyer is participating personally and substantially.

(d) As used in this Rule, the term "matter" includes:

    (1) any judicial or other proceeding, application, request for a ruling or other determination, contract, claim, controversy, investigation, charge, accusation, arrest or other particular matter involving a specific party or parties; and

    (2) any other matter covered by the conflict of interest rules of the appropriate government agency.

(e) As used in this Rule, the term "confidential government information" means information that has been obtained under governmental authority and which, at the time this Rule is applied, the government is prohibited by law from disclosing to the public or has a legal privilege not to disclose, and which is not otherwise available to the public.

Rule 1.12 Former Judge or Arbitrator

(a) Except as stated in paragraph (d), a lawyer shall not represent anyone in connection with a matter in which the lawyer participated personally and substantially as a judge or other adjudicative officer, arbitrator or law clerk to such a person, unless all parties to the proceeding consent after disclosure.

(b) A lawyer shall not negotiate for employment with any person who is involved as a party or as attorney for a party in a matter in which the lawyer is participating personally and substantially as a judge or other adjudicative officer, or arbitrator. A lawyer serving as a law clerk to a judge, other adjudicative officer or arbitrator may negotiate for employment with a party or attorney involved in a matter in which the clerk is participating personally and substantially, but only after the lawyer has notified the judge, other adjudicative officer or arbitrator.

(c) If a lawyer is disqualified by paragraph (a), no lawyer in a firm with which that lawyer is associated may knowingly undertake or continue representation in the matter unless:

    (1) the disqualified lawyer is screened from any participation in the matter and is apportioned no part of the fee therefrom; and

    (2) written notice is promptly given to the appropriate tribunal to enable it to ascertain compliance with the provisions of this rule.

(d) An arbitrator selected as a partisan of a party in a multi-member arbitrator panel is not prohibited from subsequently representing that party.

Rule 1.13 Organization as Client

(a) A lawyer employed or retained by an organization represents the organization acting through its duly authorized constituents.

(b) If a lawyer for an organization knows that an officer, employee or other person associated with the organization is engaged in action, intends to act or refuses to act in a matter related to the representation that is a violation of a legal obligation to the organization, or a violation of law which reasonably might be imputed to the organization, and is likely to result in substantial injury to the organization, the lawyer shall proceed as is reasonably necessary in the best interest of the organization. In determining how to proceed, the lawyer shall give due consideration to the seriousness of the violation and its consequences, the scope and nature of the lawyer's representation, the responsibility in the organization and the apparent motivation of the person involved, the policies of the organization concerning such matters and any other relevant considerations. Any measures taken shall be designed to minimize disruption of the organization and the risk of revealing information relating to the representation to persons outside the organization. Such measures may include among others:

    (1) asking reconsideration of the matter;

    (2) advising that a separate legal opinion on the matter be sought for presentation to appropriate authority in the organization; and

    (3) referring the matter to higher authority in the organization, including, if warranted by the seriousness of the matter, referral to the high-

est authority that can act in behalf of the organization as determined by applicable law.

(c) If, despite the lawyer's efforts in accordance with paragraph (b), the highest authority that can act on behalf of the organization insists upon action, or a refusal to act, that is clearly a violation of law and is likely to result in substantial injury to the organization, the lawyer may resign in accordance with Rule 1.16.

(d) In dealing with an organization's directors, officers, employees, members, shareholders or other constituents, a lawyer shall explain the identity of the client when it is apparent that the organization's interests are adverse to those of the constituents with whom the lawyer is dealing.

(e) A lawyer representing an organization may also represent any of its directors, officers, employees, members, shareholders or other constituents, subject to the provisions of Rule 1.7. If the organization's consent to the dual representation is required by Rule 1.7, the consent shall be given by an appropriate official of the organization other than the individual who is to be represented, or by the shareholders.

Rule 1.14 Client Under a Disability

(a) When a client's ability to make adequately considered decisions in connection with the representation is impaired, whether because of minority, mental disability or for some other reason, the lawyer shall, as far as reasonably possible, maintain a normal client-lawyer relationship with the client.

(b) A lawyer may seek the appointment of a guardian or take other protective action with respect to a client only when the lawyer reasonably believes that the client cannot adequately act in the client's own interest.

Rule 1.15 Safekeeping Property

(a) A lawyer shall hold property of clients or third persons that is in a lawyer's possession in connection with a representation separate from the lawyer's own property. Funds shall be kept in a separate account maintained in the state where the lawyer's office is situated, or elsewhere with the consent of the client or third person. Other property shall be identified as such and appropriately safeguarded. Complete records of such account funds and other property shall be kept by the lawyer and shall be preserved for a period of five years after termination of the representation.

(b) Upon receiving funds or other property in which a client or third person has an interest, a lawyer shall promptly notify the client or third person. Except as stated in this Rule or otherwise permitted by law or by agreement with the client, a lawyer shall promptly deliver to the client or third person any funds or other property that the client or third person is entitled to receive and, upon request by the client or third person, shall promptly render a full accounting regarding such property.

(c) When in the course of representation a lawyer is in possession of property in which both the lawyer and another person claim interests, the property shall be kept separate by the lawyer until there is an accounting and severance of their interests. If a dispute arises concerning their respective interests, the portion in dispute shall be kept separate by the lawyer until the dispute is resolved.

(d) Except as provided in paragraph (e), a lawyer or law firm shall establish and maintain one or more interest-bearing insured depository accounts into which shall be deposited all funds of clients or third persons that are nominal in amount or are expected to be held for a short period of time, but only in compliance with the following provisions:

(1) no earnings from such account shall be made available to the lawyer or law firm, and the lawyer or law firm shall have no right or claim to such earnings;

(2) only funds of clients that are nominal in amount or are expected to be held for a short period of time and on which interest is not paid to the clients may be deposited in such account, taking into consideration the following factors:

  (i) the amount of interest that the funds would earn during the period they are expected to be deposited;

  (ii) the cost of establishing and administering the account, including the cost of the lawyer's services and the cost of preparing any tax reports required for interest accruing to a client's benefit; and

  (iii) the capability of financial institutions to calculate and pay interest to individual clients;

(3) funds deposited in such account shall be available for withdrawal or transfer on demand, subject only to any notice period that the institution is required to observe by law or regulation;

(4) the depository institution shall be directed by the lawyer or law firm establishing such accounts:

  (i) to remit at least quarter-annually earnings from such account, net of any service charges or fees as computed in accordance with the institution's standard accounting practice, to the Missouri Lawyer Trust Account Foundation, which shall be the sole beneficial owner of the interest or earnings generated by such account; and

  (ii) to transmit with each remittance of earnings a statement showing the name of the lawyer or law firm on whose account the remittance is sent and the rate of interest applied, with a copy of such statement to such lawyer or law firm; and

(5) the lawyer or law firm shall review the account at reasonable intervals to determine if changed circumstances require further action with respect to the funds of any client.

(e) Every lawyer shall certify, in connection with this Court's annual enrollment fee statement and in such form as the clerk of this Court may prescribe, that the lawyer or the law firm with which the lawyer is associated either participates in the program as provided in Rule 1.15(d) or is exempt because the:

(1) Nature of the lawyer's or law firm's practice is such that the lawyer or law firm does not hold client or third party funds or is not required to maintain a trust account; or

(2) lawyer is primarily engaged in the practice of law in another jurisdiction and not regularly engaged in the practice of law in this state;

(3) lawyer is associated in a law firm with at least one lawyer who is admitted to practice in a jurisdiction other than the state of Missouri and the lawyer or law firm maintains a pooled interest-bearing trust account for the deposit of funds of clients or third persons in a financial institution located outside the state of Missouri and the interest, net of any service charges and fees, from the account is being remitted to the client or third person who owns the funds or to a non-profit organization or government agency pursuant to the laws or rules governing lawyer conduct of the jurisdiction in which the financial institution is located;

(4) lawyer or law firm elects to decline to maintain accounts as described in paragraph (d) in accordance with the procedures set forth in paragraph (f); or

(5) Missouri Lawyer Trust Account Foundation's Board of Directors, on its own motion, has exempted the lawyer or law firm from participation in the program when service charges on the lawyer's or law firm's trust account equals or exceeds any interest generated.

(f) A lawyer or law firm may elect to decline to maintain accounts as described in paragraph (d) for any calendar year by so notifying the Missouri Lawyer Trust Account Foundation in writing on or before January 31 of 1991 and each subsequent year. A lawyer or law firm that does not so advise the Missouri Lawyer Trust Account Foundation within any such period shall be required during the current year to maintain such accounts.

(g) For purposes of paragraph (d) of this rule:

(1) "insured depository accounts" shall mean government insured accounts at a regulated financial institution on which withdrawals or transfers can be made on demand, subject only to any notice period that the institution is required to observe by law or regulation.

(2) The Missouri Lawyer Trust Account Foundation is that not-for-profit corporation described in this Court's Order of October 23, 1984.

Rule 1.16 Declining or Terminating Representation

(a) Except as stated in paragraph (c), a lawyer shall not represent a client or, where representation has commenced, shall withdraw from the representation of a client if:

(1) the representation will result in violation of the rules of professional conduct or other law;

(2) the lawyer's physical or mental condition materially impairs the lawyer's ability to represent the client; or

(3) the lawyer is discharged.

(b) except as stated in paragraph (c), a lawyer may withdraw from representing a client if withdrawal can be accomplished without material adverse effect on the interests of the client, or if:

(1) the client persists in a course of action involving the lawyer's services that the lawyer reasonably believes is criminal or fraudulent;

(2) the client has used the lawyer's services to perpetrate a crime or fraud;

(3) a client insists upon pursuing an objective that the lawyer considers repugnant or imprudent;

(4) the client fails substantially to fulfill an obligation to the lawyer regarding the lawyer's services and has been given reasonable warning that the lawyer will withdraw unless the obligation is fulfilled;

(5) the representation will result in an unreasonable financial burden on the lawyer or has been rendered unreasonably difficult by the client; or

(6) other good cause for withdrawal exists.

(c) When ordered to do so by a tribunal, a lawyer shall continue representation notwithstanding good cause for terminating the representation.

(d) Upon termination of representation, a lawyer shall take steps to the extent reasonably practicable to protect a client's interests, such as giving reasonable notice to the client, allowing time for employment of other counsel, surrendering papers and property to which the client is entitled and refunding any advance payment of fee that has not been earned. The lawyer may retain papers relating to the client to the extent permitted by other law.

Rule 1.17 Sale of Law Practice

A lawyer or his or her law firm may sell or purchase a law practice, including good will, if the conditions set forth in this Rule 1.17 are satisfied. The seller and purchaser may agree to restrictions on the practice of law by the seller, which shall be set forth in a written agreement. The estate of a deceased lawyer may be a seller.

(a) The practice shall be sold as an entirety, except in cases in which a conflict is present or may arise, to another lawyer or law firm.

(b) Written notice shall be given to each of the seller's clients stating that the interest in the law practice is being transferred to the purchaser; that the client has the right to retain other counsel; that the client may take possession of the client's file and property; and that if no response to the notice is received within sixty days of the sending of such notice, or in the event the client's rights would be prejudiced by a failure to act during that time, the purchaser may act on behalf of the client until otherwise notified by the client.

(1) If the seller is the estate of a deceased lawyer, the purchaser shall cause the notice to be given to the client, and the purchaser shall obtain the written consent of the client to act on the client's behalf. Such consent shall be presumed if no response to the notice is received within sixty days of the date the notice was sent to the client's last known address as shown on the records of the seller or the client's rights would be prejudiced by a failure to act during such sixty-day period.

(2) In all other circumstances, not less than sixty days prior to the transfer the seller shall cause the notice to be given to the client and the seller shall obtain the written consent of the client to act on the client's behalf prior to the transfer. Such consent shall be presumed if no response to the notice is received within sixty days of the date of the sending of such notice to the client's last known address as shown on the records of the seller.

(3) The purchaser shall cause an announcement or notice of the purchase and transfer of the practice to be published in a newspaper of general circulation within the county in which the practice is located at least thirty days in advance of the effective date of the transfer.

(c) The fees charged clients shall not be increased by reason of the sale. The purchaser may, however, refuse to undertake the representation unless the client consents to pay the purchaser fees at a rate not exceeding the fees charged by the purchaser for rendering substantially similar services prior to the initiation of the purchase negotiations.

(d) If substitution of purchasing lawyer or law firm in a pending matter is required by the tribunal or this Rule 1.17, the purchasing lawyer or law firm shall provide for same promptly.

(e) Admission to or withdrawal from a partnership or professional corporation, retirement plans and similar arrangements or a sale limited to the tangible assets of a law practice is not a sale or purchase for purposes of this Rule 1.17.

COUNSELOR

Rule 2.1 Advisor

In representing a client, a lawyer shall exercise independent professional judgment and render candid advice. In rendering advice, a lawyer may refer not only to law but to other considerations such as moral, economic, social and political factors, that may be relevant to the client's situation.

Rule 2.2 Intermediary

(a) A lawyer may act as intermediary between clients if:
   (1) the lawyer consults with each client concerning the implications of the common representation, including the advantages and risks involved, and the effect on the attorney-client privileges, and obtains each client's consent to the common representation;
   (2) the lawyer reasonably believes that the matter can be resolved on terms compatible with the clients' best interests, that each client will be able to make adequately informed decisions in the matter and that there is little risk of material prejudice to the interests of any of the clients if the contemplated resolution is unsuccessful; and
   (3) the lawyer reasonably believes that the common representation can be undertaken impartially and without improper effect on other responsibilities the lawyer has to any of the clients.
(b) While acting as intermediary, the lawyer shall consult with each client concerning the decisions to be made and the considerations relevant in making them, so that each client can make adequately informed decisions.
(c) A lawyer shall withdraw as intermediary if any of the clients so requests, or if any of the conditions stated in paragraph (a) is no longer satisfied. Upon withdrawal, the lawyer shall not continue to represent any of the clients in the matter that was the subject of the intermediation.

Rule 2.3 Evaluation for Use by Third Persons

(a) A lawyer may undertake an evaluation of a matter affecting a client for the use of someone other than the client if:
   (1) the lawyer reasonably believes that making the evaluation is compatible with other aspects of the lawyer's relationship with the client; and
   (2) the client consents after consultation.
(b) Except as disclosure is required in connection with a report of an evaluation, information relating to the evaluation is otherwise protected by Rule 1.6.

ADVOCATE

Rule 3.1 Meritorious Claims and Contentions

A lawyer shall not bring or defend a proceeding, or assert or controvert an issue therein, unless there is a basis for doing so that is not frivolous, which includes a good faith argument for an extension, modification or reversal of existing law. A lawyer for the defendant in a criminal proceeding, or the respondent in a proceeding that could result in incarceration, may nevertheless so defend the proceeding as to require that every element of the case be established.

Rule 3.2 Expediting Litigation

A lawyer shall make reasonable efforts to expedite litigation consistent with the interests of the client.

Rule 3.3 Candor Toward the Tribunal

(a) A lawyer shall not knowingly:
   (1) make a false statement of material fact or law to a tribunal;

(2) fail to disclose a material fact to a tribunal when disclosure is necessary to avoid assisting a criminal or fraudulent act by the client;

(3) fail to disclose to the tribunal legal authority in the controlling jurisdiction known to the lawyer to be directly adverse to the position of the client and not disclosed by opposing counsel; or

(4) offer evidence that the lawyer knows to be false. If a lawyer has offered material evidence and comes to know of its falsity, the lawyer shall take reasonable remedial measures.

(b) The duties stated in paragraph (a) continue to the conclusion of the proceeding, and apply even if compliance requires disclosure of information otherwise protected by Rule 1.6.

(c) A lawyer may refuse to offer evidence that the lawyer reasonably believes is false.

(c) In an ex parte proceeding, a lawyer shall inform the tribunal of all material facts known to the lawyer which will enable the tribunal to make an informed decision, whether or not the facts are adverse.

Rule 3.4 Fairness to Opposing Party and Counsel

A lawyer shall not:

(a) unlawfully obstruct another party's access to evidence or unlawfully alter, destroy or conceal a document or other material having potential evidentiary value. A lawyer shall not counsel or assist another person to do any such act;

(b) falsify evidence, counsel or assist a witness to testify falsely, or offer an inducement to a witness that is prohibited by law;

(c) knowingly disobey an obligation under the rules of a tribunal except for an open refusal based on an assertion that no valid obligation exists;

(d) in pretrial procedure, make a frivolous discovery request or fail to make reasonably diligent effort to comply with a legally proper discovery request by an opposing party;

(e) in trial, allude to any matter that the lawyer does not reasonably believe is relevant or that will not be supported by admissible evidence, assert personal knowledge of facts in issue except when testifying as a witness, or state a personal opinion as to the justness of a cause, the credibility of a witness, the culpability of a civil litigant or the guilt or innocence of an accused; or

(f) request a person other than a client to refrain from voluntarily giving relevant information to another party unless:

(1) the person is a relative or an employee or other agent of a client; and

(2) the lawyer reasonably believes that the person's interests will not be adversely affected by refraining from giving such information.

Rule 3.5 Impartiality and Decorum of the Tribunal

A lawyer shall not:

(a) seek to influence a judge, juror, prospective juror or other official by means prohibited by law;

(b) communicate ex parte with such a person except as permitted by law; or

(c) engage in conduct intended to disrupt a tribunal.

Rule 3.6 Trial Publicity

(a) A lawyer shall not make an extrajudicial statement that a reasonable person would expect to be disseminated by means of public communication if the lawyer knows or reasonably should know that it will have a sub-stantial likelihood of materially prejudicing an adjudicative proceeding.

(b) A statement referred to in paragraph (a) ordinarily is likely to have such an effect when it refers to a civil matter triable to a jury, a criminal mat-ter, or any other proceeding that could result in incarceration, and the statement relates to:

    (1) the character, credibility, reputation or criminal record of a party, sus-pect in a criminal investigation or witness, or the identity of a wit-ness, or the expected testimony of a party or witness;

    (2) in a criminal case or proceeding that could result in incarceration, the possibility of a plea of guilty to the offense or the existence or con-tents of any confession, admission, or statement given by a defendant or suspect or that person's refusal or failure to make a statement;

    (3) the performance or results of any examination or test or the refusal or failure of a person to submit to an examination or test, or the identity or nature of physical evidence expected to be presented;

    (4) any opinion as to the guilt or innocence of a defendant or suspect in a criminal case or proceeding that could result in incarceration;

    (5) information the lawyer knows or reasonably should know is likely to be inadmissible as evidence in a trial and would if disclosed create a substantial risk of prejudicing an impartial trial; or

    (6) the fact that a defendant has been charged with a crime, unless there is included therein a statement explaining that the charge is merely an accusation and that the defendant is presumed innocent until and unless proven guilty.

(c) Notwithstanding paragraphs (a) and (b) (1-5), a lawyer involved in the in-vestigation or litigation of a matter may state without elaboration:

    (1) the general nature of the claim or defense;

    (2) the information contained in a public record;

    (3) that an investigation of a matter is in progress, including the general scope of the investigation, the offense or claim or defense involved and, except when prohibited by law, the identity of the persons involved;

    (4) the scheduling or result of any step in litigation;

    (5) a request for assistance in obtaining evidence and information neces-sary thereto;

    (6) a warning of danger concerning the behavior of a person involved, when there is reason to believe that there exists the likelihood of sub-stantial harm to an individual or to the public interest; and

    (7) in a criminal case:

        (i) the identity, residence, occupation and family status of the accused;

        (ii) if the accused has not been apprehended, information necessary to aid in apprehension of that person;

        (iii) the fact, time and place of arrest; and

        (iv) the identity of investigating and arresting officers or agencies and the length of the investigation.

Rule 3.7 Lawyer as Witness

(a) A lawyer shall not act as advocate at a trial in which the lawyer is likely to be a necessary witness except where:

    (1) the testimony relates to an uncontested issue;

    (2) the testimony relates to the nature and value of legal services ren-dered in the case; or

    (3) disqualification of the lawyer would work substantial hardship on the client.

(b) A lawyer may act as advocate in a trial in which another lawyer in the lawyer's firm is likely to be called as a witness unless precluded from doing so by Rule 1.7 or Rule 1.9.

Rule 3.8 Special Responsibilities of a Prosecutor

The prosecutor in a criminal case shall:
   (a) refrain from prosecuting a charge that the prosecutor knows is not supported by probable cause;
   (b) make reasonable efforts to assure that the accused has been advised of the right to, and the procedure for obtaining, counsel and has been given reasonable opportunity to obtain counsel;
   (c) not seek to obtain from an unrepresented accused a waiver of important pretrial rights, such as the right to a preliminary hearing;
   (d) make timely disclosure to the defense of all evidence or information known to the prosecutor that tends to negate the guilt of the accused or mitigates the offense, and, in connection with sentencing, disclose to the defense and to the tribunal all unprivileged mitigating information known to the prosecutor, except when the prosecutor is relieved of this responsibility by a protective order of the tribunal; and
   (e) exercise reasonable care to prevent investigators, law enforcement personnel, employees or other persons assisting or associated with the prosecutor in a criminal case from making an extrajudicial statement that the prosecutor would be prohibited from making under Rule 3.6.

Rule 3.9 Advocate in Nonadjudicative Proceedings

A lawyer representing a client before a legislative or administrative tribunal in a nonadjudicative proceeding shall disclose that the appearance is in a representative capacity and shall conform to the provisions of Rules 3.3(a) through (c), 3.4(a) through (c), and 3.5.

TRANSACTIONS WITH PERSONS OTHER THAN CLIENTS

Rule 4.1 Truthfulness in Statements to Others

In the course of representing a client a lawyer shall not knowingly:
   (a) make a false statement of material fact or law to a third person; or
   (b) fail to disclose a material fact to a third person when disclosure is necessary to avoid assisting a criminal or fraudulent act by a client, unless disclosure is prohibited by Rule 1.6.

Rule 4.2 Communication with Person Represented by Counsel

In representing a client, a lawyer shall not communicate about the subject of the representation with a person the lawyer knows to be represented by another lawyer in the matter, unless the lawyer has the consent of the other lawyer or is authorized by law to do so.

Rule 4.3 Dealing with Unrepresented Person

In dealing on behalf of a client with a person who is not represented by counsel, a lawyer shall not state or imply that the lawyer is disinterested. When the lawyer knows or reasonably should know that the unrepresented person misunderstands the lawyer's role in the matter, the lawyer shall make reasonable efforts to correct the misunderstanding.

Rule 4.4 Respect for Rights of Third Persons

In representing a client, a lawyer shall not use means that have no substantial purpose other than to embarrass, delay, or burden a third person, or use methods of obtaining evidence that violate the legal rights of such a person.

LAW FIRMS AND ASSOCIATIONS

Rule 5.1 Responsibilities of a Partner or Supervisory Lawyer

(a) A partner in a law firm shall make reasonable efforts to ensure that the firm has in effect measures giving reasonable assurance that all lawyers in the firm conform to the Rules of Professional Conduct.

(b) A lawyer having direct supervisory authority over another lawyer shall make reasonable efforts to ensure that the other lawyer conforms to the Rules of Professional Conduct.

(c) A lawyer shall be responsible for another lawyer's violation of the Rules of Professional Conduct if:

(1) the lawyer orders or, with knowledge of the specific conduct, ratifies the conduct involved; or

(2) the lawyer is a partner in the law firm in which the other lawyer practices, or has direct supervisory authority over the other lawyer, and knows of the conduct at a time when its consequences can be avoided or mitigated but fails to take reasonable remedial action.

Rule 5.2 Responsibilities of a Subordinate Lawyer

(a) A lawyer is bound by the Rules of Professional Conduct notwithstanding that the lawyer acted at the direction of another person.

(b) A subordinate lawyer does not violate the Rules of Professional Conduct if that lawyer acts in accordance with a supervisory lawyer's reasonable resolution of an arguable question of professional duty.

Rule 5.3 Responsibilities Regarding Nonlawyer Assistants

With respect to a nonlawyer employed or retained by or associated with a lawyer:

(a) a partner in a law firm shall make reasonable efforts to ensure that the firm has in effect measures giving reasonable assurance that the person's conduct is compatible with the professional obligations of the lawyer;

(b) a lawyer having direct supervisory authority over the nonlawyer shall make reasonable efforts to ensure that the person's conduct is compatible with the professional obligations of the lawyer; and

(c) a lawyer shall be responsible for conduct of such a person that would be a violation of the Rules of Professional Conduct if engaged in by a lawyer if:

(1) the lawyer orders or, with the knowledge of the specific conduct, ratifies the conduct involved; or

(2) the lawyer is a partner in the law firm in which the person is employed, or has direct supervisory authority over the person, and

knows of the conduct at a time when its consequences can be avoided or mitigated but fails to take reasonable remedial action.

Rule 5.4 Professional Independence of a Lawyer

   (a) A lawyer or law firm shall not share legal fees with a nonlawyer, except that:
      (1) an agreement by a lawyer with the lawyer's firm, partner, or associate may provide for the payment of money, over a reasonable period of time after the lawyer's death, to the lawyer's estate or to one or more specified persons;
      (2) a lawyer who undertakes to complete unfinished legal business of a deceased lawyer may pay to the estate of the deceased lawyer that proportion of the total compensation that fairly represents the services rendered by the deceased lawyer;
      (3) a lawyer who purchases the practice of a deceased lawyer, or from any person acting in a representative capacity for a disabled or disappeared lawyer, may, pursuant to Rule 1.17 of this Rule 4, pay to the estate or other representative of that lawyer the agreed-upon price; and
      (4) a lawyer or law firm may include nonlawyer employees in a compensation or retirement plan, even though the plan is based in whole or in part on a profit-sharing arrangement.
   (b) A lawyer shall not form a partnership with a nonlawyer if any of the activities of the partnership consist of the practice of law.
   (c) A lawyer shall not permit a person who recommends, employs, or pays the lawyer to render legal services for another to direct or regulate the lawyer's professional judgment in rendering such legal services.
   (d) A lawyer shall not practice with or in the form of a professional corporation, limited liability company, or association authorized to practice law for a profit, if:
      (1) a nonlawyer owns any interest therein, except that a fiduciary representative of the estate of a lawyer may hold the stock or interest of the lawyer for a reasonable time during administration;
      (2) a nonlawyer is a corporate director or officer thereof or a manager of the limited liability company; or
      (3) a nonlawyer has the right to direct or control the professional judgment of a lawyer.

Rule 5.5 Unauthorized Practice of Law

A lawyer shall not:
   (a) practice law in a jurisdiction where doing so violates the regulation of the legal profession in that jurisdiction; or
   (b) assist a person who is not a member of the bar in the performance of activity that constitutes the unauthorized practice of law; or
   (c) practice law in Missouri if the lawyer is subject to Rule 15 and, because of failure to comply with Rule 15, The Missouri Bar has referred the lawyer's name to the chief disciplinary counsel or the Commission on Retirement, Removal and Discipline.

Rule 5.6 Restrictions on Right to Practice

A lawyer shall not participate in offering or making:
   (a) a partnership or employment agreement that restricts the right of a lawyer to practice after termination of the relationship, except an agreement concerning benefits upon retirement; or

(b) an agreement in which a restriction on the lawyer's right to practice is part of the settlement of a controversy between private parties.

PUBLIC SERVICE

Rule 6.1 Pro Bono Public Service

A lawyer should render public interest legal service. A lawyer may discharge this responsibility by providing professional services at no fee or a reduced fee to persons of limited means or to public service or charitable groups or organizations, by service in activities for improving the law, the legal system or the legal profession, and by financial support for organizations that provide legal services to persons of limited means.

Rule 6.2 Accepting Appointments

A lawyer shall not seek to avoid appointment by a tribunal to represent a person except for good cause, such as:
  (a) representing the client is likely to result in violation of the rules of professional conduct or other law;
  (b) representing the client is likely to result in an unreasonable financial burden on the lawyer; or
  (c) the client or the cause is so repugnant to the lawyer as to be likely to impair the client-lawyer relationship or the lawyer's ability to represent the client.

Rule 6.3 Membership in Legal Services Organization

A lawyer may serve as a director, officer or member of a legal services organization, apart from the law firm in which the lawyer practices, notwithstanding that the organization serves persons having interests adverse to a client of the lawyer. The lawyer shall not knowingly participate in a decision or action of the organization:
  (a) if participating in the decision or action would be incompatible with the lawyer's obligations to a client under Rule 1.7; or
  (b) where the decision or action could have a material adverse effect on the representation of a client of the organization whose interests are adverse to a client of the lawyer.

Rule 6.4 Law Reform Activities Affecting Client Interests

A lawyer may serve as a director, officer or member of an organization involved in reform of the law or its administration notwithstanding that the reform may affect the interests of a client of the lawyer. When the lawyer knows that the interests of a client may be materially benefited by a decision in which the lawyer participates, the lawyer shall disclose that fact but need not identify the client.

INFORMATION ABOUT LEGAL SERVICES

Rule 7.1 Communications Concerning a Lawyer's Services

A lawyer shall not make a false or misleading communication about the lawyer or the lawyer's services. A communication is false or misleading if it:

  (a) contains a material misrepresentation of fact or law

  (b) omits a fact as a result of which the statement considered as a whole is materially misleading;

  (c) is likely to create an unjustified expectation about results the lawyer can achieve, or states or implies that the lawyer can achieve results by means that violate the Rules of Professional Conduct or other law;

  (d) compares the lawyer's services with other lawyers' services, unless the comparison can be factually substantiated.

  (e) contains a representation of, or implication of, fact regarding the quality of legal services which is not susceptible to reasonable verification by the public;

  (f) contains any statistical data or other information based on past performance which is not susceptible to reasonable verification by the public;

  (g) contains any paid testimonial about, or paid endorsement of, the lawyer, without identifying the fact that payment has been made or, if the testimonial or endorsement is not made by an actual client, without identifying that fact;

  (h) contains a simulated description of the lawyer, his partners or associates, his offices or facilities, or his services without identifying the fact that the description is a simulation;

  (i) contains any simulated representation or visualization of the lawyer, his partners or associates, his office or facilities, without identifying the fact that the representation or visualization is a simulation.

Rule 7.2 Advertising

  (a) Subject to the requirements of Rule 7.1, a lawyer may advertise services through public media, such as a telephone directory, legal directory, newspaper or other periodical, outdoor, radio, or television, or through direct mail advertising distributed generally to persons not known to need legal services of the kind provided by the lawyer in a particular matter. All advertisements that state that legal services are available on a contingent or no-recovery-no-fee basis shall also state conspicuously that the client may be responsible for costs or expenses.

  (b) A copy or recording of an advertisement or communication shall be kept for two years after its last dissemination along with a record of when and where it was used.

  (c) A lawyer shall not give anything of value to a person for recommending the lawyer's services except that:

   (1) a lawyer may pay the reasonable costs of advertising or written communication permitted by this Rule 7;

   (2) a lawyer may pay the reasonable cost of advertising, written communication or other notification required in connection with the sale of a law practice as permitted by Rule 1.17 of this Rule 4; and

   (3) a lawyer may pay the usual charges of a qualified lawyer referral service registered under Rule 10.1 or other not for profit legal services organization.

  (d) Any communication made pursuant to this rule shall include the name of at least one lawyer responsible for its content.

Rule 7.3 Direct Contact with Prospective Clients

(a) Subject to the requirements of paragraphs (c) and (d) of this Rule 7.3, a lawyer may initiate written communication, not involving personal or telephone contact, with persons known to need legal service of the kind provided by the lawyer in a particular matter, for the purpose of obtaining professional employment. All such written communications shall contain the following statement in conspicuous print:

> "ADVERTISING MATERIAL: COMMERCIAL SOLICITATIONS ARE PERMITTED BY THE MISSOURI RULES OF PROFESSIONAL CONDUCT BUT ARE NEITHER SUBMITTED TO NOR APPROVED BY THE MISSOURI BAR OR THE SUPREME COURT OF MISSOURI."

(b) A lawyer may initiate personal contact including telephone contact with a prospective client for the purpose of obtaining professional employment only in the following circumstances and subject to the requirements of paragraphs (c) and (d) of this Rule 7.3:

   (1) if the prospective client is a close friend, relative or former client, or one whom the lawyer reasonably believes to be a client;

   (2) under the auspices of a public or charitable legal services organization; or

   (3) under the auspices of a bona fide political, social, civic, fraternal employee or trade organization whose purposes include but are not limited to providing or recommending legal services, if the legal services are related to the principal purposes of the organization.

(c) A lawyer shall not initiate a written communication under paragraph (a) of this Rule 7.3 or personal contact, including telephone contact, under paragraph (b) of this Rule 7.3 if:

   (1) the lawyer knows or reasonably should know that the physical, emotional, or mental state of the person makes it unlikely that the person would exercise reasonable judgment in employing a lawyer. A written communication sent and received or a personal contact made within a reasonable period after an incident giving rise to personal injury or death is presumed to be written at a time or made at time when the writer knows or reasonably should know that the physical, emotional, or mental state of the person makes it unlikely that the person would exercise reasonable judgment employing a lawyer;

   (2) the person has made known to the lawyer a desire not to receive a communication from the lawyer; or

   (3) the communication involves coercion, duress or harassment.

(d) All communications or personal contacts made pursuant to this Rule 7.3 that state that legal services are available on a contingent or no-recovery-no-fee basis shall also state conspicuously that the client may be responsible for costs or expenses.

Rule 7.4 Communication of Fields of Practice

A lawyer may communicate the fact that the lawyer does or does not practice in particular fields of law. Any such communication shall conform to the requirements of Rule 7.1. Except as provided in subdivisions (a) and (b) of this Rule 7.4, a lawyer shall not state or imply that the lawyer is a specialist unless the communication contains a disclaimer that neither the Supreme Court of Missouri nor the Missouri Bar reviews or approves certifying organizations or specialist designations.

(a) A lawyer admitted to engage in patent practice before the United States Patent and Trademark Office may use the designation "patent attorney" or a substantially similar designation;

(b) a lawyer engaged in admiralty practice may use the designation "admiralty," "proctor in admiralty" or a substantially similar designation.

Rule 7.5 Firm Names and Letterheads

(a) A lawyer shall not use a firm name, letterhead or other professional designation that violates Rule 7.1.

(b) A lawyer's firm name shall include the name of the lawyer, the name of another lawyer in the firm or the name of a deceased or retired member of the firm in a continuing line of succession.

(c) A lawyer's firm name shall not include the name of any person other than a present member of the firm or a deceased or retired member of the firm in a continuing line of succession.

(d) Subject to paragraphs (a), (b) and (c) hereof, a law firm with offices in states other than Missouri may use the same name in Missouri as used in other states, but identification of lawyers in an office in Missouri shall indicate the jurisdictional limitations of any lawyers so listed who are not licensed to practice in Missouri.

(e) The name of a lawyer holding public office shall not be used in the name of a law firm , or in communications on its behalf, during any substantial period in which the lawyer is not actively and regularly practicing with the firm.

(f) Lawyers may state or imply that they practice in a partnership or other organization only when that is the fact.

MAINTAINING THE INTEGRITY OF THE PROFESSION

Rule 8.1 Bar Admission and Disciplinary Matters

An applicant for admission to the bar, or a lawyer in connection with a bar admission application or in connection with a disciplinary matter, shall not:

(a) knowingly make a false statement of material fact; or

(b) fail to disclose a fact necessary to correct a misapprehension known by the person to have arisen in the matter, or knowingly fail to respond to a lawful demand for information from an admissions or disciplinary authority, except that this rule does not require disclosure of information otherwise protected by Rule 1.6.

Rule 8.2 Judicial and Legal Officials

(a) A lawyer shall not make a statement that the lawyer knows to be false or with reckless disregard as to its truth or falsity concerning the qualifications or integrity of a judge, adjudicatory officer or public legal officer, or of a candidate for election or appointment to judicial or legal office.

(b) A lawyer who is a candidate for judicial office shall comply with the applicable provisions of the Code of Judicial Conduct.

Rule 8.3 Reporting Professional Misconduct

(a) A lawyer having knowledge that another lawyer has committed a violation of the Rules of Professional Conduct that raises a substantial question as to that lawyer's honesty, trustworthiness or fitness as a lawyer in other respects, shall inform the appropriate professional authority.

(b) A lawyer having knowledge that a judge has committed a violation of applicable rules of judicial conduct that raises a substantial question as to the judge's fitness for office shall inform the appropriate authority.

(c) This rule does not require disclosure of information otherwise protected by Rule 1.6.

Rule 8.4 Misconduct

It is professional misconduct for a lawyer to:

(a) violate or attempt to violate the Rules of Professional Conduct, knowingly assist or induce another to do so, or do so through the acts of another;

(b) commit a criminal act that reflects adversely on the lawyer's honesty, trustworthiness or fitness as a lawyer in other respects;

(c) engage in conduct involving dishonesty, fraud, deceit or misrepresentation;

(d) engage in conduct that is prejudicial to the administration of justice;

(e) state or imply an ability to influence improperly a government agency or official;

(f) knowingly assist a judge or judicial officer in conduct that is a violation of applicable rules of judicial conduct or other law; or

(g) manifest by words or conduct, in representing a client, bias or prejudice based upon race, sex, religion, national origin, disability or age. This Rule 4 - 8.4(g) does not preclude legitimate advocacy when race, sex, religion, national origin, disability, or age, or other similar factors, are issues.

Rule 8.5 Jurisdiction

A lawyer admitted to practice in this jurisdiction is subject to the disciplinary authority of this jurisdiction although engaged in practice elsewhere.

TERMINOLOGY

Rule 9.1 Definition of Terms

As used throughout the Rules of Professional Conduct, unless the context otherwise requires, the following terms have the following meanings:

"Belief" or "Believes" denotes that the person involved actually supposed the fact in question to be true. A person's belief may be inferred from circumstances;

"Consult" or "Consultation" denotes communication of information reasonably sufficient to permit the client to appreciate the significance of the matter in question;

"Firm" or "Law firm" denotes a lawyer or lawyers in a private firm, lawyers employed in the legal department of a corporation or other organization and lawyers employed in a legal services organization; See Comment, Rule 1.10.

"Fraud" or "Fraudulent" denotes conduct having a purpose to deceive and not merely negligent misrepresentation or failure to apprise another of relevant information;

"Knowingly," "Known," or "Knows" denotes actual knowledge of the fact in question. A person's knowledge may be inferred from circumstances;

"Partner" denotes a member of a partnership, a shareholder in a law firm organized as a professional corporation and a member of a law firm organized as a limited liability company;

"Reasonable" or "Reasonably" when used in relation to conduct by a lawyer denotes the conduct of a reasonably prudent and competent lawyer;

"Reasonable belief" or "Reasonably believes" when used in reference to a lawyer denotes that the lawyer believes the matter in question and that the circumstances are such that the belief is reasonable;

"Reasonably should know" when used in reference to a lawyer denotes that a lawyer of reasonable prudence and competence would ascertain the matter in question;

"Rule" or "Rules" denotes subdivisions of this Supreme Court Rule 4;

"Substantial" when used in reference to degree or extent denotes a material matter of clear and weighty importance.

LAWYER REFERRAL AND INFORMATION SERVICES

Rule 10.1 Lawyer Referral and Information Services

(a) The operation of this Rule 10.1 and compliance with its provisions shall be supervised by the chief disciplinary counsel. The chief disciplinary counsel shall develop and promulgate regulations, procedures and forms not inconsistent with this Rule 10.1, including the amount of the fee to register a qualified service, subject to approval by this Court.

(b) Lawyers eligible to practice in this state may participate in a service that refers them to prospective clients, but only if the service is a qualified service because it conforms to this Rule 10.1.

(c) A qualified service shall be operated in the public interest for the purpose of referring prospective clients to lawyers, pro bono and public service legal programs, and government, consumer or other agencies that can provide the assistance the clients need in light of their financial circumstances, spoken language, any disability, geographical convenience, and the nature and complexity of their problems.

(d) Only a qualified service may call itself a lawyer referral service or operate for a direct or indirect purpose of referring potential clients to particular lawyers, whether or not the term "referral service" is used.

(e) A qualified service must be open to all lawyers licensed to practice in this state who: (1) maintain an office within the geographical area served, (2) pay reasonable fees established by the service, and (3) maintain in force a policy of errors and omissions insurance in an amount at least equal to the minimum established by the chief disciplinary counsel. A qualified service shall establish and publish a procedure for admitting, suspending, or removing lawyers from its roll of panelists.

(f) No fee generating referral may be made to any lawyer who has an ownership interest in, or who operates or is employed by, a qualified service or who is associated with a law firm that has an ownership interest in, or operates or is employed by, a qualified service.

(g) A qualified service shall periodically survey client satisfaction with its operations and shall investigate and take appropriate action with respect to client complaints against panelists, the service, and its employees.

(h) A qualified service may establish specific subject matter panels, including moderate and no fee panels, foreign language panels, alternative dispute resolution panels, and other special panels that respond to the referral needs of the consumer public, eligibility for which shall be determined on the basis of experience and other substantial objectively determinable criteria.

(i) A qualified service shall:
   (1) register with the chief disciplinary counsel and demonstrate its compliance with this Rule 10.1 before commencing to operate;

    (2) update the materials filed with the chief disciplinary counsel within thirty days of any material change; and

    (3) annually file with the chief disciplinary counsel on or before June 30 a report of its operations and finances during the previous twelve months demonstrating its continued compliance with this Rule 10.1.

(j) This Rule 10.1 does not apply to:

    (1) a group or prepaid legal plan, whether operated by a union, trust, mutual benefit or aid association, corporation, or other entity or person that provides unlimited or a specified amount of telephone advice or personal communication at no charge to the members or beneficiaries, other than a periodic membership or beneficiary fee and that furnishes or pays for legal services to its beneficiaries;

    (2) a plan of prepaid legal services insurance authorized to operate in this state;

    (3) individual lawyer-to-lawyer referrals;

    (4) lawyers jointly advertising their own services in a manner that discloses that such advertising is solely to solicit clients for themselves;

    (5) any pro bono legal assistance program that does not accept any fee from clients for referrals; or

    (6) any organization maintaining a 26 U.S.C. § 501©(3) exemption that maintains a referral list only incident to its other activities.

(k) A disclosure of information to a lawyer referral service for the purpose of seeking legal assistance or for purposes of complying with the survey under Rule 10.1(g) shall be deemed a privileged lawyer-client communication.

(l) The chief disciplinary counsel may deny, suspend, or cancel any registration upon making a finding of a material violation of any provisions of this Rule 10.1. Any person who is substantially and individually aggrieved by the action of the chief disciplinary counsel may, within thirty days of receiving notice of the action, petition this Court for review of the action of the chief disciplinary counsel. This Court may direct that the issues raised in the petition be briefed and argued as though a petition for an original remedial writ has been sustained. This Court may sustain, modify or vacate the action of the chief disciplinary counsel or dismiss the petition.

(m) Any person violating the provisions of this Rule 10.1 shall be deemed to be engaged in the unauthorized practice of law.

APPENDIX B

New Hampshire's Guidelines for the Utilization of Legal Assistant Services

Several states have adopted guidelines for attorneys to best utilize paralegals, similar to the ABA's Model Guidelines. The state of New Hampshire has adopted such guidelines as Rule 35 of its Rules of the Supreme Court of New Hampshire, which follows.

NEW HAMPSHIRE STATUTES ANNOTATED RULES OF SUPREME COURT OF NEW HAMPSHIRE ADMINISTRATIVE RULES 35 TO 54

GUIDELINES FOR THE UTILIZATION BY LAWYERS OF THE SERVICES OF LEGAL ASSISTANTS UNDER THE NEW HAMPSHIRE RULES OF PROFESSIONAL CONDUCT

RULE 1.

It is the responsibility of the lawyer to take all steps reasonably necessary to ensure that a legal assistant for whose work the lawyer is responsible does not provide legal advice or otherwise engage in the unauthorized practice of law; provided, however, that with adequate lawyer supervision the legal assistant may provide information concerning legal matters and otherwise act as permitted under these rules.

RULE 2.

A lawyer may not permit a legal assistant to represent a client in judicial or administrative proceedings or to perform other functions ordinarily limited to lawyers, unless authorized by statute, court rule or decision, administrative rule or regulation or customary practice.

RULE 3.

Except as otherwise provided by statute, court rule or decision, administrative rule or regulation, or by the Rules of Professional Conduct, a lawyer may permit a legal assistant to perform services for the lawyer in the lawyer's representation of a client, provided:

A. The services performed by the legal assistant do not require the exercise of professional legal judgment;
B. The lawyer maintains a direct relationship with the client;
C. The lawyer supervises the legal assistant's performance of his or her duties; and
D. The lawyer remains fully responsible for such representation, including all actions taken or not taken by the legal assistant in connection therewith.

RULE 4.

A lawyer should exercise care that a legal assistant for whose work the lawyer is responsible does not:

A. Reveal information relating to representation of a client, unless the client expressly or implicitly consents, after consultation with the supervising lawyer and with knowledge of the consequences, or except as otherwise required or permitted, in the judgment of the supervising lawyer, by statute, court order or decision, or by the Rules of Professional Conduct; or
B. Use such information to the disadvantage of the client unless the client consents after consultation with the supervising lawyer and with knowledge of the consequences.

RULE 5.

A lawyer shall not form a partnership with a legal assistant if any of the activities of the partnership consist of the practice of law, nor practice with or in the form of a professional corporation or association authorized to practice law for a profit if a legal assistant owns an interest therein, is a corporate director or officer thereof or has the right to direct or control the professional judgment of a lawyer.

RULE 6.

A lawyer shall not share fees with a legal assistant in any manner, except that a lawyer or law firm may include the legal assistant in a retirement plan even if the plan is based in whole or in part on a profit-sharing arrangement.

RULE 7.

A legal assistant's name may not be included on the letterhead of a lawyer or law firm. A legal assistant's business card may indicate the name of the lawyer or law firm employing the assistant, provided that the assistant's capacity is clearly indicated and that the services of the assistant are not utilized by the lawyer or firm for the purpose of solicitation of professional employment for the lawyer or firm from a prospective client in violation of the relevant statutes or the Rules of Professional Conduct.

RULE 8.

A lawyer shall require that a legal assistant, when dealing with clients, attorneys or the public, disclose at the outset that he or she is not a lawyer.

RULE 9.

A lawyer should exercise care to prevent a legal assistant from engaging in conduct which would involve the assistant's employer in a violation of the Rules of Professional Conduct.

The American Bar Association has adopted Model Guidelines to assist the States in drafting their own guidelines. A copy of the Model Guidelines, with annotations and commentary, is available through the ABA Legal Assistants Department staff office. (Phone: 312/988-5616; Fax: 312/988-5677; E-Mail: legalassts@abanet.org.

The Guidelines adopted in New Hampshire, as with most states that have adopted similar Guidelines, do not offer many specifics or much detail on the utilization of paralegals. However, until a consensus is reached on paralegal regulation, guidelines for utilizing paralegals may be the best guidance the attorneys you work for have to define the legal possibilities, and limits, of your position.

Code of Ethics and Professional Responsibility of the National Association of Legal Assistants

CANON 1

A legal assistant must not perform any of the duties that attorneys only may perform nor take any actions that attorneys may not take.

CANON 2

A legal assistant may perform any task which is properly delegated and supervised by an attorney, as long as the attorney is ultimately responsible to the client, maintains a direct relationship with the client, and assumes professional responsibility for the work product.

CANON 3

A legal assistant must not (a) engage in, encourage, or contribute to any act which could constitute the unauthorized practice of law; and (b) establish attorney-client relationships, set fees, give legal opinions or advice or represent a client before a court or agency unless so authorized by that court or agency; or (c) engage in conduct or take any action which would assist or involve the attorney in a violation of professional ethics or give the appearance of professional impropriety.

CANON 4

A legal assistant must use discretion and professional judgment commensurate with knowledge and experience but must not render independent legal judgment in place of an attorney. The services of an attorney are essential in the public interest whenever such legal judgment is required.

CANON 5

A legal assistant must disclose his or her status as a legal assistant at the outset of any professional relationship with a client, attorney, a court or administrative agency or personnel thereof, or a member of the general public. A legal assistant must act prudently in determining the extent to which a client may be assisted without the presence of an attorney.

CANON 6

A legal assistant must strive to maintain integrity and a high degree of competency through education and training with respect to professional responsibility, local rules and practice, and through continuing education in substantive areas of law to better assist the legal profession in fulfilling its duty to provide legal service.

CANON 7

A legal assistant must protect the confidences of a client and must not violate any rule or statute now in effect or hereafter to be enacted controlling privileged communications.

CANON 8

A legal assistant must do all other things incidental, necessary, or expedient for the attainment of the ethics and responsibilities as defined by statute or rule of court.

CANON 9

A legal assistant's conduct is guided by bar associations' codes of professional responsibility and rules of professional conduct.

Published with permission of the National Association of Legal Assistants, 1516 S. Boston, #200, Tulsa, OK 74119, **www.nala.org.**

Appendix D

National Federation of Paralegal Associations, Inc. Model Code of Ethics and Professional Responsibility and Guidelines for Enforcement

PREAMBLE

The National Federation of Paralegal Associations, Inc. ("NFPA") is a professional organization comprised of paralegal associations and individual paralegals throughout the United States and Canada. Members of NFPA have varying backgrounds, experiences, education and job responsibilities that reflect the diversity of the paralegal profession. NFPA promotes the growth, development and recognition of the paralegal profession as an integral partner in the delivery of legal services.

In May 1993 NFPA adopted its Model Code of Ethics and Professional Responsibility ("Model Code") to delineate the principles for ethics and conduct to which every paralegal should aspire.

Many paralegal associations throughout the United States have endorsed the concept and content of NFPA's Model Code through the adoption of their own ethical codes. In doing so, paralegals have confirmed the profession's commitment to increase the quality and efficiency of legal services, as well as recognized its responsibilities to the public, the legal community, and colleagues.

Paralegals have recognized, and will continue to recognize, that the profession must continue to evolve to enhance their roles in the delivery of legal services. With increased levels of responsibility comes the need to define and enforce mandatory rules of professional conduct. Enforcement of codes of paralegal conduct is a logical and necessary step to enhance and ensure the confidence of the legal community and the public in the integrity and professional responsibility of paralegals.

In April 1997 NFPA adopted the Model Disciplinary Rules ("Model Rules") to make possible the enforcement of the Canons and Ethical Considerations contained in the NFPA Model Code. A concurrent determination was made that the Model Code of Ethics and Professional Responsibility, formerly aspirational in nature, should be recognized as setting forth the enforceable obligations of all paralegals.

The Model Code and Model Rules offer a framework for professional discipline, either voluntarily or through formal regulatory programs.

§1. NFPA MODEL DISCIPLINARY RULES AND ETHICAL CONSIDERATIONS

1.1 A Paralegal Shall Achieve and Maintain a High Level of Competence

Ethical Considerations

EC-1.1(a) A paralegal shall achieve competency through education, training, and work experience.

EC-1.1(b) A paralegal shall participate in continuing education in order to keep informed of current legal, technical and general developments.

EC-1.1(c) A paralegal shall perform all assignments promptly and efficiently.

1.2 A Paralegal Shall Maintain a High Level of Personal and Professional Integrity

Ethical Considerations

EC-1.2(a) A paralegal shall not engage in any ex parte communications involving the courts or any other adjudicatory body in an attempt to exert undue influence or to obtain advantage or the benefit of only one party.

EC-1.2(b) A paralegal shall not communicate, or cause another to communicate, with a party the paralegal knows to be represented by a lawyer in a pending matter without the prior consent of the lawyer representing such other party.

EC-1.2(c) A paralegal shall ensure that all timekeeping and billing records prepared by the paralegal are thorough, accurate, honest, and complete.

EC-1.2(d) A paralegal shall not knowingly engage in fraudulent billing practices. Such practices may include, but are not limited to: inflation of hours billed to a client or employer; misrepresentation of the nature of tasks performed; and/or submission of fraudulent expense and disbursement documentation.

EC-1.2(e) A paralegal shall be scrupulous, thorough and honest in the identification and maintenance of all funds, securities, and other assets of a client and shall provide accurate accounting as appropriate.

EC-1.2(f) A paralegal shall advise the proper authority of non-confidential knowledge of any dishonest or fraudulent acts by any person pertaining to the handling of the funds, securities or other assets of a client. The authority to whom the report is made shall depend on the nature and circumstances of the possible misconduct, (e.g., ethics committees of law firms, corporations and/or paralegal associations, local or state bar associations, local prosecutors, administrative agencies, etc.). Failure to report such knowledge is in itself misconduct and shall be treated as such under these rules.

1.3 A Paralegal Shall Maintain a High Standard of Professional Conduct

Ethical Considerations

EC-1.3(a) A paralegal shall refrain from engaging in any conduct that offends the dignity and decorum of proceedings before a court or other adjudicatory body and shall be respectful of all rules and procedures.

EC-1.3(b) A paralegal shall avoid impropriety and the appearance of impropriety and shall not engage in any conduct that would adversely affect his/her fitness to practice. Such conduct may include, but is not limited to: violence, dishonesty, interference with the administration of justice, and/or abuse of a professional position or public office.

EC-1.3(c) Should a paralegal's fitness to practice be compromised by physical or mental illness, causing that paralegal to commit an act that is in direct violation of the Model Code/Model Rules and/or the rules and/or laws governing the jurisdiction in which the paralegal practices, that paralegal may be protected from sanction upon review of the nature and circumstances of that illness.

EC-1.3(d) A paralegal shall advise the proper authority of non-confidential knowledge of any action of another legal professional that clearly demonstrates fraud, deceit, dishonesty, or misrepresentation. The authority to whom the report is made shall depend on the nature and circumstances of the possible misconduct, (e.g., ethics committees of law firms, corporations and/or paralegal associations, local or state bar associations, local prosecutors, administrative agencies, etc.). Failure to report such knowledge is in itself misconduct and shall be treated as such under these rules.

EC-1.3(e) A paralegal shall not knowingly assist any individual with the commission of an act that is in direct violation of the Model Code/Model Rules and/or the rules and/or laws governing the jurisdiction in which the paralegal practices.

EC-1.3(f) If a paralegal possesses knowledge of future criminal activity, that knowledge must be reported to the appropriate authority immediately.

1.4 A Paralegal Shall Serve the Public Interest by Contributing to the Improvement of the Legal System and Delivery of Quality Legal Services, Including Pro Bono Publico Services

Ethical Considerations

EC-1.4(a) A paralegal shall be sensitive to the legal needs of the public and shall promote the development and implementation of programs that address those needs.

EC-1.4(b)   A paralegal shall support efforts to improve the legal system and access thereto and shall assist in making changes.

EC-1.4(c)   A paralegal shall support and participate in the delivery of Pro Bono Publico services directed toward implementing and improving access to justice, the law, the legal system or the paralegal and legal professions.

EC-1.4(d)   A paralegal should aspire annually to contribute twenty-four (24) hours of Pro Bono Publico services under the supervision of an attorney or as authorized by administrative, statutory or court authority to:
1. Persons of limited means; or
2. Charitable, religious, civic, community, governmental and educational organizations in matters that are designed primarily to address the legal needs of persons with limited means; or
3. Individuals, groups or organizations seeking to secure or protect civil rights, civil liberties or public rights.

Ethical Considerations

EC-1.5(a)   A paralegal shall be aware of and abide by all legal authority governing confidential information in the jurisdiction in which the paralegal practices.

EC-1.5(b)   A paralegal shall not use confidential information to the disadvantage of the client.

EC-1.5(c)   A paralegal shall not use confidential information to the advantage of the paralegal or of a third person.

EC-1.5(d)   A paralegal may reveal confidential information only after full disclosure and with the client's written consent; or, when required by law or court order; or, when necessary to prevent the client from committing an act that could result in death or serious bodily harm.

EC-1.5(e)   A paralegal shall keep those individuals responsible for the legal representation of a client fully informed of any confidential information the paralegal may have pertaining to that client.

EC-1.5(f)   A paralegal shall not engage in any indiscreet communications concerning clients.

1.6   A Paralegal Shall Avoid Conflicts of Interest and Shall Disclose Any Possible Conflict to the Employer or Client, as well as to the Prospective Employers or Clients

Ethical Considerations

EC-1.6(a)   A paralegal shall act within the bounds of the law, solely for the benefit of the client, and shall be free of compromising influences and loyalties. Neither the paralegal's personal or business interest, nor those of other clients or third persons, should compromise the paralegal's professional judgment and loyalty to the client.

EC-1.6(b)   A paralegal shall avoid conflicts of interest that may arise from previous assignments, whether for a present or past employer or client.

EC-1.6(c)   A paralegal shall avoid conflicts of interest that may arise from family relationships and from personal and business interests.

EC-1.6(d) In order to be able to determine whether an actual or potential conflict of interest exists a paralegal shall create and maintain an effective recordkeeping system that identifies clients, matters, and parties with which the paralegal has worked.

EC-1.6(e) A paralegal shall reveal sufficient non-confidential information about a client or former client to reasonably ascertain if an actual or potential conflict of interest exists.

EC-1.6(f) A paralegal shall not participate in or conduct work on any matter where a conflict of interest has been identified.

EC-1.6(g) In matters where a conflict of interest has been identified and the client consents to continued representation, a paralegal shall comply fully with the implementation and maintenance of an Ethical Wall.

1.7 A Paralegal's Title Shall Be Fully Disclosed

Ethical Considerations

EC-1.7(a) A paralegal's title shall clearly indicate the individual's status and shall be disclosed in all business and professional communications to avoid misunderstandings and misconceptions about the paralegal's role and responsibilities.

EC-1.7(b) A paralegal's title shall be included if the paralegal's name appears on business cards, letterhead, brochures, directories, and advertisements.

EC-1.7(c) A paralegal shall not use letterhead, business cards or other promotional materials to create a fraudulent impression of his/her status or ability to practice in the jurisdiction in which the paralegal practices.

EC-1.7(d) A paralegal shall not practice under color of any record, diploma, or certificate that has been illegally or fraudulently obtained or issued or which is misrepresentative in any way.

EC-1.7(e) A paralegal shall not participate in the creation, issuance, or dissemination of fraudulent records, diplomas, or certificates.

1.8 A Paralegal Shall Not Engage in the Unauthorized Practice of Law

Ethical Considerations

EC-1.8(a) A paralegal shall comply with the applicable legal authority governing the unauthorized practice of law in the jurisdiction in which the paralegal practices.

§2. NFPA GUIDELINES FOR THE ENFORCEMENT OF THE MODEL CODE OF ETHICS AND PROFESSIONAL RESPONSIBILITY

2.1 Basis For Discipline

2.1(a) Disciplinary investigations and proceedings brought under authority of the Rules shall be conducted in accord with obligations imposed on the paralegal professional by the Model Code of Ethics and Professional Responsibility.

2.2   Structure of Disciplinary Committee

2.2(a)   The Disciplinary Committee ("Committee") shall be made up of nine (9) members including the Chair.

2.2(b)   Each member of the Committee, including any temporary replacement members, shall have demonstrated working knowledge of ethics/professional responsibility-related issues and activities.

2.2(c)   The Committee shall represent a cross-section of practice areas and work experience. The following recommendations are made regarding the members of the Committee.
1) At least one paralegal with one to three years of law-related work experience.
2) At least one paralegal with five to seven years of law related work experience.
3) At least one paralegal with over ten years of law related work experience.
4) One paralegal educator with five to seven years of work experience; preferably in the area of ethics/professional responsibility.
5) One paralegal manager.
6) One lawyer with five to seven years of law-related work experience.
7) One lay member.

2.2(d)   The Chair of the Committee shall be appointed within thirty (30) days of its members' induction. The Chair shall have no fewer than ten (10) years of law-related work experience.

2.2(e)   The terms of all members of the Committee shall be staggered. Of those members initially appointed, a simple majority plus one shall be appointed to a term of one year, and the remaining members shall be appointed to a term of two years. Thereafter, all members of the Committee shall be appointed to terms of two years.

2.2(f)   If for any reason the terms of a majority of the Committee will expire at the same time, members may be appointed to terms of one year to maintain continuity of the Committee.

2.2(g)   The Committee shall organize from its members a three-tiered structure to investigate, prosecute and/or adjudicate charges of misconduct. The members shall be rotated among the tiers.

2.3   Operation of Committee

2.3(a)   The Committee shall meet on an as-needed basis to discuss, investigate, and/or adjudicate alleged violations of the Model Code/Model Rules.

2.3(b)   A majority of the members of the Committee present at a meeting shall constitute a quorum.

2.3(c)   A Recording Secretary shall be designated to maintain complete and accurate minutes of all Committee meetings. All such minutes shall be kept confidential until a decision has been made that the matter will be set for hearing as set forth in Section 6.1 below.

2.3(d)   If any member of the Committee has a conflict of interest with the Charging Party, the Responding Party, or the allegations of misconduct, that member shall not take part in any hearing or deliberations concerning those allegations. If the absence of that member creates a lack of a quorum for the Committee, then a temporary replacement for the member shall be appointed.

2.3(e)   Either the Charging Party or the Responding Party may request that, for good cause shown, any member of the Committee not participate in a hearing or deliberation. All such requests shall be honored. If the absence of a Committee member under those circumstances creates a lack of a quorum for the Committee, then a temporary replacement for that member shall be appointed.

2.3(f)   All discussions and correspondence of the Committee shall be kept confidential until a decision has been made that the matter will be set for hearing as set forth in Section 6.1 below.

2.3(g)   All correspondence from the Committee to the Responding Party regarding any charge of misconduct and any decisions made regarding the charge shall be mailed certified mail, return receipt requested, to the Responding Party's last known address and shall be clearly marked with a "Confidential" designation.

2.4   Procedure for the Reporting of Alleged Violations of the Model Code/Disciplinary Rules

2.4(a)   An individual or entity in possession of non-confidential knowledge or information concerning possible instances of misconduct shall make a confidential written report to the Committee within thirty (30) days of obtaining same. This report shall include all details of the alleged misconduct.

2.4(b)   The Committee so notified shall inform the Responding Party of the allegation(s) of misconduct no later than ten (10) business days after receiving the confidential written report from the Charging Party.

2.4(c)   Notification to the Responding Party shall include the identity of the Charging Party, unless, for good cause shown, the Charging Party requests anonymity.

2.4(d)   The Responding Party shall reply to the allegations within ten (10) business days of notification.

2.5   Procedure for the Investigation of a Charge of Misconduct

2.5(a)   Upon receipt of a Charge of Misconduct ("Charge"), or on its own initiative, the Committee shall initiate an investigation.

2.5(b)   If, upon initial or preliminary review, the Committee makes a determination that the charges are either without basis in fact or, if proven, would not constitute professional misconduct, the Committee shall dismiss the allegations of misconduct. If such determination of dismissal cannot be made, a formal investigation shall be initiated.

2.5(c)   Upon the decision to conduct a formal investigation, the Committee shall:
   1) mail to the Charging and Responding Parties within three (3) business days of that decision notice of the commencement of a formal investigation. That notification shall be in writing and

shall contain a complete explanation of all Charge(s), as well as the reasons for a formal investigation and shall cite the applicable codes and rules;

2) allow the Responding Party thirty (30) days to prepare and submit a confidential response to the Committee, which response shall address each charge specifically and shall be in writing; and

3) upon receipt of the response to the notification, have thirty (30) days to investigate the Charge(s). If an extension of time is deemed necessary, that extension shall not exceed ninety (90) days.

2.5(d)   Upon conclusion of the investigation, the Committee may:

1) dismiss the Charge upon the finding that it has no basis in fact;

2) dismiss the Charge upon the finding that, if proven, the Charge would not constitute Misconduct;

3) refer the matter for hearing by the Tribunal; or

4) in the case of criminal activity, refer the Charge(s) and all investigation results to the appropriate authority.

2.6 Procedure For A Misconduct Hearing Before A Tribunal

2.6(a)   Upon the decision by the Committee that a matter should be heard, all parties shall be notified and a hearing date shall be set. The hearing shall take place no more than thirty (30) days from the conclusion of the formal investigation.

2.6(b)   The Responding Party shall have the right to counsel. The parties and the Tribunal shall have the right to call any witnesses and introduce any documentation that they believe will lead to the fair and reasonable resolution of the matter.

2.6(c)   Upon completion of the hearing, the Tribunal shall deliberate and present a written decision to the parties in accordance with procedures as set forth by the Tribunal.

2.6(d)   Notice of the decision of the Tribunal shall be appropriately published.

2.7 Sanctions

2.7(a)   Upon a finding of the Tribunal that misconduct has occurred, any of the following sanctions, or others as may be deemed appropriate, may be imposed upon the Responding Party, either singularly or in combination:

1) letter of reprimand to the Responding Party; counseling;

2) attendance at an ethics course approved by the Tribunal; probation;

3) suspension of license/authority to practice; revocation of license/authority to practice;

4) imposition of a fine; assessment of costs; or

5) in the instance of criminal activity, referral to the appropriate authority.

2.7(b)   Upon the expiration of any period of probation, suspension, or revocation, the Responding Party may make application for reinstatement. With the application for reinstatement, the Responding Party must show proof of having complied with all aspects of the sanctions imposed by the Tribunal.

2.8 Appellate Procedures

2.8(a)   The parties shall have the right to appeal the decision of the Tribunal in accordance with the procedure as set forth by the Tribunal.

DEFINITIONS

"Appellate Body"
means a body established to adjudicate an appeal to any decision made by a Tribunal or other decision-making body with respect to formally-heard Charges of Misconduct.

"Charge of Misconduct"
means a written submission by any individual or entity to an ethics committee, paralegal association, bar association, law enforcement agency, judicial body, government agency, or other appropriate body or entity, that sets forth non-confidential information regarding any instance of alleged misconduct by an individual paralegal or paralegal entity.

"Charging Party"
means any individual or entity who submits a Charge of Misconduct against an individual paralegal or paralegal entity.

"Competency"
means the demonstration of: diligence, education, skill, and mental, emotional, and physical fitness reasonably necessary for the performance of paralegal services.

"Confidential Information"
means information relating to a client, whatever its source, that is not public knowledge nor available to the public. ("Non-Confidential Information" would generally include the name of the client and the identity of the matter for which the paralegal provided services.)

"Disciplinary Hearing"
means the confidential proceeding conducted by a committee or other designated body or entity concerning any instance of alleged misconduct by an individual paralegal or paralegal entity.

"Disciplinary Committee"
means any committee that has been established by an entity such as a paralegal association, bar association, judicial body, or government agency to: (a) identify, define and investigate general ethical considerations and concerns with respect to paralegal practice; (b) administer and enforce the Model Code and Model Rules and; (c) discipline any individual paralegal or paralegal entity found to be in violation of same.

"Disclose"
means communication of information reasonably sufficient to permit identification of the significance of the matter in question.

"Ethical Wall"
means the screening method implemented in order to protect a client from a conflict of interest. An Ethical Wall generally includes, but is not limited to, the following elements: (1) prohibit the paralegal from having any connection with the matter; (2) ban discussions with or the transfer of documents to or from the paralegal; (3) restrict access to files; and (4) educate all members of the firm, corporation, or entity as to the separation of the paralegal (both organizationally and physically) from the pending matter. For more information regarding the Ethical Wall, see the NFPA publication entitled "The Ethical Wall - Its Application to Paralegals."

"Ex parte"
means actions or communications conducted at the instance and for the benefit of one party only, and without notice to, or contestation by, any person adversely interested.

"Investigation"
means the investigation of any charge(s) of misconduct filed against an individual paralegal or paralegal entity by a Committee.

"Letter of Reprimand"
means a written notice of formal censure or severe reproof administered to an individual paralegal or paralegal entity for unethical or improper conduct.

"Misconduct"
means the knowing or unknowing commission of an act that is in direct violation of those Canons and Ethical Considerations of any and all applicable codes and/or rules of conduct.

"Paralegal"

is synonymous with "Legal Assistant" and is defined as a person qualified through education, training, or work experience to perform substantive legal work that requires knowledge of legal concepts and is customarily, but not exclusively performed by a lawyer. This person may be retained or employed by a lawyer, law office, governmental agency, or other entity or may be authorized by administrative, statutory, or court authority to perform this work.

"Pro Bono Publico"

means providing or assisting to provide quality legal services in order to enhance access to justice for persons of limited means; charitable, religious, civic, community, governmental and educational organizations in matters that are designed primarily to address the legal needs of persons with limited means; or individuals, groups or organizations seeking to secure or protect civil rights, civil liberties or public rights.

"Proper Authority"

means the local paralegal association, the local or state bar association, Committee(s) of the local paralegal or bar association(s), local prosecutor, administrative agency, or other tribunal empowered to investigate or act upon an instance of alleged misconduct.

"Responding Party"

means an individual paralegal or paralegal entity against whom a Charge of Misconduct has been submitted.

"Revocation"

means the recision of the license, certificate or other authority to practice of an individual paralegal or paralegal entity found in violation of those Canons and Ethical Considerations of any and all applicable codes and/or rules of conduct.

"Suspension"

means the suspension of the license, certificate or other authority to practice of an individual paralegal or paralegal entity found in violation of those Canons and Ethical Considerations of any and all applicable codes and/or rules of conduct.

"Tribunal"

means the body designated to adjudicate allegations of misconduct.

Published with permission of the National Federation of Paralegal Associations, P.O. Box 33108, Kansas City, MO 64114, 816-941-4000, **www.paralegals.org.**

APPENDIX E

Directory of Paralegal Associations

NATIONAL ORGANIZATIONS

American Association For Paralegal Education
2965 Flowers Road South, Suite 105
Atlanta, GA 30341
Phone: (770) 452-9877
Fax: (770) 458-3314
E-mail: **info@aafpe.org**
Internet: **www.aafpe.org**

American Bar Association
750 N. Lakeshore Dr.,
Chicago, IL 60611
Phone: (312) 988-5000
E-mail: **info@abanet.org**
Internet: **www.abanet.org**

Association of Legal Administrators
175 E. Hawthorne Parkway, Suite 325
Vernon Hills, IL 60061-1428
Phone: (847) 816-1212
Fax: (847) 816-1213
Internet: **www.alanet.org**

Legal Assistant Management Association
LAMA Headquarters
2965 Flowers Road South, Suite 105
Atlanta, GA 30341
Phone: (770) 457-7746
Fax: (770) 458-3314
E-mail: **lamaoffice@aol.com**
Internet: **www.lamanet.org**

National Association of Legal Assistants
1516 S. Boston, #200
Tulsa, OK 74119
Phone: (918) 587-6828
Fax: (918) 582-6772
E-mail: **nalanet@nala.org**
Internet: **www.nala.org**

National Federation of Paralegal Associations
P.O. Box 33108
Kansas City, MO 64114
Phone: (816) 941-4000
Fax: (816) 941-2725
E-mail: **info@paralegals.org**
Internet: **www.paralegals.org**

DIRECTORY OF STATE AND LOCAL PARALEGAL ASSOCIATIONS

Please note that the contact information of several of the following associations changes with each change of officers and directors. For that reason, not all addresses are included in this list, and some of the following addresses may be out of date.

| **NFPA Affiliates** | **NALA Affiliates** |

Alabama

Mobile Association of Legal Assistants
P.O. Box 1852
Mobile, AL 36633

Alabama Association of Legal Assistants
P.O. Box 55921
Birmingham, AL 35255
E-mail: **president@aala.net**
Internet: **www.aala.net**

Legal Assistant Society of Southern Institute

Samford University Paralegal Association

Alaska

Alaska Association of Legal Assistants
P.O. Box 101956
Anchorage, AK 99510-1956
E-mail: Alaska@paralegals.org

Fairbanks Association of Legal Assistants

Arizona

Arizona Association of Professional
Paralegals, Inc.
P.O. Box 430
Phoenix, AZ 85001
E-mail: **Arizona@paralegals.org**

Arizona Paralegal Association

Legal Assistants of Metropolitan Phoenix

Tucson Association of Legal Assistants
P.O. Box 257
Tucson, AZ 85702
E-mail: **tala@azstarnet.com**
Internet: **www.azstarnet.com/nonprofit/tala**

Arkansas

Arkansas Association of Legal Assistants

California

California Association of Independent
Paralegals
39120 Argonaut Way, #114
Fremont, CA 94538

Legal Assistants Association of Santa Barbara
P.O. Box 2695
Santa Barbara, CA 93120-2695

Sacramento Association of Legal Assistants
P.O. Box 453
Sacramento, CA 95812-0453
Phone: (916) 763-7851
E-mail: **Sacramento@paralegals.org**
Internet:
www.paralegals.org/Sacramento/sala.htm

Los Angeles Paralegal Association
P.O. Box 8788
Calabasas, CA 91372
Phone: (818) 347-1001
Fax: (818) 222-1336
E-mail: **DavidR7944@AOL.COM**
Internet: **www.lapa.org**

NFPA Affiliates   **NALA Affiliates**

California—cont'd

Sacramento Association of Legal Assistants
P.O. Box 453
Sacramento, CA 95812-0453
Phone: (916) 763-7851
E-mail: **Sacramento@paralegals.org**
Internet:
www.paralegals.org/Sacramento/sala.htm

San Diego Association of Legal Assistants
P.O. Box 87449
San Diego, CA 92138-7449
Phone: (619) 491-1994
E-mail: **SanDiego@paralegals.org**
Internet:
www.paralegals.org/SanDiego/sdala1.htm

San Francisco Paralegal Association
P.O. Box 2110
San Francisco, CA 94126-2110
Phone: (415) 777-2390
Fax: (415) 586-6606
E-mail: **SanFrancisco@paralegals.org**
Internet: **www.sfpa.com/**

Los Angeles Paralegal Association
P.O. Box 8788
Calabasas, CA 91372
Phone: (818) 347-1001
Fax: (818) 222-1336
E-mail: **DavidR7944@AOL.COM**
Internet: **www.lapa.org**

Orange County Paralegal Association
P.O. Box 8512
Newport Beach, CA 92658-8215
Internet: **www.OCPARALEGAL.org**

Palomar College Paralegal Studies Club (San
Marcos)

Paralegal Association of Santa Clara County
P.O. Box 26736
San Jose, CA 95159-6736
Phone: (408) 235-0301
Internet: **www.sccba.com/PASCCO**

San Joaquin Association of Legal Assistants
P.O. Box 1306
Fresno, CA 93716
Internet: **www.caparalegal.org/sjala.html**

Ventura County Association of Legal Assistants
P.O. Box 24229
Ventura, CA 93002
Internet: **www.caparalegal.org/vala.html**

Colorado

Rocky Mountain Paralegal Association
P.O. Box 481864
Denver, CO 80248-1834
Phone: (303) 370-9444
E-mail: **rmpa@rockymtnparalegal.org**
Internet:
   www.rockymtnparalegal.org/index.html

Association of Legal Assistants of Colorado
606 South Nevada Avenue
Colorado Springs, CO 80903
Phone: (719) 475-0026
Fax: (719) 475-8671
E-mail: **swoop137@netzero.net**
Internet: **firms.findlaw.com/ALAC**

Connecticut

Central Connecticut Paralegal Association, Inc.
P.O. Box 230594
Hartford, CT 06123-0594
E-mail: **CentralConnecticut@paralegals.org**
Internet: **www.paralegals.org/Central
Connecticut/home.html**

Connecticut Association of Paralegals, Inc.
P.O. Box 134
Bridgeport, CT 06601-0134
E-mail: **Connecticut@paralegals.org**
Internet: **www.paralegals.org/Connecticut/home.
html**

| **NFPA Affiliates** | **NALA Affiliates** |

Connecticut—cont'd

New Haven County Association of Paralegals, Inc.
P.O. Box 862
New Haven, CT 06504-0862
E-mail: **NewHaven@paralegals.org**
Internet: **www.paralegals.org/NewHaven/home.
html**

Delaware

Delaware Paralegal Association
P.O. Box 1362
Wilmington, DE 19899
Phone: (302) 426-1362
E-mail: **Delaware@paralegals.org**
Internet: **paralegals.org/Delaware/home.html**

District of Columbia

National Capital Area Paralegal Association
P.O. Box 27607
Washington, DC 20038-7607
Phone: (202) 659-0243
E-mail: **NationalCapital@paralegals.org**
Internet: **paralegals.org/NationalCapital/home.
html**

Florida

Florida Paralegal Association, Inc.
P.O. Box 7479
Seminole, FL 33775
E-mail: **Florida@paralegals.org**

Central Florida Paralegal Association
Orlando, FL

Dade Association of Legal Assistants
Bay Harbor Island, FL

Gainesville Association of Legal Assistants
P.O. Box 2519
Gainesville, FL 32602
Phone: (352) 367-9088
Fax: (352) 367-0720

Jacksonville Legal Assistants
P.O. Box 52264
Jacksonville, FL 32201
Phone: (904) 366-8440
E-mail: **Info@jaxla.org**
Internet: **www.jaxla.org**

Legal Assistants of Southwest Florida, Inc.

Florida Legal Assistants, Inc.
Clearwater, FL

Northwest Florida Paralegal Association
P.O. Box 1333
Pensacola, FL 32596
Internet: **www.pla-net.org**

Phi Lambda Alpha Legal Assisting Society of
Southwest Florida

NFPA Affiliates   **NALA Affiliates**

Florida—cont'd

Tampa College-Brandon Student Association
Tampa, FL

Volusia Association of Legal Assistants
Ormond Beach, FL

Georgia

Georgia Association of Paralegals, Inc.   Georgia Legal Assistants
1199 Euclid Ave., NE   Alma, GA
Atlanta, GA 30307
Phone: (404) 522-1457   Professional Paralegals of Georgia
Fax: (404) 522-0132
E-mail: **Georgia@paralegals.org**   South Georgia Association of Legal Assistants
Internet: **paralegals.org/Georgia/home.htm**   Nashville, GA

Southeastern Association of Legal Assistants
  of Georgia
Pooler, GA

Hawaii

Hawaii Paralegal Association
P.O. Box 674
Honolulu, HI 96809
E-mail: **Hawaii@paralegals.org**
Internet: **paralegals.org/Hawaii/home.html**

Idaho

Gem State Association of Legal Assistants
Hailey, ID

Illinois

Illinois Paralegal Association   Central Illinois Paralegal Association
P.O. Box 8089   Bloomington, IL
Bartlett, IL 60103-8089
Phone: (630) 837-8088   Heart of Illinois Paralegal Association
Fax: (630) 837-8096   Peoria, IL
E-mail: **Illinois@paralegals.org**
Internet: **www.ipaonline.org/**

Indiana

Indiana Paralegal Association   Indiana Legal Assistants
Federal Station   c/o The Indiana State Bar Association
P.O. Box 44518   230 East Ohio Street, 4th Floor
Indianapolis, IN 46204   Indianapolis, Indiana 47204
Phone: (317) 767-7798   Internet: **www.freeyellow.com:8080/**
E-mail: **Indiana@paralegals.org**   **members/ila**
Internet: **www.paralegals.org/Indiana/**
home.html

Michiana Paralegal Association
P.O. Box 11458
South Bend, IN 46634
E-mail: **Michiana@paralegals.org**
Internet: **www.paralegals.org/Michiana/home.**
html

NFPA Affiliates	**NALA Affiliates**

Indiana—cont'd

Northeast Indiana Paralegal Association, Inc.
P.O. Box 13646
Fort Wayne, IN 46865
E-mail: **NortheastIndiana@paralegals.org**
Internet: **www.paralegals.org/NortheastIndiana/
home.html**

Iowa

Iowa Association of Legal Assistants
P.O. Box 93153
Des Moines, IA 50393
E-mail: **ialanet@forbin.com**
Internet: **www.ialanet.org**

Kansas

Kansas City Paralegal Association
P.O. Box 344
Lee's Summit, MO 64063-0344
Phone: (816) 524-6078
E-mail: **KansasCity@paralegals.org**
Internet: **www.paralegals.org/KansasCity/
home.html**

Kansas Paralegal Association
P.O. Box 1675
Topeka, KS 66601
E-mail: **Kansas@paralegals.org**
Internet: **www.ink.org/public/ksparalegals/**

Kansas Association of Legal Assistants
P.O. Box 47031
Wichita, KS 67201
Internet:
www.ink.org/public/kala/main.html

Kentucky

Greater Lexington Paralegal Association, Inc.
P.O. Box 574
Lexington, KY 40586
E-mail: **Lexington@paralegals.org**

Western Kentucky Paralegals
Murray, KY

Louisiana

New Orleans Paralegal Association
P.O. Box 30604
New Orleans, LA 70190
Phone: (504) 467-3136
E-mail: **NewOrleans@paralegals.org**
Internet:
paralegals.org/NewOrleans/home.html

Louisiana State Paralegal Association
Monroe, LA

Northwest Louisiana Paralegal Association
Shreveport, LA

Maine

Maine State Association of Legal Assistants
E-mail: **mrroy@unum.com**
Internet: **www.msala.org**

NFPA Affiliates   **NALA Affiliates**

Maryland

Maryland Association of Paralegals
P.O. Box 13244
Baltimore, MD 21203
Phone: (410) 576-2252
E-mail: **Maryland@paralegals.org**
Internet: **paralegals.org/Maryland/home.html**

Massachusetts

Central Massachusetts Paralegal Association
P.O. Box 444
Worcester, MA 01614
E-mail: **CentralMassachusetts@paralegals.org**

Massachusetts Paralegal Association
c/o Offtech Management Services
99 Summer Street, Suite L-150
Boston, MA 02110
Phone: (800) 637-4311
Fax: (617) 439-8639
E-mail: **Massachusetts@paralegals.org**
Internet: **www.paralegals.org/Massachusetts/
home.html**

Western Massachusetts Paralegal Association
P.O. Box 30005
Springfield, MA 01103
E-mail: **WesternMassachusetts@paralegals.org**

Michigan

Michiana Paralegal Association
P.O. Box 11458
South Bend, IN 46634
E-mail: **Michiana@paralegals.org**

Legal Assistants Association of Michigan
Dearborn, MI
E-mail: **goLAAM@aol.com**

Minnesota

Minnesota Paralegal Association
1711 W. County Rd. B, #300N
Roseville, MN 55113
Phone: (612) 633-2778
Fax: (612) 635-0307
E-mail: **info@mnparalegals.org**
Internet: **mnparalegals.org/**

Mississippi

Mississippi Association of Legal Assistants
Post Office Box 996
Jackson, MS 39205
Internet: **www.mslawyer.com/MALA**

University of Southern Mississippi Society
  for Paralegal Studies
Hattiesburg, MS

NFPA Affiliates   **NALA Affiliates**

Missouri

St. Louis Association of Legal Assistants
P.O. Box 69218
St. Louis, MO 63169-0218
Internet:
   www.nwmissouri.edu/~bdye/slalapage

Montana

Montana Association of Legal Assistants
E-mail: **mala@montana.com**
Internet: **www.montana.com/mala**

Nebraska

Nebraska Association of Legal Assistants
E-mail: **webmaster@meala.org**
Internet: **www.neala.org**

Nevada

Clark County Organization of Legal
Assistants
Las Vegas, NV

Sierra Nevada Association of Paralegals
Reno, NV

New Hampshire

Paralegal Association of New Hampshire
Henniker, NH

New Jersey

Prudential Insurance Company of America-
Paralegal Council
751 Broad Street
Newark, NJ 07102
E-mail: **Prudential@paralegals.org**

Legal Assistants Association of New Jersey
P.O. Box 142
Caldwell, NJ 07006
Internet:
www.geocities.com/CapitolHill/2716

South Jersey Paralegal Association
P.O. Box 355
Haddonfield, NJ 08033
E-mail: **SouthJersey@paralegals.org**
Internet: **www.paralegals.org/SouthJersey/
home.html**

New Mexico

Southwestern Association of Legal Assistants
P.O. Box 8042
Roswell, NM 88202-8042
Internet: **homepages.infoseek.com/
   ~shewolf2/sala.html**

NFPA Affiliates

NALA Affiliates

New York

Long Island Paralegal Association
1877 Bly Road
East Meadow, NY 11554-1158
E-mail: **LongIsland@paralegals.org**

Manhattan Paralegal Association, Inc.
521 Fifth Ave., 17th Floor
New York, NY 10175
Phone: (212) 330-8213
E-mail: Manhattan
Internet: **www.paralegals.org/Manhattan/
home.html**

Paralegal Association of Rochester
P.O. Box 40567
Rochester, NY 14604
Phone: (716) 234-5923
E-mail: **Rochesterparalegals.org**

Southern Tier Paralegal Association
P.O. Box 2555
Binghamton, NY 13903-2555
E-mail: **SouthernTier@paralegals.org**
Internet: **www.paralegals.org/SouthernTier/
home.html**

West/Rock Paralegal Association
P.O. Box 668
New City, NY 10956
Phone: (914) 786-6184
E-mail: **WestRockparalegals.org**

Western New York Paralegal Association
P.O. Box 207, Niagara Square Station
Buffalo, NY 14201
Phone: (716) 635-8250
E-mail: **WesternNewYork@paralegals.org**
Internet: **www.paralegals.org/WesternNewYork/
home.html**

North Carolina

Coastal Carolina Paralegal Club
Jacksonville, NC

Metrolina Paralegal Association
Charlotte, NC

North Carolina Paralegal Association
NCPA
P.O. Box 28554
Raleigh, NC 27611
Phone: (800) 479-1905, (919) 779-1903
Fax: (919) 779-1685
E-mail: **info@ncparalegal.org**
Internet: **www.ncparalegal.org**

NFPA Affiliates

NALA Affiliates

North Dakota

Red River Valley Legal Assistants
Moorhead, MN

Western Dakota Association of Legal
Assistants
Minot, ND

Ohio

Cincinnati Paralegal Association
P.O. Box 1515
Cincinnati, OH 45201
Phone: (513) 244-1266
E-mail: **Cincinnati@paralegals.org**
Internet: **www.paralegals.org/Cincinnati/
home.html**

Toledo Association of Legal Assistants
Toledo, OH

Cleveland Association of Paralegals
P.O. Box 14517
Cleveland, OH 44114-0517
Phone: (216) 556-5437
E-mail: **Cleveland@paralegals.org**

Greater Dayton Paralegal Association
P.O. Box 515, Mid-City Station
Dayton, OH 45402
E-mail: **Dayton@paralegals.org**
Internet: **www.paralegals.org/GreaterDayton/
home.html**

Northeastern Ohio Paralegal Association
P.O. Box 80068
Akron, OH 44308-0068
E-mail: **NorthEasternOhio@paralegals.org**
Internet: **www.paralegals.org/NortheasternOhio/
home.html**

Paralegal Association of Central Ohio
P.O. Box 15182
Columbus, OH 43215-0182
Phone: (614) 224-9700
E-mail: **CentralOhio@paralegals.org**

Oklahoma

Oklahoma Paralegal Association
Norman, OK

Rogers State College Association of Legal
Assistants
Claremore, OK

Rose State Paralegal Association
Midwest City, OK

NFPA Affiliates

NALA Affiliates

Oklahoma—cont'd

TCC Student Association of Legal Assistants
Tulsa, OK

Tulsa Association of Legal Assistants
Tulsa, OK

Oregon

Oregon Paralegal Association
P.O. Box 8523
Portland, OR 97207
Phone: (503) 796-1671
E-mail: **Oregon@paralegals.org**
Internet: **paralegals.org/Oregon/home.html**

Pacific Northwest Legal Assistants
Eugene, OR

Pennsylvania

Central Pennsylvania Paralegal Association
P.O. Box 11814
Harrisburg, PA 17108
E-mail: **CentralPennsylvania@paralegals.org**
Internet: **www.paralegals.org/
CentralPennsylvania/home.html**

Keystone Legal Assistant Association
Summerdale, PA

Chester County Paralegal Association
P.O. Box 295
West Chester, PA 19381-0295
E-mail: **ChesterCounty@paralegals.org**

Lycoming County Paralegal Association
P.O. Box 991
Williamsport, PA 17701
E-mail: **Lycoming@paralegals.org**

Philadelphia Association of Paralegals
P.O. Box 59179
Philadelphia, PA 19102-9179
Phone: (215) 545-5395
E-mail: **Philadelphia@paralegals.org**

Pittsburgh Paralegal Association
P.O. Box 2845
Pittsburgh, PA 15230
Phone: (412) 344-3904
E-mail: **Pittsburgh@paralegals.org**
Internet: **www.paralegals.org/
CentralPennsylvania/home.html**

Rhode Island

Rhode Island Paralegal Association
P.O. Box 1003
Providence, RI 02901
E-mail: **RhodeIsland@paralegals.org**
Internet: **paralegals.org/RhodeIsland/home.html**

NFPA Affiliates	**NALA Affiliates**

South Carolina

Palmetto Paralegal Association
P.O. Box 11634
Columbia, SC 29211-1634
E-mail: **Palmetto@paralegals.org**
Internet: **paralegals.org/Palmetto/home.html**

Central Carolina Technical College Paralegal
   Association
Sumter, SC

Charleston Association of Legal Assistants
P.O. Box 1511
Charleston, SC 29402

Grand Strand Paralegal Association (GSPA)
743 Hemlock Avenue
Myrtle Beach, SC 29577

Greenville Association of Legal Assistants
P.O. Box 10491
Greenville, SC 29603

Paralegal Association of Beaufort County
South Carolina
Beaufort, SC

Tri-County Paralegal Association, Inc. (TCPA)
P.O. Box 62691
North Charleston, SC 29419-2691

South Dakota

South Dakota Legal Assistants Association
Aberdeen, SD

National College Student Association of
Legal Assistants
Rapid City, SD

Tennessee

Memphis Paralegal Association
P.O. Box 3646
Memphis, TN 38173-0646
E-mail: **Memphis@paralegals.org**
Internet:
paralegals.org/Memphis/home.html

Greater Memphis Paralegal Alliance, Inc.
Memphis, TN
E-mail: **pcobb@tlblaw.com**

Tennessee Paralegal Association

Texas

Dallas Area Paralegal Association
P.O. Box 12533
Dallas, TX 75225-0533
Phone: (972) 991-0853
E-mail: **Dallas@paralegals.org**
Internet: **paralegals.org/Dallas/home.html**

Capitol Area Paralegal Association
Austin, TX

El Paso Association of Legal Assistants
El Paso, TX

Legal Assistants Association/Permian Basin
Midland, Texas

Northeast Texas Association of Legal
   Assistants
Longview, TX

Nueces County Association of Legal
   Assistants
Corpus Christi, TX

| **NFPA Affiliates** | **NALA Affiliates** |

Texasa—cont'd

Southeast Texas Association of Legal
Assistants
Beaumont, TX

Texas Panhandle Association of Legal
Assistants
Amarillo, TX

Tyler Area Association of Legal Assistants
Tyler, TX

West Texas Association of Legal Assistants
Lubbock, TX

Wichita County Student Association
Wichita Falls, TX

Utah

Legal Assistants Association of Utah

Vermont

Vermont Paralegal Organization
P.O. Box 5755
Burlington, VT 05402
E-mail: **Vermont@paralegals.org**

Virgin Islands

Virgin Islands Paralegal Association

Virginia

Peninsula Legal Assistants, Inc.
Poquoson, VA

Richmond Association of Legal Assistants
P.O. Box 384
Richmond, VA 23218-0384
E mail: **rala@geocities.com**
Internet:
　www.geocities.com/CapitolHill/7082

Tidewater Association of Legal Assistants
Norfolk, VA

Washington

Washington State Paralegal Association
P.O. Box 48153
Burien, WA 98148
Phone: (800) 288-WSPA
E-mail: **Washington@paralegals.org**
Internet: **paralegals.org/Washington/home.html**

NFPA Affiliates	**NALA Affiliates**

West Virginia

Legal Assistants of West Virginia
Huntington, WV
E-mail: **lawvlawv.org**

Wisconsin

Paralegal Association of Wisconsin, Inc.
P.O. Box 510892
Milwaukee, WI 53203-0151
Phone: (414) 272-7168
E-mail: **Wisconsin@paralegals.org**
Internet: **paralegals.org/Wisconsin/home.html**

Madison Area Paralegal Association
Madison, WI
E-mail: **ckorth@foleylaw.com**
Internet: **www.califex.com/mapa/index.html**

Wyoming

Legal Assistants of Wyoming
Casper, WY

Glossary

Admonition Any authoritative advice or caution from the court to the jury regarding their duty as jurors or the admissibility of evidence for consideration [the judge's admonition that the jurors not discuss the case until they are charged]. A reprimand or cautionary statement addressed to counsel by a judge [the judge's admonition that the lawyer stop speaking out of turn]. (*Black's Law Dictionary, Seventh Edition*)

American Bar Association (ABA) A voluntary national organization of lawyers. Among other things, it participates in law reform, law-school accreditation, and continuing legal education in an effort to improve legal services and the administration of justice. (*Black's Law Dictionary, Seventh Edition*)

Amicus curiae A person who is not a party to a lawsuit but who petitions the court or is requested by the court to file a brief in the action because that person has a strong interest in the subject matter. Often shortened to *amicus*. Also termed *friend of the court*. (*Black's Law Dictionary, Seventh Edition*)

Attorney–client privilege The client's right to refuse to disclose and to prevent any other person from disclosing confidential communications between the client and the attorney. Also termed *lawyer–client privilege; client's privilege*. (*Black's Law Dictionary, Seventh Edition*)

Bar association An organization of members of the bar of a state or county, or of the bar of every state, whose primary function is promoting professionalism and enhancing the administration of justice.

Billable hour Hours billed to client for legal services performed by each attorney, paralegal, or other timekeeper.

Business ethics The study and evaluation of decision making by businesses according to moral concepts and judgments.

Censure An official reprimand or condemnation; harsh criticism (the judge's careless statements subjected her to the judicial council's censure). (*Black's Law Dictionary, Seventh Edition*)

Certification Form of self-regulation whereby an organization grants recognition to an individual who has met qualifications specified by that organization.

Certified Legal Assistant (CLA) Title awarded to paralegals who pass the CLA exam and meet with other criteria established by the National Association of Legal Assistants.

Certified Legal Assistant Specialist (CLAS) Title awarded to paralegals who pass the CLA exam, at least one of the CLA specialty exams, and who meet with other criteria established by the National Association of Legal Assistants.

Chinese wall Same as ethical wall.

Civil contempt The failure to obey a court order that was issued for another party's benefit. A civil-contempt proceeding is coercive or remedial in nature. The usual sanction is to confine the contemner until he or she complies with the court order. (*Black's Law Dictionary, Seventh Edition*)

Code of conduct A written set of rules prescribing ethical behavior for all employees of an organization in accordance with the ethics policy of the organization.

Code of ethics Code or set of rules setting forth the standards and guidelines for ethical behavior and professional responsibility for a certain profession. May also be referred to as a code of professional responsibility, code of conduct, or a similar name.

Codefendant One of two or more defendants sued in the same litigation or charged with the same crime. Also termed *joint defendant. (Black's Law Dictionary, Seventh Edition)*

Commingling of funds Act of an attorney or other fiduciary in mingling funds of the client or owner of the funds with his or her own funds so that the funds lose their individual ownership identity.

Committee on Ethics and Professional Responsibility Standing committee established by the American Bar Association to issue both formal and informal advisory opinions on ethical questions as guidance to attorneys.

Competence A basic or minimal ability to do something; qualification, especially to testify (competence of a witness). *(Black's Law Dictionary, Seventh Edition)*

Confidential Entrusted with the confidence of another or with his or her secret affairs or purposes; intended to be held in confidence or kept secret; done in confidence.

Confidential communication A communication made within a certain protected relationship—such as husband-wife, attorney-client, or priest-penitent—and legally protected from forced disclosure. *(Black's Law Dictionary, Seventh Edition)*

Confidential relationship A fiduciary relationship that exists between client and attorney and others in similar circumstances. The law requires the utmost degree of good faith in all transactions between the parties in a confidential relationship.

Conflict of interest A real or seeming incompatibility between the interest of two of a lawyer's clients, such that the lawyer is disqualified from representing both clients if the dual representation adversely affects either client or if the clients do not consent. *(Black's Law Dictionary, Seventh Edition)*

Constructive contempt Contempt that is committed in outside of court, as when a party disobeys a court order. Also termed *consequential contempt; indirect contempt. (Black's Law Dictionary, Seventh Edition)*

Contingent fees A fee charged for a lawyer's services only if the lawsuit is successful or is fa-

vorably settled out of court. Contingent fees are usually calculated as a percentage of the client's net recovery (such as 25% of the recovery if the case is settled, and 33% if the case is won at trial). Also termed *contingency fee, contingency. (Black's Law Dictionary, Seventh Edition)*

Conversion Wrongful control over the property of another that violates the owner's title to, or rights in, the property.

Deposition The testimony of a witness given under oath outside of the courtroom, usually in advance of the trial or hearing, upon oral examination or in response to written interrogatories.

Diligence A continual effort to accomplish something. Care; caution; the attention and care required from a person in a given situation. *(Black's Law Dictionary, Seventh Edition)*

Direct contempt Contempt that is committed in open court, as when a lawyer insults a judge on the bench. *(Black's Law Dictionary, Seventh Edition)*

Disbarment The revocation of an attorney's right to practice law.

Disciplinary board Court-appointed board, typically consisting of a mixture of attorneys and nonattorneys, to receive complaints about attorney misconduct and oversee the disciplinary process.

Discovery A means for providing a party, in advance of trial, with access to facts that are within the knowledge of the other side, to enable the party to better try his or her case.

Document preparer An individual who prepares or assists in the preparation of legal documents at the direction of an individual who is representing himself or herself in a legal matter.

Ethical wall Fictional wall erected around a lawyer or nonlawyer within a law firm to screen that individual from a particular client and information concerning a particular client's case when that particular lawyer or nonlawyer has a conflict of interest with that client.

Ethics policy A policy adopted by an organization stating the ethical principles of the organization and standards for ethical behavior.

Evidence The means by which any matter of fact may be established or disproved. Such means include testimony, documents, and physical objects. The law of evidence is composed of rules that determine what evidence is to be admitted or rejected in the trial of a civil action or a criminal prosecution and what weight is to be given to admitted evidence.

Ex parte On or from one party only, usually without notice to or argument from the adverse party (the judge conducted the hearing ex parte). (*Black's Law Dictionary, Seventh Edition*)

Felony A serious crime, such as aggravated assault, rape, robbery, or murder, usually punishable by death or imprisonment for a term exceeding one year.

Fiduciary 1. One who owes to another the duties of good faith, trust, confidence, and candor (the corporate officer is a fiduciary to the shareholders). 2. One who must exercise a high standard of care in managing another's money or property (the beneficiary sued the fiduciary for investing in speculative securities). (*Black's Law Dictionary, Seventh Edition*)

Fiduciary duty A duty to act for someone else's benefit, while subordinating one's personal interests to that of the other person. It is the highest standard of duty implied by the law.

Firm A group of lawyers formed for the purpose of practicing law, including lawyers in a private firm and lawyers in the legal department of a corporation or other organization or in a legal services organization.

Fraud Deceit, deception, or trickery to induce another to part with anything of value, or to surrender some legal right, to his or her detriment.

Freelance paralegal A self-employed paralegal who works for several different attorneys, law firms, or corporations under the supervision of an attorney.

General retainer Fee paid to an attorney or law firm to retain their services for a specific amount of time. During that time period, the attorney and law firm may not accept any conflicting employment.

Impropriety An act of misconduct. That which is socially unacceptable.

Imputed disqualification Rule that disqualifies all of the members of a firm when one attorney is disqualified.

In camera In chambers; in private. A term referring to a hearing or any other judicial business conducted in the judge's office or in a courtroom that has been cleared of spectators.

Independent paralegal A self-employed paralegal who works directly for the public to provide legal services not considered to be the practice of law. Also known as a legal technician.

Injunction A court order commanding or preventing an action. To get an injunction, the complainant must show that there is no plain, adequate, and complete remedy at law and that an irreparable injury will result unless the relief is granted. (*Black's Law Dictionary, Seventh Edition*)

Integrated bar A bar association in which membership is a statutory requirement for the practice of law. Also termed *unified bar*. (*Black's Law Dictionary, Seventh Edition*)

Interest on Lawyers' Trust Account (IOLTA) Type of trust account designed for the pooling of funds of several clients when those funds individually are too small to earn significant interest. Interest earned on IOLTA accounts is donated to nonprofit organizations that work to deliver legal services to low-income individuals.

Interrogatory A written question (usually in a set of questions) submitted to an opposing party in a lawsuit as part of discovery. (*Black's Law Dictionary, Seventh Edition*)

Irrevocable trust A trust that cannot be terminated by the settlor once it is created. In most states, a trust will be deemed irrevocable unless the settlor specifies otherwise. (*Black's Law Dictionary, Seventh Edition*)

Legal document assistant Individual recognized in California who is authorized to provide or assist in providing, for compensation, self-help legal services to the public.

Legal ethics The standards of minimally acceptable conduct within the legal profession, involving the duties that its members owe one another, their clients, and the courts. Also termed *etiquette of the profession*. (*Black's Law Dictionary, Seventh Edition*)

Legal malpractice An attorney's failure to exercise on behalf of his client the knowledge, skill, and ability ordinarily possessed and exercised by members of the legal profession. Legal malpractice is a tort if it results in injury.

Legal technician A self-employed paralegal who works directly for the public to provide legal services not considered the practice of law. Also known as an independent paralegal.

License Permission by competent authority, usually the government, to do an act which, without such permission, would be illegal or otherwise not allowable. Permission to exercise a certain privilege, to carry on a particular business, or to pursue a certain occupation.

Mediation An alternative dispute-resolution process in which a neutral third person, the mediator, helps disputing parties to reach an agreement. The mediator has no power to impose a decision on the parties unless participation is voluntary.

Mediator Neutral third person who helps parties involved in the mediation process to reach agreement.

Misappropriation The application of another's property or money dishonestly to one's own use. *(Black's Law Dictionary, Seventh Edition)*

Misconduct A dereliction of duty; unlawful or improper behavior. *(Black's Law Dictionary, Seventh Edition)*

Misdemeanor A crime that is less serious than a felony and is usually punishable by fine, penalty, forfeiture, or confinement (usually for a brief term) in a place other than prison (such as a county jail). Also termed *minor crime, summary offense. (Black's Law Dictionary, Seventh Edition)*

Mission statement A statement formally adopted by an organization setting forth the organization's purpose and philosophy

Mitigating circumstances A fact or situation that does not justify or excuse a wrongful act or offense but that reduces the degree of culpability and thus may reduce the damages (in a civil case) or the punishment (in a criminal case). *(Black's Law Dictionary, Seventh Edition)*

Model Code of Professional Responsibility Model code adopted by the ABA that became effective in 1970. The Model Code of Professional Responsibility (Model Code) is divided into nine canons, all of which broadly prescribe ethical conduct for lawyers. Within the canons are disciplinary rules (DRs) and ethical considerations (ECs), which provide more detailed guidance on ethical issues. The Model Code of Professional Responsibility was adopted or followed closely by most jurisdictions but has since been replaced by the Model Rules of Professional Conduct by the ABA and most states.

Model Guidelines for the Utilization of Legal Assistant Services Guidelines drafted by the American Bar Association Standing Committee on Legal Assistants and adopted by the American Bar Association's House of Delegates in 1991.

Model Rules of Professional Conduct Model rules adopted by the ABA in 1983 to replace the Model Code of Professional Responsibility. Now adopted in some form in most jurisdictions in the United States.

Moral turpitude Conduct that is contrary to justice, honesty, or morality. In the area of legal ethics, offenses involving moral turpitude—such as fraud or breach of trust—traditionally make a person unfit to practice law. Also termed *moral depravity. (Black's Law Dictionary, Seventh Edition)*

National Association of Legal Assistants (NALA) A national association of legal assistants (paralegals) formed in 1975, currently representing over 18,000 members through individual memberships and 90 state and local affiliated associations.

National Federation of Paralegal Associations (NFPA) A national association of paralegals formed in 1974; currently has more than 55 state and local association members, representing more than 17,000 paralegals.

Nonintegrated bar A type of voluntary bar association that exists in some states, to which membership by attorneys practicing in that state is optional.

Paralegal Advanced Competency Exam (PACE) Exam promoted by the NFPA as a means for experienced paralegals to validate their knowledge to themselves and their employers.

Partnership An undertaking of two or more persons to carry on, as co-owners, a business or other enterprise for profit; an agreement between or among two or more persons to put their money, labor, and skill into commerce or business, and to divide the profit in agreed-upon proportions.

Per curiam [Latin] By the court as a whole. (*Black's Law Dictionary, Seventh Edition*)

Perjury Giving false testimony in a judicial proceeding or an administrative proceeding; lying under oath as to a material fact; swearing to the truth of anything one knows or believes to be false. Perjury is a crime. A person who makes a false affirmation is equally a perjurer.

Pleadings A formal document in which a party to a legal proceeding (especially a civil lawsuit) sets forth or responds to allegations, claims, denials, or defenses. In federal civil procedure, the main pleadings are the plaintiff's complaint and the defendant's answer. (*Black's Law Dictionary, Seventh Edition*)

Precedent 1. The making of law by a court in recognizing and applying new rules while administering justice. 2. A decided case that furnishes a basis for determining later cases involving similar facts or issues. (*Black's Law Dictionary, Seventh Edition*)

Probation A period during which a person who holds a job, position, or license, who has failed to perform according to acceptable standards, must either conform to such standards or suffer termination or loss of the license.

Pro bono [Latin *pro bono publico* "for the public good"] Being or involving uncompensated legal services performed especially for the public good (took the case pro bono) (50 hours of pro bono work each year). (*Black's Law Dictionary, Seventh Edition*)

Professional corporation Type of corporation that may be formed in most states by those rendering personal services to the public of a type that requires a license or other legal authorization.

Professional limited liability company Entity, similar to a professional corporation, that allows limited liability and partnership taxation status to its members, who must be professionals.

Professional responsibility A general term referring to the duties and obligations of those in the legal field; legal ethics.

Pro se For oneself; on one's own behalf; without a lawyer (the defendant proceeded *pro se*; a *pro se* defendant). Also termed *pro persona; in propria persona.* (*Black's Law Dictionary, Seventh Edition*)

Reciprocity Mutual or bi-lateral action (the Arthurs stopped receiving social invitations from friends because of their lack of reciprocity). The mutual concession of advantages or privileges for purposes of commercial or diplomatic relations (Texas and Louisiana grant reciprocity to each other's citizens in qualifying for in-state tuition rates). (*Black's Law Dictionary, Seventh Edition*)

Registration The process by which individuals or institutions meeting with certain requirements list their names on a roster kept by an agency of government or by a nongovernmental organization. Registration provides the public with a list of individuals who have met with certain requirements.

Reprimand In professional responsibility, a form of disciplinary action—imposed after trial or formal charges—that declares the lawyer's conduct improper but does not limit his or her right to practice law. (*Black's Law Dictionary, Seventh Edition*)

Request for the production of documents A request for the inspection or duplication of documents or other materials that are relevant to the subject matter of the litigation.

Sanction 1. Official approval or authorization [the committee gave sanction to the proposal]. 2. A penalty or coercive measure that results from failure to comply with a law, rule, or order [a sanction for discovery abuse]. (*Black's Law Dictionary, Seventh Edition*)

Screening A policy within a law firm to screen or shut out a disqualified attorney within the firm from representation of the client presenting the conflict.

Self-represented person A person who represents himself or herself for the purpose of resolving or completing a process in which the law is involved.

Sexual harassment As a type of employment discrimination, includes sexual advances, requests for sexual favors, and other verbal or physical conduct of a sexual nature in the course of employment prohibited by federal law (Title VII of 1964 Civil Rights Act) and commonly by state statutes.

Sole proprietorship Ownership by one person, as opposed to ownership by more than one person, ownership by a corporation, ownership by a partnership, etc.

Statute A law passed by a legislative body. (Abbr. s.; stat.) *(Black's Law Dictionary, Seventh Edition)*

Statute of limitations Statutes of the federal government and various states setting maximum time periods during which certain actions can be brought or rights enforced. After the time period set out in the applicable statute of limitations has run, no legal action can be brought, regardless of whether any cause of action ever existed.

Suspension The temporary cutting off or debarring a person, as from the privileges of that person's profession.

Traditional paralegal An individual who works as a paralegal under the direct supervision of an attorney.

Tribunal A court or other adjudicatory body. The seat, bench, or place where a judge sits. *(Black's Law Dictionary, Seventh Edition)*

Unauthorized practice of law Engaging in the practice of law without the license required by law.

Work product rule The rule providing for qualified immunity of an attorney's work product from discovery or other compelled disclosure. Fed. R. Civ. P. 26(b)(3). The exemption was primarily established to protect an attorney's litigation strategy. *Hickman v. Taylor,* 329 U.S. 495, 67 S.Ct. 385 (1947). Also termed *work product immunity; work-product privilege; work product exemption. (Black's Law Dictionary, Seventh Edition)*

Writ of quo warranto A court's written order issued to test whether a person or corporation exercising power is legally entitled to do so; intended to prevent a continued exercise of authority unlawfully asserted.

Index

ABA, 4, 5, 18

Absher Construction Company v. Kent School District No. 415, 149

Admonition, 14

Advertising and solicitation, 175–194
  false and misleading advertising, 180, 181
  Internet, 213, 214
  labeling, 183
  letterhead, 185, 188, 189
  names of law firms, 184, 185
  paralegal advertising, 188–190
  recordkeeping, 183
  referral fees, 184
  rules, 178–180
  solicitation, 185–188, 190
  specialization, 183, 184
  Supreme Court decisions, 177, 178
  timeline, 179
  type of media used, 182, 183

Agencies permitting nonlawyer representation, 47, 48

AIG Life Insurance Company, et al. v. CUNA Mutual Insurance Company, 72

Allegretti, Joseph G., 80

American Bar Association (ABA), 4, 5, 18

Astronomical awards, 80

Attorney-client privilege, 60, 62, 67–69

Attorneys
  accepting/declining representation, 112
  advertising. *See* Advertising and solicitation
  bar admission, 157–159
  client trust funds, 131–134
  compensation. *See* Legal fees
  competent representation, 108–112
  confidentiality. *See* Confidentiality

conflict of interest. *See* Conflict of interest

consequences of unethical behavior, 14, 15

diligent representation, 114–116

disciplinary matters, 159

duty of candor, 119

maintaining competence, 114

misconduct, 159–161

moral character, 158

pro bono service, 165

public image, 209

reporting judicial misconduct, 163

reporting misconduct, 161–163

responsibility for paralegal ethics, 6–9

sharing fees with nonlawyers, 141, 142, 148, 150

skills, 109–112

specialization, 112–114, 183, 184

unauthorized practice of law, and, 34, 35

zealous representation, 116–119

Attorneys' fees, 145

Bar admission, 157–159

Bar association, 3. *See* also State bar associations

Bates v. State Bar of Arizona, 177

Belli, Melvin, 175

Bill Rivers Trailers, Inc. v. Miller, 146

Billable hour, 145

Billing, 145, 146

Brooks, Garth, 82

Business ethics, 197–208
  contributions to the community, 202
  defined, 198
  diversity in workplace, 203, 204
  employee theft, 203

Business ethics—*continued*
  ethics programs, 199–201
  honesty, 202
  importance, 198
  resolving ethical dilemmas,
    205–207
  sexual harassment, 204, 205
Business transactions with clients, 92,
  93

Cellular phones, 74, 75, 212, 213
Censure, 40
Certification, 17
Certified legal assistant (CLA), 18, 19,
  123
Certified legal assistant specialist
  (CLAS), 19
Chinese wall, 89
Civil contempt, 39
CLA, 18, 19, 123
CLAS, 19
CLE courses, 114, 124
*Cleveland Area Board of Realtors v. City
  of Euclid,* 148
Cleveland Bar Association v. Scali,
  50
Client trust account, 131–134
Client trust account ledger, 144
Clinton, Bill, 81
Code of conduct, 199, 201
Code of ethics
  ABA, 4, 5
  defined, 3
  NALA, 11, 245–246
  NFPA, 12, 247–256
  state, 21–23
Codefendant, 86
Colorado v. Carpenter, 181
Commingling of funds, 134
Competence, 107
Competence/diligence
  attorneys, 108–116
  paralegals, 119–124
Competent representation, 104,
  108–112
Confidential, 61
Confidential communication, 71
Confidential relationship, 60
Confidentiality, 59–79
  attorney-client relationship, 60, 62,
    67–69
  attorney's employees/agents, 63
  cellular phones, 74, 75, 212, 213
  corporate clients, 71
  e-mail, 75, 212

  exceptions, 63–67
  facsimile (fax), 75
  model rule/code, 61
  NALA's rules, 72
  NFPA's rules, 72–74
  paralegal's perspective, 72–77
  practical considerations, 74–77
  shredding files, 76
  talking to the press, 76
  what is protected, 62, 63
  work product rule, 69, 70
Conflict of interest, 82–103
  attorney as witness, 95
  attorney's employees/agents, 95
  attorney's personal interests, 92–95
  business transactions with clients,
    92, 93
  change of employment, 89
  consenting to representation, 88
  current clients, 85–87
  defined, 83
  detecting, 90, 91
  ethical wall, 89, 90
  financial assistance to client, 93, 94
  former clients, 87
  general rule, 84, 85
  gifts to lawyers, 93
  government lawyers, 91, 92
  imputed disqualification, 88–90
  literary or media rights, 93
  model rules/codes, 85
  NALA's rules, 98
  NFPA's rules, 98, 99
  organization as client, 91
  paralegal's perspective, 97–99
  practical considerations, 99
  screening, 89, 90
Consequences of unethical behavior,
  14–16
Consequential contempt, 39
Contempt, 39
Contingent fees, 127, 128, 136–139
Continuing legal education, 114, 124
Contributions to the community, 202
Conversion, 134
Cooper, N. Lee, 211

Dayco v. McLane, 148
Decision-making check list, 206
*Depenthal v. Falstaff Brewing Corpora-
  tion,* 146
Deposition, 70
Dershowitz, Alan, 154
Devine v. Beinfeld, 100
Digital technology, 213

Diligence, 107
Diligent representation, 114–116
Direct contempt, 39
Directory of Paralegal Associations, 257–270
Disbarment, 14
Disciplinary board, 14
Disciplinary matters, 159
Discovery, 69
Diversity in workplace, 203, 204
Document preparer, 18

E-mail, 75, 211, 212
Electronic monitoring of employees, 195
Employee privacy, 195, 196
Employee theft, 203
Encryption, 212
Ethical decision checklist, 206
Ethical dilemmas
    basic rules of ethics, 8
    confidentiality, 60
    falsification of tax returns, 157
    gift to lawyer, 83
    misappropriation of trust money, 130
    resolving, 205–207
    solicitation, 176
    statute of limitations, 107
    unauthorized practice of law, 33
Ethical wall, 89, 90
Ethics, 3. *See also* Business ethics
Ethics opinion, 5
Ethics policy, 199
Ethics programs, 199–201
Ethics 2000, 211
Evidence, 66
Ex parte, 119

Facsimile (fax), 75
Fee agreements, 139, 140
Fee disputes, 139, 141
Fees. See Legal fees
Felony, 15
Ferguson v. FDIC, 148
Ferris v. Snively, 49
Fiduciary duty, 130
Financial matters
    billing, 145
    business transactions with clients, 92, 93
    client trust accounts, 131–134
    commingling of funds, 134
    legal fees, 134–142. *See also* Legal fees

misappropriation of client funds, 134
    recordkeeping, 133, 134
    trust accounting, 144
Firm, 89
Flat fee, 138
Florida v. Pascual, 50
Florida Bar v. Went For It, 186
Forbes, B.C., 129
Franklin, Benjamin, 59
Fraud, 15
Freelance paralegal, 42

Gale, John, 210
General retainer, 137
Gifts to lawyers, 93
Group legal services plan, 188
Guidelines for utilizing paralegals, 9, 41

Hale, Matthew, 153–155
Hines v. Hines, 148
Holt, John, 106
Honesty, 202
Hostile work environment sexual harassment, 204

Impropriety, 85
Imputed disqualification, 84, 88–90
In camera, 67
In re Glover-Towne, 160
In re Himmel, 163
In re Martinez, 10
In re Primus, 187
In re R.M.J., 178
In the matter of Jenkins, 191
Independent paralegal, 17, 43, 44
Indirect contempt, 39
Injunction, 39
Integrated bar, 4
Integrity of profession, 156–172
    bar admission, 157–159
    disciplinary matters, 159
    misconduct, 159–161
    paralegal's perspective, 166–171
    pro bono service, 165, 170
    reporting misconduct, 161–163
Internet
    advertising and solicitation, 213, 214
    e-mail, 211, 212
    paralegals, 217
    unauthorized practice of law, 214, 215
Interrogatories, 69, 118

IOLTA, 132
IOLTA accounts, 132, 133
Iowa State Bar Association v. Batschelet,
    115
Iowa Supreme Court Board of Profes-
    sional Ethics and Conduct v.
    Apland, 132
Irreovcable trust, 112

J.W. v. Superior Court, 32
Johnson & Johnson, 199, 200
Joint defendant, 86

Law firm names, 184, 185
Lawyers. *See* Attorneys
Legal assistant, 5, 12. *See also*
    Paralegals
Legal document assistant, 18
Legal document preparer, 39
Legal ethics, 3. *See also* Business
    ethics
Legal fees, 134–142
    contingent fees, 136–139
    fee agreements, 139, 140
    fee disputes, 139, 141
    flat fee, 138
    paralegal fee recovery, 145–148
    payment of fees, 137
    reasonable fees, 135–137
    sharing fees with nonlawyers, 141,
        142, 148, 150
Legal malpractice, 14
Legal self-help books and software,
    30, 31
Legal technician, 17
Letterhead, 185, 188, 189
Levenson, Laurie L., 58
License, 17
Limited licensure, 17
Literary or media rights, 93
Litigation explosion, 80, 81
Louisiana State Bar Asso. v. Edwins,
    50
Lying, 202

Malpractice suits, 14
Marten v. Yellow Freight System, Inc.,
    96
McGreevy v. Oregon Mutual Insurance
    Company, 148
Mediation, 33
Mediator, 39
Miller, Jay, 155
Misappropriation, 134
Misconduct
    attorneys, 159–163

defined, 157
    paralegals, 167
    reporting (attorney's duty), 161–163
    reporting (paralegal's duty),
        167–170
Misdemeanor, 40
Mission statement, 199
Missouri Rules of Professional Con-
    duct, 219–241
Missouri v. Jenkins, 146
Mitigating circumstances, 142
Model Business Principles, 201
Model Code of Professional Responsi-
    bility, 4, 5
Model Guidelines for the Utilization
    of Legal Assistant Services, 9
Model Rules of Professional Conduct,
    4, 5
Monroe v. Horwitch, 50
Moral character, 158. *See also* In-
    tegrity of profession
Moral turpitude, 142

NALA, 11
    Code of Ethics and Professional Re-
        sponsibility, 11, 241–242
    confidentiality, 72
    conflict of interest, 98
    misconduct, 167
    Model Standards and Guidelines for
        Utilizing of Legal Assistants,
    11
    overview, 12
    recognition of competence, 123,
        124
    regulation, 18, 19
Names of law firms, 184, 185
National Association of Legal Assis-
    tants. See NALA
National Federation of Paralegal Asso-
    ciations. See NFPA
Negligence, 14
New Hampshire's Guidelines for the
    Utilization of Legal Assistant Ser-
    vices, 242–244
New York v. Cassa, 70
NFPA, 11
    confidentiality, 72–74
    conflict of interest, 98, 99
    Ethics and Professional Responsibil-
        ity Committee, 13
    goals, 11, 12
    Model Code of Ethics and Profes-
        sional Responsibility, 12, 13,
        247–256
    overview, 13

paralegal's title, 189
recognition of competence, 122, 123
regulation, 19, 20
reporting misconduct, 168
standard of professional conduct, 167
Nolo Press, 31
Nonintegrated bar, 4
Non-IOLTA client trust accounts, 133
Nonlawyer representation, 47, 48
Noyce, Robert, 197

Ohralik v. Ohio State Bar, 185
Online resources (paralegal ethics research), 27
Orlik, Deborah, 58
Osias, Rosalie, 173, 174

Paralegal advanced competency exam (PACE), 19, 122
Paralegal associations, 9–13, 257–270. *See also* NALA; NFPA
Paralegal certification, 17
Paralegal fee recovery, 145–148
Paralegal licensing, 17
Paralegal registration, 18
Paralegal regulation. *See* Regulation
Paralegals
    advertising, 188–190
    billing, 145
    competence/diligence, 119–124
    continuing legal education, 124
    defined, 5
    freelance, 43
    future considerations, 215–217
    guidelines for utilization, 9, 41
    Internet, and, 217
    maintaining competence, 124
    maintaining integrity of profession, 166
    misconduct, 167
    pro bono service, 170, 171
    reporting misconduct, 167–170
    sharing fees with lawyers, 148, 150
    solicitation, 190
    traditional, 42
    unauthorized practice of law, 49, 215, 216
    unethical behavior, and, 15, 16
Parsons Technology, 31
Partnership, 184
Peel v. Attorney Registration and Disciplinary Commission of Illinois, 183
People v. Alexander, 49

People v. Culpepper, 158
People v. Fry, 40
People v. Pooley, 116
Per curiam, 40
Perez v. Eagle, 148
Perjury, 66
Phillips v. Washington Legal Fund, 133
Pleadings, 66
Practice of law, 35–37. *See also* Unauthorized practice of law
Precedent, 67
Prepaid legal services plan, 188
Pro bono service, 157
    attorneys, 165
    paralegals, 170, 171
Pro se, 36
Probation, 14
Professional corporation, 184
Professional limited liability company, 184
Professional responsibility, 3
Prosecution, 39
Public defenders, 104, 105
Punitive damages, 81

Quid pro quo sexual harassment, 204
Quo warranto, 39

Reciprocity, 34
Recordkeeping
    advertising and solicitation, 183
    client trust accounts, 133, 134
Referral fees, 141, 184, 190
Registration, 18
Regulation
    ABA's position, 18
    certification, 17
    future of, 215, 216
    licensing, 17
    NALA's position, 18, 19
    NFPA's position, 19, 20
    registration, 18
    Web site, 20
Reprimand, 14
Request for production of documents, 69
Resources for legal ethics research, 20
Retainer, 137
Rules of Professional Conduct, Missouri, 219–241

Sanchez v. California State Bar, 107
Sanction, 14
Screening, 89, 90
Self-help books and software, 30, 31

Self-representation, 30, 38, 39
Self-represented person, 18
Sexual harassment, 204, 205
Shakespeare, William, 209
Shapero v. Kentucky Bar Association, 185
Sharswood, G., 156
Shell Oil Company v. Meyer, 148
Shredding files, 76
Smith, Benjamin Nathaniel, 153
Sole proprietorship, 184
Solicitation, 185–188, 190
Solicitation letters, 185, 186
Sources of legal ethics regulation, 3–5
South Carolina v. Robinson, 52
Special retainer, 137
Specialization, 112–114, 183, 184
Specialty certification plans, 113
Standing Committee on Ethics and Professional Responsibility, 5
State bar associations, 3, 4, 7, 23–26
State code of ethics, 21–23
State judicial system, 3, 4, 7
State legislature, 4, 7
Statute, 4
Statute of limitations, 107
Suspension, 14

Talking to the press, 76
Timekeeping, 145, 146
Tobacco litigation, 56–58
Tort reform, 81
Traditional paralegal, 42
Tribunal, 35
Trust account, 131–134
Trust accounting, 144

Unauthorized practice of law, 32–55
 agencies permitting nonlawyer representation, 47, 48
 avoiding, 45–48
 basic rules, 34, 35
 case law, 49–51
 defined, 33
 enforcement, 39, 40
 guidance from paralegal associations, 44, 45
 guidelines for utilizing paralegals, 41
 Internet, and, 214, 215
 introduction, 33
 occupations most at risk, 38
 paralegal's perspective, 42–44, 215, 216
 sanctions, 49
 self-representation, 38, 39
 what constitutes, 35–38
United States of America v. The Boeing Company, 148
Upjohn v. United States, 63

Warren, Earl, 2
Williams, Merrell, 56
Williams v. TransWorld Airlines, 97
Work product, 67
Work product rule, 67, 69, 70
Workplace diversity, 203, 204
Writ, 39
Writ of quo warranto, 39

Zealous representation, 116–119